Individualism and Collectiveness in Intellectual Property Law

ATRIP INTELLECTUAL PROPERTY

Series Editors: Annette Kur, *Max Planck Institute for Intellectual Property and Competition Law, Germany* and Jan Rosén, *Stockholm University, Sweden*

The ATRIP series presents the fruit of annual meetings held by the International Association for the Advancement of Teaching and Research in Intellectual Property (www.atrip.org). Yielding unique opportunities for IP scholars from a global community to explore together the different facets of one overarching topic, the essence of those meetings is captured in the edited compilation of selected contributions contained in the volumes. Rather than employing a traditional, compartmentalized view of the different areas of IP, the ATRIP series typically applies a horizontal approach, cutting across the usual boundaries of legal categorization, with the aim to uncover hidden commonalities, and accentuate the need for differentiation where that is called for. As ATRIP counts among its members leading IP scholars from all parts of the world, and actively encourages participation of highly talented young researchers, the panel of authors contributing to the volumes does not only guarantee excellence, but also represents a full and vibrant picture of contemporary, high-level IP research in an international setting.

Titles in the series include:

The Structure of Intellectual Property Law
Can One Size Fit All?
Edited by Annette Kur and Vytautas Mizaras

Individualism and Collectiveness in Intellectual Property Law
Edited by Jan Rosén

Individualism and Collectiveness in Intellectual Property Law

Edited by

Jan Rosén

Professor of Private Law, Stockholm University, Sweden and ATRIP President

ATRIP INTELLECTUAL PROPERTY

Edward Elgar

Cheltenham, UK • Northampton, MA, USA

Published by
Edward Elgar Publishing Limited
The Lypiatts
15 Lansdown Road
Cheltenham
Glos GL50 2JA
UK

Edward Elgar Publishing, Inc.
William Pratt House
9 Dewey Court
Northampton
Massachusetts 01060
USA

A catalogue record for this book
is available from the British Library

Library of Congress Control Number: 2011932876

ISBN 978 0 85793 897 8

Typeset by Servis Filmsetting Ltd, Stockport, Cheshire
Printed and bound by MPG Books Group, UK

Contents

Contributors

Dr Irene Calboli is an Associate Professor at Marquette University Law School in the United States, where she leads the Marquette Intellectual Property and Technology Law Program. In the past several years, Professor Calboli has written numerous articles and a doctoral dissertation on topics related to Intellectual Property and Trademark Law, and has spoken extensively at conferences and workshops in the United States and abroad. Prior to going to the United States, Professor Calboli was a Research Fellow at the University of Bologna Law School, Italy, and a Visiting Scholar at the King's College, University of London. She has also been a Visiting Researcher at the Boalt Hall, School of Law, UC Berkeley, the University Complutense of Madrid, Spain, and the Max Planck Institute for Foreign and International Patent, Copyright and Competition Law, Munich, Germany.

Laura Carlson LLD is an Associate Professor at Stockholm University. She is Head of Course for American English Business Law; Head of Course for Introduction to Swedish Law; and Head of Course for European and Swedish Labour and Employment Law. Her doctoral thesis addressed access to justice issues with respect to sex discrimination and parental leave, based on a comparison of Swedish, UK, EU and US laws.

John Cross is the Grosscurth Professor of Law at the University of Louisville School of Law in Louisville, Kentucky, USA, where he teaches and researches in the areas of Intellectual Property Law, Competition Law, and the Law of Courts and Jurisdiction. Professor Cross received his undergraduate degree from Bradley University, his Juris Doctor from the University of Illinois, and a Doctor of Law degree *honoris causa* from the University of Turku in Finland.

Magnus Graner, Secretary of State, Ministry of Justice, Sweden.

Fredrik Willem Grosheide is Professor of Intellectual Property Law at Utrecht University, the Netherlands. He teaches law at the University of Utrecht as Full Professor in the field of Intellectual Property Law, particularly Copyright Law and practises law at the Amsterdam Bar with

Van Doorne. He is director of several postgraduate courses on behalf of judges, members of the bar and other practitioners in the Netherlands and abroad; Visiting Scholar a.o. Wayne State University Law School, Detroit; Berkely Centre for Law and Technology, Institute of Intellectual Property; Tokyo; Stockholm University, Sweden; Washington University School of Law, St. Louis, Fordham (USA), UNISA (S-A), Stellenbosch Universiteit (S-A), Cass Beijing (Cn).

Steven A. Hetcher, Professor of Law, Co-Director Intellectual Property Program at Vanderbilt University. He obtained his JD at Yale University, PhD (Philosophy) at the University of Illinois, MA (Public Policy) at the University of Chicago, and a BA at the University of Wisconsin. Steven A. Hetcher's research focuses on Intellectual Property, Privacy, Torts, Cyberlaw and the role of social norms in the law. In particular, he challenges the first-generation economic account of various substantive areas within the regulatory state apparatus such as Copyright, Tort, and Privacy Law. The larger substantive goal is to develop a norms-based jurisprudence of intellectual property. Hetcher joined the Vanderbilt law faculty in 1998 after practising at Arnold & Porter in Washington, D.C.

Reto M. Hilty studied mechanical engineering at ETH Zurich (1st inter-mediate exam). He studied law at the University of Zurich and obtained a Doctorate in Zurich (1989). Department Head and Board Member of the Swiss Federal Institute of Intellectual Property (1994–1997). He obtained a postdoctoral lecture qualification in Civil, Intellectual Property, Competition and Media Law at the University of Zurich (2000). He is Full Professor of Technology and Information Law, ETH Zurich. Director and faculty member of the Max Planck Institute for Intellectual Property, Competition and Tax Law (from 2002; Managing Director 2005–2006). Full Professor (ad personam) at the University of Zurich. Honorary Professor at the Ludwig Maximilians University, Munich. Areas of interest: Contract Law for intellectual property; Competition Law and protection of intellectual property; fundamental questions of property rights and new technologies; harmonization of international property rights.

Dr Silke von Lewinski, Max Planck Institute for Intellectual Property and Competition Law; Adjunct Professor, Franklin Pierce Center for IP at the University of New Hampshire Law School (USA), MIPLC, GWU summer program; Visiting Professor worldwide (Paris XI, Melbourne et al.); First Walter Minton Visiting Scholar, Columbia University; First Distinguished Visitor to IPRIA (Australia). Frequent expert to European

Commission, for example drafting and steering through process the Rental Directive; member of the EC delegation, WIPO DipCon 1996. German delegate, WIPO AV DipCon 2000. Chief legislative expert to PECO- and former Soviet countries' governments in EC's initial TA programs; work under subsequent programs worldwide. Most recent books: *The WIPO Treaties 1996* (2002; Chinese edn. 2008), with Reinbothe; *International Copyright Law and Policy* (2008); *Indigenous Heritage and Intellectual Property* (2nd edn. 2008; Chinese edn. in preparation); *Copyright throughout the World* (2008); *European Copyright Law*, with Walter (2010).

Sylvie Nérisson studied law in Paris and Berlin with a focus on Copyright and Comparative Law. She is currently completing her PhD thesis about the legitimacy of collective copyrights management societies in German and French law, supervised by Professor W. Nordemann (Humboldt Universität zu Berlin) and Professor F. Pollaud-Dulian (Paris 1). She worked as scientific assistant at the Parisian Research Institute for Intellectual Property (IRPI), at the University Paris I, and is now staff member at the Max Planck Institute for Intellectual Property and Competition Law, in Munich.

Geertrui Van Overwalle is Professor at the K U Leuven (Belgium) where she teaches Patent Law in the Master of Laws Programme in the Faculty of Law. She also teaches Intellectual Property in the BioSciences and Patent Law and Human Genetic Inventions in the Master in Biomedical Sciences at the Faculty of Medicine. She is also a professor at the Université de Liège (Belgium) where she teaches Patent Law in the Advanced Master of European Law. In October 2008 she was also appointed as Research Professor of Patent Law and New Technologies at the Tilburg Institute for Law, Technology, and Society (TILT) at the University of Tilburg (in the Netherlands).

Adejoke Oyewunmi teaches Intellectual Property Law at the Faculty of Law, University of Lagos. She holds a Bachelor of Laws Degree of the Obafemi Awolowo University, Ile-Ife, Nigeria and an Inter-Departmental Masters Degree (LLM) of the University of Lagos. Between January and December 2000, she was a World Intellectual Property (WIPO) Fellow at the Franklin Pierce Law Centre, Concord, New Hampshire, USA, where she obtained a Masters Degree in Intellectual Property Law. In the course of her teaching and research experience, she has published papers in the areas of Intellectual Property, Labour Law and other commercial and industrial law subjects.

Rudolph J.R. Peritz, Professor of Law and Director, IProgress Project, New York Law School. Professor Peritz has taught courses and seminars in Antitrust and Intellectual Property, as well as Contracts, Property, Cyberlaw and Jurisprudence. He has visited at Cardozo Law School, New York; University of Essex, UK; and Libera Università Internazionale degli Studi Sociali (LUISS), Rome. He has lectured regularly in the US and Europe. Professor Peritz has been a Langdell Fellow at Harvard Law School, Senior Research Fellow at the American Antitrust Institute, Washington, D.C., and Director, Computer-Assisted Enforcement Program, Antitrust Division, Attorney General of Texas. Before entering the legal profession, he was a systems engineer and software programmer for mainframe computer systems. He is the author of two books: *Competition Policy in America: History, Rhetoric, Law* (1996 and revised edn. 2001) and *U.S. Antitrust in Global Context* (2nd edn. 2004) (with Eleanor Fox and Lawrence Sullivan), as well as numerous articles and papers. Professor Peritz is co-editor with Steven Anderman of the book series entitled *New Horizons in Competition Policy and Economics* for Edward Elgar Publishing, Ltd. The Journal of the U.S. Patent and Trademark Office Society recently published his article entitled "Freedom to Experiment: Toward a Concept of Inventor Welfare." His current project is "The Political Economy of Progress: IP Rights and Competition".

Alexander Peukert was born in 1973; first state examination in law, Freiburg 1998; Dr. jur., University of Freiburg i.Br., 1999 (s.c.l.); second state examination, Berlin, 2001; attorney at law, Berlin, 2001–2002; Senior Research Fellow and Head of the U.S. Department, Max Planck Institute for Intellectual Property, Competition and Tax Law, Munich, 2002–2009; postdoctoral lecture qualification (Habilitation), Ludwig Maximilians University, Munich; venia legendi Civil Law, Intellectual Property Law, German and European Commercial Law, legal theory, 2008; since 2009 Professor of Civil, Commercial, and Intellectual Property Law, Goethe University Frankfurt/Main, Cluster of Excellence "Formation of Normative Orders"; http://www.jura.uni-frankfurt/peukert/

Dr Ole-Andreas Rognstad is a Full Professor in Legal Science at the Institute for Private Law, University of Oslo, Norway. Professor Rognstad holds various posts i.a. he is chairing the Norwegian Vederlagsnemnda. Rognstad has published extensively, such as the monograph *Spredning av verkseksemplar* (1999) and is co-author of a major book on EU Law, *EØS-rett* (2nd edn. 2004).

Jan Rosén LLD, Professor of Private Law, Faculty of Law, Stockholm University. Main fields of research: Intellectual Property Law,

Contracts, Competition and Media Law. Jan Rosén currently holds various commissions, among which could be mentioned the following: Pro Dean of the Stockholm Law Faculty and Chairman of the Faculty's Research Committee; Chairman of the Swedish Copyright Society; Vice President of l'Association Littéraire et Artistique International, ALAI; President of the International Association for the Advancement of Teaching and Research in Intellectual Property, ATRIP; member of the editorial board of The WIPO Journal. He is currently appointed special commissioner of the Swedish Government to revise the Swedish Copyright Act.

Jens Schovsbo, Professor dr.jur. Jens Schovsbo, PhD, is Professor of IPR at the University of Copenhagen. He is the author or co-author of nine monographs on IPR including a Danish course book and has published extensively in Danish, Scandinavian and international law journals primarily on IPR. He has taught IPR at a number of foreign universities including universities in Scandinavia, China, France (CEIPI), and the US (University of San Diego). He was a Visiting Professor at the University of San Diego in 2008–2009. In his recent research he focuses on general aspects of international IPR and especially on the relationship between IPR and Competition Law. He is a member of the Danish administrative court for trademarks and designs, and the Danish and Domain Name Panels.

Katja Weckström, IP Researcher and Lecturer, University of Turku, Faculty of Law, Finland. Lectures in Trademark Law, Comparative Law and International Intellectual Property Law. Supervisor of Master's theses and seminar papers in Trademark Law. Examiner and co-examiner for examinations and Master's theses in Property, Contract, Tort and Intellectual Property Law. Visiting Assistant Professor, University of Louisville, January 2008–June 2008, teaching a course in Trademark Law and a seminar in International Intellectual Property Law at the School of Law.

Sanna Wolk LLD is an Associate Professor at the Stockholm University. She is head of three courses at Stockholm University and the Royal Institute of Technology. She lectures at Stockholm University, Uppsala University, Lund University, Dalarna University, Örebro University, Chalmers University of Technology and the Royal Institute of Technology (KTH).

Dr Hong Xue is a Professor of Law and Director of the Institute for the Internet Policy & Law at Beijing Normal University (BNU). Professor Xue is the Fellow of Yale Information Society Project. She was elected as one of the Ten Nationally Distinguished Young Jurists by the China Law Society. Professor Xue is on the Expert Advisory Board of Diplo Foundation. After serving as a founding member of the ICANN At-Large Advisory Committee for four years (2003–2007), she was appointed on the ICANN President's Advisory Committee on Internationalized Domain Names, Nomination Committee and Fellowship Selection Committee.

Preface

The programme of the 29th ATRIP Congress, held in Stockholm 24–26 May 2010, worked under a chapeau of *Individualism and Collectiveness in Intellectual Property Law*. This heading allowed an extraordinary advanced academic gathering – some fifty prominent law professors were on the podium during the congress – to embrace fundamental, eternal and yet very contemporary elements in IP Law that they deal with in teaching and research. The emphasis was put on classic IP Law values embedded in the protection of human efforts and the creativeness of individuals, and at the same time the speakers were deploying the intrinsic phenomena of our times that lie in the enhancement of individual creativeness in a collective setting as well as the tendencies to build national, regional or global monopolies based on IP Rights. The respect for original ownership, the occasional need for collective management of IP Rights, the idiosyncrasies of co-ownership of rights and the ever-present tension to be found in encounters between exploitation of IP Rights and Competition Law were all dealt with in the arena of the scientific programme of the 2010 ATRIP Congress. This book reflects the centre field of the many aspects brought to the audience.

Opening remarks to the 2010 ATRIP Congress

The opening remarks to the 2010 ATRIP Congress by Magnus Graner, the Secretary of State at the Swedish Ministry of Justice:

First of all I would like to thank ATRIP and its President, Professor Jan Rosén, for inviting me to give this welcoming address.

The International Association for the Advancement for Teaching and Research in Intellectual Property – that is indeed an impressive name and it indicates an important goal. Rightly so, and I am more than pleased to see that the association assembles scholars and professors from all areas of Intellectual Property Law and from many countries around the whole globe. It is my understanding and hope that you share common goals in a time of increasing demands on the system of intellectual property rights.

The overall topic, or approach, of this congress – individualism and collectiveness in Intellectual Property Law – is really excellent and brings many thoughts to my mind. That is a perfect starting position.

I'll start off by making a very general remark, but still, in my mind, necessary to state. We are all aware of the importance of intellectual property rights for the development of our economies. This importance is based on societal progress. Modern economy is largely based on knowledge-based industry. This puts great demands on the system of intellectual property rights. We need to maintain the incentive to create and invest in intangible assets. But we must also take into account the interests of users and the society at large.

This could be the most important – and difficult – question related to intellectual property rights today.

Technological development and societal advancement alters the underlying conditions for creative processes, as well as the possibility to exploit intangible goods and services on the market. We need to take this into account when developing the intellectual property system. Traditionally, the intellectual property rights system is based on an individualistic point of view – it focuses on one author or one inventor at a time. Especially, copyright has traditionally been very individualistic. The moral rights are the ultimate example of this approach.

One important aspect is the exploitation of rights on the market. Traditionally, it has been difficult for copyright-holders to manage their rights individually. The advancement of new forms of mass-communication and exploitation – for example the Internet – once again puts the individualistic stance into question. To give one example: a recently published investigation, initiated by the current Swedish government and headed by the ATRIP President, Professor Jan Rosén, has proposed the introduction of a general provision on an extended collective license. This investigation is now circulated for comments among interested stakeholders. The concept of such a general provision is interesting. It is good to know that related issues will be discussed during this congress.

Another aspect is the increased collectiveness of the creative processes. Many creative goods and services are the result of collective efforts: a single product may have several rights holders, or there may be co-ownership of rights. This is especially true regarding audiovisual and multimedia products. It is important to strike a fair balance between the interests of the individual primary right holders and the interests of the exploiter to bring the creative goods onto the market.

Times change and the intellectual property rights system needs to keep up. Underlying principles must be upheld, however, maybe in an altered manner. The question is *how* we achieve a balance between legal, technological and societal demands.

Lawmakers need thorough information about the demands brought on the intellectual property rights system by the current developments of technology and society. Legal research has an important and necessary role to play in this process. I am confident that the discussions at this ATRIP conference will contribute to future policymaking.

I would like to draw attention to one aspect which doesn't always get the attention it deserves. As the system of intellectual property is under increasing criticism, I think there is a great demand for, as well as genuine need for valid information and education in this field of law. Respect for intellectual property can be established in many ways. Enforcement is one way. But the system of intellectual property rights needs legitimacy within society, among people! Information and education play a vital part in creating and sustaining this legitimacy. Therefore, you scholars and scientists have a very important role to play!

I wish you all an interesting as well as thought-provoking congress – the program, the context and yourselves are guaranteeing this.

PART I

IP rights and competition law

1. Individual, multiple and collective ownership: what impact on competition?

Reto M. Hilty*

Dealing with different forms of ownership is an appealing challenge today. In fact, awareness seems to be growing that "property" – leading to ownership – is not a predetermined concept. The content of "property" does not ensue by nature, but must be defined by law. "Property" can notably be limited in time and scope in order to pursue specific objectives in the public interest. For "property" as an institution should undoubtedly not solely realise the individual purposes of its owner (or owners); ownership, in whatever form, must ultimately take into account the social momentousness of the institution "property".[1]

This insight per se, however, does not provide a clear legal framework; instead, a great number of related issues can be grouped under the heading "ownership". And the discussion on what ownership – or property – shall encompass is, of course, also not new; on the contrary, substantial research in this area has already been accomplished.[2] If we want to narrow

* Director, Max Planck Institute for Intellectual Property and Competition Law, Munich; Professor at the Universities of Zurich and Munich. The author wishes to thank Felix Trumpke, Scholarship Holder at the Max Planck Institute for Intellectual Property and Competition Law, for his valuable support, especially with regard to searching for documents.

1   In this sense *Jefferson*: "[. . .] the exclusive right as given not of natural right, but for the benefit of society [. . .]", Thomas Jefferson to Isaac McPherson, 13 August 1883, in: *Lipscomb/Bergh* (eds.), The Writings of Thomas Jefferson, Vol. XIII, Washington 1905, at 326–38.

2   See inter alia *Peukert* (2008), Güterzuordnung als Rechtsprinzip, Tübingen, 2008, at 100 et seq.; *Demsetz* (1967), 'Toward a Theory of Property Right's, The American Economic Review [Vol. 57], at 347 et seq.; *Shavell* (2003), 'Economic Analysis of Property Law', Harvard Law and Economics Discussion Paper No. 399, available at: http://papers.ssrn.com/sol3/papers.cfm?abstract_id=370029 (accessed 03 February 2011); *Alston/Mueller* (2005), 'Property Rights and the State', in: Ménard/Shirley (eds.), Handbook of New Institutional Economics,

down the topic of ownership, this will consequently require some restrictions, which regrettably means that a great number of interesting issues cannot be addressed in the following. Such a selective discussion will not only leave numerous questions unanswered, but will also inevitably even raise new questions.

This chapter attempts to provide a certain framework aligned with the arrangement of the whole conference. It does not claim to reflect all aspects of the ongoing discussions on the tension between property regimes and liability regimes.[3] Rather, it aims at the systematisation of a number of aspects that are not always observed in a greater context. Likewise, it tries to connect certain aspects of ownership in the different fields of IP law which are quite often discussed separately.[4] The overall perspective will – as suggested by the title – focus on the impact of ownership on competition.

Dordrecht, Springer, 2005, at 573 et seq.; *Lemley* (2004), 'Property, Intellectual Property and Free Riding', Texas Law Review [Vol. 83], at 1031 et seq.; *Reed* (2004), 'What Is "Property"?', American Business Law Journal [No. 41], at 459 et seq.; *Bell/Parchomovsky* (2005), 'A Theory of Property', Cornell Law Review [Vol. 90], at 531 et seq., available at: http://papers.ssrn.com/ sol3/papers.cfm?abstract_id=509862 (accessed 03 February 2011); *Claeys* (2009), 'Property 101: Is Property a Thing or a Bundle?', Seattle University Law Review [Vol. 32], at 617 et seq.; *Gretton* (2007), Ownership and its Objects, RabelsZ [Vol. 71], at 802 et seq.; *Anderson/McChesney* (2003) (eds.), Property Rights: Cooperation, Conflict, and Law, Princeton, Princeton University Press, 2003.

[3]   See in that respect *Kur/Schovsbo* (2009), 'Expropriation or Fair Game for All? The Gradual Dismantling of the IP Exclusivity Paradigm', Max Planck Institute for Intellectual Property, Competition & Tax Law Research Paper No. 09-14, available at: http://papers.ssrn.com/sol3/papers.cfm?abstract_id=1508330 (accessed 03 February 2011); *Sterk* (2008), 'Property Rules, Liability Rules, and Uncertainty About Property', Michigan Law Review [Vol. 106], at 1285 et seq.; *Depoorter* (2008), 'Property Rules, Liability Rules and Patent Market Failure', Erasmus Law Review [Vol. 1 Issue 4], at 59 et seq.; *Crane* (2009), 'Intellectual Liability', Texas Law Review [Vol. 88], available at: http://papers. ssrn.com/sol3/papers.cfm?abstract_id=1375031 (accessed 03 February 2011); *Burk* (2009), 'Critical Analysis: Property Rules, Liability Rules and Molecular Futures. Bargaining in the Shadow of the Cathedral', in: Van Overwalle (ed.), Gene Patents and Collaborative Licensing Models, Cambridge 2009, at 294 et seq., available at: http://papers.ssrn.com/sol3/papers.cfm?abstract_id=1359216 (accessed 03 February 2011).

[4]   A growing awareness can be observed that a horizontal approach may help to reveal general principles in the area of IP law, see e.g. *Peukert* (2011), 'Individual, Multiple and Collective Ownership of Intellectual Property Rights – Which Impact on Exclusivity?', in: Kur/Mizaras (eds), Can One Size Fit All?, ATRIP Conference 2009, Cheltenham, 2011, at 196.

1. IP PROTECTION AND COMPETITION LAW – INTERACTION IN GENERAL

The interaction of IP protection on the one hand and competition law (notably antitrust law)[5] on the other continues to be of great interest in academic research.[6] However, it is broadly agreed today that a real conflict of objectives of the two areas of law does not exist – at least per se – but that their purposes are ultimately similar, and are even to some extent aligned.[7] Briefly (and incompletely) said, both areas provide for certain legal interventions based on the belief that a market situation produces "better results" *with* legal interventions compared to the situation *without*. The underlying assumption is that naturally existing, dynamic

---

[5] Regarding the interface between IP law and the – heterogeneous – approaches to regulating unfair competition, see *Hilty* (2007), 'The Law Against Unfair Competition and Its Interfaces', in: Hilty/Henning-Bodewig (eds.), The Law against Unfair Competition, Berlin, Springer, 2007, at 1 et seq.

[6] See inter alia *Drexl* (2010), Research Handbook on Intellectual Property and Competition Law, Cheltenham, Edward Elgar Publishing, 2010; *Ghidini* (2010), 'Innovation, Competition and Consumer Welfare' in Intellectual Property Law, Cheltenham, Edward Elgar Publishing 2010; *Anderman* (2005), Competition Law and Intellectual Property Rights, Oxford, Oxford University Press, 2005; *Dreyfuss* (2005), 'Unique Works/Unique Challenges at the Intellectual Property/ Competition Law Interface', in: Ehlermann/Atanasiu (eds.), European Competition Law Annual 2005: The Interaction between Competition Law and Intellectual Property Law, Oxford, Hart Publishing, 2005, available at: http://papers.ssrn.com/ sol3/papers.cfm?abstract_id=763688 (accessed 03 February 2011); *Hovenkamp/ Janis/Lemley* (2010), IP and Antitrust: An Analysis of Antitrust Principles Applied to Intellectual Property Law, 2nd edn., Austin, Wolters Kluwer Law & Business, Aspen Publishers, 2010, Vols I + II.

[7] See in this respect *Kaplow* (1984), 'The Patent-Antitrust Intersection: A Reappraisal', Harvard Law Review [Vol. 97], at 1813 et seq.; *Anderson* (ed.) (1998), 'Competition Policy and Intellectual Property Rights in the Knowledge-based Economy', Calgary 1998; *Bowman* (1973), Patent and Antitrust Law – A Legal and Economic Appraisal, Chicago, University of Chicago Press, 1973; see also *Heinemann* (2002), Immaterialgüterschutz in der Wettbewerbsordnung, Tübingen, Mohr Siebeck 2002, at 24 et seq.; *Anthony* (2000), 'Antitrust and Intellectual Property Law. From Adversaries to Partners', AIPLA Quarterly Journal [Vol. 28], at 1 et seq., available at: http://www.ftc.gov/speeches/other/ aipla.shtm (accessed 03 February 2011); *Ullrich* (2001), 'Intellectual Property, Access to Information, and Antitrust: Harmony, Disharmony, and International Harmonization', in: Dreyfuss/Zimmerman/First (eds.), Expanding the Boundaries of Intellectual Property, Oxford, Oxford University Press, 2001, at 367 et seq., 371; *US Federal Trade Commission* (2003), To Promote Innovation: The Proper Balance of Competition and Patent Law and Policy, Report, at 2 et seq., available at: http://www.ftc.gov/os/2003/10/innovationrpt.pdf (accessed 03 February 2011).

market forces as such will not – or not entirely – produce the effects that can be produced by means of (some specific forms of) legal intervention. Without intervention, some market players would enjoy advantages to the detriment of other market players and, potentially, to the detriment of the general public as a whole. Such unilateral advantages would lead to imbalances and ultimately to undesirable imperfections in the market.

If we focus on a market environment of innovation and creation, such imperfections – based on the lack of regulation of the market forces involved – might notably cause an undersupply of related intangible goods (namely innovations and creations). This might lead to what we call "market failure" in the sense of an inefficient allocation of goods and services in the relevant market.[8] In order to avoid such market failure, specific legal interventions (based on regulations) are intended to limit the freedom of action of certain market players.[9]

Basically – and again highly simplified and widely incomplete – we may identify three big areas where we find such regulations aimed at limiting the freedom of action of certain market players:

- Regulations, firstly, may focus on dysfunctional appropriation of (foreign) innovations or creations or the like, notably by means of

---

[8]   An ideal situation is a perfect free (competitive) market where an optimal allocation of goods and services exists. This state is reached and will lead to maximum social welfare when no party is able to improve his position without making another person worse off (it is *pareto-optimal*, named after Vilfredo Pareto, an Italian political scientist and economist); for further details, see *Bouckaert/De Geest* (eds.) (2001), Encyclopedia of Law and Economics, Volume II: Civil Law and Economics, Cheltenham, Edward Elgar Publishing, 2001, at 189 – 215; *Gordon* (1994), Marktversagen bei Immaterialgütern, in: Ott/Schäfer (eds.), Ökonomische Analyse der rechtlichen Organisation von Innovationen, Tübingen, Mohr, 1994, at 328 et seq. There are different sources of market failure, e.g. market power/monopoly, externalities, public goods and asymmetric information, see *Bator* (1958), 'The Anatomy of Market Failure', Quarterly Journals of Economics [Vol. 72], at 351–379; *Schäfer/Ott* (2004), The Economic Analysis of Civil Law, Cheltenham, Edward Elgar Publishing, 2004, at 86 et seq. See also *Posner* (2007), Economic Analysis of Law, 7th ed., New York, Aspen Publishers, 2007, at marginal no. 9.1. et seq.; *Besen/Raskind* (1991), 'An Introduction to the Law and Economics of Intellectual Property', The Journal of Economic Perspectives [Vol. 5], at 3 et seq.; *Landes/Posner* (1989), 'An Economic Analysis of Copyright Law', The Journal of Legal Studies [Vol. 18], at 325 – 363; *Gordon* (1992), 'Asymmetric Market Failure', University of Dayton Law Review [Vol. 17], at 853 – 869.

[9]   Accurately referred to as "competition restraints in order to boost competition" ("Wettbewerbsbeschränkung zur Förderung des Wettbewerbs") by *Lehmann*, GRUR Int. 1983, at 356, 360.

patent, design, copyright law etc.[10] To some extent, this area of regulation also includes the prohibition of an appropriation of foreign investments (as in the case of copyright neighbouring rights[11] or, in the context of EU law, the "sui generis" protection of data bases[12]).

- Regulations, secondly, may focus on dysfunctional behaviour of market participants, notably by misleading other market participants (such as consumers), mainly by means of an impairment of relevant market information. Whatever the globally different legal approaches to preventing unfair competition may be, they must all ultimately be seen in that context; for instance, "passing off" rules[13] in common law legal systems, such as England or Australia, at least from a functional

---

[10] See e.g. *Arrow* (1962), 'Economic Welfare and the Allocation of Resources for Innovations', in: Nelson (ed.), The Rate and Direction of Inventive Activity, Princeton, Princeton University Press, at 609 et seq.; *Demsetz* (1967), *supra* note 2, at 347 et seq.; *Alchian/Demsetz* (1973), 'The Property Right Paradigm', Journal of Economic History [Vol. 33], at 16–27; *Furubotn/Pejovich* (1972), 'Property Rights and Economic Theory: A Survey of Recent Literature', Journal of Economic Literature [Vol. 10], at 1137–62; *Dam* (1994), 'The Economic Underpinnings of Patent Law', Journal of Legal Studies [Vol. 23], at 247 et seq.; *Cooter/Ulen* (2008), Law & Economics, 5th ed., Boston, Pearson Addison Wesley, 2008, at 120, 122 et seq.

[11] Provided for in Art. 14 *Agreement on Trade-Related Aspects of Intellectual Property Rights* (TRIPS), for instance, but also internationally protected by the *Rome Convention for the Protection of Performers, Producers of Phonograms and Broadcasting Organisations* (RC) or in Art. 5 et seq. (Rights of Performers), Art. 11 et seq. (Rights of Phonograms) *WIPO Performances and Phonograms Treaty* (WPPT).

[12] *Directive 96/9/EC of the European Parliament and of the Council of 11 March 1996 on the legal protection of databases*; for further details, see *Benkler* (2000), 'Constitutional Bounds of Database Protection: The Role of Judicial Review in the Creation and Definition of Private Rights in Information', Berkeley Technology Law Journal [Vol. 15], at 535 et seq.

[13] Passing-off is concerned with misrepresentation made by one trader which causes damage to the goodwill of another. See generally *Wadlow* (2006), The Law of Passing-Off, 3rd edn., London, Sweet & Maxwell, 2006; *Carty* (2001), An Analysis of Economic Torts, Oxford, Oxford University Press, 2001, Chapter 8; *Cornish/Llewelyn* (2007), Intellectual Property, 6th ed., London, Sweet & Maxwell, 2007, at marginal no. 17 et seq. A controversial debate has lately arisen about the extension of the ambit of passing-off rules, in particular as a means of protecting "personal rights"; see for further details *Carty* (2004), 'Advertising, Publicity Rights and English Law', Intellectual Property Quarterly, at 209, 236 et seq.; *Learmonth* (2002), 'Eddie, Are You Okay? Product Endorsement and Passing Off', Intellectual Property Quarterly, at 306 et seq.; in a critical vein *Scanlan* (2003), 'Personality, Endorsement and Everything: The Modern Law of Passing Off and the Myth of the Personality Right', EIPR 2003, at 563–9; see also *van Bassewitz* (2008), Prominenz und Celebrity, Cologne, Heymanns, 2008, at 90 et seq.

perspective belong to this second field of regulations. The same, however, is true for trademark legislation, as well as for legislation on geographical indications or the like, as will be shown below.[14]

• Regulations, thirdly, may focus on a dysfunctional exertion of a given market position. In extreme forms, such behaviour may lead to the "misuse" of market power[15] – wherever such market power derives from and notwithstanding whether the market player in question acts individually or collectively, notably in cooperation with other market players. In the context of IP law, in particular the refusal to grant licences as well as licensing under anticompetitive conditions lie in the focus of interest.[16] The legal instrument by which such behaviour may be prohibited is usually antitrust law.

This general outline – particularly the distinction of these three areas of regulation – is of some relevance for the following reflections. With this in mind, we can make two observations:

• There is a difference between the first and the second area of regulation on the one hand and the third area of regulation on the other:
    • The first and, to a lesser extent, the second area focus on third parties, parties that shall be prohibited from entering "foreign domains".
    This goal is achieved by *granting* – more or less extensive forms of – ownership.
    • In contrast, the third area of regulation focuses on the owner. More precisely, it focuses on a control of granted ownership; the owner shall not be in a position to assert his rights in a dysfunctional – notably anticompetitive – manner.

---

[14]   See below, at Section 3.3.2.

[15]   Such behaviour, in turn, may lead to the so-called *deadweight loss*, see *Gallini/Scotchmer* (2002), 'Intellectual Property: When Is It the Best Incentive System', Innovation Policy and the Economy [Vol. 2], at 51–77; *Lemley* (2005), *supra* note 2, at 1031, 1058 et seq.; *Landes/Posner* (2003), The Economic Structure of Intellectual Property Law, Cambridge, Belknap Press of Harvard University Press 2003, at 16 et seq.

[16]   See e.g. *Drexl* (2007), Abuse of a Dominance in Licensing and Refusal to License – A 'More Economic Approach' to Competition by Imitation and to Competition by Substitution, in: Ehlermann/Atanasiu (eds.), Competition Law Annual 2005: The Interaction between Competition Law and IP Law, Oxford, Hart Publishing, 2007, at 647 et seq.; see also *Czapracka* (2009), Intellectual Property Law and the Limits of Antitrust, Cheltenham, Edward Elgar Publishing, 2009, at 36 et seq.; *Schmidt* (2010), Refusal to License Intellectual Property Rights as Abuse of Dominance, Frankfurt, Lang, 2010.

- Nevertheless, in whichever of the three areas they lie, all regulations are in principle directed at congruent aims: the freedom of action of certain market players shall be limited in order to avoid any kind of dysfunctional distortion of competition. As initially stated, all legal intervention is ultimately aimed at preventing "market failure".

Of course, as soon as we step deeper into certain details, highly complex questions arise. In particular, we must bear in mind that legal intervention is a risky undertaking since competition is dynamic, whereas regulation is necessarily of a "static" nature.[17] Additionally, in principle, our information on how market forces function is incomplete. Therefore, regulation is per se somewhat arbitrary; however we design the rules, we always risk overshooting or that the regulations remain ineffective.[18]

At this stage, the discussion on the complexity of legal regulation need not be deepened; we just have to bear this complexity in mind when responding to questions about the *impact* of any legal regulation (here: of "ownership") in the real world (here: on competition). Any answer to such questions will unavoidably be imprecise and incomplete.

2. "OWNERSHIP" – IMPACT ON COMPETITION IN GENERAL

Beside this question on the ". . .impact on competition", the given topic primarily relates to the notion of "ownership. . .". More precisely, the question is asked: what will change with regard to the "impact on competition" if we modify the rules of ownership?

A preliminary problem to this question is, of course, what impact "ownership" has on competition at all. In fact, in all three aforementioned areas of regulation, ownership, to a greater or lesser extent, seems to play a crucial role:

---

[17] See *David* (2003), The Economic Logic of "Open Science" and the Balance between Private Property Rights and the Public Domain in Scientific Data and Information: A Primer, in: Esanu/Uhlir (eds.), National Research Council, The Role of Scientific and Technical Data and Information in the Public Domain, Washington 2003, at 19, 29 (pointing out that legal intervention involves a "protracted period of waiting, and struggling to have the courts settle upon an interpretation of the law").

[18] *Hilty* (2007), Märkte und Schutzrechte, in: Beckert/Diaz-Bone/Ganßmann (eds.), Märkte als soziale Strukturen, Frankfurt/New York, Campus-Verl, 2007, at 235, 237.

- Quite clear is the situation in the **first area of regulation**, dealing with the prohibition of misappropriation. Patents, copyright-protected works, designs, etc., are by definition "owned" in a way; likewise, sound recordings, broadcastings, ("sui generis" protected) data-bases and the like can be deemed to be "owned" subject matters. Such ownership obviously has an impact on competition; at the same time it is likely that the form of ownership matters.
- Regarding the **second area of regulation**, focusing on the prohibition of the dysfunctional behaviour of market players, the impact of "ownership" is less obvious and more difficult to grasp.
  - More or less intelligible is the impact of a trademark; as a matter of principle, a trademark is "owned" by someone[19], similar to a patent or a design, etc., even if the impact *on competition* is not precisely the same. In fact, this difference is precisely why we classify trademarks in the second area of regulation and not the first, since trademark law to some extent should rather be seen as a (special) part of competition law.[20]
  - Less traceable is the situation with regard to regulations on the use of geographical indications or designations of origin etc. Insofar as such indications or designations are registered, the legal system presupposes a kind of "organisation".[21] Based on this requirement, we may conclude that a kind of "ownership" must exist – at least functionally seen – an ownership which is acquired by this "organisation".

    In contrast, if indications or designations are *not* registered, an owner – in the mere sense of the word – does not exist; rather, the impact of the regulation leads to a distinction of two types of market players:
    - those market players who are *allowed* to use geographical indications or designations of origin because they meet certain specific conditions to use them;
    - and all the other market players who are *not allowed* to use

---

19   *McClure* (1996), 'Trademarks and Competition: The Recent History', Law and Contemporary Problems [Vol. 59], at 13, 39 et seq.

20   *Hilty* (2007), *supra* note 5, at 31 et seq.; see also *Cooter/Ulen* (2008), *supra* note 10, at 134 et seq.; *McClure* (1996), *supra* note 19, at 13 et seq.

21   Art. 5 of *Council Regulation (EC) No. 510/2006 of 20 March 2006 on the protection of geographical indications and designations of origin for agricultural products and foodstuffs* speaks of a "group" which "means any association, irre-spective of its legal form or composition, of producers or processors working with the same agricultural product or foodstuff".

the indications or designations because they do not meet these conditions of use.

- In addition, the second area of regulation includes rules that belong to what we call legislation against "unfair competition", a term that is perceived differently in various legal systems, although it is based on legal protection that, in principle, is provided by international legislation.[22] Such protection generally focuses on situations in which a market player is affected with regard to his market position;[23] he may defend this position even if "ownership" does not appear to be involved, at least at first glance.[24]

  However, if we take a closer look, we realise that this observation is not convincing. Certain subject matters seem to be "owned". We just have to take the example of (trade) secrets, or as Art. 39 TRIPS names it, "undisclosed information". Whatever approach national legislators take to effectuate that legal protection, we can hardly ignore that such information – at least "factually" – "belongs" to someone.[25]

Taking an overall look at this second area of regulation, we realise that it is quite metamorphic; "ownership" does play a role and thus has a certain impact on competition, albeit not as clearly as in the first area of regulation.

- In the **third area of regulation**, focusing on the prohibition of dysfunctional exertion of market power, it is obvious that "ownership" has an impact on competition. In fact, this third area of regulation is closely connected to the first one: it is precisely the "ownership" granted in the first area – related to an IP right – that involves two kinds of risks:
    - Either this ownership allows for a unilateral misuse of existing

---

[22] Art. 10*bis Paris Convention for the Protection of Industrial Property* (PC); Art. 22 Sec. 2 (b) TRIPS. See also *Pflüger* (2010), Der internationale Schutz gegen Unlauteren Wettbewerb, Cologne, Heymanns, 2010, at 158 et seq., with an extensive analysis of the international legislation against "unfair competition". For further details, see *Pflüger* (2010), *ibid.*, at 315, 431, 455 et seq., discussing drawbacks and opportunities of a global harmonisation of the law against unfair competition.

[23] See *Pflüger* (2010), *supra* note 22, at 498 et seq.

[24] With regard to the issue of "ownership", however, one has to keep in mind that Art. 10*bis* PC tends to protect industrial *property*, and thus, the interests of an *owner* are in the field of vision, since according to the Paris Convention the protection of industrial property includes the repression of unfair competition (Art. 1 (2) PC); see in this regard *Pflüger* (2010), *supra* note 22, at 116 et seq.

[25] See below, at III. 4 (c).

market power, which as such potentially derives from that ownership (e.g. resulting in the refusal to grant a licence)[26];

- or this ownership allows the owner to impose anticompetitive conditions on a contractor (e.g. in case of a licensing agreement)[27].

In this third area of regulation it therefore seems obvious that a change in the rules on ownership may have an even remarkable impact on competition. Accordingly, the next question is to what extent the different forms of ownership really matter with regard to the impact of that ownership on competition.

3. DIFFERENT FORMS OF OWNERSHIP AND THEIR IMPACT ON COMPETITION

3.1 The Forms of "Ownership"

There are various ways to distinguish different forms of "ownership". The title, specified by the organisers of the ATRIP conference, suggests the following differentiation:

- Individual ownership – a more or less self-explanatory term;
- Multiple ownership, obviously meaning a certain – limited – number of "owners" of subject matter;
- Collective ownership, which, in contrast, seems to focus on an open number of "owners" involved.

As we will see shortly, "individual ownership" and to some extent the (rather uncommon) term "multiple ownership", subject to the understanding of such "non-technical" terms, will most probably not help to open really new perspectives, much less revolutionary ones. Distinguishing such forms of ownership, however, may clarify certain viewpoints that might oth-

---

[26] See e.g. *Hovenkamp/Janis/Lemley* (2005), 'Unilateral Refusals to License in the U.S.', in: Lévêque/Shelanski (eds.), Antitrust, Patents and Copyright, Cheltenham, Edward Elgar Publishing, 2005, at 12–56; available at: http://papers.ssrn.com/sol3/papers.cfm?abstract_id=703161 (accessed 03 February 2011); *Hovenkamp* (2002), IP and Antitrust, Gaithersburg 2002, at chapter 13; *Ruesting* (2010), When Does a Unilateral Unconditional Refusal to License or to Provide Information Become an Antitrust Concern? A United States and European Comparison, available at: http://papers.ssrn.com/sol3/papers.cfm?abstract_id=1550239 (accessed 03 February 2011); see also above, at note 16.

[27] *Czapracka* (2009), *supra* note 16, at 70 et seq.; *Hovenkamp* (2002), *supra* note 26, at chapter 21 et seq.

erwise remain unconsidered. The third form, on the other hand, "collective ownership", seems to be multifaceted, notably since the perception of the term "collective" arises, at least partially, from the current (rather political) debate expressing a certain dissatisfaction with the traditional IP system.[28]

However, whatever the possible criteria of such distinctions may be, we must be aware that the term "ownership" per se is already problematic since it does not clearly define what is allocated to a person or group of persons.[29] At the same time, precisely such an undefined term may be seen as an advantage, whereas "property" by contrast seems to be a common term. However, doctrinal discussions in different legal systems – and notably translations of the term "property" in other languages (like the German "Eigentum") – show that we by no means may detect a common understanding from the mere use of that term.[30] Rather, the lingual similarity of both tangible and intangible "property" risks leading to problematic comparisons and thus an overemphasis of the individual interest of the "proprietor".[31] Bearing this in mind, it might be wise to avoid this term and to utilise a "neutral" one, like "ownership", which, however, needs to be defined under such circumstances.[32]

Against this background, we must clarify that the use of the term "ownership" in the following does not confer any particular meaning regarding the scope of the "owned" subject matter. On the contrary, the term shall

---

[28]   See below, at Section 3.4.1.

[29]   For a detailed account, see e.g. *Gretton* (2007), *supra* note 2, at 802 et seq.; see also *Gosh* (ed.), Code: Collaborative Ownership and the Digital Age, Cambridge, Mass., MIT Press, 2005, where different forms and meanings of "ownership" with a view to "tribal societies" are discussed.

[30]   For more details concerning the notion "Intellectual Property", see *Peukert* (2010), Intellectual Property, in: Basedow/Hopt/Zimmermann (eds.), Encyclopaedia of European Private Law, Oxford 2011 (forthcoming), at 1 et seq., available at: http://papers.ssrn.com/sol3/papers.cfm?abstract_id=1550103 (accessed 03 February 2011).

[31]   See, for instance, *Rigamonti* (2001), Geistiges Eigentum als Begriff und Theorie des Urheberrechts, Baden-Baden, Nomos Verl.-Ges., 2001, at 144 et seq.; *Pfister* (2005), La properiété intellectuelle est-elle une properiété?, Revue Internationale Du Droit d'Auteur [Vol. 205], at 117; *Lemley* (1997), 'Romantic Authorship and the Rhetoric of Property', Texas Law Review [Vol. 75], at 873, 895 et seq.; *same author* (2005), *supra* note 2, at 1031; *Stallmann* (2006), 'Did You Say "Intellectual Property"? It's a Seductive Mirage', Policy Futures in Education [Vol. 4], at 334 et seq.

[32]   Admittedly, the term "ownership" is also not a purely neutral one. On the contrary, it is used in recent publications dealing with IP law (see e.g. *Peukert* (2010), *supra* note 4, at 1 et seq., but also avoiding a clear definition of "ownership"). Compared to "property", however, the notion "ownership" is rather *unusual* in academic research and thus adequate for the following rationales. See also *Gosh* (ed.), Code: Collaborative Ownership and the Digital Age, Cambridge, Mass., MIT Press, 2005.

be used precisely to mean any kind of attribution – in whatever way – of legally protected (intangible) subject matter to a person or group of persons by means of specific regulation.

3.2 "Individual Ownership"

"Individual ownership" – from the legal outset – means that one (single) right holder acquires the right in question.[33] Such ownership assumedly has a strong impact on competition. As a matter of principle, the (single) "owner" may act independently; in particular, he may exclude all others ("non-owners") from using the protected subject matter. However, the concrete impact of such individual "ownership" ultimately depends on the relevance of the protected subject matter for third parties.

The more relevant this subject matter is for "non-owners", the more dangerous unlimited ownership can be, and the more obvious it becomes that the scope of such individual ownership possibly needs to be limited. In fact, the issue of limitations (and exceptions) is highly debated today. There are basically two approaches to implementing such limitations:

- Either they derive from particular provisions within the specific legislation (notably exceptions in copyright law; compulsory licensing in patent law etc.);
- or they are rooted in the aforementioned third area of regulation, focusing on the prohibition of a dysfunctional exertion of market power, particularly the rules found in antitrust law.

At this stage, it might help to undertake a short preview of the second form of ownership: "multiple ownership". In fact, the entitlement deriving from individual ownership permits the owner to – voluntarily – create a particular form of "multiple ownership", for which a better term might be **"shared ownership"**.[34] As a matter of principle, an individually granted right may be fully or partially transferred to third parties, or third parties may at least acquire a sort of "factual ownership" (as in the case of the grant of a licence, albeit subject to the applicable legislation). The motivation of an individual owner to "share" his "ownership" usually arises from an attempt to enhance his market position – in whatever respect.

This objective makes it clear that such voluntary forms of "shared ownership" even risk intensifying negative impacts on competition (compared

---

[33]   *Peukert* (2010), *supra* note 4, at 197.
[34]   In the same vein *Peukert* (2010), *supra* note 4, at 200 (". . .individual licensing could already be qualified as a case of multiple ownership. . .").

to the merely individual use of individually granted "ownership"). These impacts, however, obviously depend on the circumstances. Patent pools, for instance, are a typical case of voluntarily created "shared ownership". Such patent pools are characterised by the fact that different patent owners bring their (individual) rights into a common pool in order to "share" and exploit these rights.[35] The effect of such a patent pool may be that it:

- either enhances efficiency from an overall perspective (e.g. if the pool contains patents related to standards, and if third parties are allowed to acquire licences to use such standards under reasonable terms and conditions);[36]
- or the pool may have a negative impact on competition (e.g. if a patent pool is aimed at the exclusion of competitors or if inaproprate licensing terms are coerced).[37]

Bearing in mind such possibilities of exploiting "individual ownership", we may conclude that this form of ownership – at least potentially – has strong impacts on competition. These impacts might be one of the reasons why the current system of IP law (mainly focusing on individual ownership) is increasingly criticised today.[38] Individual ownership as such, as well as in

---

[35]   See, for instance, *Merges* (2001), Institutions for Intellectual Property Transactions: The Case of Patent Pools, in: Dreyfuss/Zimmerman/First (eds.), Expanding the Boundaries of Intellectual Property, Oxford, Oxford University Press, 2001, at 123, 133 et seq.; *Verbeure* (2009), Patent pooling: conceptual framework, in: Van Overwalle (ed.), Gene Patents and Collaborative Licensing Models, Cambridge, Cambridge University Press, 2009, at 5 et seq.

[36]   *Verbeure* (2009), *supra* note 35, at 9 et seq.

[37]   *Ullrich* (2008), Patent Pools – Policy and Problems, in: Drexl (ed.), Research Handbook on Intellectual Property and Competition Law, Cheltenham, Edward Elgar Publishing, 2008, at 139 et seq.; *same author* (2009), 'Gene Patents and Clearing Models: Some Comments from a Competition Law Perspective', in: Van Overwalle (ed.), Gene Patents and Collaborative Licensing Models, Cambridge, Cambridge University Press, 2009, at 339, 341; *Aoki/Nagaoka* (2004), 'The Consortium Standard and Patent Pools', The Economic Review [Vol. 55], at 345–56.

[38]   See inter alia *First* (2007), 'Controlling the Intellectual Property Grab: Protect Innovation, Not Innovators', Rutgers Law Journal [Vol. 38], at 365 et seq.; *Sterckx* (2005), 'Can Drug Patents be Morally Justified?', Science and Engineering Ethics [Vol. 11], at 81 et seq.; see also *Guibault/Hugenholtz* (eds.), The Future of the Public Domain, Alphen aan den Rijn 2006; *Boyle* (2005), Fencing Off Ideas: Enclosure and the Disappearance of the Public Domain, in: Gosh (ed.), Collaborative Ownership and the Digital Economy, London 2006, at 235 et seq.; *Hilty* (2005), 'Five Lessons about Copyright in the Information Society: Reaction of the Scientific Community to Over-Protection and what Policy Makers Should Learn', Journal of the Copyright Society of the USA [Vol. 53], at 103 et seq.;

modified forms of "shared ownership", therefore undoubtedly needs to be controlled within the aforementioned third area of regulation, notably a control based on antitrust law. However, it is increasingly contested whether remedies deriving from antitrust law may really suffice.[39] These doubts are one of the reasons for the currently growing discussion about alternative regimes of "ownership", especially forms of "collective ownership".[40]

3.3   "Multiple Ownership"

If we assume that the term "multiple ownership" shall express a limited number of owners, then "shared ownership" may be deemed to be one particular form of it. As we have seen, the impacts of this particular form of (voluntary) "multiple ownership" on competition are hard to predict since it depends on the circumstances, particularly on how such ownership is organised. Nevertheless, in principle, the risk is obvious that "shared ownership" is even more likely to impair competition than ("unshared") "individual ownership".

Furthermore, "multiple ownership" may also arise from specifically designed legislation. There are basically two different constellations. One of them is rooted in the first area of regulation,[41] the other in the second area.[42]

3.3.1   First area of regulation

In the first area of regulation, "multiple ownership" evolves based on collaboration *during the process of creation or invention*:

- the common (connected or coordinated) creation of a copyright-protected work by several authors leads to co-ownership of all authors involved;[43]
- likewise, co-inventorship leads to a common entitlement to a

---

Heller (1998), 'The Tragedy of the Anticommons: Property in the Transition from Marx to Markets', Harvard Law Review [Vol. 111], at 621 – 688.; *Schovsbo* (2009), 'Increasing Access to Patented Inventions by Post-grant Measures', Science and Public Policy [Vol. 36], at 609–618, available at: http://papers.ssrn.com/sol3/papers.cfm?abstract_id=1393755 (accessed 03 February 2011).

[39]   See *van Zimmeren* (2009), Clearinghouse mechanism in genetic diagnostics. Conceptual framework, in: Van Overwalle (ed.), Gene Patents and Collaborative Licensing Models, Cambridge, Cambridge University Press, 2009, at 65 et seq. (discussing the insufficiency of antitrust law in the field of human gene patents and considering "clearinghouses" as a possible solution).

[40]   See below, at Section 3.4.

[41]   See above, at Section 1.

[42]   See above, at Section 1.

[43]   See e.g. 17 U.S.C. § 201 (a); Art. 7*bis* Berne Convention (BC).

(commonly acquirable) patent by all inventors involved (which, however, is a more theoretical approach; in real life inventors will rarely acquire a patent themselves as it is more likely that an employer or investor will file the application);
- basically the same is true for commonly created designs, etc.

All these forms of "multiple ownership" might more comprehensively be paraphrased as **"collaborative ownership"** in order to distinguish them from other constellations where a limited number of owners can be involved. If we focus on such "collaborative ownership" and ask what impact it has on competition, we may assume that specific problems will not occur. In fact, such "collaborating owners" are closely linked; they ultimately own one IP right together, which evolves from such forms of collaboration. The effects of this specific form of "multiple ownership" on third parties, therefore, basically remain the same as merely "individual ownership". Irrespective of the actual owner or the number of owners, third parties simply have to respect a granted legal right.

3.3.2   Second area of regulation
In the second area of regulation, "multiple ownership" arises from specific kinds of – market-oriented – *cooperation amongst certain market players*. In the following we will distinguish this from other forms of "multiple ownership" by labelling it **"cooperative ownership"**. There are several constellations where such "cooperative ownership" may occur:

- Firstly, "cooperative ownership" may arise from the registration of a "collective trademark".[44] Two characteristics, however, are slightly misleading:
  - Formally, only one (individual) owner exists, namely one (single) association. However, the goal of a collective trademark is ultimately the use of the trademark in question by the members of this association. Therefore, at least functionally, the members will act as "cooperative owners" of the trademark.
  - Additionally, the term "collective" trademark is imprecise, at least if we only use it for an open number of owners (as will subsequently be the case). In fact, with regard to a "collective trademark" an "open door" situation for third parties does

---

[44]   Art. 7*bis* BC; see also Lanham Act 15 U.S.C. § 1127; Arts 64–72 *Council Regulation (EC) No. 40/94* with regard to *Community Collective Marks*; Art. 15 *Directive 89/104/EC of the Council of 21 December 1988 to Approximate the Laws of the Member States Relating to Trade Marks.*

not exist; rather, in principle, the number of the members of an association that holds a "collective" trademark is limited (subject to the rules of the association).[45]

- Secondly, at first glance, a similar constellation where "cooperative ownership" seems to exist occurs with regard to "geographical indications" or "designations of origin".[46] Again, we must distinguish between two possibilities: either such indications or designations are registered – or they are not registered.

  - In cases of *registered* indications or designations, at least in Europe,[47] legal systems[48] require a kind of "organisation" of

---

[45] *Peukert* (2010), *supra* note 4, at 216, points out that the burning question is "whether outsiders have a right to access the association or group" or not.

[46] See Arts 22–24 TRIPS. See also *Frankel* (2008), Trademarks and Traditional Knowledge and Cultural Intellectual Property, in: Dinwoodie/Janis (eds.), Trademark Law and Theory: A Handbook of Contemporary Research, Cheltenham, Edward Elgar Publishing, 2008, at 433 et seq.

[47] There have been a lot of international negotiations with regard to the implementation of international protection and registration of geographical indications. According to Art. 5 of the *Lisbon Agreement on Appellations of Origin* (1958), for instance, an application of origin should be registered in the International Register of WIPO; however, not more than twenty countries joined this Agreement. Further attempts by the WIPO in this respect, e.g. the *Draft Treaty on the Protection of Geographical Indications* (available at: http://www.wipo.int/mdocsarchives/ TAO_II_75/TAO_II_2_E.pdf, accessed 03 February 2011), failed as well. In more detail in this regard, see *O'Connor* (2003), Geographical Indications in National and International Law, Brussels, O'Connor & Company, 2003, at 21, 29 et seq.; *Heath* (2005), Geographical Indications: International, Bilateral and Regional Agreements, in: Heath/Kamperman Sanders (eds.), New Frontiers of Intellectual Property Law, Oregon, Hart Publishing, 2005, at 97, 101 et seq.

Apart from the issue concerning the establishment of a multilateral register for geographical indications, it is highly debatable if the protection of Art. 23 TRIPS should be extended to products other than wines and spirits; in more depth in this regard, see *Goldberg* (2001), 'Who will Raise the White Flag? The Battle between the United States and the European Union over the Protection of Geographical Indications', University of Pennsylvania Journal of International Economic Law [Vol. 22], at 107–152; *Kamperman Sanders* (2005), Future Solutions for Protecting Geographical Indications Worldwide, in: Heath/Kamperman Sanders (eds.), New Frontiers of Intellectual Property Law, Oregon, Hart Publishing, 2005, at 133 et seq.; see also *Ragnekar* (2002), Geographical Indications: A Review of Proposals at the TRIPS Council. UNCTAD/ICTSD Capacity Building Project on Intellectual Property Rights and Sustainable Development, available at: http://www.iprsonline.org/uncta dictsd/docs/GI%20paper.pdf (accessed 03 February 2011), at 23 et seq.; *O'Connor* (2007), The Law of Geographical Indications, London, Cameron May Ltd, 2007, at 389 et seq.; *Correa* (2007), Trade Related Aspects of Intellectual Property Rights. A Commentary on the TRIPS Agreement, Oxford 2007, at 235, 236 et seq.

[48] See e.g. *Council Regulation (EC) No. 2081/92 of 14 July 1992 on the protec-*

the potential users of the indication or designation.[49] To some extent, this requirement reminds us of the "collective trademark"; in other words, subject to the legal form of such an organisation, something like "ownership" of the indication or designation is likely to exist.

However, in the case of registered geographical indications or designations of origin, unlike the "collective trademark", we are faced with an "open door" situation for third parties, provided such third parties are willing to comply with the conditions related to the use of the indication or designation in question.[50] Insofar, registered indications or designations rather resemble "collective ownership" which will be discussed later on – at least functionally seen.

- In the case of *non*-registered indications or designations, "owners" of such indications or designations in the mere sense of the word do not exist. Rather, as already mentioned, the effect of the legal regulation is basically that we must distinguish between two kinds of market players: those whose products or services meet certain conditions and who are therefore allowed to use the indication or designation, on the one hand, and those whose products or services do not meet the required conditions and who are therefore not allowed to use them, on the other.

Returning to the question of the impact on competition, we may observe the following:

---

tion of geographical indications and designations of origin for agricultural products and foodstuffs; *Council Regulation (EC) No. 510/2006 of 20 March 2006 on the protection of geographical indications and designations of origin for agricultural products and foodstuffs*. For a detailed account, see *O'Connor* (2003), *supra* note 47, at 83 et seq.; *same author* (2007), *supra* note 47, at 123 et seq.; see also *Knaak* (2001), 'Case Law of the European Court of Justice on the Protection of Geographical Indications and Designations of Origin Pursuant to EC Regulation No. 2081/92', IIC 2001, at 375 et seq.

[49]   See Art. 5 *Council Regulation (EC) No. 510/2006 of 20 March 2006 on the protection of geographical indications and designations of origin for agricultural products and foodstuffs*, speaking of a "group" which "means any association, irrespective of its legal form or composition, of producers or processors working with the same agricultural product or foodstuff."

[50]   Art. 10 (2) PC; Art. 5 (3) *Council Regulation (EC) No. 510/2006 of 20 March 2006 on the protection of geographical indications and designations of origin for agricultural products and foodstuffs*; see also *Correa* (2007), *supra* note 47, at 210.

● The collective trademark, to some extent, reminds us of the afore-mentioned (voluntarily) "shared ownership",[51] since it is based on the decision of a group of market participants to cooperate by introducing such a trademark on the market and subsequently to use it commonly. Consequently, similar considerations regarding its impact on competition may apply.

As a matter of principle, we may assume that a collective trademark tends to be used more extensively than an individual trademark, although there may of course be exceptions. Notably in view of the fact that the owner of an individual trademark may also – even extensively – grant licences and thereby allow its use by other market participants, both the individual as well as the collective trademark may lead to simultaneous usage by a large number of users.[52]

Nevertheless, it must generally be assumed that a collective trademark is used by a number of parties, whereas in the case of the individual trademark, such constellations may only occur based upon specific agreements. Therefore, the average number of users of an individual trademark will presumably be smaller than the users of a collective trademark. In view of this, an impairment of competition by collective trademarks seems more likely, since a – dysfunctional – coordination of the conduct of a substantial number of market participants can be effected more easily.

Contrariwise, the use of a collective trademark may also enhance the diffusion of relevant information about the trademark in question (e.g. about the quality of certain products labelled with that trademark[53]). This may ultimately also lead to advantages for the consumer and may thereby potentially have a particularly positive impact on competition.[54]

---

[51] See above, at Section 3.2.

[52] *Peukert* (2010), *supra* note 4, at 217.

[53] Pursuing this objective, some legislations recognise a particular form of a collective trademark that shall not be discussed in detail in the following, namely the "Guarantee or Certification Trademark" – a sign, that is used by several enterprises under the control of the owner of the mark and which serves to guarantee the quality, geographical origin, type of manufacture or other characteristics common to goods or services of such enterprises, see e.g. Art. 21 Swiss Trademark Act (*Bundesgesetz über den Schutz von Marken und Herkunftsangaben*). See also Sec. 20 (6) German Act against Restraints of Competition (*Gesetz gegen Wettbewerbsbeschränkungen*), where it is stated that an objectively unjustified refusal to become a member of a quality mark association is prohibited.

[54] See *Ricolfi* (2009), Geographical Symbols in Intellectual Property Law: the Policy Options, in: Hilty/Drexl/Nordemann (eds.), Schutz von Kreativität und

- This latter aspect is of even greater relevance with regard to geographical indications or designations of origin. The legal regulations are aimed precisely at the – correct – use of such distinctive signs which provide relevant market information.[55] To give a concrete example: the use of the designation "Parmesan" for cheese, which (1) has been produced in Parma, and (2) according to the specific requirements of the production of "real" Parmesan, provides important information to a consumer interested in buying this particular type of cheese, whereas the use of the designation "Parmesan" for other types of cheese would be dysfunctional. The use of incorrect information would most likely mislead consumers and ultimately risk impairing competition.

To put it in a nutshell, "multiple ownership" may have a broad range of different impacts on competition subject to the manner in which such ownership is exploited in a particular market situation:

- In the form of "collaborative ownership", as well as in the form of "cooperative ownership" arising from specifically designed legislation, "multiple ownership" does not typically impair competition. This is notably the case if an open-door situation exists, which means that any third party meeting the requirements for the use of an indication or designation is allowed to do so.
- Voluntarily created forms of "multiple ownership" – notably "shared ownership" and a form of "cooperative ownership", which do not lead to an open-door situation – risk amplifying those potentially negative impacts on competition that "individual ownership" already tends to have.

3.4 "Collective Ownership"

3.4.1 The notion of "collective ownership"
A definition of the term "collective ownership" is not easy; to some extent this notion may be understood as a – merely "hypothetical" – legal construction, based on certain (theoretical) considerations on how a more cooperative world might be organised within the current legal system.[56] In

---

Wettbewerb, FS Loewenheim, Munich, Beck, 2009, at 231, 235 et seq.

[55] See also *Peukert* (2010), *supra* note 4, at 217.

[56] See, for instance, *Schovsbo* (2010), The Necessity to Collectivize Copyright – and Dangers Thereof, 2010, available at: http://papers.ssrn.com/sol3/papers.cfm?abstract_id=1632753 (accessed 03 February 2011).

fact, as we will see later, particular legal provisions upon which "collective ownership" might be constructed are absent.

On the other hand, the term "collective ownership" tends to reflect the reaction of those groups that are concerned about increasingly observed excesses within the first area of regulation, where the appropriation of protected subject matters is extensively prohibited.[57] In fact, it is this prohibition per se that is sometimes perceived as the source of negative impacts on competition,[58] or – in an even broader sense – of the impairment of interests of the general public.[59]

Against this background, "collective ownership" can hardly be paraphrased more precisely than involving an indefinite number of owners.[60] Beyond that, as already mentioned above,[61] neither the term "ownership" per se nor the term "collective" is self-explanatory, quite the contrary. The latter may be utilised for a number of constellations but does not provide a clear perception of the relationship between the persons involved. Rather, the reasons why such collective ownership evolves may be quite different.

In view of this, it may help to understand the nature of "collective ownership" by introducing the notion "open". This notion can basically be found in three fields:[62]

---

[57]   See, for instance, *Rai/Boyle* (2007), 'Synthetic Biology: Caught Between Property Rights, the Public Domain, and the Commons', PLoS Biology [Vol. 5], at 0389 et seq.; *Maurer/Scotchmer* (2006), Open Source Software: The New Intellectual Property Paradigm, in: Hendershott (ed.), Handbook of Economics and Information Systems, Amsterdam, Elsevier, 2006, at 285 et seq.; *Winickoff/Saha/Graff* (2009), 'Opening Stem Cell Research and Development: A Policy Proposal for the Management of Data. Intellectual Property, and Ethics', Yale Journal of Health Law, Policy and Ethics, at 52 et seq.

[58]   *Bessen/Meurer* (2008), 'Do Patents Perform Like Property?', The Academy of Management Perpectives 2008 [Vol. 22], at 8 et seq.; *Stirnimann* (2004), Urheberkartellrecht, Zurich 2004, at 34 et seq.

[59]   See e.g. *Boyle* (2003), 'The Second Enclosure Movement and the Construction of the Public Domain', Law & Contemporary Problems [Vol. 66], at 33 et seq.; *Heller/Eisenberg* (1998), 'Can Patents Deter Innovation? The Anticommons in Biomedical Research', Science [Vol. 280], at 698 et seq.

[60]   According to *Peukert* (2010), *supra* note 4, at 212, "collective ownership" is characterised by the fact that *one IP right is held by a plurality of persons* and shall include joint ownership and collective trademarks or geographical indications. Both joint ownership and collective trademarks or geographical indications, however, have already been labelled "collaborative or cooperative ownership" as a case of "multiple ownership", see above, at Section 3.3.

[61]   See above, at Section 3.1.

[62]   See *Petrusson/Pamp* (2009), Intellectual Property, Innovation and Openness, in: Arup/van Caenegem (eds.), Intellectual Property Policy Reform. Fostering Innovation and Development, Cheltenham, Edward Elgar, 2009, at 154 et seq.

- "Open source" – related to software – was the first field, where the term was utilised to express the opposite of proprietary (in the sense of exclusively protected) software.[63]
- "Open access" began to be used as a term about one decade ago; it mainly focuses on the access to scientific information in contrast to commercially disseminated information sources (notably by scientific publishers).[64]
- "Open innovation" is finally a rather new, but increasingly used term, albeit a rather cloudy one, addressing certain rather theoretical approaches.[65]

---

[63] For further details, see the *Free Software Foundation*, at http://www.fsf. org/ (accessed 03 February 2011) and the *Open Source Initiative*, at http://www. opensource.org/history (accessed 03 February 2011); see also *S. Weber* (2004), The Success of Open Source, Cambridge, Harvard University Press, 2004; *Rosen* (2004), Open Source Licensing, Upper Saddle River, Prentice Hall PTR, 2004; *Lerner/Tirole* (2005), 'The Scope of Open Source Licensing', Journal of Law, Economics, and Organization [Vol. 21], at 20–56; *McGowan* (2001), 'Intellectual Property Challenges in the Next Century: Legal Implications of Open-Source Software', University of Illinois Law Review, at 241–304; *Hope* (2009), Open Source Genetics. Conceptual Framework, in: Van Overwalle (ed.), Gene Patents and Collaborative Licensing Models, Cambridge, Cambridge University Press, 2009, at 171, 173 et seq. (with regard to implementing open source in the field of human genetics); *R.H. Weber* (2001), 'Does Intellectual Property Become Unimportant in Cyberspace?', International Journal of Law and Information Technology [Vol. 9], at 171 et seq.

[64] See in that respect *Berlin Declaration on Open Access to Knowledge in the Sciences and Humanities*, available at: http://oa.mpg.de/lang/en-uk/berlin-prozess/ berliner-erklarung/ (accessed 03 February 2011); see also *Hilty/Seemann* (2009), Open Access – Zugang zu wissenschaftlichen Publikationen im schweizerischen Recht, Rechtsgutachten im Auftrag der Universität Zürich, Zurich 2009, available at: http://www.oai.uzh.ch/ index.php?option=content&task=view&id=445&Itemi d=324&mos_lng=en (accessed 03 February 2011).

[65] See, for instance, *Chesbrough* (2003), Open Innovation: The New Imperative for Creating and Profiting from Technology, Boston, Harvard Business School Press, 2003, at 155 et seq.; *same author* (2006), Open Innovation: A New Paradigm for Understanding Industrial Innovation, in: Chesbrough/Vanhaverbeke/West (eds.), Open Innovation: Researching a New Paradigm, Oxford, Oxford University Press, 2006, at 1 et seq.; *West/Vanhaverbeke/Chesbrough* (2006), Open Innovation: A Research Agenda, in: Chesbrough/Vanhaverbeke/West (eds.), Open Innovation: Researching a New Paradigm, Oxford, Oxford University Press, 2006, at 285 et seq.; *Dahlander/Gann* (2010), 'How open is innovation?', Research Policy [Vol. 29], at 699 et seq.; see also *Strandburg* (2009), 'Evolving Innovation Paradigms and the Global Intellectual Property Regime', Connecticut Law Review [Vol. 41], at 861 et seq. (criticising TRIPS and its failure to account adequately for the far-reaching changes caused by (open) innovation).

3.4.2   Characteristic of "openness" with regard to copyright law

The first two "open approaches" provide a more or less clear perception. In fact, they both ultimately depend on the existence of copyright law. Copyright law as a matter of principle accrues by the mere act of creation, without any further (formal) effort on the part of the author.[66] In other words, "ownership" is provided anyway, independent of whether the creator wants to acquire that ownership or not.

At the same time, it is precisely this ownership upon which special licensing regimes may be built (usually designated "creative common licences").[67] Such special licensing regimes basically allow for the use of the protected subject matter, however, by imposing certain conditions

---

[66]   In this sense *Cohen/Ryan* (cited by *Guadamuz González* (2005), Open Science: Open Source Licences in Scientific Research, available at: http://papers. ssrn.com/sol3/papers.cfm?abstract_id=764064 (accessed 03 February 2011), at 19 fn. 91): "Copyright [. . .] flows from the nib of a pen."

[67]   *Creative Commons* is a worldwide project that was founded inter alia by *Michael Carroll, Molly Shaffer Van Houweling* and *Lawrence Lessig* in 2001 to provide for standardised open content licensing terms and to make copyright "more accessible and negotiable". This concept allows the creator in a very easy and fast way to define the conditions upon which his work may be reutilised. Due to the easily understandable symbols a user knows exactly what rights he has. All licences are royalty-free and grant the right to copy, distribute, and publicly perform the work for non-commercial use. They all require attribution. Currently, there are six different possible licences: (1) *Attribution* (= user is free to share and to remix, but he has to attribute the work in the manner specified by the author or licensor); (2) *Attribution Share Alike* (= user is free to share and to remix, but he *and* may distribute derivative works only under a licence identical to the licence that governs the original work); (3) *Attribution No Derivatives* (= user is free to share, but he must attribute the work and is not allowed to make derivative works); (4) *Attribution Non-Commercial* (= user is free to share and to remix, but he has to attribute the work and is not allowed to use the work for commercial purposes); (5) *Attribution Non-Commercial Share Alike* and (6) *Attribution Non-Commercial No Derivatives*. *Creative Commons* licences have now been developed in 53 jurisdictions. For further details, see http://creativecommons.org/about/licenses/ (accessed 03 February 2011); with regard to the history of *Creative Commons*, see http://creativecommons.org/about/history/ (accessed 03 February 2011). For an excellent and comprehensive overview, see *Fitzgerald* (2007), A Short Overview of Creative Commons, in: Fitzgerald (ed.), Open Content Licensing: Cultivating the Creative Commons, Sydney 2007, at 3 et seq., available at: http://eprints.qut. edu.au/6677/1/6677.pdf (accessed 03 February 2011); see also *Hietanen* (2008), The Pursuit of Efficient Copyright Licensing, Lappeenranta, Lappeenrannan Teknillinen Yliopisto, 2008, at 42 et seq.; *Lessig* (2004), Free Culture, New York, Penguin Press, 2004, at 275 et seq.; in a critical vein, see *Elkin-Koren* (2006), Exploring Creative Commons: A Sceptical View of a Worthy Pursuit, in: Guibault/Hugenholtz (eds.), The Future of the Public Domain. Identifying the

and requirements. The most relevant requirement is that "creative uses" of the subject matter in question (meaning its use for further, additional steps of creation) are permitted insofar as the result of this further or additional creation likewise remains "open" for any further (creative) use by third parties.[68] One of the most prominent examples in this respect might be Wikipedia. Indeed, under www.wikipedia.com we find a huge number of apparently integrative works (text, pictures), which, however, only exist due to the contribution of an indefinite number of creators.[69] All these works are concurrently subject to any further addition and creation.

Bearing these characteristics in mind, one might indeed be seduced into talking of a "collective ownership" of such works. Nevertheless, formally, the "collectiveness" is limited to the fact of the described form of cooperation of different individuals, resulting in one – or possibly more than one – integrative work. Consequently, this result as such is not owned collectively, but is ultimately nothing more than a combination of numerous individual ownerships of the same work or works.[70] Each piece of

---

Commons in Information Law, Alphen aan den Rijn, Kluwer Law International, 2006, at 325 et seq.

68   This provision is called "Share-Alike" ["⊚"], i.e. licensees may distribute derivative works only under a licence identical to the licence that governs the original work. This licence condition was inspired by the Free Software Foundation's GNU *General Public License* (GPL) which was the first *copyleft* licence; for a detailed account, see *Carver* (2006), 'Share and Share Alike: Understanding and Enforcing Open Source and Free Software Licenses', Berkeley Technology Law Journal [Vol. 20], at 443–480. The "Share-Alike" provision has also been criticised in the literature, see, for instance, *Katz* (2006), Pitfalls of Open Licensing: An Analysis of Creative Commons Licensing, IDEA – The Intellectual Property Law Review [Vol. 46], at 391, 399 et seq., arguing that the CC-licence scheme could create systematic and unexpected problems since certain licences may be incompatible with others. Notably the Share-Alike licence may regulate derivative works in a way that could impede the creation of new works; this is particularly the case if a derivative work is based on multiple pre-existing works subject to different Share-Alike licences.

Concerning the validity of the *copyleft* clauses, see *Guadamuz González* (2004), "Viral Contracts or Unenforceable Documents? Contractual Validity of Copyleft Licences", EIPR 2004, at 331, 334 et seq.

69   See e.g. *Rimmer* (2009), Wikipedia, collective authorship and the politics of knowledge, in: Arup/van Caenegem (eds.), Intellectual Property Policy Reform. Fostering Innovation and Development, Cheltenham, Edward Elgar Publishing, 2009, at 172, 178.

70   Similarly *Gosh* (2005), Creativity and Domains of Collaboration, in: Gosh (ed.), Code: Collaborative Ownership and the Digital Economy, Cambridge, Mass., MIT Press, at 8.

individual ownership is based on all pre-existing individual ownerships of the pre-existing parts of the work in question,[71] and only encompasses the newly created part.

Interestingly, the combination of these – to some extent "tied" – individual ownerships is even the key to the fact that the system as such remains open: only based on such ownership is it possible to establish and to enforce this special ("open") licensing regime.[72] In other words, "open source" or "open access" first of all requires the existence of individual ownership,[73] although such ownership is not collectively exerted in an exclusive manner, but in a way to ensure openness on a sustainable basis for any further, additional steps of creation related to the work or works in question.[74]

3.4.3   Characteristic of "openness" with regard to patent law

In contrast, open innovation is based on a different legal framework. With regard to the related right – mostly a patent right – (formal) legal owner-ship does not accrue from the mere act of innovation. Rather, a kind of

---

[71]   In this sense: "[. . .] Creativity and innovation rely on a rich heritage of prior intellectual endeavour. We stand on the shoulders of giants by revisiting, reusing, and transforming the ideas and works of our peers and predecessors [. . .]", at: http://wiki.creativecommons.org/Legal_Concepts (accessed 03 February 2011); see also *Nelson/Winter* (1982), An Evolutionary Theory of the Economic Change, Cambridge, Belknap Press of Harvard University Press, 1982, at 130 (pointing out that innovation "[. . .] consists to a substantial extent of a recombination of conceptual and physical materials that were previously in existence"); see also *Treiger-Bar-Am* (2007), Authors' Rights as a Limit to Copyright Control, in: Macmillan (ed.), New Directions in Copyright Law, Vol. 6, Cheltenham, Edward Elgar Publishing, 2007, at 359, 364 et seq.; see also *Laddie* (1996), Copyright: over-strength, over-regulated, over-rated?, EIPR 1996, at 253, 259: "[. . .] The whole of human development is derivative [. . .]"; *Landes/Posner* (2003), *supra* note 15, at 66, 67; *Lemley* (1996), The Economics of Improvement of Intellectual Property Law, at 9, 10 (but in a sceptical vein at 53 et seq.), available at: http://papers.ssrn.com/sol3/ papers.cfm?abstract_id=1274199 (accessed 03 February 2011).

[72]   *Dreyfuss* (2010), 'Does IP Need IP? Accommodating Intellectual Property Production outside the Intellectual Property Paradigm', Cardozo Law Review [Vol. 31], at 1437, 1449.

[73]   *Elkin-Koren* (2005), 'What Contracts Can't Do: The Limits of Private Ordering in Facilitating a Creative Commons', Fordham Law Review [Vol. 74], at 101, 119 et seq., 133.

[74]   See *Creative Commons*, License Your Work: "[. . .] With a Creative Commons license, *you keep your copyright* but allow people to copy and distribute your work [. . .]", available at: http://creativecommons.org/choose/ ?lang=en_GB (accessed 03 February 2011).

"factual ownership" initially comes into existence, namely in the form of what Art. 39 TRIPS calls "undisclosed information".[75]

Based on this factual ownership,[76] the inventor in the first instance has three possibilities. He (1) may keep the information undisclosed, (2) may disclose it without acquiring formal legal ownership (in other words, he does not apply for a patent), or (3) may apply for formal legal ownership (a patent) which at a certain stage of procedure unavoidably leads to the publication of his application and thereby to disclosure of the related information even before grant of the patent (and actually without protection if the requirements are not met).

In the first case, "openness" of the innovation will not be achieved, whereas in the second case, "openness" ensues, although the inventor no longer has any control over the further use of his innovation by third parties. In the third case, assuming the patent is finally granted, the

---

[75]   Interestingly, during the negotiations of the TRIPS Agreement it was highly debated if "undisclosed information" should be deemed as a form of "property" and therefore as a category of "intellectual property" (see e.g. the wording of the proposal of the United States: "[. . .] To maintain legal protection, the owner of a trade secret may be required to make efforts reasonable under the circumstances to maintain such secrecy [. . .]", Suggestion by the United States for Achieving the Negotiating Objective, MTN.GNG/NG11/W/14/Rev. 1, of October 17, 1988, at 6 et seq.; see also the response of India: "[. . .] Trade Secrets cannot be considered to be intellectual property rights. [. . .]", Standards and Principles Concerning the Availability, Scope and Use of Trade-Related Intellectual Property Rights, MTN. GNG/NG11/W/37, of July 1989, at paragraph 46 et seq.).

However, the idea that undisclosed information should be subject to unfair competition rules prevailed in the end; see *Correa* (2007), *supra* note 47, at 367, 368; with regard to the legislative history of Article 39 TRIPS, see *de Carvalho* (2008), The TRIPS Regime of Antitrust and Undisclosed Information, The Hague, Kluwer Law International, 2008, at 207 et seq. (marginal no. 39.2.1. et seq.).

That is why the agreement does not mention words such as "property" and "proprietary" and uses instead "control", see Art. 39 (2) TRIPS: "Natural and legal persons shall have the possibility of preventing *information lawfully within their control* from being disclosed [. . .]". Nevertheless, irrespective of the legal nature of "undisclosed information" it is undisputed that the *holder* has *possession* of the information in question. See *de Carvalho* (2008), *ibid.*, at 226 (marginal no. 39.2.38); see also *UNCTAD* (2005), Resource Book on TRIPS and Development, Chapter 28: Undisclosed Information, at 526 et seq., available at: http://www.iprsonline.org/unctadictsd/ ResourceBookIndex.htm (accessed 03 February 2011).

With regard to this "property approach" in national law, see e.g. *Cornish* (1975), Der Geheimnischutz im englischen Recht, GRUR Int. 1975, at 153 et seq.; *The American Law Institute* (ed.), Restatement of Law (Third) of Unfair Competition, S. Paul 1995, at 426, 439 et seq.

[76]   *Correa* (2007), *supra* note 47, at 368.

outcome to some extent resembles copyright law, albeit with different legal characteristics.

As a matter of principle, as already mentioned, filing a patent application involves disclosure of the information related to the innovation. In other words, unlike copyright law, where access to information is the controversial issue (e.g. scientific information stored electronically in a database, which cannot be accessed freely, but is secured by technical protection measures applied by the scientific publisher running the database), the question of access to information is not an issue under patent law.[77] On the contrary, it is precisely the aim of patent law to reveal the related information, on the one hand, but to prohibit the use of it once the patent is granted, on the other hand.[78] Additionally, subject to the applicable patent legislation,[79] filing the application may already cause a kind of anticipated effect of the subsequently granted exclusive right. In contrast, copyright law – once access to information is achieved – does not prohibit the use of the related information.[80]

Once the patent is granted, there are basically two possibilities to achieve openness:

● The patent owner himself (who might be, but is not necessarily, the former inventor) may take the decision to "open" the system. In

---

[77]   *Régibeau/Rockett* (2007), IP Law and Competition Law: An Economic Approach, in: Anderman (ed.), The Interface between Intellectual Property Rights and Competition Policy, Cambridge, Cambridge University Press, 2007, at 505, 517; *Boettinger/Burk* (2004), 'Open Source Patenting', Journal of International Biotechnology Law [Vol. 1], at 224, 225.

[78]   *Ghidini* (2006), Patent Protection of Innovations: A Monopoly with a Wealth of Antibodies, in: Ghidini (ed.), Intellectual Property and Competition Law. The Innovation Nexus, Cheltenham, Edward Elgar Publishing, 2006, at 13, 25 et seq.; *Landes/Posner* (2003), *supra* note 15, at 294, 295.

[79]   See Art. 67 (1) *European Patent Convention* (EPC) ("A European patent application shall, from the date of its publication, provisionally confer upon the applicant the protection provided for by Article 64 [. . .]") granting the same full protection as a European patent. None of the Contracting States of the EPC, however, has implemented such provision, but limited protection instead (pursuant to Art. 67 (2) EPC), e.g. compensation remedy. Similarly, according to 35 U.S.C. Sec. 154 (d) (1) "a patent shall include the right to obtain a reasonable royalty" for any infringement committed "during the period beginning on the date of publication of the application for such patent [. . .] and ending on the date the patent is issued". See also Art. 29 *Patent Cooperation Treaty* (PCT); Art. 9 (3) *Eurasian Patent Convention*; *Pahlow* (2008), Erfindungsschutz vor Patenterteilung, GRUR 2008, at 97–103.

[80]   See Article 9 Sec 2 TRIPS, or Article 2 WIPO Copyright Treaty (WCT); see also 17 U.S.C. Sec. 102 (b).

particular, based on patent law – equal to creative common licences based on copyright law – he may establish a special licensing regime and thereby allow for certain uses under specific conditions and requirements, notably the requirement of ongoing openness for any further – downstream – innovation related to his patent.[81]

- Even if the patent owner does not opt for a special licensing regime but, on the contrary, insists on the exclusivity of his patent, a degree of "openness" may arise from the applicable legislation. In fact, most patent legislations (pursuant to Art. 31 lit. (l) TRIPS),[82] provide for the establishment of a compulsory licence in the case that "a patent ('the second patent') . . . cannot be exploited without infringing another patent ('the first patent')", if a number of requirements are met.[83]

---

[81] See, for instance, the *Creative Commons Public Patent License*, available at: http://wiki.creativecommons.org/CC_Public_Patent_License (accessed 03 February 2011). See also the *Open Invention Network* (OIN), which acquires patents and makes them available by granting a royalty-free licence to any company or individual that agrees not to assert its patents against Linux; for more details, see http://www.openinventionnetwork.com/ (accessed 03 February 2011); *Feldman* (2005), 'The Open Source Biotechnology Movement: Is it Patent Misuse?', Minnesota Journal of Law, Science & Technology [Vol. 6], at 132, 140, 141 (also discussing if this licensing regime is impermissible due to patent misuse, which – according to *Feldman* – is not the case); see also *Science Commons*, available at: http://sciencecommons.org/ (accessed 03 February 2011); *International HapMap Project*, available at: http://hapmap.ncbi.nlm.nih.gov/index.html.en (accessed 03 February 2011).

[82] See in this regard *Julian-Arnold* (1993), International Compulsory Licensing: The Rationales and the Reality, IDEA: The Journal of Law and Technology, at 350, 358, 359 et seq. (pointing out that "a provision of this nature may indeed serve to foster technical progress" and "provide an incentive for the furtherance of technical and economic development").

[83] See, for instance, Sec. 24 (2) German Patent Act (*Patentgesetz*); Art. 36 Swiss Patent Act (*Bundesgesetz über die Erfindungspatente*); in the U.S., however, legal provisions for compulsory licences in patent law are missing. See in that respect *Frost* (1946), 'Legal Incidents of Non-Use of Patented Inventions Reconsidered', The George Washington Law Review [Vol. 14], at 273 et seq.; for an overview concerning "compulsory licences" in general, see *Julian-Arnold* (1993), *supra* note 82, at 349 et seq.; *Salamolard* (1978), La licence obligatoire en matière de brevets d'invention, Genève 1978.

For further details concerning Art. 31 lit. (l) TRIPS, see *de Carvalho* (2010), The TRIPS Regime of Patent Rights, 3rd ed., Alphen aan den Rijn, Kluwer Law International, 2010, at 508, 511 et seq. (discussing the similarity of compulsory licences for dependent patents with the essential facilities doctrine and pointing out that it is impossible to imply the essential facilities doctrine to patent law); *Ghidini* (2006), *supra* note 78, at 13, 36 et seq.; see also Art. 5 (2) PC.

In the first case, if the patent owner establishes a special licensing regime, the effect may be similar to the creative common licences in the open source (software) or open access (publishing) environment, provided that every subsequent inventor behaves in the same way, namely either by initially disclosing the information containing his further invention without acquiring formal legal ownership, or by acquiring a patent and establishing a special licensing regime. In the latter case, every such subsequent inventor per se is an individual owner of a patent. However, ownership – collectively – is not exercised exclusively, but in a manner so as to ensure openness on a sustainable basis in view of any further or additional steps of innovation. Thus, as we have seen with regard to copyright law, the term "collective ownership" is again imprecise, even if it describes certain effects of such a special licensing regime in a comprehensible way.

In the second case, if a compulsory licence is granted, we also face one (or possibly more than one) subsequent owner(s) of one (or more) younger patent(s). However, such owners of younger ("dependent") patents are not usually committed to establishing a special licensing regime. Rather, they exercise their individual rights exclusively and as far as possible independently. In other words, there is no foundation for the term "collective ownership".

3.4.4   Impacts of "open approaches" on competition

Now, in view of the outlines of such "open approaches", which to some extent lead to what may (imprecisely) be paraphrased as "collective ownership", what are their impacts on competition?

For a start, we may assume that the collective "understanding" of a group of (ultimately individual, but deliberately "connected") owners not to exercise their ownership in an exclusive manner will generally have a positive impact.[84] This assumption is based on the consideration that network effects – under certain conditions, particularly in view of innovation or creation processes – produce positive effects. In truth, we know that creation and innovation do not happen in isolation. The single creator and particularly the single inventor rarely exist in reality; the generation of something "new" in most cases is a cooperative process. Insofar, we may

---

[84]   *Bessen/Maskin* (2009), 'Sequential Innovation, Patents, and Imitation', RAND Journal of Economics [Vol. 40], at 611, 619 et seq.; *Olivieri/Marchegiani* (2007), Open Source Software and Technological Innovation: Competitive Issues, in: Gellini/Cozzi (eds.), Intellectual Property, Competition and Growth, Houndmills, Palgrave Macmillan, 2007, at 47, 59 et seq.; *Maurer/Scotchmer* (2006), *supra* note 57, at 285 et seq.; similarly *David* (2003), *supra* note 17, at 19, 28 et seq.

suppose that well-designed forms of "collective ownership" – or rather the establishment of special (i.e. open) licensing regimes – will potentially increase stimulation to invent or create.[85]

The question, however, is whether we may consequently conclude that "collective ownership" – in the sense of "openness" – will have a positive impact on competition.[86] In fact, the answer to this question might depend on a number of further factors, as competition hardly (or at least not only) takes place at the level of innovators or creators. In reality, creators are rarely in a (negotiating) position to maintain legally acquired "ownership", but rather have to assign their copyrights to employers, producers, investors etc.[87] Worse still is the situation of inventors, who do not even acquire the related patents themselves, since the applications are usually initially filed (and patents ultimately acquired) by those parties who will subsequently exploit the patent or license it to third parties.

But even the veritable owner of an IP right is not necessarily the ultimate player on the market, since he is not usually the "entrepreneur" who exploits the protected subject matter. In other words, the impact of IP law on competition at the end of the day does not depend on the actions of creators or inventors themselves and possibly not even of subsequent owners of the related rights.[88] Rather, we have to focus on those particular entrepreneurs who exploit patents, copyrights, etc., as economic assets on the market.[89] Such entrepreneurs obviously do not have the same interests as inventors or creators, who may themselves benefit from open systems when their own innovations are based on pre-existing protected subject matter. Entrepreneurs, on the contrary, do not have any reason why they should not exert their "ownership", which they have contractually

---

[85] See *Litman* (2007), The Economics of Open Access Law Publishing, Lewis & Clark Law Review [Vol. 10], at 101 et seq.; see also *Bessen/Maskin* (2009), *supra* note 84, at 619, 628 (arguing that strong intellectual property rights could inhibit innovation when discoveries are *sequential* (i.e. that "each successive invention builds in an essential way on its predecessors").

[86] *Feldman* (2005), *supra* note 81, at 164 et seq.

[87] See *Hugenholtz* (2000), The Great Copyright Robbery. Rights allocation in a digital environment, A free information ecology in a digital environment, Conference NYU School of Law 2000, available at: www.ivir.nl/publications/hugenholtz/thegreatcopyrightrobbery.pdf (accessed 03 February 2011).

[88] *Drexl* (2006), Droit d'auteur et information scientifique – Analyse concurrentielle, protection des bases de données et perspective allemande, in: IRPI (ed.), La propériété intellectuelle en question(s) – Regards croisés européens, Paris, Litec, 2006, at 73.

[89] For more details concerning the limitation of exclusivity, see *Peukert* (2010), *supra* note 4, at 204 et seq.

acquired by purchase, under unrestricted exclusivity in order to generate as much income as possible.[90]

The more such conduct by entrepreneurs becomes a reality, the more important it may be under certain conditions to limit their freedom to exert their "ownership" exclusively.[91] On the one hand, this can be achieved by the implementation of statutory limitations, notably the aforementioned system of compulsory licences.[92] On the other hand, however – and this is precisely the important observation here – we must be aware of the potential benefits of open systems (and insofar the benefits of approaches named "collective ownership"). In fact, as long as it is up to the creator or inventor to permit certain uses of his creation or invention under certain conditions, the freedom of any subsequent owner to exploit the legal title exclusively may remain limited, subject to the applicable legislation.[93] After all, open systems – and thus the permission for subsequent creators

---

[90]   See, for instance, *The Wellcome Trust* (2003), Economic analysis of scientific research publishing. A report commissioned by the Wellcome Trust, Cambridgeshire 2003, at 19 et seq., available at: http://www.wellcome.ac.uk/stellent/groups/corporatesite/@policy_communications/documents/web_document/wtd003182.pdf (accessed 03 February 2011); see also *Montagnani/Borghi* (2008), Positive Copyright and Open Content Licences: How to Make a Marriage Work by Empowering Authors to Disseminate their Creations, International Journal of Communications Law & Policy [Vol. 12], at 244, 251 et seq.

[91]   In the same sense *Montagnani/Borghi* (2008), *supra* note 90, at 244, 252 et seq.; *Peukert* (2010), *supra* note 4, at 204.

[92]   In more depth in this regard, see *Hilty* (2009), Renaissance der Zwangslizenzen im Urheberrecht? Gedanken zu Ungereimtheiten auf der urheberrechtlichen Wertschöpfungskette, GRUR, Beck, 2009, at 633 et seq.; see also *Reichman* (2001), 'Of Green Tulips and Legal Kudzu: Repacking Rights in Subpatentable Innovation', Vanderbilt Law Review [Vol. 53], at 1743 et seq. (suggesting a compensatory liability regime).

[93]   An interesting proposal is made by *Montagnani/Borghi* (2008), *supra* note 90, at 244, 269 et seq., suggesting a limitation on freedom of copyright contracts. This so-called "Non-Commercial Dissemination Provision" (NCDP) is conceived as an "inalienable and unwaivable right" providing authors with the possibility of disseminating their works after a first commercial exploitation. According to the NCDP *authors shall be entitled to distribute and communicate to the public their works as a web digital resource for non-commercial purposes whenever the exercise of rights granted for commercial purposes no longer engenders substantial revenue.* The last condition, the exhaustion of the commercial value of the work, however, is hard to define. Therefore, *Montagnani/Borghi* propose a tentative test to determine *ex post facto* this exhaustion of commercial value; for further details, see *Montagnani/Borghi* (2008), *supra* note 90, at 271 et seq.; see also *Aigrain* (2005), Positive Intellectual Rights and Information Exchanges, in: Gosh (ed.), Code: Collaborative Ownership and the Digital Economy, Cambridge, Mass., MIT Press, 2005, at 287, 297 et seq., arguing for a *positive* approach to IPRs that centres

or inventors to use pre-existing creations or inventions – are based on contractual relationships;[94] in the case of a transfer of the related legal title (the copyright, patent etc.) to third parties, such contractual relationships must be sufficiently sustainable. If this is not the case – in other words, if by acquiring an exclusive right, prior contractual permission to other parties can be negated – open systems unavoidably fail. Consequently, the applicable legislation needs to ensure that any subsequent holder of an acquired exclusive right is not in a position to prohibit further "creative uses" of the protected subject matter. Ultimately, the suitability of the legal framework depends on an appropriate resolution of conflict arising between contractual (so-called "relative") rights and exclusive ("absolute") rights.[95] At the same time, this is the weak point of the whole construction of open systems.

3.4.5 Alternative understanding of "open innovation"

For the sake of completeness, it should be added that the aforementioned is not the only or even necessarily the common understanding of "open innovation". Beyond that, some industries are increasingly becoming aware of the fact that cooperation with other market participants (possibly even competitors) may ultimately increase their potential for technical improvements.[96] Based on this awareness, such industries are tending to reconsider their former policies of "exclusivity" and, instead, some are currently "opening" their research and development activities to others.[97]

---

on the needs of creators and emphasising that these "positive rights" should be the basic principle in order to promote innovation.

[94] Regarding the *copyleft* licences and the relevance of third-party rights, see *Guadamuz González* (2004), *supra* note 68, at 331, 336 et seq.

[95] In more depth in this regard, see *Hilty* (2001), Lizenzvertragsrecht, Bern, Stämpfli, 2001, at 107 et seq.

[96] *Chesbrough* (2006), *supra* note 65, at 1 et seq.; *Alexy/Criscuolo/Salter* (2009), 'Does IP Strategy Have to Cripple Open Innovation?', MIT Sloan Management Review [Vol. 51], at 71–8; *Hunter/Stephens* (2010), 'Is open innovation the way forward for big pharma?', Nature Reviews Drug Discovery [Vol. 9], at 87.

[97] See *Chesbrough/Vanhaverbeke/West* (eds.), Open Innovation: Researching a New Paradigm, Oxford, Oxford University Press, 2006, Part I (at 15 et seq.); *Laursen/Salter* (2006), 'Open for innovation: the role of openness in explaining innovation performance among UK manufacturing firms', Strategic Management Journal [Vol. 27], at 131–50; *König/Battiston/Napoletano/Schweitzer* (2009), The Efficiency and Evolution of R&D Networks, Paris 2009, available at: http://www.ofce.sciences-po.fr/pdf/dtravail/WP2008-31.pdf (accessed 03 February 2011); see also *Verbeure* (2009), *supra* note 35, at 3 et seq.; *Shapiro* (2000), Navigating the Patent Thicket: Cross Licenses, Patent Pools, and Standard Setting, available at: http://groups.haas.berkeley.edu/iber/cpc/pubs/Publications.html#2000

This more "open" behaviour is sometimes also called "open innovation", although it is not necessarily comparable to initiatives that have been undertaken by "open source" or "open access" communities, at least not insofar as these industries at the end of the day rely on the exclusive rights provided by patent law. Rather, the intention of such cooperation may ultimately lead to what we have been discussing under the term "shared ownership" as one (voluntary) form of "multiple ownership".[98] As we have seen, the impacts on competition of such forms of ownership are hard to predict; however, at least it does not seem likely that "shared ownership" will unleash similar synergies as we may assume in an environment of truly open forms of cooperation.[99]

Beyond that, some industries may open the system even more and include undetermined market participants so that (some) results of their own research and development activities will be – more or less fully – disclosed to third parties for the sake of technical progress. However, the impact on competition of this kind of "openness" ultimately depends on the overall behaviour of such industries. The more they commonly share knowledge in a long-term perspective and the less they insist on exclusive rights after having achieved a certain state of the art, the more likely it is that such openness will indeed increase the potential for further progress and thus probably foster a competitive environment.

4.   EXCURSUS

4.1   Collective Rights Management

The term "collective" brings to mind the management of rights – notably within the area of copyright law – which may operate in such a way that "collecting societies" are involved. This latter term obviously focuses on one of the main tasks of such organisations, namely the "collection" of royalties from the users of copyright-protected works in order to fulfil the second main task of such organisations,[100] namely to distribute the income

---

(accessed 03 February 2011); *same author* (2001), Setting Compatibility Standards: Cooperation or Collusion, in: Dreyfuss/Zimmerman/First (eds.), Expanding the Boundaries of Intellectual Property, Oxford, Oxford University Press, 2001, at 81 et seq.; *van Zimmeren* (2009), *supra* note 39, at 63 et seq.

[98]   See above, at Section 3.2.

[99]   See above, at Section 3.4.4.

[100]   See generally *Fiscor* (2002), Collective Management of Copyright and Related Rights, Geneva, WIPO, 2002, at 15 et seq.; *Gervais* (2010), Collective

amongst the different right holders. The common term for these activities is "collective rights management", which has to be seen in contrast to "individual rights management". Individual rights management – notably in the form of individual licensing – in principle applies to constellations in which the right holder himself is in a position to contract directly with the user(s) of his work(s).

This freedom, however, may be limited in order to ban potential misuse by individually exploiting copyrights. Notably so-called "derivate right holders" – industries[101] that purchase copyrights from the original right holders (the creators), like editors, producers etc. – tend to leverage the anticompetitive potential of copyright law by bundling a sufficient number of titles (e.g. scientific articles, music) and to build market power upon certain particular – usually online – business models.[102] One remedy against such behaviour is an obligation to contract with collecting societies in order to allow the latter to grant usage licences to interested third parties (e.g. to libraries).

Therefore, in some legal systems a number of exploitation rights may not be administered individually, and right holders must involve collecting societies.[103] Moreover, in Nordic countries a special form of "enforced"

Management of Copyright: Theory and Practice in the Digital Age, in: Gervais (ed.), Collective Management of Copyright and Related Rights, 2nd edn., Alphen aan de Rijn, Wolters Kluwer, 2010, at 1 et seq.; for an overview of collective rights management in different parts of the world, see *Gervais* (ed.), Collective Management of Copyright and Related Rights, 2nd ed., Alphen aan de Rijn, Wolters Kluwer, 2010, at 135 et seq.; see also *Kretschmer* (2002), The Failure of Property Rules in Collective Administration. Rethinking Copyright Societies as Regulatory Instruments, EIPR 2002, at 126–136.

[101]   For more details concerning the price and distribution policies of these industries, see *Hilty* (2005), *supra* note 38, at 118 et seq.; *same author* (2006), Das Urheberrecht und der Wissenschaftler, GRUR Int. 2006, at 179 et seq.; see also *European Commission* (2006), Study on the economic and technical evolution of the scientific publication markets in Europe, Final report, available at: http://ec.europa.eu/research/science-society/pdf/scientific-publication-study_en.pdf (accessed 03 February 2011).

[102]   See *Helfer* (2010), Collective Management of Copyright and Human Rights: An Uneasy Alliance, in: Gervais (ed.), Collective Management of Copyright and Related Rights, 2nd ed., Alphen aan de Rijn, Wolters Kluwer, 2010, at 75, 90 et seq.; see also *The Wellcome Trust* (2003), *supra* note 90, at 19 et seq., available at: http://www.wellcome.ac.uk/stellent/ groups/corporatesite/@policy_communica tions/documents/web_document/wtd003182.pdf (accessed 03 February 2011).

[103]   See e.g. Germany, where the right of cable retransmission may be exercised by a collecting society only, Sec. 20 (b) German Copyright Act (*Gesetz über Urheberrecht und verwandte Schutzrechte*), or according to Sec. 52 (a) German Copyright Act (public accessibility for tuition and research), remuneration can only

collective rights management is known under the title "extended collective licences".[104] A licence agreement between an organisation of right owners

---

be asserted through a collecting society; for a detailed account, see *Plate* (2003), Die Verwertungsgesellschaftspflicht für urheberrechtliche Vergütungsansprüche und ausschließliche Verwertungsrechte, Berlin, Berliner Wiss.-Verl., 2004, at 71 et seq.; see also *Hilty* (1995) (ed.), Die Verwertung von Urheberrechten in Europa, Basel, Helbing & Lichtenhahn, 1995; *same author* (2010), Kollektive Rechtewahrnehmung und Vergütungsregelungen: Harmonisierungsbedarf und –möglichkeiten, in: Leistner (ed.), Europäische Perspektiven des Geistigen Eigentums, Tübingen, Mohr Siebeck, 2010, at 123 et seq.

[104]   This legal model has been used in the Nordic countries since the early 1960s; see generally *Koskinen-Olsson* (2010), Collective Management in the Nordic countries, in: Gervais (ed.), Collective Management of Copyright and Related Rights, 2nd ed., Alphen aan de Rijn, Wolters Kluwer, 2010, at 283 et seq.; *Olsson* (2005), The Extended Collective License as Applied in the Nordic Countries, available at: http://www.kopinor.no/en/copyright/extended-collective-license/documents/ The+ Extended+Collective+License+as+Applied+in+the+Nordic+Countries.748.cms (accessed 03 February 2011); *Christiansen* (1991), The Nordic Licensing System – Extended Collective Agreement Licensing, EIPR 1991, at 346 et seq.; *Riis/ Schovsbo* (2010), Extended Collective Licenses and the Nordic Experience – It's a Hybrid but is it a Volvo or a Lemon?, Columbia Journal of Law and the Arts [Vol. 33 Issue IV] (forthcoming), at 1 et seq., available at: http://papers.ssrn.com/sol3/ papers.cfm?abstract_id=1535230 (accessed 03 February 2011).

Since Extended Collective Licences "have the effectiveness of compulsory licences but at the same time leave right holders in control of the use of their works" (see *Riis/Schovsbo* (2010), *ibid.*, at 2), they have attracted more and more international attention; see *Spurgeon* (2003), License or Limit? On-Line Educational Uses: Alternatives for Preserving the Exclusive Rights of Copyright Owners, at 12 et seq., available at: http://portal.unesco.org/culture/en/files/11061/ 10675961831Spurgeon_E.pdf/Spurgeon%2BE.pdf (accessed 03 February 2011); *European Commission* (2008), Green Paper on Copyright in the Knowledge Economy, COM (2008), at 16 et seq., available at: http://ec.europa.eu/internal_ market/copyright/docs/copyright-infso/greenpaper_en.pdf (accessed 03 February 2011); *European Commission* (2009), Creative Content in European Digital Single Market: Challenges for the Future, A Reflection Document of DG INFSO and DG MARKT, at 14 et seq., available at: http://ec.europa.eu/avpolicy/docs/other_ actions/col_2009/reflection_paper.pdf (accessed 03 February 2011).

Despite their usefulness, one has to keep in mind, that Extended Collective Licences have to be seen in the cultural context of the Nordic societies, see in particular *Riis/Schovsbo* (2010), *ibid.*, at 2, 23 et seq. However, in Scandinavia there is an ongoing discussion about broadening the provisions on Extended Collective Licences, e.g. a general rule concerning Extended Collective Licences was recently introduced in Denmark, Sec. 50 (2) Denmark Copyright Act (DCA), allowing the parties to enter into agreements in all cases where organisations and users find the use of an agreement to be helpful; for further details, see *Riis/Schovsbo* (2010), *ibid.*, at 6; similar rules are being considered in other Nordic countries. Other proposals are made concerning library distribution of digitised material or the making (copyright holders) and users *is extended by law* to right owners who are *not* members of the organisation.[105]

However, even if collective rights management is mandatory, the term "collective" as such is to some extent misleading. This form of management of rights does not involve an alteration from "individual ownership" to any other form of ownership. Rather, the term focuses on the, ultimately merely organisational, issue of the "management" of rights. Admittedly, this management may not only be based on a merely fiduciary appearance of collecting societies on the market (exploiting *foreign* rights in their own name), but rather the related copyrights as such may be assigned to the collecting society in order to enable the society to act as the right holder instead of the "actual" right holder, notably claiming royalties for the use of its *own* rights and in its own name. The internal relationship between "actual" right holders on the one hand and collecting societies on the other, however, is limited by the purpose of the contract: a collecting society acts instead of the right holder, but ultimately on his behalf.

The consequence of such a construction is that we are neither faced with a kind of "shared ownership" nor with truly "collective ownership". Even after assigning copyrights to collecting societies, we are still dealing with – transferred – "individual ownership". Nevertheless, this transfer is not without relevance with regard to the question of the impact on competition. For collecting societies are able to bundle a huge number of individual copyrights and at the same time, subject to the applicable legislation, they may act independently insofar as competing collecting societies in the same (national) territory may possibly not exist.[106] Therefore, the involvement of collecting societies in the administration of copyrights

---

of copies at places of work including digital work, see *Swedish Government Official Report* (SOU 2010:24), at 10, 232, 241 et seq., available at: http://www.sweden. gov.se/content/1/c6/14/33/63/a1746577.pdf (accessed 03 February 2011). See also (for Canada), *Gervais* (2003), Extended Collective Licensing Regime in Canada: Principles and Issues Related to Implementation, available at: http://aix1.uottawa. ca/~dgervais/publications/extended_licensing.pdf (accessed 03 February 2011).

[105]   The organisation of right holders has to represent a substantial number of right holders in the field concerned. Unrepresented right holders must be given equal treatment to those who are directly represented by the organisation, i.e. that both members and non-members shall receive the same distribution. The foreign right owners also have a right to individual remuneration and the possibility to opt out of the agreement; the latter, however, is seldom used in practice; for further details, see *Koskinen-Olsson* (2010), *supra* note 104, at 283, 291 et seq.

[106]   *Handke/Towse* (2007), Economics of Copyright Collecting Societies, IIC 2007, at 940, 941.

is of considerable interest to competition authorities.[107] However, this is not due to any specific form of ownership but is simply based on the particular structure of the market.[108] In the following, we will therefore not deepen this discussion.

4.2 The Notion of "Common Land" (Allmende)

Occasionally the discussion on alternatives to the traditional "proprietary" approaches of IP law focuses on the fact that the protected subject matter in question is of such public interest that "common ownership" by the whole community concerned would be the only feasible approach.[109] Laurence Lessig[110] notably discussed the notion of what in German is

---

[107]   See e.g. *European Commission* (2005) Recommendation 2005/737/EC of 18 May 2005 on collective cross-border management of copyright and related rights for legitimate online music services, available at: http://eur-lex.europa. eu/LexUriServ/site/en/oj/2005/l_276/l_27620051021en00540057.pdf (accessed 03 February 2011).

[108]   See for further details *Hollander* (1984), Market Structure and Performance in Intellectual Property: The Case of Copyright Collectives, International Journal of Industrial Organization [Vol. 2], at 199 et seq.; *Besen/Kirby* (1989), Compensating Creators of Intellectual Property – Collectives that Collect, The Rand Corporation 1989, available at: http://www.rand.org/pubs/reports/2007/ R3751.pdf (accessed 03 February 2011); *Handke/Towse* (2007), *supra* note 106, at 941 et seq.; for a more critical view, see *Katz* (2005), The Potential Demise of Another Natural Monopoly: New Technologies and the Future of Collective Administration of Copyrights, Journal of Competition and Law and Economics Vol. 1 Issue 4], at 541–593.

[109]   See, for instance, *Rose* (2003), Romans, Roads, and Romantic Creators: Tradition of Public Property in the Information Age, Law and Contemporary Problems [Vol. 66], The Public Domain, at 89–110; *Shiffrin* (2001), Lockean Arguments for Private Intellectual Property, in: Munzer (ed.), New Essays in the Legal and Political Theory of Property, Cambridge, Cambridge University Press, 2001, at 138 et seq.; *Boyle* (2003), *supra* note 59, at 33– 74; *Hess/Ostrom* (2003), Ideas, Artifacts, and Facilities: Information as a Common-Pool Resource, available at: http://www.law.duke.edu/shell/cite.pl?66+Law+&+Contemp.+Prob s.+111+(WinterSpring+2003) (accessed 03 February 2011); *Lessig* (2001), The Future of Ideas, New York, Random House, 2001, at 85 et seq.; for a more "moderate" approach, see e.g. *Heverly* (2003), The Information Semicommons, Berkeley Technology Law Journal [Vol. 18], at 1127 – 1189, pointing out that information ownership could be seen as a form of ownership "that acknowledges the dynamic relationship between private and common uses" (called *semicommons*).

[110]   *Lessig* (2001), *supra* note 109, at 19, 85 et seq.; *same author* (2002), The Architecture of Innovation, Duke Law Journal [Vol. 51], at 1783, 1788 (". . .By a commons I mean a resource that is free. . .").

called "Allmende" – basically "common land" – belonging to all concerned individuals in equal measure.[111]

In fact, the current (individual) property approach is not God-given; certain indigenous communities may have different perceptions of what "ownership" involves.[112] To some extent even from the perspective of a "Western" country it seems logical that certain kinds of "collective goods" should be treated differently, be it by a "non-property" approach but with collective responsibility (like protection of the environment), or by a kind of "ownership" with specific responsibility borne by the common organisation of the community (e.g. a "state").[113]

However, in the field of – newly created or invented – intangible goods, it is questionable whether such comparisons are really convincing. Even if one may not necessarily believe in all aspects of the "incentive theory",[114] some of the arguments behind it are persuasive. It is improbable that substantial investments would be made by individuals (or companies, like the drug or the movie industries) if the outcome at the end of the day could

---

[111]   The term "common land", or "commons", means land or resources that is/are *collectively* owned. The notion "commons", however, has been used extensively in legal scholarship in different ways, see e.g. *Hardin* (1968), The Tragedy of the Commons, Sciences [Vol. 162], at 1243 et seq.; *Heller* (1998), The Tragedy of the Anticommons, Harvard Law Review [Vol. 111], at 621 et seq.; *Buchanan/Yoon* (2000), Symmetric Tragedies: Commons and Anticommons, Journal of Law & Economics [Vol. 43], at 1 et seq.; *Eggertsson* (2003), Open access versus common property, in: Anderson/McChesney (eds.), Property Rights: Cooperation, Conflict, and Law, Princeton, Princeton University Press, 2003, at 73 et seq.; *Alston/Mueller* (2005), *supra* note 2, at 573 et seq. According to *Munzer* (2005), The Commons and the Anticommons in the Law and Theory of Property, in: Golding/Edmundson (eds.), The Blackwell Guide to Philosophy of Law and Legal Theory, Oxford, Blackwell, 2005, at 150, 151 and *Eggertsson* (2003), *ibid.*, at 74, the notion "commons" has two different arrangements: *open-access resources* (owned by no one, i.e. no one has a legal right to exclude anyone from using a resource) and *common property* (members of a group collectively have rights with respect to the resources including the right to exclude non-members from using that resource); for further details, see *Eggertsson* (2003), *ibid.*, at 74 et seq.; *Ciriacy-Wantrup/Bishop* (1975), "Common Property" as a Concept in Natural Resource Policy, Natural Resources Journal [Vol. 15], at 713, 715.

[112]   See e.g. *Strathern* (2005), Imagined Collectivities and Multiple Authorship, in: Gosh (ed.), Collaborative Ownership and the Digital Age, Cambridge, Mass., MIT Press, 2005, at 13 et seq.

[113]   For an overview, see *Peukert* (2008), *supra* note 2, at 104 et seq.

[114]   See in that respect *Boldrin/Levine* (2005), Intellectual Property and the Efficient Allocation of Social Surplus from Creation, Review of Economic Research on Copyright Issues [Vol. 2], at 45 et seq.

not be allocated to the investor (at least to some extent and for a certain period of time).[115]

This does not necessarily mean that intangible goods should be owned "individually" before turning to "collective ownership". Traditional knowledge or different forms of cultural heritage, for instance, may be deemed to be "collective ownership", even if such goods may until now have been "individually owned", as they constitute a kind of "undisclosed information".[116] However, the more such goods are utilised, the more the primary "owner" loses control and thus the goods become "common".

This transformation admittedly happens more distinctly if IP rights are involved, namely at the moment when they expire. Certainly, the "impact on competition" changes more or less substantially the moment formerly (and formally) protected intangible goods fall into the public domain, albeit subject to the circumstances of the individual case (e.g. according to the remaining relevance of the subject matter in question in view of the public interest). In principle, as regards competition, we may assume that the situation turns for the better insofar as more market participants are in a position to use the subject matter in question. However, it is erroneous to conclude that an acceleration of such – creeping or terminated – transformation from "individual ownership" to "common ownership" would generally be a valuable approach. The more we value

---

[115]   *Dreyfuss* (2010), Does IP Need IP? Accommodating Intellectual Property Production outside the Intellectual Property Paradigm, Cardozo Law Review [Vol. 31], at 1437, 1447 et seq.; *Lemley* (1997), *supra* note 71, at 989, 994 et seq.; *Gilbert* (2010), A World Without Intellectual Property? Boldrin and Levine, Against Intellectual Monopoly, Journal of Economic Literature, forthcoming 2011, available at: http://escholarship.org/uc/item/3h7363s3#page-1 (accessed 03 February 2011); *Depoorter/Parisi* (2002), Fair Use and Copyright Protection: A Price Theory Explanation, International Review of Law and Economics [Vol. 21], at 453, 465; *Elkin-Koren/Salzberger* (1999), Law and Economics in Cyberspace, International Review of Law and Economics [Vol. 19], at 553, 559 et seq.; in a sceptical vein, see *Boldrin/Levine* (2005), *supra* note 114, at 45, 51 et seq.; *same authors* (2008), Perfectly Competitive Innovation, Journal of Monetary Economics [Vol. 55], at 435 et seq.

[116]   For more details concerning the possibilities and problems of legal protection in developing countries with regard to their cultural heritage, see *Hilty* (2009), Rationales for the Legal Protection of Intangible Goods and Cultural Heritage, IIC 2009, at 883 et seq.; see also *Taubman/Leistner* (2008), Traditional Knowledge, in: von Lewinsky (ed.), Indigenous Heritage and Intellectual Property, 2nd ed., Alphen aan den Rijn, Kluwer Law International, 2008, at 59 et seq.; *Peukert* (2010), *supra* note 4, at 217 et seq.; *Munzer/Raustiala* (2009), The Uneasy Case for Intellectual Property Rights in Traditional Knowledge, Cardozo Arts & Entertainment Law Journal [Vol. 27], at 37 et seq.

new ideas and seek creations, inventions, etc., the less we should blindly stress competition issues, and the less likely "common" approaches will be to promise relief.

Undeniably, the conviction exists that certain protected subject matter – notably information (including technical information, e.g. regarding the positive effects of substances to cure disease), but also the vague term "culture" etc. – should not be "monopolised" in a way that impairs the interests of the general public.[117] This aim, however, is not only to be achieved at the cost of denying the possibility of individual ownership. Rather, the negative impacts of such individual ownership should be compensated by the application of specifically designed limitations in order to safeguard such general interests.

In other words, the very form of "collective ownership" that epitomises the notion of "Allmende" – "common land" – is hardly a genuinely valuable alternative to balance the interests involved,[118] at least not insofar as it risks failing to promote new creations and innovations.[119] However, environments may exist where common approaches, in the sense of truly "collective" forms of ownership, seem apt to foster newly emerging information, culture etc. Such alternative legal regimes should, of course, not be rejected out of hand. Instead, if we strive for positive impacts of legal regulations on competition, we will most probably have to accept that a plurality of approaches with respect to "ownership" exists.[120] Depending on the specific environment of creation or invention, one or another approach may provide us with appropriate answers.

5. CONCLUSIONS

Any question related to "impacts on competition" primarily requires identification of the relevant market players. These market players are rarely those to whom "ownership" of intangible goods is initially granted. Rather, a diverse assortment of entrepreneurs constitute the driving factors of competition, and it is obvious that the question of "ownership" is only one factor amongst many others to determine how these market

---

[117] *Peukert* (2010), *supra* note 4, at 222, 223; see also *Munzer/Raustiala* (2009), *supra* note 116, at 37 et seq.

[118] See above, at Section 3.4.1.

[119] *Dreyfuss* (2010), *supra* note 115, at 1437, 1447 et seq.

[120] See e.g. *Dreyfuss* (2010), *supra* note 115, at 1437, 1465 et seq., where it is argued that mixed regimes, i.e. different forms of creative development, may be in the field of vision in the future.

players truly act and how their role as entrepreneurs impacts competition. In other words, focusing on ownership alone would be too narrow.

Apart from this important conclusion, observation of the period of time during which ownership is originated is also of interest, notably in view of the fact that the creator or inventor may, subject to the applicable legislation, indeed be in a position to influence the "destiny" and further use of his original property by subsequent owners. From this viewpoint, we must be aware that basically two worlds exist side by side:

- In one world, innovations or creations are kept open to be used by subsequent inventors or creators. In order to enable the original inventors or creators to keep the system open, "individual ownership" is required; this ownership is the basis for the – collective – control and safeguarding of the "openness" of the whole system in the long run.

  Presumably such an open world would tend not to have negative impacts on competition at whatever level. On the contrary, in this world, there would be a level playing field for all market players to co-invent or co-create and thereby add their own contributions to the utilised, pre-existing subject matter. In other words, the open world tends to generate perfect competition: at the end of the day it will be the best creator or inventor who produces the best results. To some extent this might be to his own benefit (depending on his own further marketing strategy), but also to a great extent to the benefit of the general public.

- In the other world, legal protection is implemented in order to generate (or to maintain) individually owned and individually exploited property. We are increasingly aware that such a proprietary world risks having negative impacts on competition, which, however, cannot simply be changed by a modification of the legal rules of ownership. For individual ownership is the starting point for both worlds – the open as well as the proprietary one. Without granting individual ownership (IP rights), even the open world would not work, because sustainable openness could not be ensured based on a special licensing regime.

Based on this awareness, and if our assumption is correct that the open world rather than the proprietary one produces positive impacts on competition, our primary interest should not lie in how to shape different forms of ownership in the best possible way. In truth, "individual ownership" is the basis for both worlds. Therefore, we should rather reflect on possibilities to enhance the incentives for creators and inventors to take the path that will ultimately lead us to a more open world.

However, we have to accept that, regardless of all such incentives, a great number of them will opt to take such a path anyway. In fact, we should not put too much energy into the creation of an "ideal" – open – world. Rather, we should focus on legal regulations enabling us to control the use and enforcement of individually granted ownership based on the rules of the proprietary world. Such control of the use of individually granted ownership may ensue:

- either within the aforementioned third area of regulation (basically on the basis of antitrust law). However, experience shows that the currently existing legal settings of antitrust law are hardly able to remedy the situation efficiently;
- or based on specific regulations within the property regimes (that is to say, in the first and second area of regulation, namely under patent, copyright, design, trademark law etc.) by introducing limitations and exceptions; and particularly with a view to competition by introducing provisions to facilitate (compulsory) licensing.[121]

In other words, as sweet as dreams of an open, collective world may be, they should not hinder us from tackling the hard (political) work of bringing back more balance to the reality of IP law, in the predominantly

---

[121] This instrument, however, is currently not common in trademark law. At the same time, the *Federal Trade Commission* (FTC) ruled in the *ReaLemon Case* (FTC (1978), Borden, Inc., FTC Decisions [Vol. 92], at 669 et seq., that Borden, Inc., shall grant a ten-year licence of its "ReaLemon" trademark to any competitor, since Borden, Inc. had unlawfully monopolised the market for lemon juice by using the trademark in an anticompetitive manner; see *FTC* (1978), Borden, Inc., FTC Decisions [Vol. 92], at 669, 774 et seq., available at: http:// www.ftc.gov/os/decisions/docs/vol92/FTC_VOLUME_DECISION_92_(JULY_-_ DECEMBER_1978)PAGES_660-836.pdf#page=10 (accessed 03 February 2011). For more details, see *Schmalensee* (1979), On the Use of Economic Models in Antitrust: the ReaLemon Case, University of Pennsylvania Law Review, at 994–1050. Although no similar claims have since been brought by the *FTC* or the *Department of Justice*, it is repeatedly highlighted in the literature that there are situations where compulsory licensing of trademarks might be useful, see e.g. *Babin* (1974), Abuse of Trademarks: A Proposal for Compulsory Licensing, University of Michigan Journal of Law Reform, at 644, 662 et seq. (proposing a statutory codification of compulsory trademark licensing); in a critical vein, *Palladino* (1978), Compulsory Licensing of a Trademark, The Trademark Reporter [Vol. 68], at 522, 530 (but pointing out that 15 U.S.C. § 1064 (Sec. 14 Lanham Act) may be read to approve compulsory licences); *Lane* (1988), Compulsory Trademark Licensing, Southern Economic Journal [Vol. 54], at 643–655.

See also *Julian-Arnold* (1993), *supra* note 82, at 349 et seq.; *Hilty* (2009), *supra* note 92, at 633 et seq.

existing proprietary world. In view of this challenge, the role of the legislature should primarily be to abstain from any one-sided ruling.[122] Today it is one-sided; we are living in a mainly proprietary world. Further legislation, therefore, should not be blindly directed at the further enhancement of legal protection within this proprietary world.[123] Legislation should rather be as "neutral" as possible. The law is there to ensure as much freedom as possible, since freedom is the best ingredient for workable competition. Freedom, however, also encompasses the freedom to choose one of the two worlds. This freedom does not exist if the legislature does not take action to ensure the coexistence of different "ownership regimes". Such coexistence is only ensured if the decision of a creator or inventor to contribute to the open world is sustainable; and if there are sufficiently strong legal remedies to defend the open world against being overrun by the proprietary one.

---

[122]   Similarly *David* (2003), *supra* note 17, at 19, 23.
[123]   See generally *van den Houwe* (2001), Public Choice, Constitutional Political Economy and Law and Economics, in: Bouckaert/De Geest (eds.), Encyclopedia of Law & Economics, Volume I, Cheltenham, Edward Elgar Publishing, 2001, at 603 et seq.; *Becker* (1983), A Theory of Competition among Pressure Groups for Political Influence, Quarterly Journal of Economics [Vol. 98], at 371 et seq.

2. The law and economics of progress: IP rights and competition policy

Rudolph J.R. Peritz

1. INTRODUCTION

The *New York Times* and other respected voices of the press have been observing that the economics profession is in turmoil after its failure to predict the Great Recession that still threatens us. Indeed, it was modern economics' overconfidence in its algorithmic routines and its faith in free market abstractions that drove the collapse in financial markets and its aftermath by enchanting the judgment of players from hedge fund strategists to investors to regulatory agency officials. But unpredicted financial panics and recessions are nothing new, of course. And economics has long been a troubled enterprise, aspiring to the heights of mathematics to escape its historical roots in moral philosophy and to avoid a behavioralist future as a branch of social psychology. Like the commerce it scrutinizes, modern economic analysis can itself be described as cyclical, with episodic developments, bubbles, panics, inflations, depressions, and recessions, all neatly plotted by the criticisms of esteemed practitioners from John Maynard Keynes and John Kenneth Galbraith to Nobel Laureates Amartya Sen and George Stiglitz, and Paul Krugman just two years ago.

It should come as no surprise, then, that there has long been trouble brewing in the IP economics that prevails in the United States. (By the way, my references in this chapter to IP are intended as a shorthand for only patent and copyright.) Given economics' powerful influence on public policy, the trouble has spilled into IP jurisprudence as well. The trouble with IP economics recently reached its boiling point with the admission by William Landes and Richard Posner, the Chicago School's dynamic duo of law and economics, the admission that there is no ground for the dominant view of IP economics, no ground for the view that an incentive theory can justify, explain, or rationalize IP rights. They made this confession in their book entitled *The Economic Structure of IP Law*. The book has received wide attention and much praise. But the public confession of incentive theory's failure has been largely ignored.

At virtually the same moment, a related but separate development bubbled to the surface of IP jurisprudence: in a recent series of surprising opinions, the US Supreme Court weakened patent and trade dress protection, and in the process emphasized the role of competition as an engine for promoting economic progress. The opinions were surprising because they run against the dominant view that pits an IP domain of exclusionary rights against an entirely separate antitrust domain of free access. The recent opinions have destabilized this binary opposition between IP rights and competition.[1]

In tandem, the failed economics and the unstable state of IP jurisprudence have thrown the dominant approach to IP rights into crisis. This crisis is an emergent form of a long-term problem at the heart of both the economics and the jurisprudence of IP rights, and it cannot be easily resolved.

On the economics side, informed policy makers have long recognized that economic progress is driven by two engines – not only IP rights but also free competition. Economist Kenneth Arrow wrote in his landmark 1962 paper that the great difficulty lies in determining an optimal balance between them. Some years earlier, economist Joseph Schumpeter had already sought to merge the two engines in his vision of competition as serial monopoly, his perennial gale of creative destruction.[2]

As for the jurisprudence, the US Constitution has been interpreted as instructing Congress to balance the exclusionary rights of IP protection and the open access of free competition. The Constitution empowers Congress to enact copyright and patent protection for the explicit purpose of promoting the progress of science and useful arts – what we would call

---

[1]   This chapter takes up the theme of IP law as a competition regime explored in my earlier writing, beginning with my *Report to the IP Academy of Singapore* (2002–2003) (revised and published *sub nom* 'Competition policy and its implications for intellectual property rights in the United States', in *The Interface Between Intellectual Property Rights and Competition Policy* (Steven D. Anderman, ed.) (Cambridge, UK: Cambridge University Press, 2006) and variously investigated in other writing. The theme is a special case of the complex relationship between private property rights and competition policy in American political economy, which I first developed in the domain of antitrust (*Hastings L Rev* 1989, *Duke L Rev* 1990), and then extended to other domains in *Competition Policy in America: History, Rhetoric, Law* (NY: Oxford University Press, 1996, 2001). This chapter sketches the contours of a larger project, whose working title is 'The Political Economy of Progress: IP Rights and Competition'.

[2]   Schumpeter, *Capitalism, Socialism and Democracy* ([1942] 3d edn., 1950); Kenneth J. Arrow, "Economic welfare and the allocation of resources for invention," in *The Rate and Direction of Inventive Activity: Economic and Social Factors*, R. Nelson, ed., at p. 609 (Princeton, New Jersey: Princeton Univ. Press, 1962).

the progress of knowledge and industrial technology. So copyright and patent protections are not rewards; nor are they natural rights. They are incentives – private means to a public end. No question about that. But when does the private incentive of IP protection promote the public benefits of progress? When does patent and copyright protection produce more progress than would accrue without it? The answer to this question of balancing has proved elusive to both theorists and empirical researchers.[3]

In my view, it is this open question at the very core of IP policy that has put analysts and decision makers, including federal judges, in an untenable position – what Texans call being squeezed between a rock and a hard place: on the one side, policy makers are pressed to make decisions; on the other, they are blocked from making rational decisions because there is no analytical methodology at hand. Not only between the rocks and hard places of Texas but throughout the United States, policy makers have sought to extricate themselves by taking a fall-back position, the position that maximizing the means maximizes the ends, the position that greater IP protection naturally leads to more invention and thus to more progress. In my view, this fall-back position explains the so-called propertization of IP rights that has increasingly transformed them into natural property rights since the 1980s.

This fall-back into natural rights is not surprising, given the powerful ideology of private property rights in the United States. But it makes no logical sense. Nor is it supported in theory or fact. Indeed, it is well-known that too much IP protection as well as too little can stifle innovation and impede economic progress. So both the economics and the law present IP policy makers with a Goldilocks problem. But there is no calculus for determining what amount of IP rights is just right, particularly in a unitary system that does not discriminate among different kinds of inventions. At the same time, it must be recognized that there is no clear justification for simply eliminating IP rights entirely as a means to encourage invention and thus to promote economic progress.

So, what's to be done? In my view, the answer is surprisingly clear: Change the fall-back position. Reverse the presumption. In choosing between two rules or standards, adopt the one that expresses the policy of free competition unless the superiority of the exclusionary rule or standard

---

[3]   For a close analysis of these issues, see my essay, 'Thinking about economic progress: Arrow and Schumpeter in time and space', in *Liber Amicorum: for Hanns Ullrich* (Josef Drexl, ed.) (Munich, Germany: Max Planck Institute) (Bruxelles: Larcier Pub., 2009). I do not address in this paper the fundamental question of what should be encompassed in the goal of economic progress in addition to economic growth.

is shown.[4] But given the indeterminate economic value of both competition and IP rights in encouraging invention, why the presumption favoring rules that promote the open access of free competition?

Why? Because competition produces a tie-breaker for its economic stalemate with IP rights. The tie-breaker is competition's superior distributional effects. When patents and other IP rights produce monopoly prices, they create welfare losses in both static and dynamic terms. In the short run, consumers pay higher prices or go to second-best substitutes. In the longer run, follow-on inventors also pay higher prices or go to second-best substitutes, causing some combination of a decline and a substitution in follow-on inventive activity. In this light, any rule or policy that would expand IP rights should first be shown to promote greater progress than would occur without the expansion.

That is all I will say today about the economics. My presentation at the Munich conference addressed the failure of incentive theory as the justification for IP protection. That paper is available in Annette's fine collection. And I have a paper that will appear in a collection edited by Steve Anderman that develops the residual IP economics of competition. Today, my focus is on the US jurisprudence of patent protection.

In the time that remains, I sketch the dominant and emergent approaches seen in the patent jurisprudence, and then give an example of change to patent policy that would come of extending the emergent view and, I am convinced, the better view, the view that the domain of patent rights is fundamentally a competition regime.

Adopting this emergent strain can produce what complexity theorists call the butterfly effect – a radical change in system behavior produced by a small change in initial conditions. The familiar image for this is a butterfly in New York City's Central Park whose fluttering wings alter the course of an entire weather system in the Amazon rain forest.[5] Perhaps a more timely example is an Icelandic volcano altering the course of global airline travel. A presumptive shift in patent jurisprudence to competition

---

[4] Two examples: active directory in the EU Microsoft case; industrial policy legislated to target incentive, to channel invention in, eg, green technology, or even more specifically, solar or wind energy, without regard to economic effects more broadly, ie, without regard to effects on economic growth.

[5] And so this tertium quid can be understood as radical incrementalism. The concept of sensitive dependence on initial conditions in René Thom's catastrophe theory, later in chaos theory, and even later in complexity theory: small differences in the initial condition of a dynamic system may produce large variations in the long term behavior of the system. Chaos pre-Theory: Edward Lorenz, MIT in 1961.

policy is a small change, certainly within the traditional view that free competition promotes economic progress. But the shift can produce sharp and surprising turns in patent policy, turns to the better for promoting progress in science and useful arts.[6]

But first the dominant view of patent policy. The Supreme Court long ago declared: "Since the primary aim of the patent laws is to promote the progress of science and useful arts, an arrangement which diminishes the incentive is said to be against the public interest."[7] More specifically, the Supreme Court declared that "[t]he primary purpose of our patent system . . . is directed to disclosure of advances in knowledge which will be beneficial to society; it is . . . an incentive to disclosure."[8] In other words, patents publicize new knowledge which would otherwise be hidden under the blanket of trade secrecy. The public value of new knowledge

---

[6] This effect is an extreme form of the tipping phenomenon derived from mathematician René Thom's Catastrophe Theory: a sudden and irreversible change in direction from a preceding course that was steady and reversible. I want to tip the law and economics of IP rights from the current steady course driven by an unfounded incentive theory.

[7] *Transparent-Wrap Mach. Corp. v. Stokes & Smith Co.,* 329 U.S. 637, 646 (1947) (Douglas, J.)

[8] "The primary purpose of our patent system is not reward of the individual but the advancement of the arts and sciences. Its inducement is directed to disclosure of advances in knowledge which will be beneficial to society; it is not a certificate of merit, but an incentive to disclosure." *Sinclair & Carroll Co. v. Interchemical Corp.,* 325 U.S. 327, 330 (1945). "The basic quid pro quo contemplated by the Constitution and the Congress for granting a patent monopoly is the benefit derived by the public from an invention with substantial utility." *Brenner v. Manson,* 383 U.S. 519, 534 (1966). ". . . the public may have the full benefit thereof, after the expiration of the patent term." *Bonito Boats, Inc. v. Thunder Craft Boats, Inc.,* 489 U.S. 141, 147 (1989).

Still, the Supreme Court has long expressed skepticism about the incentive value of IP rights. For example, in the *Marconi Wireless* case of 1943, the Chief Justice remarked: "For all I know the basic assumption of our patent law may be false, and inventors and their financial backers do not need the incentive of a limited monopoly to stimulate invention. But whatever revamping our patent laws may need, it is the business of Congress to do the revamping." *Marconi Wireless T. Co. of America v. U.S.,* 320 U.S. 1, 63-4 (1943).

Economic analysis of disclosure: Patent right and disclosure obligation is the right strategy for those inventions not adequately protected as trade secrets. In this light, patented inventions are those most likely to be disclosed anyway and so the public really gains very little if anything. Note tension between this account and traditional norms and incentives to disclose in scientific community, tensions increased with increased propertization and thus incentive to withhold disclosure until patent application filed. Note also patent doctrine's disincentives to read patents, especially intentional infringement liability for multiple damages.

goes beyond the enlightenment virtue of edification. It has use value for follow-on inventors: Disclosure reduces the costs of competition by invention. In short, the public benefit of disclosure is the free competition that results from free riding on the patented efforts of prior inventors.[9]

This insinuation of free competition is not exceptional. Indeed, monopoly has long been disfavored in the United States. As Thomas Jefferson put it over 200 years ago, the patent system must draw "a line between the things which are worth to the public the embarrassment of an exclusive patent, and those which are not."[10]

What patent law has always favored is free competition. Still, this line drawing pinpoints a fundamental tension that Supreme Court Justice Sandra Day O'Connor identified, a tension "between the need to encourage innovation and the avoidance of monopolies which stifle competition." Twenty years ago, Justice O'Connor wrote that "free exploitation of ideas will be the rule, to which the protection of a federal patent is the exception." There is, she explained, a "baseline of free competition upon which the patent system's incentive to creative effort depends."[11]

Here are three instances of recent Supreme Court patent jurisprudence that reflect this view:[12]

The first involves the requirement that a patented invention be nonobvious in light of prior art. Nonobviousness draws the line between patent monopoly and free competition, between exclusionary rights and open access. Since the 1980s, the nonobviousness requirement has been increasingly trivialized. For example, in 1999, the Federal Circuit Court ordered that the US Patent Office issue a patent to an applicant – I cannot bear to call him an inventor – an applicant who decorated large black plastic garbage bags with orange pumpkin faces. The Federal Circuit declared that this combination of garbage bags and Halloween decoration, each

---

[9]   Of course this would apply as well to cooperative invention, which I leave to another day.

[10]   13 *Writings of Thomas Jefferson* at 335 (Memorial edn. 1904), cited in, e.g., Bonito Boats, 489 U.S. 141, 148 (1989). This passage and others suggest the possibility that for the 18th century founding fathers, property rights had a natural incentive effect. In this view, there was no fundamental distinction between property as natural rights and as incentives.

[11]   *Bonito Boats, Inc. v. Thunder Craft Boats, Inc.*, 489 U.S. 141, 145-7 (1989).

[12]   I discuss the patent opinions in 'The Roberts Court after two years: Antitrust, intellectual property rights, and competition policy', 53 *Antitrust Bulletin* 153 (2008) (Symposium on Antitrust and the Roberts Court), reprinted in 35 *Giurisprudenza Commerciale* 1028 (2008) (Rome, Italy) and in 8 *Criterio Jurídico* 283 (2008) (Pontificia Universidad Javeriana, Cali, Columbia), available at SSRN URL http://ssrn.com/author=75649.

element itself obvious, was a nonobvious combination that merited a patent.[13] In 2003, the Federal Trade Commission issued a widely praised Report criticizing patent protection's descent into triviality.[14]

Then, in 2007, the Supreme Court published a decision that raised the nonobviousness requirement for the largest category of patents, those like the Halloween garbage bag, that involve combinations of prior art. The decision instructed the Patent Office to reject applications for combination that show only "ordinary creativity" or common sense.[15] The Patent Office has since rejected on the ground of obviousness a number of applications for combination patents, and the courts have regularly upheld those rejections.

While the Supreme Court made no explicit mention of competition in this opinion, the clear context is the FTC's competition policy concern. And the clear result is that competitors now have open access to make, use, and sell products that would have been protected by combination patents under the lower level of creativity.

A second important Supreme Court decision recently elevated the requirement for obtaining an injunction against a patent infringer. The more stringent requirement means that infringing competitors are not so easily restrained from making, using, and selling patented inventions; instead, the remedy of compulsory licenses opens competition to patent infringers who would otherwise have been excluded from the market.[16] A concurring opinion by Justice Anthony Kennedy makes numerous references to the FTC Report on patents and competition.

In a third case, Justice Stephen Breyer recently made reference not only to the FTC Report but also quoted Justice O'Connor's "baseline of competition" opinion to express the concern that too much patent protection, whether for basic scientific relationships or for business methods, would upset the "careful balance" that "the federal patent laws . . . embod[y]."[17]

---

[13] In *re Dembiczak*, 175 F.3d 994 (Fed. Cir. 1999).

[14] *To Promote Innovation: The Proper Balance of Competition and Patent Law and Policy*.

[15] *KSR Int'l. Co. v. Teleflex Inc.*, 127 S.Ct. 1727, 1743 (2007).

[16] *eBay Inc. v. MercExchange*, L.L.C., 126 S.Ct. 1837 (2006). Of course the infringing user must be a reasonable royalty as determined by the court. This can be understood as shifting from the patent holder to the court the power to determine royalties. In consequence, the patent holder cannot hold up would-be competitors in what is typically a one-sided monopoly bargaining scenario that does not promise the efficient solution generally attributed to settlements and bargain contracts more generally, per the Coase Theorem.

[17] *Laboratory Corp. of America Holdings v. Metabolite Laboratories, Inc.*, 126 S.Ct. 2921 (2006) (dissenting).

These recent opinions reflect the emergent view, actually the re-emergent view of the patent domain as a competition regime. In the first, the Court raised the level of nonobviousness for patentability. In the second, it eliminated the practice of automatic injunctions that had kept accused patent infringers out of the market. These two decisions narrowed first the scope and second the anti-competitive effects of patent monopolies.[18] Finally, Justice Breyer's opinion, though a dissent, raised questions about the proper reach of patent monopoly, questions addressed in the two other opinions and currently under consideration in a closely watched pending case – *Bilski v. Doll*, in which almost 70 amicus briefs were filed.

These three decisions signal the re-emergence of the competition baseline for patent protection. Moreover, let me remind you that the dominant approach's reliance on incentive theory is like riding a dead horse.[19] It cannot take even one step of progress because it lacks logical or economic life. What does make sense, both in economic and jurisprudential terms, is a baseline of free competition. And so I close with an example of significant change that could result from the shift from an incentive theory to a competition baseline.

My example is the experimental use defense to patent infringement. Almost twenty-five years ago, the Federal Circuit transformed unauthorized experimental use into patent infringement. The rationale lay in a questionable extension of the already questionable logic of incentive theory. The court determined that a patent holder's power over the invention should extend beyond commercial profit to control of its every use. Why? The court began by attributing a "business interest" to everyone from garage tinkerers to research scientists, a business interest that was itself seen as endangering the incentive value of patents. An unlicensed researcher could overcome this powerful presumption of a business interest only when the purpose was literally the "idle curiosity" of a "dilettante affair."[20] Since the doctrine's announcement, not one

---

[18]   An earlier paper written before these decisions gave injunctions and nonobviousness as two examples of improvements to patent policy that would result from treating the patent domain as a competition regime. See AALS talk, available on SSRN.

[19]   There is an English language idiom – beating a dead horse – meaning that continuing the same course of conduct is futile: The horse will not respond. Riding a dead horse – particularly one stuffed and mounted by a taxidermist – is intended to reflect an even more absurd course of conduct for making progress. The English artist William Hogarth might have called it the Taxidermist's Progress.

[20]   *Roche Prods. v. Bolar Pharma. Co.*, 733 F.2d 858 (Fed. Cir. 1984) (citing as most persuasive precedent *Pitcairn v. U.S.*, 547 F2d 1106 (Ct. Cl. 1976)). This

published decision has reported a successful experimental use defense to patent infringement.

The demise of the traditional privilege to engage in unauthorized experimental use of a patented invention is an instance of the propertization trend that has been expanding IP protection in the United States. It is a particularly harmful instance because experimental use is the most important form of competition during the patent term. If unauthorized experimentation were seen instead as presumptively competitive conduct, then the patent holder would be required to prove actual commercial injury and public harm, all of which results not from imagined intentions but from actual commercial conduct, from making, using, and selling. In short, a viable experimental use defense would not harm patent holders' legitimate interests in exclusive rights to commercial profit during the patent term.

Moreover, the current stranglehold on unlicensed experiment disserves the public interest in three ways. First, it in effect extends the twenty-year patent monopoly by the time necessary for rivals to engage in research and development of products for offer on the market.[21] Second, the current regime empowers patent holders to control too much of follow-on research, a power inconsistent with the unlimited availability of improvement patents to all who meet the statutory requirements. Patent's open door policy for follow-on research is in sharp contrast to the Copyright Act's treatment of derivative works, whose protection is available only to the holder of the underlying copyright.[22] Third, the patent holder's control over research also channels and restrains the production of new knowledge intended to replenish the public domain. More widespread competition and cooperation in research during the patent term would produce public benefits by lowering the costs, expanding the field of improvement patents, opening the production of new knowledge, and finally, limiting the patent term to its statutory boundary.

Were there more time, I could give numerous other examples within patent policy as well as in the IP domain more broadly. Moreover, consistently adopting this baseline of competition would change the current US view of IP and antitrust as antithetical regimes, as a binary opposition

---

expanded view of patent rights is a natural result of viewing them through the prism of property logic.

[21] Cf. *Brulotte v. Thys Co.*, 379 U.S. 29, 32 (1964) (licensing agreement extending beyond patent term per se violation of federal patent law); *Pitney Bowes, Inc. v. Mestre*, 701 F.2d 1365 (11th Cir. 1983) (same).

[22] The current treatment of derivative works also reflects overprotection, in this author's view.

between monopoly and competition, between exclusion and access.[23] What would emerge is a more functional and progressive view of IP and antitrust as two intertwined regimes comprising policies of both exclusion and access, policies that regulate relationships of competition and cooperation. I leave these ideas to another day and to my ongoing project about the political economy of progress. Thank you for your kind attention.

---

[23]   The conflict between antitrust and IP is sometimes expressed in terms of ends – allocative efficiency versus dynamic efficiency – and other times in terms of means – the open access of competition and exclusionary rights of IP protection.

3. The multiplicity of territorial IP rights and its impact on competition

Ole-Andreas Rognstad

1. INTRODUCTION

When discussing the impact on competition of various kinds of IPR-ownership, it is important to note in particular that the notions of multiple and collective ownership are far from clear and that the terms can be defined in different ways.[1] Regardless of the definitions or the classification of terms, the main issue to be discussed when addressing the question of the impact on competition of individual, multiple and collective ownership is the impact the *ownership structure* in itself has on competition in relevant markets. In this respect a natural starting point is to consider the ownership structure within a particular IPR regime. It is reasonable to presume that professor Hilty has implicitly taken this starting point in his survey and analysis in Chapter 1.[2] It is also possible, however, to analyze the consequences for competition of

---

[1] Compare Peukert (2011) pp. 195 et seq., with Hilty (Chapter 1 of this book). Peukert defines multiple ownership as the situation where "not only one, but a plurality of IP rights is relevant for a certain product" (p. 200), whereas collective ownership occurs where "only one IP right is at stake" (p. 212). Pursuant to Hilty's definitions, multiple ownership entails a limited number of owners, contrary to collective ownership, which comprises an open number of owners. A third understanding of the concept of collective ownership seems to follow from Schovsbo in Chapter 8 of this book, who focuses on collective rights administration, a phenomenon which according to Peukert's approach is considered as a solution to problems related to multiple ownership (see Peukert p. 214), whereas Hilty's definition seems to imply that collective rights management is a way of handling individual or multiple ownerships. It is also possible to say that Peukert's and Schovsbo's definitions of collective ownership presuppose the property structure of IPRs, whereas Hilty's definitions imply that collective ownership is the alternative open solution to the property solution.

[2] See Hilty, Chapter 1 of this book.

the IPR-ownership structure from a more global point of view, taking into consideration all possible IPR regimes. Doing this, the perspective changes, as individual rights in this situation are transformed into multiple rights as a consequence of the territorial nature of intellectual property rights.[3] To the extent that the multiple territorial rights put the right owner in a position to prevent cross-border transactions, competition problems *may* arise as a *result* of multiple ownerships, even in the situation where the original right owner herself holds the bundle of territorial rights. In addition, the assignment or licensing of the various parallel rights to different persons or undertakings may also cause specific problems for competition.

The competition problems to be discussed in this context are not territorial restrictions in international trade as such, but the problems that occur as a result of the multiplicity of territorial IP rights, in contrast to the conceivable situation that the right owner were granted one unified IP right at a global level. The competition problems that occur in this context relate to the fact that the right holder may be in a position to block cross-border transactions between the territories for which the IPR in question is held.[4] Though the competition concerns in this respect should mainly be considered to result from *multiple* (territorial) ownerships related to the same subject matter, additional problems may arise in the context of *collectivization* of rights, as will be shown below.[5]

When discussing the impact on competition of the multiplicity of territorial rights, it must be noted that the application of *competition law* in these situations will have to depend on national or regional competition rules. Even though there are signs of competition concerns in the TRIPs agreement, efforts to establish a global competition regime have thus far failed to be successful and are hardly realistic in the near future.[6]

---

[3]   Cf. Peukert (2011).

[4]   Indeed, competition problems also arise from the very fact that the legal protection may differ from state to state. This, however, is more a problem of lack of legal harmonization (or of possibilities for harmonization) than the multiplicity of ownership in itself and will not be dealt with specifically here.

[5]   The term collectivization is here used in the same sense as that used by Schovsbo in Chapter 8 of this book, implying that the term comprises situations where different IP rights to different subject matters are gathered at one entity.

[6]   See for example Drexl (2008), p. 279 concerning the realism of reform; see also Anderson (2008).

2. MULTIPLE TERRITORIAL RIGHTS AS AN IMPEDIMENT TO CROSS-BORDER TRANSACTIONS

As outlined above, the possible problems for competition resulting from the multiplicity of territorial IP rights relate to the right holder's ability to block cross-border transactions. To the extent that the national or regional IP rights put the right holder in a position to prevent goods or services from other countries or territories, the existence and exercise of multiple territorial rights *may* affect competition on relevant markets. However, it is not necessarily so that the IPRs will entitle the right holders to block cross-border transactions.

Firstly, it will depend on *choice of law rules* whether the IPRs in the country of destination are at all applicable. Although there is as yet no uniform choice of law regulation on a global level, the rule of *lex loci protectionis* – the applicable law is the law in the country for which protection is claimed – is generally accepted as the prevailing choice of law rule in the IP field, at least as far as the existence, validity, scope and duration of the rights are concerned.[7] Applying *lex loci protectionis* will imply in many cases the law of the country of destination, but not necessarily so. For example, in the context of satellite distribution in Europe, the application of lex loci protectionis implies the country of transmission, since Article 1(2)(b) of the Satellite/Cable Directive[8] states that "[t]he act of communication to the public by satellite occurs solely in the Member State where, under the control and responsibility of the broadcasting organization, the programme-carrying signals are introduced into an uninterrupted chain of communication leading to the satellite and down towards the earth". Consequently, under lex loci protectionis, and given that the right holder has consented to the communication in the country of transmission, it will not be possible to invoke the copyrights in the remaining European countries in order to prevent the satellite transmission from taking place

---

[7] See Ulmer (1978) pp. 11–14, pointing out that *lex loci protectionis* is not to be confused with *lex fori*, the country where a legal action is sought, and that in an action for infringement of rights, the application of the rules of the protecting country depends upon the infringement having been committed in that country. In European law, the *lex loci protectionis* rule now follows from the Rome II regulation on the law applicable to non-contractual obligations as far as IP infringement cases are concerned, cf. Regulation 864/2007, OJ 2007 L 299 pp. 40–49, Article 8(1), see Dickinson (2008) pp. 447–470, for the drafting history and the interpretation of the provision.

[8] Council Directive 93/83/EC, OJ 1993 L 248 pp. 15–21.

there.[9] Hence, the multiplicity of European copyrights has no impact on competition in this situation. The fact that the European market for satellite distribution is still to a large extent territorially divided owes to contractual arrangements combined with technical protection measures, not the territorial nature of copyright.[10]

Secondly, even if the law of the country of destination is applicable, it depends on the *content* of its internal IP rules whether the right holder is in a position to prevent the transaction from taking place. The country of transmission rule mentioned above may also serve as an example in this respect.[11] Moreover, at least as far as distribution of goods is concerned, a principle of international *exhaustion (first sale doctrine)* may apply, so that the right holder will not be able to prevent goods put on the market with her consent in another state from being imported (parallel imports). Neither in this case will competition problems occur *as a result* of the multiple territorial rights. Again, it is possible instead that the right owner will attempt to reinforce her rights by way of private arrangements. To the extent that this is problematic from a competition point of view, it is nevertheless not due to the multiplicity of IPRs and therefore not relevant in this context

In the present situation, no universal exhaustion rule exists, not even for the distribution of tangible objects (goods). Symptomatically, TRIPs article 6, states that "([f]or the purposes of dispute settlement) nothing in this Agreement shall be used to address the issue of exhaustion of IPRs."[12] In European law, the exhaustion rule – based on the principle of free

---

[9] It is important to note that Article 1(2) is not itself a choice of law rule, but a rule on substantive law, see for example Dreier (2010), pp. 410, who proclaims that "even if a national conflict of laws rule declared the copyright law of one or more of the reception States applicable, that State's copyright law would not be infringed by the mere fact that reception of satellite signals took place in this state". Here it shall be added that the substantive rule of country of transmission also will have the effect that the IP law in the reception state will not at all be applicable as long as the principle of *lex protectionis* is applied, because the country of transmission rule implies that protection is claimed for the country of transmission as far as the right to communication to public is concerned, not the country of reception. Cf. Torremans (2001) pp. 57–63.

[10] See Dreier (2010) pp. 414–415, pointing out that "under the Directive, exclusivity can only be achieved on an in personam basis, i.e. no longer by transferring rights, but only on the basis of a contractual obligation of the original right holder towards the broadcasting organization in [the transmission] state . . . Also, the signals have to be encrypted and decoders to be distributed only in the area conceded by the contract."

[11] Cf. the citation from Dreier, note 9 supra.

[12] See for example Gervais (2008) at pp. 197–202 for the background and the interpretation of this provision.

movement of goods – which applies in trade between countries pertaining to the European Economic Area (the European Union plus the EFTA states Norway, Iceland and Liechtenstein) is inapplicable to trade from countries outside the EEA.[13] By contrast, in the trademark, design and copyright fields, the states have an obligation to refrain from exhaustion as far as trade from non-EEA countries is concerned.[14] In the US, the picture is somewhat unclear and much depends on the particular IPR in question, but there is certainly no general rule of international exhaustion.[15] In other countries and regions, the exhaustion regimes differ to a large extent.[16] Consequently, the multiplicity of territorial rights in many situations will put the right holder in a position to block parallel imports of goods. The question as to the extent to which this is a problem for competition will be dealt with under Section 3 below.

For IP-related transactions other than distribution of goods, which can be denoted by the general term "provision of services", a general exhaustion rule certainly does not apply. The European Court of Justice (ECJ) has rejected that the principle of free movement of services within the European Union (EEA) leads to exhaustion of television broadcasting rights.[17] Similarly, the EU Copyright Directive[18] Article 3(3) confirms that the right of communication to the public, including the making available right (on demand right), "shall not be exhausted by any act of communication to the public or making available to the public". Recital 29 of the same directive underscores that "[t]he question of exhaustion does not arise in the case of services and on-line services in particular" and that "[t]his also applies with regard to a material copy of a work or other subject-matter made by a user of such a service with the consent of the rightholder".[19] In US law, the somewhat different approach to online distribution implies that exhaustion may occur in

---

[13]   See in particular case 51/75, *EMI v. CBS*, [1976] ECR 811 (trade marks) and case 270/80, *Polydor v. Harlequin*, [1982] ECR 329 (copyright).

[14]   See Parliament and Council Directive 2008/95/EC, OJ 2008 L 299 pp. 255–33, Article 7(1), cf. (inter alia) case C-355/95, *Silhouette v. Hartlauer*, [1998] ECR I-4799 (trade marks); Council Directive 2001/29/EC, OJ 2001 L 197 pp. 10–19 (copyright), cf. case C-479/04, *Laserdisken v. Kulturministeriet*, [2006] ECR I-8089 (copyright); Council Directive 98/71, OJ 1998 L 289 pp. 28–35, Article 15 (designs).

[15]   For an overview, see for example Forsyth and Rothnie (2007) pp. 441–445.

[16]   See Forsyth and Rothnie (2007) pp. 438–441 and 448–455.

[17]   Case 62/79, *Coditel v. Cine Vog (I)*, [1980] ECR 881.

[18]   Note 14 supra.

[19]   See further for example Tai (2003) and Wiebe (2009) for different opinions on the implications of this regulation.

certain situations, but it has hardly any substantial, practical impact for the problems discussed here.[20] The general picture, in Europe and US as well as in other countries or regions, is that the multiplicity of territorial IP rights puts the right holder in a position to prevent transnational provision of services, provided that the applicable law is that of country of destination.

In any event it is important to note that impediments to cross-border transactions are not tantamount to restraints on competition. Although an exhaustion rule *may* serve to solve competition problems in international trade, there are also other considerations behind this rule, for example free trade and market integration concerns or the argument that the essential function of a trademark is to serve as a guarantee for the origin of the goods and services in question, and that this function is not affected by a rule of international exhaustion. This is to say that the multiplicity of territorial rights does not necessarily have a negative impact on competition in the stricter sense, even if the applicable law is that of the country of destination and no exhaustion rule or similar applies. Whether the right holder's position to block cross-border transaction restricts competition in the relevant market depends on market definitions, market conditions and market structure. This is not the place to elaborate thoroughly on the issue, which is vast, but a short overview of relevant considerations could be given.

3.   MULTIPLE TERRITORIAL OWNERSHIPS – A PROBLEM FOR COMPETITION?

The point of departure is where a single IPR is invoked in order to block cross-border transactions of goods or services which have been distributed in other territories with the consent of the right holder. In relation to distribution of goods, it is a question of preventing parallel imports from occurring.[21] In this situation, the IPR will represent a vertical restraint on competition. The goods in question may be imported to and distributed in the import state, but only through channels authorized by the right

---

[20]   The US first sale doctrine seems to apply to copies downloaded on a physical medium with the consent of the right holder, see Forsyth and Rothnie (2007) p. 454 and further Nimmer, volume 2 § 8-12 [E].

[21]   The normal and simple, although broad, definition of the term parallel imports in the context of intellectual property being lawfully produced goods imported from abroad without the consent of the right owner in the importing country.

holder. In other words the intra-brand or intra-technology competition will be affected, but not the inter-brand or inter-technology competition. To what extent vertical restraints represent a competition problem is a long-disputed issue. However, taking a strict competition policy view, leaving aside broader market integration considerations, it is plausible to claim that vertical restraints harm competition only in the event the right holder has some degree of market power.[22] Parallel imports are first and foremost good for price competition, and the right holder will only be in a position to charge excessive prices if she holds a dominant position on the market.[23] Whether there is market dominance depends on the definitions of the relevant market, that is, both the product market and the geographical market.

Potential competition problems increase if there are horizontal elements involved, that is, contractual arrangements or concerted practice

---

[22] This view is now also generally accepted on an EU-level, cf. the EU Commission's Notice on Guidelines on vertical restraints, OJ 2000 C 291 pp. 1–43, paragraph 6, where it is emphasized that "for most vertical restraints, competition concerns can only arise if there is insufficient inter-brand competition, i.e. if there is some degree of market power at the level of the supplier or the buyer or at both levels. If there is insufficient inter-brand competition, the protection of inter- and intra-brand competition becomes important."

[23] For an example of a case where that was an issue, cf. T-198/98, *Micro Leader Business v. Commission*, [1999] ECR II-3989, where the European Court of First Instance (now the General Court) found that the Commission in a case concerning a complaint forwarded by a parallel importer of software had failed to investigate whether Microsoft abused its dominant position by invoking its non-exhausted distribution right in France in order to prevent parallel imports from Canada of French language versions of Microsoft's software. The Court held, inter alia, that:

> whilst it is true that, under Article 4(c) of Directive 91/250 [the Software Directive], the marketing by MC [Microsoft Corporation] of copies of software in Canada does not, in itself, exhaust MF's [Microsoft France] copyright over its products in the Community . . ., the factual evidence put forward by the applicant constitutes, at the very least, an indication that for equivalent transactions, Microsoft applied lower prices on the Canadian market than on the Community market and that the Community prices were excessive . . . The extract from MF's information bulletin of 27 September 1995 . . ., suggests that the products imported from Canada were in direct competition with the products marketed in France and that their resale price in France was significantly lower, despite the expense of importing them into the Community from a third country . . . In the present case, therefore, the Commission could not argue, without undertaking further investigation into the complaint, that the information in its possession at the time it adopted the contested decision did not constitute evidence of abusive conduct by Microsoft.

between competitors holding different IPRs.[24] In this context we can speak of collectivization of rights.[25] But even in the case of market dominance and horizontal elements, there might be grounds for accepting the territorial restraints. There might be objective justifications for the blocking of cross-border transactions – for example that territorial restrictions in specific situations promote dynamic competition and hence the incentives to innovate.[26]

Although this is not the place for a broad analysis of the competition problems that result from the territorial scope of IPRs, an example of the dilemmas and considerations at stake may be given. By also bringing in the aspect of collectivization of rights, the controversy regarding European collective management of music performance rights (copyright) in the digital age may serve as an illustration of competition problems related to the multiplicity of territorial IP rights.

The clearing of music performance rights is traditionally based on collective management at a territorial level. Based on collectivization of (copy)rights, the collective societies are often monopolies as regards the services they offer (management of rights to right holders and granting of licenses to users).[27] Whether, or to what extent, the monopoly position of collective societies is economically inefficient, or whether and to what extent there are objective justifications for monopolies in this field,

---

[24]   See for example the EU Commission Notice. Guidelines on the application of the EC Treaty to technology transfer agreements, OJ 2004 C 101 pp. 2–235, paragraphs 26–33 on the distinction between competitors and non-competitors in technology transfer agreements, and Antitrust Guidelines for the Licensing of Intellectual Property, Issued by the US Department of Justice and the Federal Commission of Trade (1995), available at http://www.justice.gov/atr/public/guide lines/0558.htm, paragraph 3.3, where it is underlined that "identification of [horizontal] relationships is . . . an aid in determining whether there may be anticompetitive effects arising from a licensing arrangement", but that "such a relationship need not give rise to an anticompetitive effect".

[25]   See note 5 supra as regards the terminology in this respect.

[26]   See for example case 261/82, *Coditel v. Cine Vog (II)*, [1982] ECR 3381, paragraph 16, concerning exclusive licenses for broadcasting of a film in Belgium, used in order to block the retransmission of the film from Germany, where the ECJ stated that "the characteristics of the cinematographic industry and of its markets in the Community, especially those relating to dubbing and subtitling for the benefit of different language groups, to the possibilities of television broadcast, and to the system of financing cinematographic production in Europe serve to show that an exclusive exhibition license is not, in itself, such as to prevent, restrict or distort competition".

[27]   See Drexl (2007) pp. 6–8.

is disputed.[28] Nonetheless, the European Court of Justice found that the reciprocal representation contracts between collective societies in Europe, whereby the national societies gave each other the right to grant authorizations for public performance of musical works within their territories, were not in themselves restrictive of competition in the *offline* environment.[29] In the *online* environment, however, the territorially based clearance system has been challenged at different levels by the European Commission, partly on the basis of a "soft law" recommendation on collective cross-border management of copyright and related rights for online music services[30] partly by actions for breach of the EU competition rules.[31] The underlying concept for the application of both instruments is that territorial monitoring of rights is not necessary in the online environment and that consequently there is a potential for competition between

---

[28] See for example Thowes and Handke (2007).

[29] See the French Discotheque cases, case 395/87, *Ministère Public v. Tournier*, [1989] ECR 2521 paragraphs 19-20 and joined cases 110/88, 241/88 and 242/88, *Lucazeau and others v. SACEM*, [1989] ECR 2811, paragraphs 13-14, where the ECJ stated that:

it is apparent that reciprocal representation contracts between copyright-management societies have a twofold purpose: first, they are intended to make all protected musical works, whatever their origin, subject to the same conditions for all users in the same Member State, in accordance with the principle laid down in the international provisions; secondly, they enable copyright-management societies to rely, for the protection of their repertoires in another State, on the organization established by the copyright-management society operating there, without being obliged to add to that organization their own network of contracts with users and their own local monitoring arrangements,

and that "it follows from the foregoing considerations that the reciprocal representation contracts in question are contracts for services which are not in themselves restrictive of competition in such a way as to be caught by Article 85(1) of the Treaty". Note, however, that the Court at the same time added that "the position might be different if the contracts established exclusive rights whereby copyright-management societies undertook not to allow direct access to their repertoires by users of recorded music established abroad".

[30] Commission Recommendation of 18 May 2005 on Collective Cross-border Management of Copyright and Related Rights for Legitimate Online Music Services (2005/737/EC, OJ [2005] C 276 pp. 54–57).

[31] See Commission Decision of 08.10.2002 in case COMP/C2/38.014 (*IFPI Simulcasting*), OJ [2003] L 107 pp. 58–84; Commission Statement of Objection of 29.04.2004 in case COMP/C2/38.126 (*Santiago Agreement*), cf. Press Release IP/04/586; Commission Decision of 16.07.2008 in case COMP/C2/698 (*CISAC*), appealed to the General Court (case T-442/08).

collective societies for the benefit of the users.[32] In other words, the fact that the copyrights are territorial is not considered justification for keeping up the system whereby rights are cleared by the collective society of the territory of the user.

On the other hand, there is an important difference between the approach taken in the recommendation and the Commission's application of the competition rules. Whereas the recommendation seeks to encourage competition between collective societies in general, that is, also with regard to which repertoire to represent,[33] the application of the competition rules does not necessarily do away with the one stop shop principle, namely the principle that the rights should be cleared at one point for the entire repertoire.[34] Hence, whereas the recommendation has resulted in the emergence of different collective societies representing different repertoires, a possible result of the mere application of the competition rules could be that a multiterritorial and multirepertoire license can be received from one collective society at the choice of the user.

It is evident that the traditional rights management model was based on the multiplicity of territorial copyrights (and related rights). The collective societies in each state administered the rights in the states for which the works were used. This was true also with regard to the reciprocal agreements between collective societies, since each society granted the others licenses to rights in the territory of the licensee. And even the now expired Santiago and Barcelona agreements, which provided for multiterritorial exploitation rights for online use of musical works, was based on the concept of multiple territorial rights.[35] The model excluded to a large extent, at least in practice, competition between the collective societies,

---

[32] See the recommendation (note 30 supra) paragraph 7–11; Simulcasting decision (note 31 supra) paragraph 61; the press release in the Santiago case (note 31 supra) and CISAC decision (note 31 supra) paragraph 60.

[33] See the Commission Staff Working Document. Study on a Community Initiative on the Cross-border Collective Management of Copyright of 07.07.2005, available at http://ec.europa.eu/internal_market/copyright/docs/management/study-collectivemgmt_en.pdf, p. 36.

[34] See Simulcasting decision (note 31 supra) paragraph 86; the press release in the Santiago case (note 31 supra); CISAC decision (note 31 supra) paragraphs 236 and 241.

[35] See the press release in the Santiago case (note 31 supra): The traditional licensing framework would require a commercial user wishing to offer to its clients such musical work to obtain a copyright license from every single relevant national society. The Santiago Agreement therefore seeks to adapt the traditional framework to the online world by envisaging the possibility of one-stop licenses allowing for the provision of legitimate services such as music downloading or streaming.

whereas both the approaches of the Commission promote such competition. At first glance it is therefore natural to conclude that the traditional model is anti-competitive, contrary to the actions of the Commission.

However, as usual, things are not quite as simple as they seem. Firstly, in order to evaluate the impact on competition, it is important to make clear what competition concept is pursued – competition as a means to promote allocative efficiency or dynamic competition in the sense of competition promoting creativity.[36] Secondly, and closely linked to the first aspect, it is essential to consider whether or to what extent restraints on competition in the upstream markets of administration of rights and licenses to users is necessary in order to achieve competition in downstream markets, e.g. the markets for online music downloading or streaming services. Neither of the two aspects seems to have been analyzed thoroughly by the EU Commission. A possible objection to the system promoted by the Commission's recommendation (DG MARKT) is that it encourages competition in favor of mainstream music to the detriment of cultural diversity.[37] Moreover, the abandonment of the one stop shop principle may reduce the transparency of the rights clearance system and make it more difficult at least for small or medium enterprises to establish businesses in the downstream market. The application of the competition rules by the EU Commission (DG COMP) is not necessarily subject to these arguments, but it is possible to question whether the benefits gained from price competition between collective societies on administrative costs outweighs the transaction costs entailed in breaking up the seemingly well-functioning CISAC model for collective licensing, provided it opened up for multiterritorial licenses, as was done through the Santiago and Barcelona agreements. This is not to claim that the Commission was wrong in intervening against this model, but it is reasonable to say that the Commission has based its decisions on competition and market integration paradigms rather than an analysis of market effects.

The general point in this context is that although multiple territorial rights may indeed cause competition problems in international trade, and even more so if they are doubled with collectivization of rights, there might be reasons for accepting market solutions based on it. An analysis of the impact for competition should firstly include the concept of dynamic competition and secondly take into consideration its ancillary functions aimed at promoting competition in the downstream market. It is also important to note that territorial segmentation of markets is not only a consequence

---

[36] Drexl (2007) pp. 16–22.
[37] Drexl (2007) p. 22.

of territorial IP rights. Hence, despite the introduction of the principle of the single right clearance in the Satellite/Cable Directive,[38] the market is still territorially divided by way of agreements. Likewise, even though "online music shops" have received licenses for several territories, they are still operating on a national basis with no cross-border competition.[39] Thus, it is an open question whether the Commission has started at the right end by concentrating on competition in the upstream markets for rights administration and licenses for professional users rather than the downstream market for music end use.

4.   CONCLUDING REMARKS

To the extent that the multiplicity of territorial rights puts the right holder in a position to block or limit cross-border transactions of goods and services, this may have negative impact on competition if the right holder has some degree of market power and/or there are horizontal elements involved. In innovative and creative markets, however, it is important to have a broader outlook on competition, and include concepts of dynamic and creative competition, rather than focusing merely on allocative efficiency. Moreover, restraints of trade and competition at one level may promote competition at a different level. The multiplicity of territorial rights is therefore not tantamount to unacceptable restraints on competition, even if it leads to some restraints on cross-border transactions.

A considerable problem with regard to cross-border trade, however, is the lack of cross-border regulation of the IP/competition interface on a global level. There is certainly a need for an improved international framework, both in the sense of uniform protection rules, for example common international principles of exhaustion of IP rights, and an international regime for handling cross-border competition issues at a global level, but as pointed out above the realism of such a project is rather slight. All this is relevant if we concentrate on regulations to control the use of individual, multiple and collective ownerships in the property sense.[40] An alternative path is to seek collective ownerships in the sense of open solutions *instead of* property solutions.[41] In view of the uncertainty created by the

---

[38] See note 8 supra.
[39] See Farrand (2009).
[40] See Hilty, Chapter 1 of this book.
[41] Hilty, Chapter 1 of this book.

complexity of competition assessments and the lack of an international framework to deal with the problems, the open solutions could indeed solve many of the competition problems that the property solutions bring about. As pointed out by Professor Hilty in Chapter 1, the problem – and the challenge – in this respect lies in the creation of *incentives* for creators and inventors to choose the path of the open solutions.[42]

REFERENCES

Anderson, Robert (2008), 'Competition policy and intellectual property in the WTO: more guidance needed', in J. Drexl (ed.), *Research Handbook on Intellectual Property and Competition Law*, Cheltenham, UK and Northampton, US: Edward Elgar, pp. 451–473.

Dickinson, Andrew (2008), *The Rome II Regulation. The Law Applicable to Non-Contractual Obligations*, Oxford: Oxford University Press.

Dreier, Thomas (2010), 'Satellite and cable directive', in Michel Walter and Silke von Lewinski (eds), *European Copyright Law. A Commentary*, Oxford, New York: Oxford University Press.

Drexl, Josef (2007), *Collecting Societies and Competition Law*, available at http://193.174.132.100/shared/data/pdf/drexl_-_crmos_and_competition.pdf (accessed 28 August 2010).

Drexl, Josef (2008), 'Intellectual property and competition: sketching a competition-oriented reform of TRIPs', in Antonina Bakardijeva Engelbrekt, et al. (eds), *Festskrift till Marianne Levin*, Stockholm: Norstedts, pp. 261–280.

Farrand, B. (2009), 'The case that never was: an analysis of the Apple iTunes case presented by the Commission and potential future issues', *European Intellectual Property Review*, **31**, 508–513.

Forsyth M. and W.A. Rothnie (2007), 'Parallel imports and exhaustion', in Steven Anderman (ed.), 'Intellectual Property Rights and Competition Policy', Cambridge: Cambridge University Press.

Gervais, Daniel (2008), *The TRIPS Agreement. Drafting History and Analysis*, Third Edition, London: Sweet and Maxwell.

Nimmer, Melvine B. and David Nimmer, *Nimmer on Copyright*, Newark and San Francisco: Matthew Bender Publications (loose-leaf).

Peukert, Alexander (2011), 'Individual, multiple and collective ownership of intellectual property rights. Which impact on exclusivity?', in Annette Kur & Vitautas Mizaras (eds), *The Structure of Intellectual Property Law*, Cheltenham, UK: Edward Elgar Publishing.

Tai, Eric Tjong Tjin (2003), 'Exhaustion and online delivery of digital works', *European Intellectual Property Review*, **25**, 207–211.

Thowes R. and C. Handke (2007), 'Economics of copyright collecting societies', *International Review of Intellectual Property and Competition Law*, **38**, 937–957.

Torremans, P. (2001), 'The law applicable to copyright', *Revue Internationale du Droit d'Auteur*, **188**, 37–115.

---

[42]   See Hilty, Chapter 1 of this book.

Ulmer, Eugen (1978), *Intellectual Property Rights and the Conflict of Laws*, Deventer: Kluwer.

Wiebe, Andreas (2009), 'The principle of exhaustion in European copyright law and the distinction between digital goods and digital services', *Gewerblicher Rechtsschutz und Urheberrecht, Internationaler Teil*, **58**, 114–118.

PART II

Individualism and collectiveness in patent law

4. Individualism, collectivism and openness in patent law: from exclusion to inclusion through licensing

Geertrui Van Overwalle

1. INTRODUCTION

Recently, a shock wave swept through the biotechnology community when Judge Robert W. Sweet of the District Court for the Southern District of New York decided to deny patent protection for isolated human genes and associated diagnostic methods. The case related to genetic tests for familial breast and ovarian cancer developed by Myriad Genetics.[1] Although the decision has been appealed [2] and may well be reversed in light of the *Bilski* case,[3] many of the concerns relating to the impact of gene patenting, which are extensively discussed in this case, will continue to exist. The Myriad case is an exponent of a systemic problem. The disputed issues in the Myriad case point to the uneasy relationship between human genomic science and intellectual property (IP). The debate particularly revolves around the alleged hindering effect of single, blocking patents, on the one hand, and patent thickets, on the other hand, in the area of genetics.

Inspired by the ongoing exchange of ideas on distinct modes of ownership and their respective impact on exclusivity and competition,[4] the

---

[1]   *Association for Molecular Pathology v. USPTO, Southern District of New York* (March 29, 2010). For details and discussion of the Myriad decision, see Geertrui Van Overwalle, 'Turning patent swords into shares', 330 *Science*, 2010, 1630–1631; Isabelle Huys, Geertrui Van Overwalle and Gert Matthijs, 'Gene and genetic diagnostic method patents. A comparison under current European and US patent law', *European Journal of Human Genetics (EJHG)*, 2011, June 8.

[2]   The notice of appeal was filed on June 16, 2010.

[3]   *Bilski v. Kappos*, US Supreme Court (June 28, 2010).

[4]   Reto Hilty, 'Individual, multiple and collective ownership – what impact on competition?', Chapter 1 in this volume; Alexander Peukert, 'Individual, multiple

present chapter is an attempt to analyse the current problems in gene patenting through the lens of individual, multiple and collaborative ownership. The objective of this chapter is to systematize the relation between modes of ownership, modes of licensing and their effect on access.[5]

The underlying (normative) starting point of the present study is the legitimacy of IP ownership over human genes.[6] Another assumption is the merit of openness for fostering research and development in genetics.[7] The central question of the present chapter is which measures can be taken to assist patent law in responding to the alleged hindering effect of various forms of ownership and the intensified appeal for access in genetics. The core question is not what will change if the rules or forms of IP *ownership* are modified in genetics, but what might change if the conventional modes of *licensing* are altered. In other words, the key question does not revolve around proprietary or non-proprietary approaches in genetics, but around access improving license management structures.

The central question will be dealt with in two steps. First, we will examine different forms of ownership and their effect on access: do different forms of ownership have a different effect on access in genetics? Then, we will explore different forms of licensing and their effect on openness: do different forms of licensing result in different degrees of access?

Section 2 defines the contours of individual ownership, discusses its potential hindering effect on access and use in genetics, and suggests possible individual license policies and their effect on (re)establishing openness. Section 3 analyses the various forms of multiple ownership, looks into their effect on access and use in biotechnology, and investigates various collaborative licensing models and their effect on openness. Section 4 explores how these individual and collaborative license policies may assist in achieving "open biotechnology". Section 5 sets forth the most striking conclusions and suggests some avenues for further research.

---

and collective ownership of intellectual property rights – Which impact on exclusivity?', in *Can One Size Fit All?*, Kur/Mizaras (eds.), ATRIP *The Structure of Intellectual Property*, Cheltenham: Edward Elgar, 2011, available at http://papers.ssrn.com/sol3/papers.cfm?abstract_id=1563990

[5]   The current chapter does not seek to look into issues relating to ownership and access (to knowledge) in patent law, but is interested to learn about the effect of ownership on access *and* (legitimate) use of patented knowledge. Hence, the issue of (enabling) disclosure, and its contribution to access to knowledge, will not be dealt with here. Also see *infra*, section 4.1.

[6]   This starting point is substantiated *infra* (see section 3.3.), where we explain why we will not enter into the debate on the patentability of human genes.

[7]   Empirical evidence and economic analysis would be helpful in providing a wider scientific basis for this assumption.

The present study will conclude that in genetics, individual and multiple ownership have different effects. Individual ownership may result in blocking patent positions and multiple ownership may lead to hindering patent thickets. Both phenomena frustrate follow-on innovation. The effect of individual and multiple ownership, blocking patents and patent thickets may be attenuated by the creative design of (new) individual, collaborative and collective (voluntary and compulsory) licensing models, leading to semi-open or totally open biotechnology infrastructures.

2.   INDIVIDUAL OWNERSHIP

2.1   Concept

Ownership refers to any kind of attribution of legal protection of (intangible) subject matter to a person or group of persons by way of specific regulation.[8] [9] **Individual ownership** refers to a single person acquiring a single protection right. Translated into the patent context individual ownership refers to one inventor [10] holding one patent right [11] (also see Table 4.1).

2.2   Individual Ownership and "Blocking Patents"

At first sight, the exclusivity provided for by individual ownership seems predestined to have a problematic impact on access and use in genetics. This derives from the very nature of human genes and the character of patent claims on genes. Patent claims on genes are generally difficult, if

---

[8]   Based on Hilty (*supra* note 4): "the term [ownership] shall be used precisely to mean any kind of attribution – in whatever way – of *legally protected* (intangible) subject matter to a person or group of persons by means of specific legal regulation" (My Italics). In the definition set forth by Hilty, it is difficult to understand that ownership is the attribution (by means of regulation) of subject matter *that is already legally protected.*

[9]   In the context of the present chapter we will not enter into the (debated) distinction between the concepts of "property" and "ownership", but opt for the term "ownership". For more on the "property"–"ownership" discussion, see Hilty (*supra* note 4), and the references cited there.

[10]   As Hilty rightly remarks, the patent applicant or patent holder may be different from the inventor. The patent applicant/holder may well be an employer (of the inventor) to whom the right to (apply for) protection has been transferred or to whom the granted patent right (or patent application) has been sold. The inventor mostly is not the market player exploiting the patent (Hilty, *supra* note 4). We will not go into the consequences of this reality.

[11]   Cf. Hilty, *supra* note 4; Peukert, *supra* note 4.

not impossible, to invent around. Consequently, gene patents emerge as blocking IP entitlements. We define a **blocking patent** as a patent covering *essential* features of an invention which cannot be invented around,[12] [13] bearing in mind that a blocking patent is a *relative* concept. It is a relative concept as it relates to the presence of two distinct components or layers: an essentiality component and an instrumentality component.[14] Given that a certain activity or function is envisaged (instrumentality component), an assessment is required as to which elements are essential to perform that activity or function and whether these essential elements are claimed by the patent at stake (essentiality component). Only when the elements are indispensable or essential to achieve a specific result – in other words, when the essential elements are a necessary means to an end – and only when they are claimed in the patent, the patent concerned is a blocking patent.[15] In other words, a **blocking patent** appears when the patent covers essential features of an invention relevant for achieving a specific result. In the area of genetic diagnostics, a patent encompassing claims on the entire (or relevant part of the) gene sequence, on a common pathogenic mutation or on the fundamental method to determine the association between a mutated gene and an inherited disease, is blocking for carrying out the genetic test based on nucleotide analysis for that disease. A patent including the same claims is most likely not blocking when it comes to carrying out the test based on an analysis at the protein level (a so-called protein determination assay).[16]

Some recent data suggest that a substantial number of gene patent claims are indeed hard or impossible to circumvent and therefore qualify as blocking patents.[17] Blocking patents do not per se have a negative

---

[12] Geertrui Van Overwalle, 'Of thickets, blocks and gaps: designing tools to resolve obstacles in the gene patents landscape', in *Gene Patents and Collaborative Licensing Models. Patent Pools, Clearinghouses, Open Source Models and Liability Regimes*, Geertrui Van Overwalle (ed.), Cambridge, Cambridge University Press, 2009, 381–463.

[13] In a wider sense, *any* patent is by definition a blocking patent, as a patent confers upon its proprietor the right to stop others from making, using, offering for sale, selling, or importing the patented invention (See Art. 28.1 TRIPs Agreement). Used in this sense, the notion blocking patent is a tautology.

[14] Van Overwalle, *supra* note 12.

[15] Van Overwalle, *supra* note 12.

[16] Van Overwalle, *supra* note 12.

[17] Isabelle Huys, Nele Berthels, Gert Matthijs & Geertrui Van Overwalle, 'Legal uncertainty in the area of genetic diagnostic testing', **27**, *Nature Biotechnology*, 2009, 903–909.

impact on openness.[18] Whether blocking patents have an unfavourable impact on access and form a threat to openness, largely/totally depends on the licensing policy applied by the individual right holder.

2.3 Licensing and Openness

2.3.1 Bilateral or cross licences

A single right holder may be willing to share the benefit of his (blocking) gene patent with others in an attempt to enhance his market position.[19] Sharing with *one* person usually takes place under the form of a one-to-one bilateral license [20] in return for a fee or for a license,[21] resulting in restricted access (see Table 4.1*)*. Sharing with *multiple* (though limited in number) persons may take place by granting a bilateral license to each of them, resulting in a series of bilateral licenses and royalty fees, but still resulting in restricted access (see Table 4.1). In both cases, only **restricted access** is created, as access and use is limited to a number of well-identified licensees (see Table 4.1).[22] Both access regimes confer access upon payment of a fee, resulting in **conditional,** [23] restricted access.

2.3.2 License of right

The individual right holder who wants to share the use of his patented invention with an even wider circle of persons, or, in other words, who is willing to provide access and use to an *unlimited* number of users, may do so by opting for a "license of right" (see Table 4.1). The **"license of right"** is a legal mechanism by which a patent holder voluntarily chooses to give access to the patented invention to *anyone* else.

Licenses of right are not new. They already appear in the national patent

---

[18]   The terms "access" and "openness" are used alternately. Access and openness refer to access to *and* use of patented technology, see *infra* section 4.1.

[19]   Cf. Hilty, *supra* note 4.

[20]   The term license refers to license in the pure commercial sense, excluding Material Transfer Agreements (MTAs), cf. Esther van Zimmeren, Sven Vanneste & Geertrui Van Overwalle, *Patent Licensing in Medical Biotechnology,* Leuven, Acco, 2011, at 41.

[21]   Hence the term cross-license. The term cross-license refers to a special variant of a bilateral license: it is generally an agreement between two patent owners, where the patent owners grant each other a license for the exploitation of the subject-matter claimed in the relevant patents. Both patent owners act as licensor and licensee, see van Zimmeren et al., *supra* note 20, at 59.

[22]   On "restricted access", also see *infra*, section 4.1.

[23]   On "conditional" versus "unconditional", also see *infra*, section 4.1.

legislation of various EU member states[24] and were envisaged in the framework of the Community Patent Convention of 1975[25] and the Community Patent Agreement of 1989.[26] Nowadays, they figure in the proposed Community Patent Regulation which provides that "[t]he proprietor of a Community patent may file a written statement with the Office that he is prepared to allow any person to use the invention as a licensee in return for appropriate compensation. In that case, the renewal fees for the Community patent which fall due after receipt of the statement shall be reduced."[27]

The license of right option also captured some attention in patent practice. IBM launched a proposal for a "soft" Community patent endorsing a license of right.[28] Furthermore, a recent study by legal and economic scholars suggests that a remuneration-based license of right would be attractive for various kinds of patent owners and might encourage a more efficient exploitation of patented knowledge.[29] The study recommends further empirical research on the use and impact of licenses of right in the various EU member states and on the overall effectiveness of a remuneration system.

Licenses of right grant access to the patented invention to *anyone* else, thus creating **general access**.[30] The patent owner agrees to receive a predetermined remuneration for the use of his invention and if the user pays the required amount, the patent owner has no right to prevent the grantee

---

[24]   They exist in several countries, like for instance the United Kingdom, Germany, France and Switzerland. For more details, see van Zimmeren & Van Overwalle, *supra* note 31.

[25]   76/76/EEC: Convention for the European patent for the common market (Community Patent Convention), 26 January 1976, [1967] OJ L 17/1 (Article 43).

[26]   89/695/EEC: Agreement relating to Community patents – Done at Luxembourg, 15 December 1989, [1989] OJ L 401/1 (Article 43).

[27]   Article 20, Proposal for a Council Regulation on the Community patent, Brussels, 1.8.2000 COM(2000) 412 final, see http://ec.europa.eu/internal_market/indprop/patent/index_en.htm#system.

[28]   IBM, *The European Community Patent – A Realisable Dream*, IBM Discussion Paper, available at http://www.epip.eu/conferences/epip02/lectures/European%20Interoperabily%20Patent%201.1.pdf. The authors of the discussion paper promote "soft IP", which would serve both open and proprietary innovation, and argue in favor of an EU patent which endorses a license of right in line with the idea of "soft IP".

[29]   Robert Cowan, Wim Van der Eijk, Francesco Lissoni, Peter Lotz, Geertrui Van Overwalle & Jens Schovsbo, *Policy Options for the Improvement of the European Patent System*, Report commissioned by STOA (Scientific Technology Options Assessment) of the European Parliament and coordinated by Bjørn Bedsted of The Danish Board of Technology/ETAG, 2007, 67. (http://www.europarl.europa.eu/stoa/publications/studies/stoa16_en.pdf).

[30]   "General access", "total access" or "global access" are used as synonyms here. On "general access", also see *infra*, section 4.1.

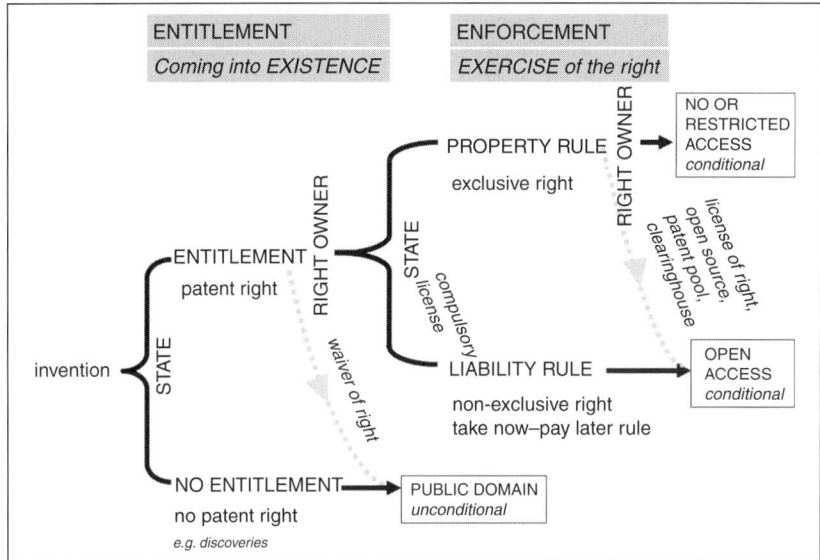

Note: Illustration of the various strategies of a knowledge holder [RIGHT OWNER] to establish openness. One way is to waive his (potential) entitlement, resulting in his creation falling into the public domain (*unconditional* openness). Another way is to license his entitlement to all others, individually through a "license of right" or an open source license, or collaboratively/collectively through a pool or a clearinghouse, resulting in *general*, *conditional* openness. In some cases, the legislature [STATE] enforces *semi-open* or *total*, *conditional* openness, by way of compulsory licenses.

Figure 4.1   Strategies a right owner may use to establish openness

from using the invention anymore.[31] Hence, the terms "remuneration right" and **conditional** access (see Figure 4.1).

2.3.3   Open source license [32]

The term "open source" originally came up in the context of copyrighted software. Over time, the term acquired several layers of meaning. Some

---

[31]   Esther van Zimmeren & Geertrui Van Overwalle, 'Compulsory license regimes for public health in Europe', *International Review of Intellectual Property and Competition Law (IIC)*, 2011, 4–40. Also see Geertrui Van Overwalle, 'The implementation of the biotechnology directive in Belgium and its aftereffects. The introduction of a new research exemption and a compulsory license for public health', **37** *International Review of Intellectual Property and Competition Law (IIC)*, 2006, 889–920.

[32]   This section is largely based on Van Overwalle, *supra* note 12.

scholars refer to a set of licensing criteria to define open source. A license is **open source** if "it allows *anyone*, anywhere, for any purpose, to copy, modify and distribute the software (where distribution takes place either for free or for a fee) without having to pay royalties to the (copyright) owner",[33] it being understood that the software program includes source code.[34] According to other scholars, emphasizing the licensing component is "excessively formalistic".[35] Rather than referring to the legal architecture and the details of licenses to characterize open source, open source refers to a mode of production, centering around "open and collaborative research".[36] Yet other observers recognize that the call for open source can refer to both approaches: "a licensing structure [. . .] granting access on the condition of reciprocal access" (= open source as a model or template), as

---

[33] Janet Hope, 'Open source genetics: a conceptual framework', in *Gene Patents and Collaborative Licensing Models. Patent Pools, Clearinghouses, Open Source Models and Liability Regimes*, Geertrui Van Overwalle (ed.), Cambridge, Cambridge University Press, 2009, 171–93, with reference to Lawrence Rosen, *Open Source Licensing: Software Freedom and Intellectual Property Law,* New Jersey, Prentice Hall, 2004. As to distribution, the Open Source Definition provides the following: "1. Free Redistribution: The license shall not restrict any party from selling or giving away the software as a component of an aggregate software distribution containing programs from several different sources. The license shall not require a royalty or other fee for such sale." (see http://opensource.org/osi3.0/node/4).

[34] As to source code, the Open Source Definition provides the following: "2. Source Code. The program must include source code, and must allow distribution in source code as well as compiled form. Where some form of a product is not distributed with source code, there must be a well-publicized means of obtaining the source code for no more than a reasonable reproduction cost preferably, downloading via the Internet without charge. The source code must be the preferred form in which a programmer would modify the program. Deliberately obfuscated source code is not allowed. Intermediate forms such as the output of a preprocessor or translator are not allowed" (see http://opensource.org/osi3.0/node/4).

[35] Arti Rai, 'Critical commentary on "Open Source" in the life sciences", in *Gene Patents and Collaborative Licensing Models. About Patent Pools, Clearing Houses, Open Source Models and Liability Regimes in Human Genetics*, Geertrui Van Overwalle (ed.), Cambridge, Cambridge University Press, 213–218.

[36] Arti Rai, 'Open and collaborative research: a new model for biomedicine', in *Intellectual Property Rights in Frontier Industries: Software and Biotechnology*, Robert W. Hahn (ed.), 2005, (131), 137: a model is open – and Mertonian – in the sense that "scientists work openly without secrecy and the usual sorts of exclusionary proprietary rights"; a model is collaborative – and goes beyond Merton – if it requires "scientists [to] work closely with others outside their own lab or small firm". As Rai points out, the term 'open and collaborative' was invoked in a letter to the WIPO (available at http://www.cptech.org/ip/wipo/kamil-idris-7july2003.pdf), but does not specify the terms.

well as "a general pattern for structuring networks of [. . .] researchers" (= open source as a metaphor).[37] In the framework of the present chapter, we opt for the rather narrow legalistic definition.

Open source is characterized by three essential elements, namely credible commitment, competition and, optionally, copyleft.[38] Credible commitment means that to be open source, a technology must be protected by IP or other proprietary rights and distributed on terms that are perceived to be legally enforceable.[39] A technology that is made available under the open source model is indeed not in the public domain,[40] but is owned by the licensor, who makes a legally enforceable promise via the license agreement not to interfere with others' freedom to use, improve or circulate the technology[41] and thus not to lock them in a web of IP. Competition refers to a level playing field between the licensor and the licensees of open source technologies with respect to the legal freedom to use and commercialise both the technology itself and any downstream innovations.[42] In that regard, an open source license may not impose field-of-use or territorial restrictions, nor may it prevent a licensee to start a new branch of collaborative development ("code the fork"). Copyleft imposes an obligation on the licensee to make any downstream innovations that it chooses to distribute beyond the boundaries of its own organisation available under the same terms as the original technology.[43]

Open source models may have various advantages for both the owner-user and the follow-up users.[44] Addressing the issue of uncertainty of innovation is one of them. Open source functions as a form of incomplete contract when there is uncertainty and informational problems, because

---

[37] Antony Taubman, 'Several kinds of "should": the ethics of open source in life sciences innovation', in *Gene Patents and Collaborative Licensing Models. About Patent Pools, Clearing Houses, Open Source Models and Liability Regimes in Human Genetics*, Geertrui Van Overwalle (ed.), Cambridge, Cambridge University Press, 219–44.

[38] Hope, *supra* note 33.

[39] Hope, *supra* note 33.

[40] Similarly, Richard Jefferson, 'Science as a social enterprise. The CAMBIA, BiOS Initiative', 1 *EconPapers,* issue 4, 2006, 13–17. Contra, Rai, *supra* note 35, 213–218: ". . . various other flavors of open source essentially amount to a dedication of source code to the public domain. Those who improve upon source code distributed under BSD licenses may feel a [social] norm-based obligation to contribute their improvements back, but they are under no legal obligation to do so".

[41] Hope, *supra* note 33.

[42] Hope, *supra* note 33.

[43] Hope, *supra* note 33.

[44] Hope, *supra* note 33.

knowledge is part of ongoing cumulative innovation.[45] But open source models may also entail some risks. Open source models may lead to anti-trust concerns.[46] Whether open source models always follow a free access rationale rather than a business strategy, needs to be examined more closely.

The archetypal open source copyleft license is the General Public License (GPL).[47] [48] The GPL allows anyone to use the licensed program, to study its source code, to modify it, and to distribute (un)modified versions to others, under the same terms as the initial license.[49] It is this final proviso that makes the GPL a copyleft licence, giving it its "viral" character.[50]

Open source principles are currently being tested in other technical areas than software, such as genetics. Some working examples of open source have emerged in the life sciences, mainly in the field of agricultural biotechnology. A prominent example is the Biological Open Source (BiOS) License from the Centre for Applications of Molecular Biology in International Agriculture (CAMBIA), a private non-profit research institute located in Canberra.[51] Founded by molecular biologist Richard Jefferson about fifteen years ago, CAMBIA pioneered, and subsequently

---

[45]   Reiko Aoki, 'Access to genetic patents and clearinghouse model. An economic perspective', in *Gene Patents and Collaborative Licensing Models. About Patent Pools, Clearing Houses, Open Source Models and Liability Regimes in Human Genetics*, Geertrui Van Overwalle (ed.), Cambridge, Cambridge University Press, 171–93, referring to free revealing users and user-owners.

[46]   See Hanns Ullrich, 'Gene patents and clearing models. Some comments from a competition law perspective', in *Gene Patents and Collaborative Licensing Models. About Patent Pools, Clearing Houses, Open Source Models and Liability Regimes in Human Genetics*, Geertrui Van Overwalle (ed.), Cambridge, Cambridge University Press, 2009, and the references cited there, amongst which Böcker, L., 'Mit freier Software gegen den Wettbewerb? Die General Public License (GPL) als horizontale Wettbewerbsschränkung', *Festschrift F. Säcker*, Berlin, 2006, 69.

[47]   See http://www.gnu.org/.

[48]   Linux is the contraction of Linus' Minix (Minix was version UNIX which Linus Torvalds enhanced). The name Linux was chosen by the developer (Linus Torvald) to refer to the *kernel* of the "GNU/Linux" operating system.

[49]   See http://www.gnu.org/licenses/gpl.html.

[50]   Hope, *supra* note 33. Similarly, Sara Boettiger & Dan Burk, 'Open source patenting', 1 *JIBL*, 2004.

[51]   See http://www.bios.net/daisy/bios/home.html. Also see Nele Berthels, 'CAMBIA's Biological Open Source Initiative (BiOS)', in *Gene Patents and Collaborative Licensing Models. About Patent Pools, Clearing Houses, Open Source Models and Liability Regimes in Human Genetics*, Geertrui Van Overwalle (ed.), Cambridge, Cambridge University Press, 2009, 194–203.

patented the GUS[52] and TransBacter[53] technology serving as a prominent research tool in agricultural biotechnology. The BiOS initiative was launched in 2004[54] and is intended to make these biological research tools widely available on open source conditions.[55] Another example is the open source style license policy promoted by Diversity Arrays Technology (DArT) Proprietary Limited.[56]

The translation of open source software principles does not seem to constitute insurmountable obstacles as to the very first key requirement, namely, credible commitment. Although the term "credible commitment" might not always be employed, this feature seems to be well understood by entrepreneurs active in the realm of biotech: "The idea of using patent licenses not to extract a financial return from a user of a technology, but rather to impose a covenant of behaviour, is the single feature of BiOS that is most resonant with Free and Open Source Software."[57] The implementation of the second requirement, competition, in the genetic field may prove

---

[52] The GUS technology relates to the β-glucuronidase (GUS) gene fusion system, and to the cloning and characterisation of the β-glucuronidase and glucuronide permease genes of *Escherichia coli*. Because of the abundance and availability of useful substrates for β-glucuronidase enzyme, GUS gene fusions may serve as a superior reporter gene system as well as an effective means of altering cellular phenotype. There are also implementations in conjunction with recombinant glucuronide permease, which may be used to render host cells permeable to β-glucuronidase substrates (see http://www.cambia.org/daisy/cambia/2539.html). Also see R.A. Jefferson, T.A. Kavanagh and M.W. Bevan, 'GUS fusions: Beta-Glucuronidase as a sensitive and versatile gene fusion marker in higher plants', **6**(13) *European Molecular Biology Organization Journal,* 1987, 3901–07. For information on the GUS patents, see Van Overwalle, *supra* note 12.

[53] The TransBacter technology relates generally to technologies for the transfer of nucleic acids molecules to eukaryotic cells. In particular non-pathogenic species of bacteria that interact with plant cells are used to transfer nucleic acid sequences. The bacteria for transforming plants usually contain binary vectors, such as a plasmid with a vir region of a Ti plasmid and a plasmid with a T region containing a DNA sequence of interest (see http://www.cambia.org/daisy/cambia/2538.html). For information on the TransBacter patents, see Van Overwalle, *supra* note 12.

[54] C. Dennis, 'Biologists launch "Open-Source Movement", **431** *Nature (News),* 2004, 30 September 2004, 494.

[55] See Berthels, *supra* note 51.

[56] See A. Kilian, 'Case 9. Diversity arrays Technology Pty Ltd.: Applying the open source philosophy in agriculture', in *Gene Patents and Collaborative Licensing Models. About Patent Pools, Clearing Houses, Open Source Models and Liability Regimes in Human Genetics*, Geertrui Van Overwalle (ed.), Cambridge, Cambridge University Press, 2009.

[57] Jefferson, *supra* note 40.

to be rather problematic from a principle point of view,[58] but may hardly pose a problem as a practical matter.[59] The final key element, copyleft, has equally raised concern in a life sciences context. Some critical observers fear that the BiOS License bears resemblance to grant back provisions, thus establishing a "club atmosphere", a "tit for tat" approach, rather than true openness.[60] Rather than strictly corresponding to open source features in every detail, open source efforts in the biotech area deliver "open source-*style*" licenses[61] which are "loosely" [62] based on open source principles.

Open source licenses, encompassing as a matter of principle a promise not to interfere with others' freedom to use, improve or circulate the patented technology, dismantle the exclusivity principle of patent law. They transform the right to exclude others into a duty to include others, on the condition that these others behave in the same sharing way, in exchange for unhampered access to improvement innovations. Open source thus creates **total,**[63] **conditional openness,** the condition not being monetary remuneration, but covenanted sharing behaviour (see Table 4.1). The subsequent user can realize his commitment to sustain openness in various ways: he can disclose the knowledge relating to his improvement without applying for a legal entitlement (patent), or he can apply for a patent and then establish a special license regime.[64]

2.3.4 Compulsory license

Real problems arise when blocking gene patents are not licensed or licensed very restrictively. Imagine a patent with claims covering (some or more) DNA sequences that are essential for the diagnosis of a genetic disease, the production of a test kit or the development of a therapy, and which patent is licensed exclusively to one or two laboratories around the world or not licensed at all. Third parties would be restrained from using (part of) the technology deemed necessary to carry out a diagnosis or manufacture a test or develop a therapy. Such restrictive licensing behavior may result in barriers to research,[65] hinder development that is instrumen-

---

58   See Hope, *supra* note 33.

59   Rai, *supra* note 35, with reference to E. Raymond, 'The Magic Cauldron', 1999 (available at http://www.catb.org/~esr/writings/magic-cauldron/magic-cauldron.html).

60   Hope, *supra* note 33.

61   Kilian, *supra* note 56.

62   Kilian, *supra* note 56.

63   "General access", "total access" or "open access" are used as synonyms here. On "total access", also see *infra*, section 4.1.

64   Cf. Hilty, *supra* note 4.

65   In some empirical studies a negative impact of "blocking" gene patents

tal to public health, restrict clinical access and decrease the availability of high quality tests and therapies for patients. The Myriad case represents a key example of such a restrictive license policy, resulting in restrained openness and public disapproval.[66] Several studies have documented other restrictive licensing practices in the area of gene-based diagnostic genetic services as well.[67]

In the case of blocking gene patents and restrictive license behavior, openness can be achieved by way of compulsory licenses. In response to the Myriad case, various European legislatures have introduced a compulsory license for public health.[68] Depending on the specific national regime, these compulsory licenses create **semi-open** [69] or **general access** [70] (see Table 4.1).

2.4 Conclusion

Gene patents are prone to be blocking. However, individual ownership of (blocking) gene patents does not per se hamper access and use. Rather

---

could not be found (e.g. John P. Walsh, Wesley M. Cohen, & Charlene Cho, 'Where excludability matters: material versus intellectual property in academic biomedical research', **36** *Research Policy*, 2007, 1184–1203. That can be explained by the fact that these studies focused on biomedical *research* rather than downstream product development.

[66]   R. Gold & J. Carbone, *Case Study, Myriad Genetics: In the Eye of the Policy Storm.* 2008 (see http://www.theinnovationpartnership.org/en/ieg/cases/); T. Caulfield, T. Bubela & C.J. Murdoch, 'Myriad and the mass media: the covering of a gene patent controversy', **9**, *Genetics in Medicine,* 2007, 850–55.

[67]   M.K. Cho, S. Illangasekare, M.A. Weaver, D.G.B. Leonard & J.F. Merz, 'Effects of Patents and Licenses on the Provision of Clinical Genetic Testing Services', **5**(1), *Journal of Molecular Diagnostics,* 2001, 3; Gert Matthijs, in *Gene Patents and Public Health,* Geertrui Van Overwalle (ed.), Bruylant, Brussels, 2007, 27–44; 'Case studies prepared for the Secretary's Advisory Committee on Genetics, Health, and Society (SACGHS)', *Genetics in Medicine,* Volume **12**, Issue 4 (2010).

[68]   For a detailed discussion, see van Zimmeren & Van Overwalle, *supra* note 31.

[69]   Semi-open access refers to access for a certain category of users (see *infra,* section 4.1.). Under Belgian law, for example, the applicant for a compulsory license must demonstrate that he has, should the compulsory license be granted to him, the resources or the bona fide intention to obtain resources that are necessary for actual and continual manufacture and/or application in Belgium of the patented invention (article 31bis § 2 of the Belgian Patent Act of 1984, inserted April 28th 2005). See Van Overwalle, *supra* note 69. Also see van Zimmeren & Van Overwalle, *supra* note 69.

[70]   "General access", "total access" or "open access" are used as synonyms here. On "general access", also see *infra,* section 4.1.

than the individual ownership of gene patents as such, it is the subsequent licensing behavior which leads to potential access problems. If the individual patent owner non-exclusively licenses such patent to *multiple* interested users, the impact of the blocking patent may be reduced substantially. If the individual patent owner decides to license his patent by way of a license of right to *any* user, a blocking patent no longer forms an obstacle at all. Especially in the case where the patent owner only grants exclusive licenses or no licenses at all, real problems of access may emerge, which, however, might be attenuated by taking recourse to a compulsory license (when available).

Licenses to multiple users, beneficial as they may be, only create restricted, conditional access. In contrast, the license of right, the open source license and the compulsory license, transform the exclusive right of the individual patent owner, into a right to use, thereby creating semi-open or general access. In the case of the license of right and the compulsory license, access is conditioned upon the payment of a fee, thus turning the exclusive right into a right of remuneration or take-now-pay-later rule. In the case of open source, access is awarded in exchange for a sharing behavior (see Figure 4.1).

3.   MULTIPLE OWNERSHIP

3.1   Concept

Multiple ownership has been circumscribed and catalogued before. Hilty defines multiple ownership by referring to "a certain – limited – number of 'owners' of subject matter".[71] He suggests that a particular form of multiple ownership may be created by the individual owner ("shared ownership"),[72] or may evolve from collaboration during the process of creation or invention ("collaborative ownership").[73] Hilty further defines collective ownership, involving "an open number of 'owners'",[74] as being distinct from multiple ownership.

The picture sketched is somewhat unclear as different criteria are being employed to spell out multiplicity. Multiplicity is being defined, on the one hand, by looking at the way an IP right *comes into being*,[75] and, on the

---

[71]   Hilty, *supra* note 4.
[72]   Hilty, *supra* note 4.
[73]   Hilty, *supra* note 4.
[74]   Hilty, *supra* note 4.
[75]   See Hilty's definition on collaborative ownership (Hilty, *supra* note 4).

other hand, by looking at the way in which the IP right is *exercised* and the effect of licensing on accessibility for third parties.[76] The landscape portrayed is opaque because *legal* ownership [77] and *factual* ownership [78] are muddled.[79] This chapter opts for a more rigid approach and defines the various modes of multiple ownership on the basis of legal ownership. The main reason is that in patent law, legal ownership comes into being by the attribution of a protection right to the inventor by an authorized body (patent office), or by the formal transfer of that right by way of contract by the patent owner to another party. Legal ownership does not come into being through licensing of the right by the patent owner to another party. A license involves the attribution of a right to use to the other party, not the adjudication of a right of ownership.

All this brings us to the following definition of multiple ownership. **Multiple ownership** refers to *multiple* persons each acquiring a *single* protection right, resulting in a series of independent rights, or in other words, *multiple* protection rights. Translated into patent parlance, multiple ownership refers to multiple, independent inventors each holding one, single patent right, resulting in many different patent rights[80] (see Table 4.1). Multiple ownership needs to be distinguished from **collaborative** or **joint ownership** which refers to *multiple* persons acquiring *one* single right, in other words, *various* inventors collaborating [81] together, developing *one*

---

[76] See Hilty's definition of shared ownership (Hilty, *supra* note 4). Cf. Peukert (*supra* note 4): ". . . individual licensing could already be qualified as a case of multiple ownership".

[77] See Hilty's definition of collaborative ownership (Hilty, *supra* note 4).

[78] See Hilty's definition of shared ownership and collective ownership (Hilty, *supra* note 4).

[79] A typical example where *attribution* of rights (creating an IP entitlement for the knowledge holder) and *use* of rights (not creating any kind of IP entitlement, only a right to use for others) are mingled, and where *legal* ownership (of the knowledge holder) and *factual* ownership (of others) are – wrongly – muddled is Hilty's concept of "shared ownership" (Hilty, *supra* note 4: "In fact, the entitlement deriving from individual ownership permits the owner to – voluntarily – create a particular form of multiple ownership, for which a better term might be 'shared ownership'. As a matter of principle, individually granted rights may be transferred to third parties, or at least third parties may acquire sort of factual ownership, like in the case of the grant of a license") (this volume). Cf. Peukert (*supra* note 4): "individual licensing could already be qualified as a case of multiple ownership".

[80] Hilty, *supra* note 4; Peukert, *supra* note 4.

[81] On the distinction between collaborative and collective, see *infra*, section 3.3. Joint ownership in patent law can be characterized as collaborative ownership, but not as collective ownership.

invention and acquiring *one* patent right (see Table 4.1). **Collective owner-ship** also involves ownership of *multiple* persons holding *one* single right, but does not result from prior collaboration between the right holders.

Individual, multiple, collaborative and collective *ownership* (which are based on the form of legal ownership) is further distinguished from bilat-eral, collaborative and collective *licensing* (which is based on the various forms of licensing), and from individual and shared *use* (which is based on the scope of actual use)[82] (see Table 4.1).

The categorizations and qualifications suggested here are meant to be helpful intellectual tools to analyze complex legal architectures. Only a correct understanding of essential features can lead to correct starting assumptions, and can result in opening certain perspectives and crafting adequate responses. It goes without saying, however, that definitions and typologies are not an end in themselves. The debate on ownership and licensing should not be led astray by semantic subtleties and incongruities. What counts is the effect licensing measures achieve in fulfilling the objec-tive of accessibility and sharing in practice, disregarding the way in which ownership and licensing arrangement can be qualified.

3.2   Multiple Ownership and "Patent Thickets"

Multiple ownership may have a negative impact on access when it accu-mulates into a patent thicket. Although the term "patent thicket" has been widely used over the past years, its exact meaning and scope is still not clear. Merges defines an intellectual property thicket as "a tangled, twisted mass of intellectual property rights, which criss-cross the established walk-ways of commerce" and where progress requires "numerous contracts with multiple, independent right holders".[83] Shapiro speaks of "a dense

---

[82]   Confusingly termed "factual ownership" by some authors.

[83]   Robert P. Merges, 'Contracting into liability rules: intellectual property rights and collective rights organizations', **84** *Calif. Law Rev.*, 1996, 1293–1393. Merges already introduced the "thickets" metaphor in this article: "Intellectual property experts, especially scholars, have responded to this burgeoning *thicket* of rights. . ." (p. 1386) and "This Article is aimed at providing conceptual guidance for those who need to traverse the new *thicket* of intellectual property rights. Each vine, each plant, standing in one's path represents a distinct IPR owned by an individual. To pass through, one needs a license from each owner. Where a single right blocks the path, this is easy: a single licensing contract does the trick. Today, however, business people more often than not encounter a tangled, twisted mass of IPRs, which criss-cross the established walkways of commerce. Progress along this path does not come cheaply: rather, it requires numerous contracts with multiple, independent right holders." (p. 1295)

web of overlapping intellectual property rights that a company must hack its way through in order to actually commercialize new technology".[84] Careful reading of these definitions suggests that a patent thicket is likely to emerge when multiple patents are held by multiple patent owners. However, various questions are left unanswered. Merges and Shapiro do not clarify whether a patent thicket is only present when the patents are numerous, or also when the patents are confined. Although their wording suggests the presence of a large number of patents, it may very well be that in a certain field of technology a relatively small number of scattered patents leads second comers to decide not to engage in related research. Neither do Merges and Shapiro articulate whether a thicket only appears when the many patents at stake are essential, or also when they are independent of one another. Shapiro says that "overlapping" patent rights create a patent thicket, suggesting that a patent thicket is present when a set of somehow "related" patents needs to be aggregated to develop a certain technology. Based on these insights and experiences from experts in genetics,[85] we define a **patent thicket** as the existence of *multiple, essential* (blocking) patents necessary to develop *one* product or process, which are held by *multiple,* independent patent owners.[86]

A patent thicket raises concern because the negotiation of a number of licenses can be so difficult and costly, that it can become impossible "to

---

[84] Carl Shapiro, 'Navigating the patent thicket: cross licenses, patent pools and standard setting' in E. Jaffe et al. (eds.), *Innovation Policy and the Economy* (Vol. I), MIT Press, 2001, 119–150.

[85] Larry Horn suggests that a patent thicket is really present if there is a "critical mass of essential patent holders with a critical mass of essential patents" (*see* Larry Horn, 'Case 1. The MPEG LA® licensing model. What problem does it solve in biopharma and genetics ethics and patents for genetic diagnostic tests', in *Gene Patents and Collaborative Licensing Models. About Patent Pools, Clearing Houses, Open Source Models and Liability Regimes in Human Genetics*, Geertrui Van Overwalle (ed.), Cambridge, Cambridge University Press, 2009); Jeorge Goldstein says that "If multiple patent owners hold patents over different mutational correlations, and all of them are necessary for a successful test, then a thicket may appear" (*see* Jeorge A. Goldstein, 'Critical analysis of patent pools', in *Gene Patents and Collaborative Licensing Models. About Patent Pools, Clearing Houses, Open Source Models and Liability Regimes in Human Genetics*, Geertrui Van Overwalle (ed.), Cambridge, Cambridge University Press, 2009); Birgit Verbeure refers to "the existence of multiple patents held by multiple patent owners" and argues that "a patent-thicket occurs when multiple patents cover the same application or technology" (Birgit Verbeure, 'Patent pooling for gene-based diagnostic testing. Conceptual framework', in *Gene Patents and Collaborative Licensing Models. Patent Pools, Clearinghouses, Open Source Models and Liability Regimes*, Geertrui Van Overwalle (ed.), Cambridge, Cambridge University Press, 2009, 3–32).

[86] Van Overwalle, *supra* note 12.

work naturally coherent pieces of technology".[87] The transaction costs related to patent thickets may lead to royalty stacking and ultimately result in a "tragedy of the anti-commons".[88] Patent thickets, per definition, have a higher negative impact on access than blocking patents: even if all patent holders involved display a favourable licensing policy, aggregation problems remain, and the cost of trading patent rights (searching and bargaining costs, cost of multiple license fees, etc.)[89] can still be prohibitive.

As of now, empirical data have not yet confirmed the existence of a wide patent thicket in genetics at large.[90] However, several surveys clearly

---

[87]   Ullrich, *supra* note 46. Ullrich subtly adds, however, that the patent thicket is more a matter of the number and of the strategic positioning of patents than of the number of patentees.

[88]   Michael A. Heller & Rebecca S. Eisenberg, 'Can patents deter innovation? The anticommons in biomedical research', **280** *Science,* 1998, 698–701. Cf. Adam B. Jaffe & Josh Lerner (*Innovation and Its Discontents,* Princeton-Oxford, Princeton University Press, 2004, at 5): "[. . .], valuable technologies have become snarled in a web of litigation and licensing negotiations. [. . .] The accumulation of fees paid for the use of multiple patents makes the product development process more expensive, limiting the rate at which companies can bring new products to market. And some companies, given the choice of paying royalties or facing litigation on as-yet unproven new products, may simply drop the project altogether".

[89]   The present chapter will not look into solutions "ignoring the norm". See Van Overwalle, *supra* note 12, and the references cited there.

[90]   Most empirical studies focus on the *issuance* of human gene patents by patent authorities. See M.M Hopkins, S. Mahdi, P. Patel and S. Thomas, 'DNA patenting: the end of an era?', **25** *Nature Biotechnology,* 2007, 185–7; M.M. Hopkins, S. Mahdi, P. Patel and S. Thomas, *The Patenting of Human DNA: Global Trends in Public and Private Sector Activity* (A Report for the European Commission – PATGEN Project – 6th FP-2003- LifeSciHealth-II), Brighton, Science and Technology Policy Research (SPRU) – University of Sussex, 2006, 14 (available at: http://www.sussex.ac.uk/spru/documents/patgen_finalreport.pdf); K. Jensen, and F. Murray, 'Intellectual property landscape of the human genome', **310** *Science,* 2005, 239–40; National Research Council of the National Academies (Committee on intellectual Property Rights in Genomic and Protein Research and Innovation), *Reaping the Benefits of Genomic and Proteomic Research: Intellectual Property Rights, Innovation, and Public Health,* Washington, National Academies Press, 2005, 161; Birgit Verbeure, Gert Matthijs and Geertrui Van Overwalle, 'Analysing DNA patents in relation with diagnostic genetic testing', **14** *European Journal of Human Genetics (EJHG),* vol. 1, January 2006, 26–33; J.P. Walsh, C. Cho, and W. M. Cohen, *Patents, Material Transfers and Access to Research Inputs in Biomedical Research* (Final Report to the National Academy of Sciences Committee [on] Intellectual Property Rights in Genomic and Protein-Related Research Inventions), Washington, National Academies Press, 2005, 172. Few empirical studies focus on the set of gene patents that have been asserted in *court* to assess the actual restrictive effect of patents. See C.M. Holman, 'The impact of human gene patents on innovation and access: a survey of human gene patent

point to potential problems in the field of diagnostic testing.[91] Moreover, it is quite possible that thicket problems in genetic diagnostics grow with the switch from monogenetic testing to multifactorial testing (multiplex diagnostics) and the shift towards diagnostics based on genome-wide association studies driven by the high-throughput of SNP platforms and the next-generation sequencing possibilities.[92] Although the Myriad case is not an illustrative example of this phenomenon, the Myriad decision has invigorated concerns about the potential negative effects of a dispersed patent landscape affecting further research and development, and harming clinical and patient access in the long run.

3.3 Licensing and Openness

Various strategies have been suggested to mitigate the alleged hindering effect of patent thickets and to facilitate access to genome-related inventions. One way to achieve this goal is to narrow down patentable subject matter.[93] As valuable as such an approach may be, it is more easily said than done, given the (global) change in legislation it would require. Another approach, oriented to cut down on the mass of "trivial patents" of dubious merit, is to strengthen patentability requirements and "raise the bar", or to apply existing standards more stringently and reserve patent protection for "high quality patents".[94] Reserving the patent premium

---

litigation', **76** *University of Missouri-Kansas City Law Review,* 2007, 295–362 (also available at http://papers.ssrn.com/sol3/papers.cfm?abstract_id=1090562).

[91]   See references in previous footnote. Also see T. Caulfield, R.M. Cook-Deegan, F.S. Kieff and J.P. Walsh, 'Evidence and anecdotes: an analysis of human gene patenting controversies', **24** *Nature Biotechnology,* 2006, (1091), 1092.

[92]   J.H. Barton, **24** *Nat. Biotechnol.,* 2006, 939–41; Secretary's Advisory Committee on Genetics, Health, and Society (SACGHS), *Revised Draft Report on Gene Patents and Licensing Practices and Their Impact on Patient Access to Genetic Tests,* Approved by SACGHS May 2, 2010 (see http://oba.od.nih.gov/SACGHS/sacghs_documents.html); Van Overwalle, *supra* note 12.

[93]   See e.g., the Genomic Research and Accessibility Act, introduced in 2007 by US Congressmen Xavier Becerra and Dave Weldon, to amend § 106 of the Patent Act, as follows: 'Notwithstanding any other provision of law, no patent may be obtained for a nucleotide sequence, or its functions or correlations, or the naturally occurring products it specifies.' H.R. 977, 110th Cong. (2007), at http://thomas.loc.gov/cgi-bin/query/z?c110:H.R.977. See also 'Rights to human genes. Time has come to reassess the benefits of the present practice of patenting human genetic material', Editorial, **127** *Nature Immunology* 2009.

[94]   Dietmar Harhoff offers a useful and rather comprehensive definition of 'high quality patent', see his paper presented at the European Patent Conference (EUPACO), Brussels, May 15, 2007 at http://www.eupaco.org/eupaco2.

for high-quality inventions is a must, and various initiatives seem to be under way to implement this idea.[95] But even if only high-quality inventions are awarded patent protection, patent thickets may emerge. Yet another – complementary – option is to explore solutions which focus on the exercise of high-quality patent rights. Swift and plastic responses to the current proliferation problem in patent law might be helped by contractual tools resulting from party autonomy, rather than from legal reform measures resulting from an initiative of the legislator. A first approach in this regard may be the large-scale use of individual measures such as licenses of right or open source licences. In a world of technology covered increasingly with IP rights, and in which companies are spending large amounts of time and resources in order to obtain licenses to prevent hold-ups from right-owners, large-scale use of specially crafted individual measures can already significantly reduce these problems.[96] An alternative strategy may be the design of tools organizing the transaction of IP rights more effectively, such as patent pools or clearinghouses. A distinction can be made between collaborative and collective tools. To collaborate means "working jointly with others or together especially in an intellectual endeavour".[97] **Collaborative licensing measures** thus refer to measures where people *work together*. Hence, some efforts, such as patent pools, are collaborative in nature, as they presuppose active cooperation between the various rights owners.[98] Collective means "involving all members of

---

[95] For Europe, see Cowan et al., *supra* note 31; European Patent Office (EPO), *Scenarios for the Future* 105 (2007) at http://www.epo.org/topics/patent-system/scenarios-for-the-future.html; European Patent Office (EPO), *Annual Report* 2008, Munchen, Gerber, 2009, more in particular the section *Quality Over Quantity: On Course to Raise the Bar* 8 –11. Quite significant in this section is the admission that '[w]hile the volume of applications the EPO has to examine has been on an upward trend, the same cannot be said of their quality. Applications that are inconsistent with the EPC standards, the many procedural steps through which they must pass – and the legal uncertainties that sometimes result – have all engendered a backlog at the EPO and a rethink of quality management.' For the US, see Dan L. Burk and Mark A. Lemley, *The Patent Crisis and How the Courts Can Solve It*, Chicago-London, The University of Chicago Press, 2009, 220; Martin Enserink, 'Biomedical patents: U.S. Patent Office may raise the bar on gene claims', 287 *Science,* 2000, 1196.

[96] Cowan et al., *supra* note 31.

[97] The term "open and collaborative" was invoked in a letter to the WIPO, but does not specify the terms (see http://www.cptech.org/ip/wipo/kamil-idris-7july2003.pdf). The present explanation is taken See *Merriam-Webster's Online Dictionary* – also for further etymological background – available at http://www.merriam-webster.com.

[98] In our previous research we catalogued open source as a collaborative

a group as distinct from its individuals".[99] **Collective licensing measures** thus refer to measures which *involve* all members. Hence some other initiatives, such as clearinghouses, are collective as they affect all rights holders, without presupposing prior collaboration between them (see Table 4.1).[100]

Both the impact of joint ownership on access and the effect of licensing on openness largely follow the lines of individual ownership,[101] and will therefore not be further discussed here.

3.3.1 Patent pools[102]

Concept The term "patent pool" has acquired different meanings. In its widest sense a patent pool refers to a loose collection of patents held by

---

licensing mechanism (see Van Overwalle, *supra* note 12). But, open source can be introduced starting from the willingness of *one* legally entitled patent owner, hence we classify it here under individual license mechanisms. As the success of open source will depend on the attitude of subsequent knowledge holders to share under the same open source conditions, it might still be qualified as a collaborative licensing measure as well.

[99] See *Merriam-Webster's Online Dictionary* – also for further etymological background – available at http://www.merriam-webster.com.

[100] Although we previously made a distinction between collaborative and collective measures as a matter of principle, we classified pools and clearinghouses both as collaborative licensing models (see Van Overwalle, *supra* note 12). However, rethinking these definitions, it seems more adequate to qualify pools as *collaborative* efforts (as they presuppose active, mutual collaboration between patent holders to conclude a set up agreement) and clearinghouses as *collective* measures (as they involve various patent holders, but do not require their mutual collaboration). See below. Also see Geertrui Van Overwalle, 'Designing models to clear patent thickets in genetics', in *Working within the Boundaries of Intellectual Property,* Rochelle Dreyfuss, Harry First & Dianne Zimmerman (eds.), Oxford, Oxford University Press, 2010, 305–324.

[101] Similarly, Hilty (*supra* note 4): "The effects of this specific form of [. . .] ownership for third parties, therefore basically remain the same as in case of merely individual ownership: irrespective of the person of the owner [. . .] third parties simply have to respect a granted legal protection". Cf. Peukert (*supra* note 4): "Joint ownership concerns one subject matter of protection only. Since there is only one object, there is also only one IP right. [. . .] the general limits of exclusivity apply unmodified. The reason is that there is only one IP right in one subject matter held by one group of people – as in the paradigm case of individual exclusivity".

[102] This section is largely based on earlier work, see Geertrui Van Overwalle, Esther van Zimmeren, Birgit Verbeure & Gert Matthijs, 'Models for facilitating access to patents on genetic inventions', 7 *Nature Review Genetics*, February 2006, 143–8; Geertrui Van Overwalle, *supra* note 100; Birgit Verbeure, Esther van Zimmeren, Gert Matthijs & Geertrui Van Overwalle, 'Patent pools and diagnostic

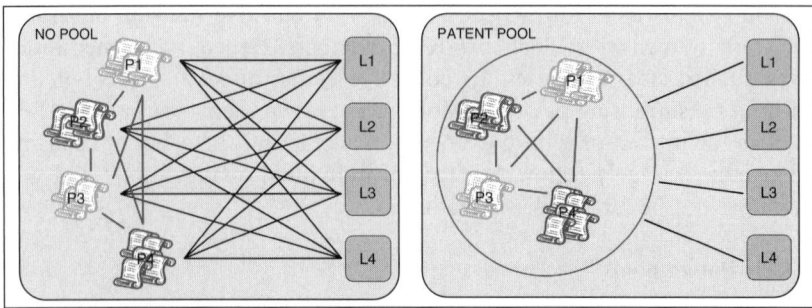

Note: Comparative illustration of the different licenses needed in the absence or presence of a patent pool. P1–P4 represents the patent holders. L1–L4 represents the licensees. In the absence of a patent pool, licensees have to enter into negotiations with all the patent holders, which is a time consuming and expensive process. By contrast, in the presence of a patent pool licensees turn to the patent pool for acquiring the rights as one package, which results in simplification and a significant reduction of transaction costs.

Source: Reprinted from Verbeure (2006), *supra* note 102, at 116, with permission from Elsevier.

Figure 4.2   Licenses needed in the absence or presence of a patent pool

different patent owners. In a more narrow sense, and as employed here, a **patent pool** points to an agreement between two or more patent owners to license one or more of their patents to one another, and to license them as a package to third parties who are willing to pay the royalties that are associated with the license.[103] Licenses are provided to the licensee, either directly by the patentee, or indirectly through a new entity that is specifically set up for the administration of the pool (see Figure 4.2).

---

testing', **24** *Trends in Biotechnology (TIB)*, Vol. 3, March 2006, 115–120; *Gene Patents and Collaborative Licensing Models. Patent Pools, Clearinghouses, Open Source Models and Liability Regimes*, Geertrui Van Overwalle, ed., Cambridge, Cambridge University Press, 2009, 477.

[103]   Jeanne Clark et al., *Patent Pools: A Solution to the Problem of Access in Biotechnology Patents?* (United States Patent and Trademark Office, Dec. 2000) at http://www.uspto.gov/web/offices/pac/dapp/opla/patentpool.pdf; Robert P. Merges, 'Of property rules, Coase and intellectual property', **94** *Colum. L. Rev.*, 1994, 2655. See also Robert P. Merges, 'Institutions for intellectual property transactions: the case of patent pools', in *Expanding the Boundaries of Intellectual Property*, Rochelle Dreyfuss, Diane L. Zimmerman, & Harry First (eds.), Oxford, Oxford University Press, 2001 (123–65), at 123, 129; US Department of Justice – Antitrust Division, *Business Review Letter from Joel I. Klein to Gerrard R. Beeney* (Letter 98-C relating to MPEG LA L.L.C., et al.), June 1997, at http://www.usdoj.gov/atr/public/busreview/215742.pdf.

Patent pools may have significant benefits. In a nutshell, pools may eliminate stacking licenses,[104] reduce licensing transaction costs through the introduction of a system of "one stop licensing" for non-member licensees,[105] decrease patent litigation and contribute to the institutionalized exchange of technical information that is not covered by patents, through a mechanism for sharing technical information relating to the patented technology, which would otherwise be kept as a trade secret.[106] As well as providing a possible solution to the problem of patent thickets, the creation of a patent pool might also stimulate funding for research and development, benefiting all partners in the pool.

Patent pools might also carry some risks. In brief, pools might shield invalid patents[107] and entail inequitable remunerations.[108] Additionally, patent pools might cover for a cartel and, subsequently, have anti-competitive effects.[109]

Examples   Patent pools are not new, having been used occasionally but regularly since the 19th century. The first licensing pool was established in 1856 among members of the sewing machine industry.[110] A further prominent example of an early patent pool is the 1917 aircraft pool that was formed between almost all US aircraft manufacturers.[111] This patent pool was crucial to the US government entering World War I.

● Information, communication and entertainment (ICE) technology
In the 1990s the patent pool model gained wide interest in the ICE-sector and several pools with worldwide coverage were formed. In contrast to the early patent pools, those modern pools usually cover relevant patents for one particular standard, rather than covering all patents of an industry.

---

[104]   Clark, *supra* note 103.

[105]   Merges, *supra* note 103, at 144.

[106]   Clark, *supra* note 103; Merges, *supra* note 103, at 139; Shapiro, *supra* note 84.

[107]   Shapiro, *supra* note 84.

[108]   *Business Review Letter from Joel I. Klein to Gerrard R. Beeney*, *supra* note 103.

[109]   Merges, *supra* note 103; Shapiro, *supra* note 84; US Department of Justice – Antitrust Division, *Business Review Letter from Charles A. James to Ky P. Ewing* (Letter 02-4 relating to 3G Patent Platform Partnership), Nov. 2002, at http://www.usdoj.gov/atr/public/busreview/200455.htm; Steven C. Carlson, 'Patent pools and the antitrust dilemma', 16 *Yale J. on Reg.*, 1999, 359.

[110]   Robert P. Merges, *Who Owns the Charles River Bridge? Intellectual Property and Competition in the Software Industry*, (Boalt Working Papers in Public Law, Paper 64, 1999); Merges, *supra* note 103.

[111]   Harry T. Dykman, 'Patent licensing within the Manufacturer's Aircraft Association', **46** *J. Patent Office Soc'y* 646 (1964); Merges, *supra* note 103, at 134–8.

Further, their licensing rules are more complex than those of the early licensing pools.[112]

A key example of a modern patent pool in the ICE area is the pool related to the digital video compression standard known as MPEG-2.[113] The MPEG-2 pool emerged as a consequence of MPEG-2 having been established as international standard by the International Standards Organization (ISO) in 1995. The MPEG-2 technology is covered by more than 425 essential patents owned by some 21 patent holders.[114] In the presence of the pool, users of the technology can acquire access to the bulk of patents with one, single license.[115] The MPEG-2 pool has a central entity, MPEG LA,[116] which administers the patent pool on behalf of its members based on a set of formal codified internal rules. These rules also organize the admission of new members to the pool, after having been evaluated in detail by experts, and the resulting changes in the licensing profits among the members.[117]

A second trendsetting patent pool of the 1990s is the DVD pool. Similar to the MPEG-2 pool, this pool emerged within a consortium setting a standard for the DVD technology. However, the consortium did not lead to one single pool, but to two distinct pools. A first pool, the so-called DVD4C patent pool, united four of the ten core DVD developers and was cleared by the Department of Justice (DoJ) in 1998.[118] A second pool, the DVD6C patent pool, assembled six other core members and covered more than 840 patents.[119] The pool was cleared by the DoJ in 1999.[120]

---

[112]   Merges, *supra* note 110.

[113]   For more details, see Horn, *supra* note 85. Also see Merges, *supra* note 103 at 147–50 and 1612.

[114]   Baryn S. Futa (CEO and Manager, MPEG LA, LLC), *Statement Before the United States Department of Justice Antitrust Division and the Federal Trade Commission Joint Hearings on Competition and Intellectual Property Law and Policy in the Knowledge-Based Economy*, 1997, available at http://www.ftc.gov/opp/intellect/020417barynfuta.pdf.

[115]   *Business Review Letter from Joel I. Klein to Gerrard R. Beeney, supra* note 103.

[116]   See http://www.mpegla.com.

[117]   Merges, *supra* note 110.

[118]   US Department of Justice – Antitrust Division, *Business Review Letter from Joel I. Klein to Garrard R. Beeney* (Letter 98-11 relating to Koninklijke Philips Electronics N.V., Sony Corporation of Japan and Pioneer Electronic Corporation of Japan), December 16, 1998, available at http://www.usdoj.gov/atr/public/busreview/2121.pdf. Also see Merges, *supra* note 103 at 150–54 and 161–2.

[119]   See http://www.dvd6cla.com.

[120]   US Department of Justice – Antitrust Division, *Business Review Letter from Joel I. Klein to Carey R. Ramos* (Letter 99-2 relating to Hitachi Ltd., Matsushita

● Biotechnology

Transplanting the patent pool concept from ICE to genetics was suggested by the Organisation for Economic Co-operation and Development (OECD). The OECD considered the patent pool concept to be interesting for biotechnology, but called for further study.[121] The OECD feared that the fact that biotechnological companies rely heavily on their IP and foster what has been called a "bunker mentality" might cause difficulties in the process of creating a pool.

Notwithstanding the scepticism of the OECD, some patent pools have already been set up in genetics. A first, instructive genetic patent pool which gained wide attention, is the Golden Rice pool. Potrykus succeeded in genetically enriching rice grains with β-carotene[122] and wanted to transfer the Golden Rice materials to developing countries for further breeding in order to introduce the trait into local varieties that are consumed in these countries. Six key patent holders were approached and an agreement was reached that allowed Potrykus to grant licenses, free of charge, to developing countries, with the right to sub-license.[123] This agreement is an example of how private and public organizations, in a combined effort, dealt with the surrounding patents to create a non-profit humanitarian (and therefore probably a-typical) patent pool in the form of a single licensing authority.[124]

Another genetic pool, supported by the World Health Organization (WHO), is the Severe Acute Respiratory Syndrome (SARS) corona virus

---

Electric Industrial Co. Ltd., et al.), June 10, 1999, available at http://www.usdoj. gov/atr/public/busreview/2485.htm.

[121] Organisation for Economic Co-operation and Development (OECD), *Genetic Inventions, Intellectual Property Rights and Licensing Practices – Evidence and Policies*, 2002, available at http://www.oecd.org/pdf/M00031000/M00031448. pdf.

[122] Peter Beyer et al., 'Golden rice: introducing the beta-carotene biosynthesis pathway into rice endosperm by genetic engineering to defeat vitamin A deficiency', 132 *J. Nutr.* 506 (2002).

[123] *Golden Rice Collaboration Brings Health Benefits Nearer* (Zeneca (now Syngenta) press release issued May 16, 2000); *International Rice Research Institute Begins Testing Golden Rice* (Zeneca press release issued January 22, 2001; Syngenta to Donate Golden Rice to Humanitarian Board. (Zeneca press release issued October 14, 2004).

[124] Gregory Graff & David Zilberman, 'Towards an intellectual property clearinghouse for ag-biotechnology', 3 *IP Technology Today,* 2001; Gregory Graff et al., 'The public-private structure of intellectual property ownership in agricultural biotechnology', 21 *Nature Biotechnology,* 2003, 989; Randall Parish & Reiner Jargosch, R., 'Using the industry model to create physical science patent pools among academic institutions', 15 *J. Ass'n U. Tech. Managers*, 2003, 65.

pool. The relevant patent holders have been identified and agreement has officially been gained by the signing of a letter of intent.[125] The SARS pool highlights the opportunities that are offered by the patent-pool concept for biomedical genetic inventions. However, the pool is no longer actively being pursued, because with no further outbreaks of SARS, the economic driver for the formation of such a pool has been removed.[126]

Effect on openness   Patent pools, requiring as a matter of competition law open and non-discriminatory licensing policies vis à vis everyone, convert the exclusivity principle of patent protection into a liability regime – a "take now, pay later" regime [127] introducing a rule that takes the form of "an automatic license without the power to exclude".[128] The major difference between an IP right and a liability rule is that a liability rule, in contrast to an IP right, does not allow to control follow-on applications: a liability rule allows companies within a defined period of time, to borrow one another's innovation, on the condition that they contribute to the costs of development [129] (see Figure 4.1). A patent pool is an example of a contractually-constructed liability regime, created when "contracting parties start with property rule entitlements, and wind up subject to a collectively-determined liability rule",[130] which takes place when stake-

---

[125]   James Simon, 'Dealing with patent fragmentation: The SARS patent pool as a model', in *Gene Patents and Public Health,* Geertrui Van Overwalle (ed.), Brussel, Bruylant, 2007, 115–20. See also Carmen E. Correa, 'IP fragmentation and patent pools: the SARS case', in *Gene Patents and Collaborative Licensing Models. About Patent Pools, Clearing Houses, Open Source Models and Liability Regimes in Human Genetics,* Geertrui Van Overwalle (ed.), Cambridge, Cambridge University Press, 2009.

[126]   Personal Communication with James Simon, Jan. 21, 2009.

[127]   Merges, *supra* note 83, at 1302.

[128]   See Jerome H. Reichman, 'Of green tulips and legal Kudzu: repackaging rights in subpatentable innovation', **53** *Vanderbilt Law Review,* 2000, 1743–98; Jerome H. Reichman & T. Lewis, 'Using liability rules to stimulate innovation in developing countries: application to traditional knowledge', 337 *International Public Goods and Transfer of Technology Under a Globalized Intellectual Property Regime,* Keith E. Maskus & Jerome H. Reichman (eds.), 2005, 337–366. Also see Annette Kur & Jens Schovsbo, 'Expropriation or fair game for all? The gradual dismantling of the IP exclusivity paradigm', *Max Planck Institute for Intellectual Property, Competition and Tax Law Research Paper Series,* No 09–14 (available at http:// papers.ssrn.com/sol3/papers.cfm?abstract_id=1508330); Ben Depoorter, 'Property rules, liability rules and patent market failure', **1** *Erasmus Law Review,* 2008, 59–74.

[129]   See Reichman, *supra* note 129. Also see Reichman & Lewis, *supra* note 129.

[130]   See Merges, *supra* note 83, at 1303, who called the process of creating "contracting into liability rules", and the resulting organizations "private liability rule organizations". Also see Merges, *supra* note 103, at 132.

holders voluntarily seek to obtain private ordering with outcomes that differ from what the default rules of IP law might otherwise provide.[131]

Patent pools create **general,** but **conditional openness**, the condition being payment of a fee. In exchange for a fee, they turn exclusive patent rights into commonly shared assets (see Table 4.1).[132]

3.3.2   Clearinghouses [133]

Concept   Clearinghouse models might be another approach to facilitate access when many patents are present. The term "clearinghouse" is derived from banking institutions and refers to the mechanism by which cheques and bills are exchanged among member banks to transfer only the net balances in cash. Nowadays the concept has acquired a broader meaning and the term **clearinghouse** refers to any mechanism by which providers and users of goods, services and/or information are matched.[134] (See Figure 4.3).

Based on the various functions a clearinghouse may fulfil, five types can be distinguished.[135] Two models merely provide *access* to (protected) information: the information clearinghouse and the technology exchange clearinghouse. The information clearinghouse provides a mechanism for exchanging technical information and/or information that is related to the IP status of that information.[136] The technology

---

[131]   See Jerome Reichman & Paul Uhlir ('A contractually reconstructed research commons for scientific data in a highly protectionist intellectual property environment', **66** *Law and Contemporary Problems*, 2003, 315–462) from whom the term "contractually-constructed liability regime" has been drawn. Also see Reichman, *supra* note 129. Also see Reichman & Lewis, *supra* note 129.

[132]   Van Overwalle, *supra* note 12, at 381.

[133]   This section is largely based on previous work, *see* references *supra* note 102 and Esther van Zimmeren, Birgit Verbeure, Gert Matthijs & Geertrui Van Overwalle, 'A clearinghouse for diagnostic testing: the solution to ensure access to and use of patented genetic inventions?', *Bulletin of the World Health Organization*, 2006, 352–9.

[134]   Anatole F. Krattiger, 'Financing the bioindustry and facilitating biotechnology transfer', **8** *IP Strategy Today*, 2004; van Zimmeren et al., *supra* note 133.

[135]   For a more extensive description of the different types of clearinghouses and their respective pros and cons, see Esther van Zimmeren, 'Clearinghouse mechanisms in genetic diagnostics: conceptual framework', in *Gene Patents and Collaborative Licensing Models. Patent Pools, Clearinghouses, Open Source Models and Liability Regimes*, Geertrui Van Overwalle, ed., Cambridge, Cambridge University Press, 2009, 63–119.

[136]   Krattiger, *supra* note 134 at 1–45; Graff & Zilberman, *supra* note 124; Graff et al., *supra* note 124 at 989–95; van Zimmeren et al., *supra* note 133.

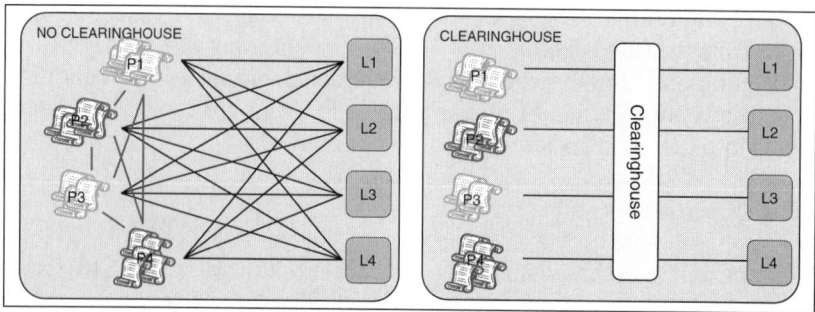

Note: Comparative illustration of the different licenses needed in the absence or presence of a clearinghouse. P1–P4 represents the patent holders. L1–L4 represents the licensees. In the absence of a clearinghouse, licensees have to enter into negotiations with all the patent holders. In the presence of a clearinghouse, licensees turn to the clearinghouse entity for acquiring the rights.

Figure 4.3   Licenses needed in the absence or presence of a clearinghouse

exchange clearinghouse is inspired by the internet-based business-to-business (B2B) model and provides an information service that lists the available technologies to allow technology owners and/or buyers to initiate negotiations for a license. Additionally, it may provide more comprehensive mediating and managing facilities.[137] It is important to underline that actual access to the patented inventions is not usually granted by the technology exchange clearinghouse but by the individual patent holder after one-to-one licensing negotiations have taken place with the licensee. These negotiations are, however, based on the information on the inventions which was provided by the clearinghouse.[138] Although the technology-exchange clearinghouse model is generally cheap to maintain and generates only low operating costs, it might be difficult to bring together the critical mass of genetic patents that would be needed to turn platforms of this type into useful tools. At present, most of the platforms offer only a small proportion of the market and a low density of patents, and one has to search various websites (sometimes paying considerable registration fees). Moreover, this model might only be suitable for technologies that can be easily defined and valued. Therefore, it might be limited as a model for general-purpose research methods, such as Polymerase Chain Reaction (PCR), and for patents

---

[137]   Krattiger, *supra* note 134; Graff & Zilberman, *supra* note 124; van Zimmeren et al., *supra* note 133.
[138]   van Zimmeren et al., *supra* note 133.

that protect specific and well-defined improvements to familiar downstream products or processes.[139]

Three more elaborate models provide access and also standardize the use of the (patented) inventions: the open access clearinghouse, the standardized licenses clearinghouse and the royalty collection clearinghouse. The open access clearinghouse not only fosters open access to information about inventions to everyone, as its name may suggest, but also offers exchange and use of inventions at no charge.[140] Open access clearinghouses might be a readily available model for sharing and exchanging unpatented technology. However, most genetic inventions are the outcome of long-lasting research that requires high levels of investment. Both private enterprises and universities wish to recover those investments and so do apply for patent protection. Therefore, the scope of application for this model might be limited in the area of genetic inventions, at least in the near future.[141]

The standardized licenses clearinghouse provides access to and standardizes licenses for the use of protected inventions.

The royalty collection clearinghouse comprises all the functions of the information clearinghouse, the technology exchange clearinghouse and the standardized licenses scheme.[142] In addition to these functions, the royalty collection clearinghouse sets up a mechanism to collect license fees from users on behalf of the patent holders in return for the access to and use of the inventions.[143] The patent holder is reimbursed by the clearinghouse pursuant to a set allocation formula, which has been negotiated beforehand.[144]

Examples

● General examples

Examples of *information* clearinghouses include general patent search sites, either freely accessible, such as Espacenet from the European Patent Office (EPO), [145] or fee-based, like Delphion [146]or Micropatent.[147]

An interesting example of a global *technology* exchange model is

---

[139]   Graff & Zilberman, *supra* note 124; Krattiger, *supra* note 134; van Zimmeren et al., *supra* note 133.

[140]   van Zimmeren et al., *supra* note 134; van Zimmeren, *supra* note 135.

[141]   van Zimmeren et al., *supra* note 134; van Zimmeren, *supra* note 135.

[142]   van Zimmeren et al., *supra* note 134; van Zimmeren, *supra* note 135.

[143]   Merges, *supra* note 83.

[144]   van Zimmeren et al., *supra* note 133.

[145]   See http://www.espacenet.com.

[146]   See http://www.dephion.com.

[147]   See http://www.micropatent.com/static/index.htm.

TechTransferOnline.[148] It is an internet-based platform that brings together offers and demands for innovations, and provides services dedicated to finding and facilitating contacts between technology holders and technology seekers. More than 102,000 technologies are currently searchable by investors, entrepreneurs and scientists who are looking for new business or scientific opportunities.

An example of the *standardized* license clearinghouse is Creative Commons (CC).[149] CC has already been in operation for a couple of years facilitating the use of copyrighted material, such as music, movies, photos, books, course materials, scientific and medical literature (e.g. PLoS Biology) by way of standardized, simplified licenses and has been very successful.

Classical examples of *royalty* collection clearinghouses include copyright societies such as ASCAP (the American Society of Composers, Authors and Publishers) [150] or other national agencies.[151]

- Biotechnology

For quite some time, the Human Genome Organization (HUGO), the OECD and various other international and national bodies have suggested that clearinghouses should be set up in the field of patents and genetic inventions as well.[152] And, indeed, the clearinghouse model found

---

[148]   See http://www.techtransferonline.com. Recently, TechTransferOnline acquired another technology exchange model named BirchBob (see Esther van Zimmeren & Dirk Avau, 'BirchBob: an example of a technology exchange clearing house, in *Gene Patents and Collaborative Licensing Models. Patent Pools, Clearinghouses, Open Source Models and Liability Regimes*, Geertrui Van Overwalle (ed.), Cambridge, Cambridge University Press, 2009) (see www. TechTransferOnline.com, Press Release September 30, 2008).

[149]   See http://creativecommons.org.

[150]   See http://www.ascap.com.

[151]   Eg, Sabam in Belgium (http://www.sabam.be). See Jan Corbet, 'The collective management of copyright and neighbouring rights. An example of a royalty collection clearing house', in *Gene Patents and Collaborative Licensing Models. About Patent Pools, Clearing Houses, Open Source Models and Liability Regimes in Human Genetics*, Geertrui Van Overwalle (ed.), Cambridge, Cambridge University Press, 2009, 151–60.

[152]   Australian Law Reform Commission, *Gene Patenting and Human Health, Discussion Paper* 68, at 636–39, (2004) (also available at http://www.austlii.edu. au/au/other/alrc/publications/dp/68); HUGO Intellectual Property Committee, Statement on the Scope of Gene Patents, Research Exemption and Licensing of Patented Gene Sequences for Diagnostics, Dec. 2003 (also available at http://www.hugo-international.org/img/ip_gene_2003.pdf); E. Richard Gold, 'Biotechnology patents: strategies for meeting economic and ethical concerns', **30** *Nat. Genet.* 359 (2002); Graff & Zilberman, *supra* note 124; Krattiger, *supra* note

some reception in the biotech area. A well-known example of a biotech *information* clearinghouse is Patent Lens.[153] Patent Lens is established in the framework of the Biological Open Source (BiOS) initiative and offers a free, fully text-searchable database of US, European and Australian agricultural and life science patents, as well as complementary advisory and educational services.[154]

Specific healthcare *technology* exchange platforms include Innovaro Pharmalicensing [155] or TechEx.[156] They provide online partnering support that enables companies in the biopharmaceutical and biomedical industry to find licensing partners and conclude licensing contracts. Specific bio-technology clearinghouses include PIPRA (Public Intellectual Property Resource),[157] a collaboration between universities, foundations and non-profit research institutions to make agricultural technologies more easily available for humanitarian use.

A well-known example of an *open access* clearinghouse in the life sciences is the SNP Consortium.[158] The goal of the non-profit SNP Consortium is to identify and collect single nucleotide polymorphisms (SNPs) and create and make the SNP map of the human genome publicly available, without any proprietary rights retained by the members of the clearinghouse, in order to enable further drug discovery.

An example of a *standardized* biotech license clearinghouse is Science Commons.[159] This constellation aims to encourage data sharing,

---

134; Nuffield Council on Bioethics, *The Ethics of Patenting DNA, A Discussion Paper* 93 (2002); OECD, *Guidelines for the Licensing of Genetic Inventions,* point 39 and 46 (2006) (available at http://www.oecd.org/dataoecd/39/38/36198812. pdf).

[153]   See http://www.patentlens.net/. See Berthels, *supra* note 51.

[154]   See http://www.bios.net/daisy/bios/home.html.

[155]   See http://www.pharmalicensing.com.

[156]   See http://www.techex.com.

[157]   See http://www.pipra.org. See Alan B. Bennett & Sara Boettiger, 'The public intellectual property resource for agriculture. A standard license public sector clearinghouse for agricultural IP', in *Gene Patents and Collaborative Licensing Models. About Patent Pools, Clearing Houses, Open Source Models and Liability Regimes in Human Genetics*, Geertrui Van Overwalle (ed.), Cambridge, Cambridge University Press, 2009, 135–42.

[158]   See http://snp.cshl.org.

[159]   See http://sciencecommons.org. See Thinh Nguyen, 'The science commons material transfer agreement project. A standard license clearing house?', in *Gene Patents and Collaborative Licensing Models. About Patent Pools, Clearing Houses, Open Source Models and Liability Regimes in Human Genetics*, Geertrui Van Overwalle (ed.), Cambridge, Cambridge University Press, 2009, 143–50; van Zimmeren et al., *supra* note 133.

technology transfer and IP licensing, by stimulating stakeholders to adopt standardized licenses in order to create greater transparency.

At present, an example of a *royalty* collection clearinghouse is on its way in the field of patents and genetics. The Unitaid-Medicines Patent Pool aims at establishing a voluntary licensing mechanism to enhance the availability of improved, affordable and high-quality medicines for the treatment of HIV/AIDS in developing countries. The pool will work towards obtaining voluntary licenses for HIV/AIDS medicine(s) patents from patent holders and then make such licenses available to qualified third parties (such as generic manufacturers). The Medicines Patent Pool is an independent legal entity based in Geneva, Switzerland, established with the support of Unitaid. Unitaid is an innovative Global Health financing mechanism, whose mission is to contribute to scaling up access to treatment for HIV/AIDS, malaria and tuberculosis in low- and middle-income countries.[160] Although the Unitaid HIV/AIDS patent initiative is termed a pool, close examination of its structure and tasks[161] leads us to conclude that it is not a pool proper, but a clearinghouse. It is a one-stop-shop or "hub" that facilitates in- and out-licensing of HIV/AIDS-related patents: patent holders unilaterally out-license their patents to the "hub"; qualified users in-license patents of their choice from the hub in exchange for a fee, after which the hub distributes the collected royalties among the patent holders.

Effect on openness   Standardized and royalty collecting clearinghouses, if characterized by *ex ante* disclosure of standardized licensing and royalty conditions, also convert the exclusivity principle of patent protection into a liability regime (see Figure 4.1), thereby creating **general, conditional access**, the condition being payment of a fee. This type of clearinghouse also turns the exclusive patent right into shared use (see Table 4.1).[162] However, if the licenses offered by the clearinghouse are only available for qualified users (e.g. generic manufacturers, as in the Unitaid pool case),

---

[160]   For more details, see http://www.unitaid.eu/en/The-Medicines-Patent-Pool-Initiative.html. Also see Jorge Bermudez & Ellen 't Hoen, 'The UNITAID patent pool initiative: bringing patents together for the common good', **4** *The Open AIDS Journal*, 2010, 37–40.

[161]   See   UNITAID   factsheet   (http://www.unitaid.eu/images/NewWeb/documents/Publications_July2010/pp_facts_en_jul10.pdf) and Frequently Asked Questions (http://www.unitaid.eu/images/NewWeb/documents/Publications_July2010/pp_q&a_en_jul10.pdf).

[162]   Geertrui Van Overwalle, *supra* note 12, at 381.

the effect, strictly speaking, would be **restricted** access, even though such an effect might be negligible in practice, as – apart from the qualified users – no one would probably apply.

Technology exchange clearinghouses do not trigger this transformation from a right to exclude to a right to remuneration, as they mainly serve as a marketplace to find licensing partners, where the patent holder keeps the authority to exclude certain licensees, and where – in the event the licensee is accepted – licenses are individually crafted.

3.3.3   Open source licenses

A license is **open source** if "it allows anyone, anywhere, for any purpose, to copy, modify and distribute the software (where distribution takes place either for free or for a fee) without having to pay royalties to the (copyright) owner".[163] An open source license regime can get started from individual ownership, in particular with the willingness of *one* legally entitled patent owner. Hence, we have classified open source under the range of individual license mechanisms. As the success of open source will largely depend on the attitude of subsequent knowledge holders to share under the same open source conditions, open source may also be qualified as a collaborative licensing measure as well.[164]

Effective as it may be from a blocking perspective, it remains to be seen to what extent open source licensing can deal with cumulative technology and subsequent patent fragmentation.[165] Some cases clearly demonstrate that the open source license model is a viable commercial strategy through the provision of accessory genotyping services in the context of the licensed core technology package, but it is unclear to what extent the open source-style license offering access to the core technology has facilitated and simplified uptake of this technology.[166] Furthermore, the DArT experience seems to suggest that the open source philosophy will

---

[163]   See section 2.3.3.

[164]   As we did in our previous work, See Van Overwalle, *supra* note 12.

[165]   Sara Boettiger and Brian D. Wright, 'Open source in biotechnology: open questions', *Innovations,* 2006, 45–63. On patent fragmentation and patent thickets, see *supra.*

[166]   This conclusion is based on Kilian, *supra* note 56: "Under this [the present] arrangement, CAMBIA offers *DArT* through its BiOS initiative while we at DArT PL are offering a licence to practice the technology in the context of a *complete technology package*". ". . .as the list of BiOS licensees is not publicly available it is impossible to judge the extent of DArT's uptake or development through this channel." And also on Kilian: "Interestingly, a few years after the separation of DArT PL from CAMBIA the level of interest in licensing just *the right to practice the technology in general* is very low (practically non-existent), while at the same

be difficult to be put to practice in market segments aiming at the largest potential profit margins, such as the biomedicine sector, unless a specific niche can be identified, likely in an area of limited financial opportunity, where competition with "mainstream" companies would be less intense.[167]

3.4   Conclusion

Multiple ownership (the occurrence of multiple, independent inventors each holding one – or more – single patent) is likely to create problems of access in the area of genetic diagnostics, because multiple ownership may give rise to patent thickets (the existence of multiple, independent inventors all holding multiple, essential (blocking) patents necessary to develop one product or process).

Individual licensing, taking the form of licenses of right or open source licenses, may help to mitigate patent thickets. However, collaborative and collective licensing may attenuate the effect of multiple ownership more adequately and facilitate access to a web of gene patents even more effectively. **Collaborative licensing models**, presupposing mutual collaboration between the various patent holders, include patent pools. Patent pools create **general, conditional** openness, the condition being payment of a fee (see Table 4.1). **Collective licensing models**, involving all patent holders without requiring prior collaboration, include clearinghouses. Standardized and royalty collecting clearinghouses create global, conditional access, the condition being payment of a fee (see Table 4.1). Open source licenses, encompassing as a matter of principle a promise not to interfere with others' freedom to use, also create **global, conditional** openness, the condition being covenanted sharing behaviour (see Table 4.1).

4.   OPEN BIOTECHNOLOGY

4.1   Concept and Typology of Access

So far, we have discussed the impact of (individual and multiple) ownership on access and use in biotechnology. In doing so, we have used the terms access and openness alternately. **Access** and **openness** refer to

---

time the level of interest in our *genotyping services and technology provision* in general is rapidly increasing." [Author's italics]
[167]   Cf. Kilian, *supra* note 56.

access and use of patented technology,[168] establishing freedom to operate.[169] Access encompasses both access for end-users (e.g. geneticists using as a matter of routine in their daily work the recombinant DNA technology patented by Cohen and Boyer) and for follow-on innovators (e.g. molecular scientists aiming to improve the recombinant DNA technology).

Restricted access refers to access which is restricted to a limited, well-defined number of users (e.g. a series of clearly identified companies). **Semi-open access** refers to access for a certain category of users (e.g. generic manufacturers). **General, total** or **global access** refers to access which is awarded to an indefinite number of users and where nobody can be excluded.

Conditional access refers to access which is possible in exchange for a certain (monetary or non-monetary) compensation (quid pro quo). Bilateral licenses create restricted, conditional access, where a fee has to be paid. Cross licenses also create restricted, conditional access, but differ in the condition which has to be met: access to one's own technology, rather than a fee has to be given in return for access. Compulsory licenses induce semi-open or totally open, conditional access. Licenses of right, patent pools, standard clearinghouses and royalty collecting clearinghouses are examples of general, conditional access, where a royalty fee has to be paid to obtain access. Open source creates general, conditional access where a certain behaviour has to be displayed in return for access. **Unconditional access** refers to access which is possible without compensation (free access). Access can be achieved by knowledge holders themselves through formal rules of contract [170] (individual or collaborative/collective license agreements) or by the legislator through formal legal rules (e.g. compulsory license regimes).

Licenses result in **shared use,** as the legally entitled (individual, multiple

---

[168] Cf. van Zimmeren et al., *supra* note 133: "A clearing house for diagnostic testing: the solution to *ensure access to and use of* patented genetic inventions?" (My Italics).

[169] "Freedom to operate" is generally defined as a situation where "the commercial production, marketing and use of a product, process or service does not infringe the patent rights of others ('third party patent rights')", see van Zimmeren, *supra* note 20.

[170] For the distinction between formal *legal* rules and formal rules of *contract,* see Tom Dedeurwaerdere, 'The role of law, institutions and governance in facilitating access to the scientific research commons' in *Gene Patents and Collaborative Licensing Models. About Patent Pools, Clearing Houses, Open Source Models and Liability Regimes in Human Genetics*, Geertrui Van Overwalle (ed.), Cambridge, Cambridge University Press, 2009, at 365.

Table 4.1   Overview of different forms of ownership in patent law, their 'constituting elements', differing licensing strategies and their effect on openness

Coming into EXISTENCE of rights				EXERCISE of rights			
Number of inventors	Number of rights awarded	individual ownership	Potential problem	Number of licensees	Type of license	Effect on openness	individual use / shared use ***
one inventor	one right	individual ownership	blocking patent	(a) no one		no access*	individual use
				(b) one 3rd party	bilateral license	restricted, conditional** access	shared use ***
				(c) multiple others	multiple bilateral licenses	restricted, conditional access	
				(d) indefinite number of others	"license of right"	global, conditional access	
					open source license	global, conditional access	
					compulsory license	semi-open or global conditional access	

inventors	rights	ownership	(legitimate use)	access means	instrument	licensing	access	use
multiple inventors	multiple rights	**multiple ownership**	patent thicket	(a) one another	cross-licenses		"club", restricted access	**shared use** [no collective use]
				(a') one other (platform)	license			
				(b) indefinite	sublicenses patent pool (a) + (b)	**collaborative licensing**	global, conditional access	
					clearinghouse (a') + (b)	**collective licensing**	global conditional access	conditional access
								conditional access
multiple inventors	one right **joint ownership**	**collaborative ownership**		(a) one				
				(b) multiple				
				(c) indefinite				
one/ multiple inventors	no IP						open *unconditional access*	*unconditional* access
								public domain

Notes:

The 'constituting elements' include number of knowledge holders and number of attributed rights.

* access means: access *and* (legitimate) use.

** *monetary* condition: payment of fee; *non-monetary* condition: sharing behavior.

*** *shared* use (points to relation between owner and user) and user): use shared between the legal owner and licensee(s), whereby the licensor and the licensee(s) can exert their right independently; *collective* use (points to relation between users): use shared between connected licensees, whereby the licensees exert their right as a group.

or joint) grantees all share the benefit of exclusive right of the IP owner, albeit on certain conditions. Licenses usually do not seem to establish a form of **collective use,** where the legitimate other users exert their right of use in dialogue with one another.[171]

4.2   Concept and Typology of Open Biotechnology

Recently, scholars have introduced the term "open biotechnology",[172] a term that calls for some explanation. At first sight, the term encompasses a variety of projects, ranging from open journals such as PLoS,[173] new bioinformatic tools,[174] databases,[175] big science projects such as HapMap or the Human Genome Project,[176] projects to facilitate access to biotech research tools, such as BiOS,[177] or a combination of these. **Open biotechnology** seems to be used as a container term for all kinds of projects and approaches fostering open research in the biotechnology sector.

At closer sight, these projects differ greatly in terms of ownership, however. A first type of open biotechnology projects can be catalogued as **public domain** initiatives. Public domain status is achieved by *renouncing* any form of (potential and available) IP entitlements (see Figure 4.1), thus creating total openness (see Table 4.1). Examples here include big science projects, such as HapMap and the Human Genome Project.

A second type of projects relates to **open access** endeavors. The term "open access" was originally used in a copyright context. Open access refers to the free and unrestricted online availability of peer reviewed literature, to all scientists, scholars, teachers, students, and other curious minds, permitting them to read, download, copy, distribute, print, search, or link to the

---

[171]   Similarly, Hilty, *supra* note 4.

[172]   Yann Joly, 'Open biotechnology: licenses needed', **28** *Nature Biotechnology*, 2010, 417–419.

[173]   E.g. Public Library of Science, see http://www.plos.org/.

[174]   E.g. the BioMoby messaging standard, for interoperability between biological data hosts and analytical services. The Moby-S system defines an ontology-based messaging standard through which a client will be able to automatically discover and interact with task-appropriate biological data and analytical service providers, without requiring manual manipulation of data formats as data flows from one provider to the next, see http://biomoby.open-bio.org/.

[175]   E.g. NIH db GaP, a database of genome wide association studies, see http://www.ncbi.nlm.nih.gov/projects/gap/cgi-bin/about.html.

[176]   For HapMap, see http://hapmap.ncbi.nlm.nih.gov/) and for the Human Genome Project, see http://www.ornl.gov/sci/techresources/Human_Genome/home.shtml.

[177]   http://www.cambia.org/daisy/cambia/home.html.

full texts of these articles, crawl them for indexing, pass them as data to software, or use them for any other lawful purpose, without financial, legal, or technical barriers other than those inseparable from gaining access to the internet itself.[178] The basis of open access is the willingness of the (individual or multiple) *copyright* holder(s) to allow access. Open access in this context creates total and unconditional (?) access. Examples here include open journals, such as PLoS. The term "open access" could also be used in a patent context, referring to access and use of patented technology.[179]

A third type of projects embraces **open source** or **open patent**. "Open patent" is a translation of the open source principles into *patented* software technology. The basic idea is to change the rules in such a way that they are beneficial to participants in solving the problems of software patents.[180] Stated differently, the open patent movement seeks to build a portfolio of patented inventions that can freely be distributed under a copyleft-like license.[181,182] Open source creates general, conditional access. Examples here include projects such as Cambia Bios.[183]

All these initiatives are genuine attempts to (re)establish **open science**. Open science refers to a research climate where openness of knowledge and the ethos of sharing prevail. Traditionally, the concept of scientific progress, dating from the 16th to 17th centuries, has been linked with an ideal of free and open dissemination of scientific information.[184] Scientific knowledge was wholeheartedly qualified and supported as a true public good,[185]

---

[178]   Definition applied in the Budapest Open Access Initiative. *See* Budapest Open Access Initiative, http://www.soros.org/openaccess/read.shtml.

[179]   Supra, section 4.1.

[180]   *See* OpenPatents.org, http://www.openpatents.org.

[181]   *See* Wikipedia, Open Patent, http://en.wikipedia.org/wiki/Open_patent.

[182]   The open patent movement should not be confused with the open patents initiative, an interface for those looking for new free ideas to patent, or to deposit ideas which are never going to be patented. Open Patents is a platform where "bright and good people from around the world donated their free ideas for you to patent, and many entrepreneurs are waiting for your ideas, right now!" , see http://www.openpatents.net/.

[183]   On CAMBIA BiOS, also see section 2.3.3.

[184]   William Eamon, 'From the secrets of nature to public knowledge: the origins of the concept of openness in science', XXIII(3) *Minerva* (1975), 335 and 338–40.

[185]   Dana Dalrymple, 'Scientific knowledge as a global public good: contributions to innovation and the economy' in *The Role of Scientific and Technical Data and Information in the Public Domain,* Washington DC, National Academies Press, 2003, p. 35 and p. 48; Inge Kaul, Isabelle Grunberg and Marc Stern (eds.) (1999) *Global Public Goods*, New York, UNDP (United Nations Development Programme).

characterized by non-excludability and non-rivalry.[186] Open availability of scientific data, full disclosure of results, freedom to read and freedom to use were regarded as cornerstones of academic research, long upheld by the scientific community. Universities were depicted as "the realm of truth" and as "the gift of nonproperty"[187] and scientific research institutes were portrayed as "gift economies"[188] where independent scientists, driven by curiosity, inspire knowledge and share insights with one another. Scientific norms of openness were not codified or necessarily explicit. Rather, they operated as "prescriptions, proscriptions, preferences and permissions [. . .] legitimated in terms of institutional values [. . .] transmitted by precept and example and reinforced by sanctions".[189] Over time, a growing strain emerged on universities and scientific institutes to appropriate knowledge and to cash in the commercial potential created by their research. Both universities and individual academics are increasingly prone to regard their knowledge as targets for opportunities for creating income through patents and secrecy.[190] At present various initiatives emerge aiming to recapture

---

[186]   Anyone can use the knowledge (non-excludability) and the use by one does not preclude the use by another (non-rivalry). *See* Paul A. David (1993), 'Intellectual property institutions and the panda's thumb: patents, copyrights and trade secrets in economic theory and history' in *Global Dimensions of Intellectual Property Right in Science and Technology* (M.B. Wallerstein, M.E. Mogee and R.A. Schoen (eds.), Washington, National Academy Press), p. 1–61. Also see Patrick Croskery (1989), 'The intellectual property literature: a structured approach' in *Owning Scientific and Technical Information. Value and Ethical Issues,* V. Weil and J. Snapper (eds.), New Brunswick, Rutgers University Press, p. 268, 269; Michael Lehmann, 'Property and intellectual property' in *International Review of Industrial Property and Copyright Law,* 1989, p. 13–14; Kaul et al, *supra* note 186, at 3–8.

[187]   Corynne McSherry, *Who Owns Academic Work? Battling for Control of Intellectual Property,* Cambridge, Harvard University Press, 2001, 20.

[188]   Warren O. Hagstrom, *The Scientific Community,* New York, Basic Books, 1965.

[189]   Robert King Merton, 'The Normative Structure of Science in *Social Theory and Social Structure,* New York: Free Press, 1957, 550–61. Also see Geertrui Van Overwalle, 'Reconciling patent policies and university mission', 13 *Ethical Perspectives,* 2006, 231–47; Geertrui Van Overwalle, 'Octrooien op maat? Naar een evenwicht tussen publieke opdracht en privaat goed' ['Patents Fit All? Towards an Equilibrium Between Public Mission and Private Good'], *in Tussen Markt en Agora. Over het statuut van universitaire kennis [Between Market and Agora. About the Status of Academic Knowledge],* Bart Pattyn and Geertrui Van Overwalle (eds.), Leuven, Peeters, 2006, 181–214.

[190]   See Van Overwalle, *supra* note 189. Also see Arti Kaur Rai, 'Regulating scientific research: intellectual property rights and the norms of science', **94**, *Nw. U. L. Rev.* 77, at 109–111 (1999); Rebecca S. Eisenberg, 'Proprietary rights and the norms of science in biotechnology research', **97** *Yale L. J.,* 1987, 177, at 230–31.

the spirit of the open science tradition. Such initiatives take many forms and "open access" initiatives to copyrighted scientific literature is one of them. This explains why open access and open science are sometimes used as synonyms.[191]

Linking the findings in this chapter with the open biotechnology discourse, leads us to conclude that (individual and multiple) ownership of knowledge may contribute to the accomplishment of open biotechnology, *if* well crafted (individual, collaborative or collective) license models are put to work, taking the form of licenses of right, open source licenses, patent pools and standard or royalty collecting clearinghouses.[192]

5. FINAL CONCLUSION

The debate on the role of knowledge and IP protection in genetics has been very intense over the past decade, as concerns have deepened over access and use in the field of human genetics and health care. Individual ownership of gene patents is cumbersome for it may result in blocking patents. Multiple ownership of gene patents is disquieting as it may lead to hindering patent thickets. Blocking patents and patent thickets may ultimately frustrate research and development instrumental to public health, restrict clinical access and decrease the availability of therapies for patients.

The alleged detrimental impact of individual and multiple ownership may be mitigated by the use of creative individual licensing regimes and the establishment of collaborative and collective platforms facilitating the fluid exchange of patents from patent holders to third-party users. The effect of blocking patents and patent thickets may be attenuated by well-tailored individual and collaborative/collective licensing mechanisms.

The experience with special license regimes in the life sciences is fascinating because it depolarizes the debate around proprietary and non-proprietary regimes.[193] In cases of individual and multiple IP ownership, formal rules of contract [194] taking the form of licenses of right, open source

---

[191]　See for example in the definition provided by Science Commons (http://sciencecommons.org/resources/readingroom/principles-for-open-science/).

[192]　Public domain knowledge may also contribute to the set up of open biotechnology projects, assuming it is not appropriated and then licensed restrictively. An in-depth discussion of the contribution of public domain to openness is beyond the scope of the present chapter.

[193]　Cf. Taubman, *supra* note 37.

[194]　For the distinction between formal *legal* rules and formal rules of *contract,* see Dedeurwaerdere, *supra* note 170, at 365.

licenses, pools and clearinghouses, create (quasi-)total openness. Through the shaping of license policies, exclusive or proprietary rights are used to leverage access, to promote dissemination, and to safeguard downstream use rights. Imaginative and solid IP license management is a powerful tool for advancing both private and public interest.[195] The notion of promoting access through rights that exclude is indeed the underlying paradox of IP law and policy.[196]

The paradoxical effect of collaborative and collective mechanisms on private entitlements was suggested by Robert Merges as early as 1996.[197] He found that these organizations ease some of the tensions created by strong IP rights and may play a valuable role in facilitating transactions in IP rights.[198] However, his efforts (as well as later writings from other scholars)[199] have mainly focussed on collaborative and collective measures, such as patent pools and copyright collecting societies, in specific industries such as ICE and music. This chapter has aimed at carrying the debate further by reflecting upon the potential role of both collaborative/collective and individual licensing measures in different technological areas, such as genetics. Both individual license schemes, taking the form of a license of right or an open source license, and collaborative/collective license structures, taking the form of patent pools, standardized clearinghouses or royalty collecting clearinghouses, moderate the effect of IP exclusivity and turn the individual and multiple IP ownership regime into (semi-)open infrastructures.

Recent studies have tried to recast the debate on managed-access property initiatives and develop a theoretical framework based on the work of Elinor Ostrom.[200] These scholars take up the challenge of better understanding the governance of environments where the resources to be produced are pieces of information – cultural and scientific knowledge – which are distributed through institutions supporting pooling and sharing

---

195   Cf. Sam Dryden, in his foreword to *Intellectual Property Management in Health and Agricultural Innovation,* Anatole Krattiger (ed.), MIHR, PIPRA, Oswaldo Cruz Foundation and bioDevelopments-International Institute, 2007, (XIX), XIX.

196   Cf. Taubman, *supra* note 37.

197   Merges, *supra* note 83.

198   Merges, *supra* note 103.

199   Josh Lerner, Marcin Strojwas and Jean Tirole, 'The Design of Patent Pools: The Determination of Licensing Rules', The RAND Journal of Economics, Volume **38**, Issue 3, pages 610–625, Autumn 2007; Shapiro, *supra* note 84.

200   Michael J. Madison, Brett M. Frischmann & Katherine J. Strandburg, 'Constructing commons in the cultural environment', **95** *Cornell L. Rev.*, 2010, 658.

of knowledge, and lead to "constructed cultural commons". They antici-pate that social ordering both depends on and generates a wide variety of formal and informal institutional arrangements and that the logical and normative priority assigned to proprietary rights and government intervention may turn out to be misplaced. Further reflection is needed on the concept of "reconstructed"[201] or "positive commons"[202] as well as the way in which individual and collaborative/collective licensing measures reshape the patent and exclusive ownership regime into such a recon-structed commons, and on the validity of arguments fully dismantling proprietary rights.

Another issue meriting further attention relates to the "sustainability" of openness, established by special licensing regimes. Most totally open regimes – created through licenses of right, compulsory licenses, patent pools or clearinghouses – only establish "first generation", "one shot" or "relative" openness: openness is established towards a first subse-quent user, after which openness comes to an end. Yet, one open regime – namely the regime created through open source – has the capacity to warrant openness towards "further generations" and constructs a "chain" of openness: openness towards the first subsequent user, the second fol-low-on innovator, and so on. So, openness does not end with the first sub-sequent user but is being ensured to all downstream users. Can licensing scenarios, other than open source, also enforce a chain of openness? How can follow-on openness be secured, and can first and later subsequent users be prevented from prohibiting further use?[203] Can such sustainable openness be crafted by formal rules of contract or is a legislative interven-tion, establishing formal legal rules, necessary?

Further research is also called for to investigate the economic viabil-ity of open biotechnology infrastructures in a for-profit context. Recent

---

[201] The term "reconstructed commons" is drawn from Reichman & Uhlir, *supra* note 132, at 315. Also see Van Overwalle, *supra* note 189.

[202] A positive commons is "a common in which resources are jointly owned and so use of those resources by any one commoner depends on all the common-ers having consented", see Peter Drahos, 'The Commons, The Public Domain and (Monopoly) Commerce', paper presented at the conference *The Politics and Ideology of IP*, organized by the Transatlantic Consumer Dialogue (TACD) Brussels, 20–21 March 2006 (http://www.tacd.org/); Peter Drahos, 'A defence of the intellectual commons', **16** *Consumer Policy Review,* May/June 2006, 3–5. Also see Geertrui Van Overwalle, 'L'intérêt général, le domaine public, les *commons* et le droit des brevets d'invention', in S. Dussolier and M. Buydens (eds.), *L'intérêt général et l'accès à l'information en propriété intellectuelle*, Brussels, Bruylant, 2008, 149–75.

[203] Is this what is meant by Hilty, *supra* note 4?

experiences in the genetic sector suggest that collaborative/collective models are more easily established in genetics when they serve social and humanitarian motives in a not-for-profit context.[204] Can open licensing models be efficient and adequate enough to deal with knowledge production, protection, exchange and translation, in markets served by the profit motive? Can licensing regimes fostering openness be viable in a for-profit context? Can such models be crafted in a way that they are not only economically viable, but also yield socially acceptable outcomes? The introduction of open patent regimes in a for-profit context should only be contemplated, to the extent that such regimes prove to be economically viable without overriding social motives.

---

[204]   See Van Overwalle et al., *supra* note 102. Also see Verbeure B. et al., *supra* note 102.

PART III

Individualism and collectiveness in copyright law

5. Collectivism and its role in the frame of individual contracts

Silke von Lewinski*

1. INTRODUCTION: PRESENTATION OF THE PROBLEM

This short panel contribution focuses on the question of whether, and if so, how, collectivism may be a means to strengthen the typically weak bargaining position of authors or performers in individual licensing contracts with exploitation businesses, such as publishers, producers, or broadcasting organizations, in order to enable them to receive an equitable remuneration for the exploitation of their rights. The problem is a longstanding one that is present worldwide, and it is widely perceived as not having found, in most cases, an appropriate solution.

At the outset, the respective interests of both contractual parties are the same: both have a strong interest in being able to control the exploitation of the work or performance at stake, not least in order to best benefit therefrom. Since, however, the marketing is usually not undertaken by the author or performer but by a publisher or other exploitation company, authors and performers regularly assign or license their exclusive rights to such companies in order to enable such marketing. From this moment on, the authors' and performers' interests are focused on receiving an equitable remuneration for the exploitation of the work or performance. Given their typically weak bargaining position as compared to exploitation companies, their chances to receive such equitable remuneration are often somewhat limited in practice. In order to remedy this situation in favour of authors and performers, different legislative models have been developed in different countries.

---

* Max Planck Institute for Intellectual Property and Competition Law, Munich; Adjunct Professor at Franklin Pierce Center for IP at the University of New Hampshire Law School, Concord, N.H., USA.

2.   SOLUTIONS TO THE PROBLEM

2.1   Statutory Rules on Individual Copyright Contracts

While in many countries especially of the *droit d'auteur*-system, legislative provisions on copyright contracts aim at a strengthening the position of authors or performers in different ways, the weakness of these provisions is rooted in the fact that the solution here is sought where the problem is located, namely, within the same delicate, individual contractual relationship between authors or performers, on the one hand, and exploitation businesses, on the other one. In many cases, the author will not dare to insist on the application of such provisions because he may then face more far-reaching consequences for his future possibilities to gain money from his works or performances, namely, when the publisher or other company will no longer be willing to conclude contracts with him in the future; in view of the current, widespread media concentration, one may even better understand that authors and performers often do not make use of their rights under legislative rules on copyright contracts.[1] Indicatively, only after their deaths, their widows have frequently started relevant legal proceedings.

2.2   Solutions Based on Collectivism

2.2.1   Labour law
In contrast, legislative models that are not based on the individual relationship but that introduce a collective element in order to strengthen the individual author or performer in the form of a group replacing him in negotiations with the exploitation companies have been more successful. First, the model of labour law is to be mentioned. In the USA, for example, all audiovisual performers participating in a film made under US law, even if they there do not enjoy performers' rights in their performances, in principle must become members of a labour union or guild before concluding a contract with a film producer on their participation in a film. Likewise, US film producers under most guild agreements are obliged to conclude contracts only with performers who are members of the relevant guilds. Due to this obligation as well as to the sheer size of the

---

[1]   Schricker, Gerhard, *Efforts for a better Law on Copyright Contracts in Germany – A Never Ending Story?* (35) IIC, 2004, p. 850, 856/857, pointing at the decision of Regional Court (Oberlandesgericht) München, ZUM 2001, 427, confirmed by Supreme Court (BGH) of 17 June 2004 – I ZR 136/01.

US film industry and the enormous, worldwide market for this industry, as well as due to the right of performers to go on strike (and thereby to cause considerable losses of revenues not only for the film production industry, but also for any related industries that are indirectly involved through delivery of products and services), these audiovisual performers are much more powerful than they could be in mere individual relations with the producers and thus have obtained, in the framework of their collective bargaining, quite favourable contractual conditions, which apply to all of the members of the guilds.[2]

At the same time, this model only works for employed authors and performers rather than for freelancers; also, it may work well only in countries where similar obligations to join such unions exist or where unions are strong for other reasons. However, especially in countries with small markets (for example, due to narrow language areas or culturally specific demands of consumers), such labour law solutions may not show any success that would be comparable to that of US-audiovisual performers.

2.2.2 German Copyright Contract Law of 2002

Another example of the replacement of individual negotiations by collective action is the German Copyright Contract Law of 2002.[3] In essence, it grants authors and performers a right to receive an equitable remuneration as a guaranteed counterpart for the grant of licences. While the claim to obtain such equitable remuneration (if this is not anyway provided in the individual contract) still must be made by the individual author against his publisher or other contractual partner, the collective element plays its role in the negotiation of what is to be considered as 'equitable'. Such determination may either be made in negotiations between labour unions, on the one hand, and employers of authors and performers, on the other hand, or, in their absence – and this is the main innovation of the 2002 copyright contract law – in negotiations between associations of

---

[2] For a presentation of this situation in the USA, see Reber, Nikolaus, *Die Beteiligung von Urhebern und ausübenden Künstlern an der Verwertung von Filmwerken in Deutschland und den USA*, 1998, p. 308 ff (in part published under the title 'Film Copyright, Contracts and Profit Participation', IIC Studies no 19 (Weinheim 2000)). See also von Lewinski, Silke, *The Protection of Performers in the Audio-Visual Field in Europe and the United States*, in: Hungarian ALAI group (ed.), Creators' Rights in the Information Society. Proceedings of the ALAI Congress September 14–17, 2003, pp. 885 ff and *International Copyright Law and Policy* (Oxford University Press, 2008), 18.05.

[3] For an English translation and a presentation, see (33) IIC 2000, p. 842 ff, and Dietz, Adolf, *Amendment of German Copyright Law in order to Strengthen the Contractual Position of Authors and Performers*, ibid p. 828 ff.

authors or performers, on the one hand, and individual publishers or their associations, on the other hand.[4] Such collective negotiations would set standards of what is to be regarded as 'equitable' in different branches, such as for translators of fiction works, authors of children's books, etc. The individual author may then claim from his contractual partner payment of a remuneration according to this standard (if the remuneration is not settled in the contract) or he may claim the consent by his contractual partner to altering the contents of the contract according to such standard, if the agreed remuneration is lower than this standard (sec. 32(1) of the German Copyright Act).

So far, this model has shown only limited positive effects for authors. Apart from publishers' strategies to prolong negotiations or otherwise avoid a speedy agreement on such standards,[5] the lack of associations of authors or performers in many branches is among the practical obstacles to a broad application in practice of this model. Authors and performers tend to be individualists and generally have little interest in joining in associations. Accordingly, for most branches of authors or performers, negotiations on standards of 'equitable remuneration' have not even started and might never start. The main systemic obstacle to success of this model is, however, the fact that in the end, it is still the individual author or performer who must address his publisher or other contractual partner to make a claim for such equitable remuneration – even where standards have been agreed on collectively. Thus, the above described problem of authors who may not dare to make such claims[6] is not removed, because the problem in the end still must be resolved within this delicate, individual contractual relationship.

2.2.3   The model of the EC Rental Directive

Presentation of the model   In contrast, a third legislative model on which this contribution will focus avoids the above-mentioned deficiencies of the other models. It is the model first realized in Article 4 of the EC Rental Rights Directive of 1992.[7] Although the scope of application of this model

---

[4]   Sec 36 of the German Copyright Act.

[5]   See von Lewinski, Silke, *Rechte des Übersetzers an seinem Werk*, MDÜ (Mitt. für Dolmetscher und Übersetzer) 6/2004, pp. 42 ff, in particular 44.

[6]   See fn 1, above.

[7]   Council Directive 92/100/EEC of 19 November 1992 on Rental Right and Lending Right and on Certain Rights related to Copyright in the Field of Intellectual Property, O.J. L 346/61 of 27 November 1992; the Directive has been consolidated (Article 4 is now Article 5), though not amended regarding Article 4,

in this directive is limited to the exclusive rental right, it could in principle (and in some countries already has done so) serve as a model for other economic rights. It was invented by the author of this contribution, when she was an expert to the European Commission and drafted a proposal for that directive.[8] She then faced the following situation: on the one hand, there was a strong tendency and pressure in favour of choosing an exclusive right as the appropriate form for a right covering rental activities; on the other hand, in particular Germany had already had positive experiences with its statutory remuneration right for rental administered by collective management organisations (CMOs), so that from this perspective, it seemed preferable to keep (and introduce EC-wide) such a remuneration right instead of an exclusive right. In particular, it was felt that authors and performers could get better shares of the revenues from rental through collective administration of this right than on the basis of individual licensing contracts based on an exclusive right, due to the collective power in the framework of CMOs. In fact, the perception in particular in Germany was that any possible replacement of the existing statutory remuneration right through an exclusive right without any further mechanism would result in lower income from rental for authors and performers, because the latter would license the exclusive rental right to their producers and would receive their remuneration according to the contract, which would mostly reflect the unequal bargaining position of both parties to the disadvantage of authors and performers. It was clear that also mandatory rules on copyright contract law as they existed in many Member States would not be able to fully remedy this situation of imbalanced negotiation powers, because these rules would remain inside the individual contract, where this imbalance subsists.

The author of the draft directive and of this contribution finally solved this conflict between different existing models through a combination of the advantages of both concepts. Given the strong pressure in favour of an exclusive right and the claimed need of producers to take market decisions on the basis of exclusive rights in order to best amortize their investments, the rental right was principally conceived as an exclusive right for authors and neighbouring right owners, namely, for authors of works, performers,

---

see O.J. L 376/28 (Directive 2006/115/EC). On Article 4 of the Rental Directive, see in particular Reinbothe and von Lewinski, *The EC Directive on Rental and Lending Rights and on Piracy* (London 1993), p. 65 ff; and von Lewinski, Silke, 6.4.1 ff, in Walter, Michel M and von Lewinski, Silke (eds), *European Copyright Law – A Commentary* (Oxford: Oxford University Press, 2010).

[8] Therefore, she does not object it being given the short name of 'Lewinski-model'.

phonogram producers, and film producers. Accordingly, the advantage of an exclusive right on the market and its strength when compared to a mere remuneration right was safeguarded. At the same time, the advantage of a statutory remuneration right administered by CMOs, i.e., a regularly better share for authors and performers than under individual contracts, was added to the exclusive right in an innovative way, namely, by safeguarding for authors and performers, after they have transferred or assigned the exclusive right or granted a licence, a residual remuneration right that would ideally be administered through CMOs. This part of the solution aimed at solving the problem of the typically weak bargaining position of authors and performers in individual contracts and at ensuring that authors and performers would indeed benefit from the rental right granted to them under the law.

This model is now presented in a graph and explained in more detail, and its most effective ways of implementation are presented (Figure 5.1).

This model applies where an author or performer has transferred or assigned[9] a particular exclusive right[10] concerning her work or performance to a producer, publisher, or other exploitation company,[11] as is the rule regarding exclusive rights. Also, a transfer or assignment presumed by law would be covered by this model. For this situation, the law must determine that the author and performer retains, even after such transfer or assignment, the right to obtain an equitable remuneration for the relevant use. One might interpret this right as a residue of the exclusive right. The law must state that this remuneration right cannot be waived by authors and performers and, ideally,[12] that it can be transferred only to a CMO and has to be entrusted for administration to a CMO representing authors or performers. The law should best specify that the remuneration must be claimed from the professional user, such as the rental outlet, who received an exploitation licence from the producer or other company.[13]

---

[9]   Also the particular German concept of *Einräumung* would work in this respect.

[10]   Due to its limited scope of application, Article 4 of the EC Rental Directive only applies to the rental right and arguably to the lending right; however, it could serve as a model for other rights.

[11]   Due to its limited scope of application, Article 4 of the EC Rental Directive only applies to the relationship with a phonogram producer or film producer.

[12]   Due to early influence by the film industry, the initially planned mandatory collective administration could not be inserted in the initial proposal of the directive, nor in the final version.

[13]   The Directive leaves the determination of who is the debtor of the remuneration to the Member States; however, a study found out that the aim of this model is best reached, if the debtor is the professional user, see the study by Vanheusden,

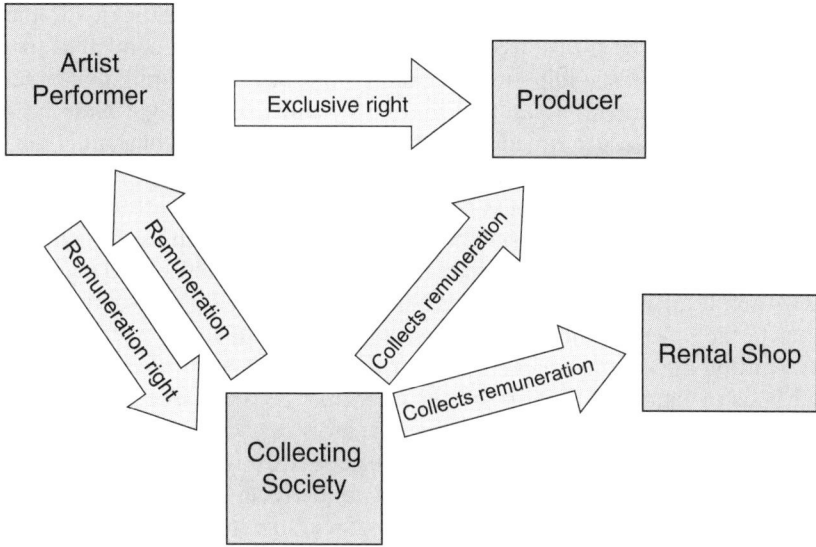

Figure 5.1   Art 4 EC Rental Directive (1992; consolidated 2006)

Thus, this innovative combination of an exclusive right and, for authors and performers only, a residual right to equitable remuneration subject to collective management is based on the general assumption that the author or performer regularly cannot obtain an equitable remuneration for granting licences or transfer/assignment of his rights in individual contracts and should instead obtain such remunerations outside of these contracts, namely through the intervention of CMOs that administer their separate, unwaivable remuneration rights by collecting the revenues from the professional users and distributing them directly to authors and performers. By this way of 'outsourcing' the delicate questions on remuneration from the individual contract with business partners to a 'service organization' (a CMO), this model avoids the disadvantages of the above mentioned models that function inside the individual contract.

In order to be efficient as a means to remedy the typically unbalanced situation in individual licensing contracts, it is, however, crucial that this model integrates the following five factors: (1) the statutory basis for

Els for AEPO/ARTIS, *Performers' Rights in European Legislation: Situation and Elements for Improvement*, June 2007, p. 57, http://www.aepo-artis.org/usr/AEPO-ARTIS%20Studies/Study%20Performers%20Rights%20in%20Acquis_AEPO-ARTIS.pdf.

the remuneration right; (2) the unwaivable nature of the right; (3) the fact that it can be transferred only to a CMO; (4) mandatory collective administration of the remuneration right, and the professional user being the debtor of the remuneration. Firstly, the remuneration right under this model is based on a statute rather than on the individual contract. Thus, the law itself provides for the right to claim an equitable remuneration, irrespective of any contractual agreements. Secondly, the author and performer is strengthened by the nature of the right as an unwaivable right; thus, an author or performer could not be forced in the individual contract with any legal effects to waive the right. This element is a necessary corollary to the independent, statutory remuneration right.

Thirdly, the fact that the remuneration right can be transferred only to a CMO is to guarantee that the author/performer does not 'lose' this right to an exploitation business on the basis of the individual contract. Fourthly, in relying on the central role of collecting societies through mandatory collective administration, the model reveals its underlying philosophy, namely, the perceived need to withdraw the issue of remuneration from the delicate individual contractual relationship in order to import it into the framework of collecting societies where authors and performers no longer individually face their publishers and other exploitation businesses but may benefit from their stronger bargaining position as a group. Also, CMOs are existing in most fields of authors' rights and related rights, and the typical individualism of authors and performers is less of an obstacle to join a CMO than it seems to be to join a professional organisation that would be needed for the purposes of the German Copyright Contract Law of 2002. In other words, this model is built on the experience that an enhanced bargaining power through a collective element may in practice be more efficient than legal provisions, that have to be enforced by the individual author on the basis of the individual contract, like traditional copyright contract rules. The capacity of a collecting society to collectively administer rights of authors and performers, who thereby gain an increased bargaining power makes it suitable to fulfil the function of balancing the interests of authors and performers against those of publishers and other exploitation businesses.

Finally, the model is most effective if the law clearly determines the professional user as the debtor of the remuneration for authors and performers.[14] Of course, the professional user in such a case must be made aware of the fact that he will be faced not only with the publisher or other business in order to obtain a licence subject to payment, but that in addition, he must expect a separate claim for remuneration from a collective manage-

---

[14]   See the preceding footnote 13.

ment organisation on behalf of authors and/or performers. If he takes into account this overall legal situation before concluding the licensing contract, he may from the outset be prepared to conduct the licensing negotiations accordingly. Such a situation is not unique; for example, broadcasting organisations are traditionally faced with the need for obtaining licences from authors (or their collective management organisations) and, at the same time, the need for paying statutory remuneration rights of performers and phonogram producers (or their collective management organisations) for the use of phonograms for their broadcasting activities.

The potential of the model This model was devised in the framework of the EC Rental Directive only for the rental right; however, given its generally valid purpose and its basic mechanism, there is no reason not to extend it to other rights. In fact, at the time of the implementation of the EC Rental Directive, the German Government had already recognised the potential and fundamental importance of this model with a view to balancing interests of authors/performers and exploitation businesses in general: it observed that it might consider this model in the framework of the then future reform of copyright contract law.[15] In addition, this model was adopted for the exclusive cable retransmission right, which has been supplemented by an unwaivable right to equitable remuneration for authors and performers.[16]

In the meantime, this model has also been introduced, in particular in Spain regarding the right of making available[17] and in Poland regarding other rights.[18] While the model may not be appropriate for rights in respect of all kinds of uses, one should explore its further application, even beyond the rights of making available and of cable retransmission;

---

[15] Governmental Proposal, BT Drucks. 13/115 of 21 December 1994, p. 14; see for the same vision von Lewinski, *Die Umsetzung der Richtlinie zum Vermiet- und Verleihrecht*, ZUM 1995, 442, 447. Unfortunately, though, the Government did not do so but essentially based this reform of copyright contract law as adopted in 2000 on the individual relationship between authors/performers and exploitation businesses and made applicable a collective element (the collective negotiation of remuneration standards) again in the individual framework.

[16] § 20b(2) of the German Copyright Act; for performers, see § 78(4) in respect of § 20b, and § 27(2) phr. 2 in respect of the rental right.

[17] See Xalabarder, Raquel, *Spain,* in Walter, Michel M and von Lewinski, Silke, *European Copyright Law – A Commentary* (Oxford: Oxford University Press, 2010), p. 1127.

[18] See Czajkowska-Dąbrowska, *Poland,* in Walter, Michel M and von Lewinski, Silke, *European Copyright Law – A Commentary* (Oxford: Oxford University Press, 2010), p. 373.

for example, in countries where an exclusive right for secondary uses of phonograms has been introduced in favour of phonogram producers and performers, instead of the traditional remuneration right as set out, e.g., in Article 12 of the Rome Convention, applying this model to the exclusive rights of broadcasting and communication might help to safeguard for performers their share of 50 per cent regularly applied by CMOs to these rights.

Given the strength of this model as compared to traditional copyright contract law or the above mentioned, other solutions, it may be astonishing that for a long time, it has not met with wider attention, even if it has been introduced into discussions from time to time.[19] It is possible that the model, which deviated from traditional copyright doctrine, was too inventive to be easily accepted, or that it was premature at a time when the conflicts of interest may have seemed to be less accentuated than today. Yet, it seems that today is a time when the need for such a model is increasingly recognised. Indeed, a study made for AEPO-ARTIS has focussed, among others, on this model, on the basis of an analysis of implementation of Article 4 of the EC Rental Directive in selected EC Member States.[20] In addition, the result of a series of seminars organised by WIPO regarding the protection of performers, and audiovisual performers in particular, shows that the performers themselves have recognised the potential of this model. They consistently stated that, according to their experience or estimation, they would best benefit from such a combination of an exclusive right and a remuneration right; explicit reference is made in this context to the model of the EC Rental Directive.[21] Most recently, it seems also to be discussed in the framework of legislative debates in Mexico and India. Also, the SAA (Society of Audiovisual Authors) in its White Paper of

---

[19]   See, for example, its discussion in the framework of the international Congress of ALAI 1997, which was entirely devoted to the thought that the typically weaker bargaining power of authors and performers within individual contracts could be remedied by three parallel mechanisms, namely, mandatory legislative rules on copyright contracts, collective agreements under labour law, and the mandatory exercise of rights by collecting societies. See in particular *von Lewinski*, Introduction, in: G. Roussel (ed.), *Actes du XLIe Congres de l'ALAI* (Montreal 1998), p. 30 ff.; the author of this contribution had also co-conceived the scientific program of the Congress.

[20]   Vanheusden, Els, *Performers' Rights in European Legislation: Situation and Elements for Improvement*, June 2007, pp. 50 ff, http://www.aepo-artis.org/usr/ AEPO-ARTIS%20Studies/Study%20Performers%20Rights%20in%20Acquis_AE PO-ARTIS.pdf.

[21]   WIPO doc SCCR/17/3 of 17 October 2008, paragraph 27, especially at footnote 12.

February 2011, pp. 26ff., advocates this model. Moreover, the European Commission in its Audiovisual Green Paper of July 2011 discusses this model as an option to secure adequate remuneration to authors and performers (parts 4.1 and 4.2 and questions 16 and 18 in particular).

3. CONCLUSIONS

The model of the EC Rental Directive has been highlighted for its potential to enable authors and performers to receive an equitable remuneration for the exploitation of their rights by outsourcing the issue of remuneration from the individual contractual relationship to the services of a CMO and thus by using the collective power of an intermediate representative to strengthen their position. This model may also be a strong counterargument to those who may want to throw out the baby with the tap water when they argue that authors' rights protection should be limited to statutory remuneration rights (fully replacing exclusive rights) because authors do not sufficiently well benefit from exclusive rights. Against this background, the model discussed here may even be welcome by exploitation businesses. It allows keeping the advantages of an exclusive right for all right owners while safeguarding an equitable remuneration to authors and performers. Therefore, authors, performers and their CMOs should more strongly urge legislators to adopt this model for relevant rights in order to remedy the worldwide and long-standing problem of typically unbalanced bargaining powers within individual contracts and their negative consequences for authors and performers.

6. Ownership of copyright and investment protection rights in teams and networks: need for new rules?

Sylvie Nérisson*

This chapter addresses the question of how collective management should be approached by lawmakers to tackle problems with copyright ownership and investment protection rights.

The chapter is structured in seven parts. As a preliminary point, it is necessary to stress the delicate delineation of copyright and investment protection rights for the author in this comment. In the second part, I shall introduce the function of collective management as a remedy to (one of) the paradox(es) of copyright. The third part focuses on the difficult and fragile rationale of collective management and demonstrates the necessity that apart from authors, publishers join collective management societies (CMS) as well. The arguments for this admission will be discussed in the fourth part. The fifth part provides two illustrative German cases attesting the conflicting interests of publishers and authors in the bosom of CMS. The danger of ignoring this conflict and the necessary distinction between first right owners (creators) and derivative right holders (investors such as publishers) will be demonstrated in the sixth part. To this aim I shortly and critically present consequences of the European Commission Recommendation of 18 October 2005 on collective cross-border management of copyright and related rights for legitimate online music services.[1] The final part calls for legislative intervention with regard to the collective management of copyrights.

* Research Fellow at the Max Planck Institute for Intellectual Property and Competition Law. I wish to deeply thank Annette Kur and Jan Rosen for the invitation to participate in the Stockholm ATRIP conference and to this book. Moreover, I also need to thank Tobias Bednarz and Gilles Vercken for discussions and critical comments. All errors are my own.
[1] No 2005/737/EC, see OJ L 276/54 21.10.2005. On this Recommendation, see Drexl (2007).

1. INVESTMENT PROTECTION RULES: INTRUDERS IN THE AUTHORS' RIGHTS SYSTEM

Being French and working in Germany, I translate the term *copyright* and think of *droit d'auteur* or *Urheberrecht*. I therefore consider the protection of investment to be only a secondary effect of the protection of the creation, since *authors' rights* do not reward the time and the investment necessary for the creation (French copyright law expressly excludes the merit of the author as a protection criterion[2]) but serve as a guarantee to the creator of a work that his/her personal relation to his/her creation will be respected.[3] The essence of copyright is to protect and enhance the creation of intellectual works independently of any consideration of industrial efficiency.[4] The fundamental rationale for protection by the *Urheberrecht* is the author's personality, and that of *Droit d'auteur* is the indissoluble tie between the creator and his/her works.[5] Financial performance, however, can hardly be considered to reflect one's personality, which is the decisive criterion for a work to be eligible for the protection granted by the *Droit d'auteur* and the *Urheberrecht*. Therefore, the introduction, during the last 30 years, of investment protection rights, as such, into the authors' rights system continues to be a proverbial stumbling stone. To accord first ownership of an *oeuvre collective* to the editor,[6] to grant neighbouring rights to film producers, broadcasters, or to give sui generis protection to databases are, in my opinion, intrusions into the classical copyright system protecting the creators of musical, artistic and scientific works. The object of my studies has been the author; a human being inspired by the world and inspiring his/her fellows. In other words, the aim of copyright

---

[2] See Art. L. 112-1 of the French *Code de propriété intellectuelle*.

[3] Moreover the value of a scientific article or a poem, of a picture, a movie, a song or a symphony does not depend on the time spent on its elaboration or the means involved. Its value is mostly a cultural issue. In this respect, consider the definition of *cultural industries* in the Green paper 'Unlocking the potential of cultural and creative industries' (COM(2010)183/3) of the Education and culture DG of the European Commission : '"Cultural industries" are those industries producing and distributing goods or services which at the time they are developed are considered to have a specific attribute, use or purpose which embodies or conveys cultural expressions, irrespective of the commercial value they may have.'

[4] Industrial efficiency is a decisive factor in patent law and maybe trade mark law, but definitely not in copyright law understood as 'authorship law'.

[5] For a thorough, subtle and historically founded analysis of *droit d'auteur* first ownership issues, see Gaudrat (2001).

[6] See L. 113-2 al. 3 of the French *Code de propriété intellectuelle*. On the historical roots of this 'inversion of the ordinary law', see Gaudrat (2001) pp. 170 et seq.

is, in my opinion, to find the means for him/her not to be systematically disappointed by the way the world deals with his/her creations. I would wish that authors' rights help him/her to be able to continue creating and to encourage him/her to make his/her works public. In contrast, if we consider investment protection, we are dealing with industrial efficiency sought by merchants who are inspired by the market and exploiting it. Publishers' and producers' tasks consist of buying works, or rights in works, exploiting them, and then selling licences to users at a higher price. To buy and sell are the concerns of merchants, not those of creators. Making such a distinction does not preclude a person from having both types of skills and activities but it underlines that it is not necessary to reward or to protect the investment with legal tools conceived to foster creation. The protection of publishers, producers and other investors is not in itself a key element in protecting and enhancing creation for itself.[7] These investors are of course helpful satellites of the creation process and their interests shall be taken into consideration, when tailoring the scope of protection. But still they remain merchants, professionals able to make money with virtually anything. There is no reason to offer them stronger legal protection than that offered by general law simply because they deal with copyrighted works. They know how to deal with commercial law, corporate law, etc. Therefore, they might also be able to deal with the copyrights of creators without requiring their own.

Nevertheless, bearing in mind that 'my' creating individual needs investors and merchants for his/her work to be enjoyed on a larger scale, I must acknowledge the merchants' needs as they market the works of 'my' author. And while merchants and investors transform risk into money, what they need most is some amount of legal certainty. That is what the legislator should take into account the most when designing the copyright law. And this is where collective management comes into play.

2.   THE FUNDAMENTAL PARADOX OF COPYRIGHT

There is a mysterious and wonderful phenomenon in my studies: the paradox of author's rights. The *droit d'auteur* system protects works because they are an effluent of the author's personality, which means it is a highly personal and individual issue. But beyond the first licence of a work,

---

[7]   Even if it has been the decisive point for legislators to acknowledge copyrights and *droits d'auteur*; see Gaudrat (2001) and Gervais (2010).

allowing it to be used and disseminated, an author, unless in exceptional situations entailing extraordinary bargaining power, is not able to appropriately defend his/her interests in negotiations with the powerful investors that commercial users mostly are. Of course, copyright gives him/her the right to forbid the exploitation of his/her work. The right to exclude does not strengthen his/her bargaining power that much though. The remedy is rather to find someone he/she can entrust with his/her rights, someone able to negotiate his/her rights on an equal footing with the merchants, someone who would do it on his/her behalf, and someone who would thereby represent his/her interests as a creator: the missions of societies operating the collective management of copyrights.[8] To put this copyright paradox in a nutshell: the personal and individual copyright needs collective exercise so as to actually be effective in all cases of mass-scale use.

3. COLLECTIVE MANAGEMENT OF COPYRIGHT, COPYRIGHT FIRST OWNERS AND INVESTORS

In continental Europe, collective management societies (CMS) appeared shortly after the enactment of copyright law itself.[9] They appeared as private societies of authors, founded upon the contractually enforced will of their parties, authors. The very first authors' societies assembled creators to lobby for an acknowledgement of copyright by legislators, but their actual business purpose soon became the negotiation with users on equal footing and the achievement of the respect of copyright by users such as theatres[10] and lastly to enforce those rights in court.[11]

---

8   For a deeper description, see Gervais (2010) pp. 6 et seq.
9   Best examples can be found in Austria and Germany. In Austria the first law protecting non-dramatic musical works was enacted in 1885 (Gesetz über den Schutz des Urheberrechts), and the AKM, Society for authors, composers, and publishers was founded in 1897; in Germany the society for dramatic authors and composers (Deutsche Genossenschaft dramatischer Autoren und Komponisten) was founded in 1871, in order to apply the law of North Germany of 1870 (Gesetz für den norddeutschen Bund vom 11. Juni 1870 betreffend das Urheberrecht an Schriftwerken, Abbildungen, musikalischen Compositionen und dramatischen Werken), and the association of German composers (which founded in the same year the AFMA, grandmother of the current GEMA, German CMS for copyright in musical works) has been founded in 1903, after the copyright law of 1901 entered into force in 1902. See Dümmling (2003), pp. 26–67.
10   See the *société de législation dramatique*, founded by Beaumarchais for dramatists to be recognized a right against actors of the *Comédie Française*, cf. Gervais (2010), pp. 3–4.
11   See SACEM founded around the composer Bourget, who sued a restaurant

CMS flourished since then[12] and adapted their business models to accommodate the needs of new users such as radio and television broadcasters. This happened not only because they are highly advantageous for the first owners of copyright but also because they are useful to commercial users,[13] investors. It is better for merchants to negotiate a single blanket license with a strong representative of most (if not all) authors than to exploit the weak bargaining power of single authors. Contracts with single authors or publishing houses are only beneficial in the short term or when dealing with single works. As users exploiting numerous works, to acquire rights on a work-by-work or repertoire-by-repertoire basis, would be under the constant threat of the individual copyright exercise by single authors (such as co-authors whose rights have not been assigned to the same publishing houses, those who recovered their right after a first licence, or left the publishing house the user contracted with).[14] Moreover, the transaction costs would be tremendous if users had to negotiate for each individual work. Furthermore, it is better for first owners of copyright to be represented by a CMS specifically dealing with their interests than to be represented by investors, naturally motivated by commercial interests which may or may not coincide with the interests of creators.

Therefore, to offer blanket licences facilitating mass-scale use of copyrighted works has been the very keystone of the flourishing of CMS. Blanket licences allow users to predict the costs associated with the use of copyrighted works, offer legal certainty, and give them a wide choice of works to be performed and/or reproduced thanks to the reciprocal representation system of most CMS in the world which grants all participating societies a worldwide repertoire.[15] CMS are therefore only efficient if they

---

for playing his works without authorisation or payment. Cf. Kretschmer (2002), pp. 141–2.

[12]   The International Confederation of Societies of Authors and Composers (CISAC) was founded in 1926 and, at the time, represented 18 members acting in 18 countries. It currently has a membership of 229 CMS, acting in 121 countries.

[13]   For example, the mandatory collective management of the cable retransmission right as stated in the 'Council Directive 93/83/EEC of 27 September 1993 on the coordination of certain rules concerning copyright and rights related to copyright applicable to satellite broadcasting and cable retransmission' (OJ L 248, 6.10.1993, p. 15) is thought to serve the interests of cable operators, see recital 28 and arts. 9 and 10 of the Directive.

[14]   In this respect, see recital 28 of Directive 93/83/EEC, stating that the mandatory collective exercise of rights is a way to ensure 'that the smooth operation of contractual arrangements is not called into question by the intervention of outsiders holding rights in individual parts of the programme'.

[15]   See, for this very consideration of the legal certainty granted to users by contracting with CMS, Vercken (1996) no 10.

are able to assemble as many authors as possible. The bigger the network of authors and works they represent,[16] the stronger they can stand up against commercial users, and at the same time, the higher the legal certainty they can offer to the merchants they contract with.

This leads us to more closely examine the role of investors in the collective management of copyright or, conversely, the boundaries between the protection of creation and that of investment. Given the need of CMS to offer an exhaustive repertoire, one indeed has to ask whether the proper place for investors is within these societies, together with creators, or not. To put it differently: should the repertoire of a CMS only be exhaustive in respect of the rights held by authors, or in respect of all the rights in works which must be cleared in order to use them? The latter possibility requires derivative holders of copyright to be also represented by these authors' organisations, while the former would facilitate the distinction of interests at stake. As a matter of fact one has to differentiate between rights holders on the one hand, and commercial users on the other hand, since it becomes tricky when considering publishers who actually have a foot on each side of the boundary. It is not only creators who belong to the side of right-holders but their publishers as well. The latter are derivative rights holders, since they possess licensee rights that they acquire from the creators by virtue of their investments. But being assignees and investors, they should actually be considered as commercial users too. For this chapter, however, we define *rights holders* as individuals who entrust CMS with copyrights, that means first rights owners (in other words authors or creators) and derivative rights holders (publishers); and we consider *commercial users* as being those obtaining from CMS licences to use works.

Since their inception, CMS of authors of musical and literary works accepted investors such as publishers as their members.[17] This has not been without raising problems though.

4. THE PRESENCE OF PUBLISHERS IN THE BOSOM OF AUTHORS' CMS

The presence of publishers in the bosom of the authors' network established through the collective management system is an old issue. Their

---

[16] Pointing out the need of CMS for being able to offer licence rights in an exhaustive repertoire, see Uchtenhagen (2005) no 10.

[17] German writers actually tried to build a CMS without publishers, but soon had to abandon this plan and found a new CMS with the publishers. This is the story of the still active VG Wort; see Melichar (1991) p. 7.

presence is the rule in CMS dealing with musical works and literature[18] and this is the way CMS for musical and literary works developed.[19] There are mainly two reasons for this evolution.

Firstly, in order to join a CMS administering rights in musical or literary works, a creator must have already exploited and marketed such works. For example, recordings of musical works must have been made available on the market or performed a certain number of times before their authors and composers could be allowed to join SACEM (French CMS for musical authors and lyricists, and publishers thereof) or GEMA (German CMS for musical authors and lyricists, and publishers thereof).[20] This allows the societies to deal exclusively with professional authors by avoiding the management of works which have not been exploited yet, and hereby save the costs of administrating useless data.[21] In the writing branch, rights managed by CMS are mostly those for public lending and reprography, and it would actually be hard to lend or photocopy unpublished works. Therefore, authors must have assigned their rights (at least the reproduction rights) to a publisher before being able to join a CMS.[22]

Secondly, uses which only involve a single type of right are rare. On the contrary, a single use of a copyrighted work usually affects a number of different rights in that work.[23] One example is the mechanical rights asso-

---

[18]   It is not the case in other branches, like in the French SACD (CMS for dramatical works), the French SCAM (CMS for documentary films), the French ADAGP and SAIF (CMS for pictures and sculptures) and the German VG Bildkunst (CMS for visual arts).

[19]   For a detailed and historical presentation of this issue, see Kretschmer (2002), pp. 141–7.

[20]   This could now change in light of the new possibilities offered by the digitisation and the Internet. For example, SACEM (French CMS for authors of musical works) now allows composers to join if their work has been downloaded against a fee a certain number of times).

[21]   See e.g. art. 5 of the rules (*règlement général*) of SACEM and sec. 3 of the admission's rules (*Geschäftsordnung für das Aufnahmeverfahren*) of GEMA.

[22]   This requirement is not absolute in Germany due to the obligation laid in § 6 of the German Law of Copyright Administration (*Wahrnehmungsgesetz*), which makes it obligatory for German CMS to administer rights of any rights holder whose works belong to its business purpose. The admission in GEMA is then possible for a composer attesting five works that he/she composed. However, in order to become a member with voting rights among the assemblies of the society, he/she must attest the exploitation of his/her works. Moreover, it is noteworthy that this necessary preliminary step of a licensing contract with publishers leads some scholars to ask the exactly opposite question: why are there authors in CMS since they assigned their rights to publishers before their admission in the CMS, see Kretschmer (2002), pp. 152-153.

[23]   See Gervais, 'fragmentation', cf. Gervais (2010), pp. 10 et seq.

ciated with the performance or broadcasting of a work.[24] In fact, publishers are the owners of the reproduction rights necessary to the massive uses collective management deals with.[25] In practice, therefore, on the day an author joins a CMS, his/her publisher must join it as well for the CMS to be able to protect the entire spectrum of rights in the works of the author.

This symbiosis of publishers and authors is advantageous in two respects.[26] Users obtain a comprehensive licence from CMS assembling authors and publishers, and publishers enjoy the collective protection of authors. Furthermore, it allows small publishers not to be excluded from the market when competing with the giants of the industry.[27] In addition, all publishers benefit 'politically' from the nice romantic image of creators. The drawback of this symbiosis appears obvious: the interests of authors get confused with those of merchants.

Let's take a closer look at these arguments.

5. THE INTEREST OF COMMERCIAL USERS TO OBTAIN COMPREHENSIVE LICENCES ENDANGERED BY THE INCREASING POWER OF PUBLISHERS IN THE BOSOM OF CMS

There is an obvious benefit for users to get a single licence covering all rights necessary for the type of use they want to make of works; it is the same argument for dealing with one collective body rather than numerous individual rights holders, namely to reduce transaction costs and enjoy legal certainty almost equivalent to a presumption that any use covered by the licence indeed concerns all works available on the market, world wide. Yet, problems arise in situations in which even such a comprehensive licence is not sufficient to clear all necessary rights. Then, in addition to the CMS, still another rights holder must be negotiated with in order to obtain the necessary consent.

---

[24] Regarding mechanical rights, see Ficsor (1989) no 60.

[25] Publishers are the derivative owners of these rights in Continental Europe; they mostly are their first owners in Great Britain and in the USA.

[26] The main positive aspects are summarised in the decisions of the German Patent Office (the supervisory body in respect of CMS) of 6 June 1977, [1978] UFITA 81, 348 and of 26 October 1981, [1982] UFITA 94, 364. In these cases a composer argued that the publisher members of GEMA were accorded too much voting power within GEMA's inner structure.

[27] Such as the 'big four': Universal Music Publishing Group, Sony/ATV Music Publishing, EMI Group Publishing and Warner/Chappell Music.

In Germany, such an instance arose in relation to mobile phone ring tones. Publishers claimed that the licence acquired from GEMA by commercial users to make and sell online ring tones did not cover the affected moral rights arguing that a ring tone was an adaptation of the underlying musical works.[28] As the adaptation right was assigned to the publishers and not to GEMA, the publishers contended that only they were able to license that right. In other words, the publishers, actually members of GEMA, argued that commercial users exploiting ring tones should not only pay GEMA for the economic rights, but also themselves for the adaptation and the moral rights at stake. This was absurd; not only because the licence obtained from GEMA thereby became useless but also because moral rights are not intended to help the economic interests of copyright assignees, as publishers are, but to protect the highly personal relation of a creator to his/her works. However, this verdict of absurdity had to be established by the German Supreme Court, which stated that under German copyright contract law the licence offered by GEMA must be interpreted as covering the adaptation required to transform a song into a cell phone ring tone.[29] This followed the principle that a licensing contract should, in case of doubt, be interpreted as covering all rights affected by the use licensed, including the changes and alterations predictable at the moment of the assignment.[30] However, if neither the author nor the publisher entrusted GEMA with the right to use a melody as a mobile phone ring tone, a commercial user seeking those rights would have to contract with both the author (or the publisher if the exercise of moral rights have been assigned to him) for obtaining the licence to adapt the melody into a cell phone ring tone, and with GEMA, for the licence to make it available.[31] Such association of collective and individual management can be

---

[28]   The decisions in this instance have been issued based on both § 23 (adaptation right) and § 14 (right to the integrity) of the German Copyright law (UrhG). Since CMS mostly deal with mass-scale uses of works of authorship, it is unquestionable that CMS only manage economic rights. And the exception to this principle does not concern uses being so numerous.

[29]   German Supreme Court (BGH) 18 December 2008 – Case I ZR 23/06, GRUR Int. 2009, p. 616.

[30]   While this line of argument could be based on the '*Zweckübertragungsprinzip*' of § 31(5) of the *Urheberrechtsgesetz*, the German Supreme Court relied on § 39, which states that 'alterations to the work and its title which the author cannot reasonably refuse shall be permissible'. The Court considered that authors assigning the right to license their songs for cell phone ring tones to GEMA had to assume their works would be altered for this purpose.

[31]   See *Klingeltöne für Mobiltelefone II,* German Supreme Court (BGH), Case I ZR 18/08, 11 March 2010, GRUR 2010 p. 920, no 29 et seq.

wonderful,[32] if the individual treatment serves only the moral or intellectual interests of the creator whereas the CMS grants to users some legal certainty with the help of an easily predictable and single price thanks to tariffs and the clear notice made to users that they also need the consent of the author; and if it ensures authors a fair share of the revenues drawn from the use at stake. The historical example of such a combination dates from the 19th century. French SACD combines collective and individual management regarding theatrical works. The rate for a theatre to play a drama belonging to the SACD repertoire is unique, following tariffs set up by the CMS. But the SACD will only license the theatre if the author gives his consent for the intended play (according to the director, to the conditions of the play etc). The recently introduced § 1h of the contract by which any member of GEMA entrusts it with his/her right[33] took the split into account but does neither remedy the absurdity mentioned above regarding moral rights, nor go in the 'wonderful' direction. In conjunction with § 1i, § 1h states that GEMA and rights holders have to notify each other when a request is done by a commercial user for a licence concerning a mobile phone ring tone. Furthermore, this section allows rights holders (the publisher and/or the author) to withdraw the rights at stake in order to manage them individually after the notification. Such a constellation seems to preclude that the CMS keeps any influence on the licence between commercial users and rights holders. Moreover, nothing impedes that moral rights are abusively used by publishers to increase their revenue. § 1i has actually been written for the production of movies, in order to allow an author to withdraw his/her rights from the CMS for assigning them to a film producer. Therefore, one cannot help thinking that the very aim of this new scope of the possible individual management ruled by § 1i is to satisfy the greed of publishers who found in the moral rights necessary for the making of a ring tone a new source of income which escapes from the distribution scheme of GEMA. Benefits are huge for those merchants: in going the individual way, the price of the licence can be freely negotiated (without the tariffs schemes of the CMS); and rights holders enjoy a stronger bargaining power since the statutory obligation to contract with

---

[32]   Vercken speaks of 'combined management' (Vercken (1996) no 110); Ficsor calls the way such association is exercised in France by the SACD for dramatic works 'not a form of full collective administration: it is of an agency-type administration' (Ficsor (1989) nos 77 and 86).

[33]   '*Berechtigungsvertrag*', last amended on 23–24 June 2009, available at http://www.gema.de/fileadmin/inhaltsdateien/presse/Publikationen/Jahrbuecher/ Jahrbuch_09_10/Berechtigungsvertrag__Neufassung_v._23.-24._Juni_2009_S.170 _ff.pdf.

any users concerns only CMS.[34] This could be wonderful for authors, but one has to bear in mind that it is probably the publishers who take advantage of this, without redistributing any significant share to authors and without taking into account actually intellectual considerations regarding the alteration of the work. In such a combination, the collective management becomes useless as it helps neither commercial users in terms of providing legal certainty, nor authors to enforce their rights in the way the Copyright Act enshrined them. It only helps publishers enhance their economic power as buyers and sellers, which is, as already said, not the point of copyright law, and should not therefore be the point of CMS either. It is not only the fault of GEMA whose decisions apparently are too publisher-friendly; it is also the fault of judges admitting that moral rights are used to make money and not to defend the very specific relation that an author has to his/her work.

Another case currently pending in Germany illustrates a similar uncomfortable split of rights' ownerships regarding a single use as it highlights the uncertainty that exists if the different rights necessary for a certain use are held by several owners and not all of them are assembled in a CMS.[35] This case regards the website myvideo.de, which – similar to YouTube – allows users to make videos available online. Myvideo obtained a licence from GEMA covering the online uses. But similar to the ring tone case, the publisher, EMI Music Publishing Europe Limited, maintained that it also had to be asked and paid for authorisation. In particular, it argued that GEMA could not license the necessary mechanical reproduction rights.[36] In fact, as a consequence of the European Commission Recommendation of 18 October 2005,[37] the 'big four' publishers withdrew the mechanical online reproduction rights in their Anglo-American repertoire from the collective rights management system. The case primarily touches the question whether under German law the necessary rights to exploit a musical work on the Internet could legitimately be split into an online performing (making available right) and an online reproduction right (mechanical

---

[34] § 11 of the Wahrnehmungsgesetz states that a CMS may not refuse to contract with a user wishing to acquire a licence on rights that it managed.

[35] Whereas practitioners often speak of 'copyright split', e.g. among publishing houses occurring in cases of remixes, Daniel Gervais speaks of 'fragmentation', Gervais (2010), pp. 10 et seq.

[36] *EMI v myvideo*. Munich District Court (LG München), Case 7 O 4139/08, 25 June 2009, ZUM 2009 p. 788; Munich Court of Appeal (OLG München), Case 29 U 3698/09, 29 April 2010, ZUM 2010 p. 709. The case has been appealed; therefore the German Supreme Court will have to decide on the issue.

[37] On this Recommendation, see Drexl (2007).

right) which were held by different entities. While this is not the place to consider this issue in more detail, what seems important is the following.

Be it for the exploitation of mobile phone ring tones or musical works on the Internet, when the CMS can no longer act as one-stop shops, their very *raison d'être* disappears, since the licences that they offer in these cases do not meet the users' need which is to acquire the necessary rights on a wide repertoire through a single and safe licence.[38] And, coming back to the issue of publishers being in the bosom of the CMS, it appears that the weight of publishers in the CMS should be restrained in order to avoid that the CMS lose their rationale as reconciling or balancing means, and hence avoid that they become simple commercial tools for merchants.

6. THE DANGER OF IGNORING THE CONFLICTING INTERESTS

Authors and publishers do have a common interest in an intensive and successful exploitation of 'their' works. However, let us forget for the purposes of this chapter the intellectual interest everybody shares in seeing their works spread without barriers, for the enlightenment and the education, for helping one to realise the grace of being human and hence enabling to live in peace and enjoy the magnificence of a novel, the reflexion of a demonstration of a scientific article, the transcendence of a picture, the extraordinary power of a piece of music, be it an adoring cantata or a dancing tune. . . And then think back to money: it is undeniable that two people having to share a cake have conflicting interests. No footnotes listing tremendous studies seem necessary to prove that publishers and authors have conflicting interests when they both are members in the same CMS collecting fees for works in which they both have rights. And what is more, the German case law shows that publishers can become hurdles for the smooth clearing and licensing of copyrights when they act outside CMS.

Let me illustrate the danger of not recognising the conflict between these interests with one example. The observation of the interdependent development of copyright laws and CMS does not only lead to the recognition

---

[38] The fact that Youtube tries (and sometimes succeeds) to negotiate licences with CMS on a national level attests that the pan-European licences fostered by the European Commission are not interesting as long as they do not cover a world wide repertoire. The announcement of a deal closed between Youtube and SACEM illustrates it; see the press release on 30 September 2010, available at http://www.sacem.fr/cms/home/la-sacem/derniers-communques_2/sacem-you-tube.

of those societies as necessary enforcement tools of copyright. The CMS is furthermore regarded as the scapegoat of the whole copyright system. This shift of the blame on CMS for any difficulties met by the 'creative content industries' can be found in comments of the DG Markt[39] of the European Commission about the slow development of legal paying online music offers in the EU. In a study, published in July 2005, DG Markt stated:

> In 2004, US online revenues were almost eight times higher than those achieved in Western Europe. (. . .) This gap between US and Western European online music revenue needs to be redressed. It is of little value to speculate as to the different reasons for this revenue gap, when the Commission can identify at least one issue where action is required at Community level in order to narrow this gap. This issue is the way in which copyright for online music services is cleared across the 25 Members States that comprise the EU.[40]

Beside this easy way (not) to consider the 'different reasons of the revenue gap', all papers that the DG Markt issued in relation to the Community initiative on the Cross-border Collective Management of Copyright share one fault: neither authors nor creators ever appear in these considerations; the DG Markt systematically considers rights holders as a whole and thus fails to promote or defend the creators' concerns. This study established three possible ways to react to the lack of pan-European licences for musical works on the Internet: doing nothing, favouring stronger competition among collecting societies for users or favouring a stronger competition among collecting societies for right-holders.[41] The second option would have been consistent with the DG Comp *IFPI Simulcast* decision[42] which called for the elimination of territorial restrictions and discriminatory provisions in the reciprocal representation agreements between CMS. But the DG Markt chose the third one: 'give right-holders the choice to authorize collecting societies of their choice to manage their online rights for the entire EU'. At first glance, it seems appealing to free 'right-holders' from the burden CMS place on their members,[43] above all when readers

---

[39] Internal Market and Services Directorate General.

[40] See *Commission Staff Working Document, Study on a Community Initiative on the Cross-border Collective Management of Copyright*, available at http://ec.euro pa.eu/internal_market/copyright/docs/management/study-collectivemgmt_en.pdf, p. 6.

[41] On these options, see Ricolfi (2007), pp. 294–6

[42] Case COMP/C2/38.014. 8 October 2002, OJEC 2003 No. L 107 p. 58.

[43] However; it is noteworthy that these burdens are not the result of the arbitrary will of advisory boards of CMS. As a matter of fact, European authorities recognised that these burdens represented the legitimite interests of CMS and authors in several decisions; see especially the 'SABAM decision', *BRT v SABAM,*

interpret these to mean authors, or at least the creative side. However, by not distinguishing among rights holders and thereby confusing publishers and authors, the DG Markt did not pay attention to the very sensitive difference between, on the one hand, single authors rightly defended by CMS and the reciprocal representation network built by them and, on the other hand, huge publishing companies holding extraordinarily large and attractive repertoires which have strategic interests in creating scarcity. As a matter of fact, this recommendation invited collecting societies to compete for rights holders – without differentiating within this large side – since the DG Markt 'simply' turned its back to the reciprocal representation system, encouraging CMS to grant licences to users only covering their very own repertoire. In other words, those societies – who anyway were disoriented by upcoming business models, the globalization of uses of protected contents, the refusal of the European Commission to approve the Santiago Agreement,[44] and this new position of the Commission – now had to comply with the requirements of rights owners holding the most demanded repertoire.[45] This does not mean the needs of the majority of authors, but those of the biggest publishers, since these players always had to compete for the most demanded repertoire. Later, representatives of this DG stated that they had expected this recommendation to create flexibilities for authors and not publishers. This is a bit worrying as they show that either there has been a lot of unofficial influence of those whose interests have been served by this recommendation, or quite some naivety on the side of the lawyers drafting the Recommendation.

While no one really knows today what pan-European online licensing models will look like in a few years, it is certain that the collective

---

ECJ 21 March 1974, Case 127/73, [1974] ECR 313; the 'Tournier decision', *Ministère public v Tournier*, ECJ 13 July 1989, Case 395/87, [1989] ECR 2521; and the 'Daft Punk decision' of the European Commission, *Banghalter and Homem Christo v SACEM*, Europ. Commission, Case COMP/C2/37.219, 12 August 2002, available on the website of the European Commission at http://ec.europa.eu/competition/antitrust/cases/decisions/37219/fr.pdf

[44] This standard agreement organised a one-stop-shop system with the help of the reciprocal representation agreements between CMS of the CISAC, allowing users to get a single licence for a worldwide online use. The Santiago agreement covered performing rights and a similar Agreement had been concluded in Barcelona for reproduction rights. The Santiago agreement has been notified to the Commission (see Case COMP/C2/38126); the Commission mainly criticized the economic residency clause; see press release IP/04/586 of 3 May 2004 and the notice of 17 August 2005, OJ C 200/11. These agreements have not been extended beyond the end of 2004.

[45] For a thorough and critical discussion of the line held by the Commission in this recommendation, see Drexl (2007).

management system which allowed users to get licences covering the world-wide repertoire by only negotiating with a single CMS has already disappeared regarding the online use of musical works.[46] Offers made by GEMA, SACEM and PRS for pan-European online uses in the musical sectors are now defined by the repertoires of publishers who withdrew their right from the 'traditional' collective management in order to entrust societies they choose with the online uses.[47] Such commercial tailoring of the scope of the repertoire which can be licensed by copyright management societies may only, however, by chance support the interest of creators and cultural diversity. Moreover, no similarly banging move by single authors and independent publishers has been observed after the recommendation. On the contrary, rights in works of authors which do not fall into the mainstream repertoire of the 'big four' now can only be licensed for international uses by the collecting society they joined, since the whole reciprocal representation system collapsed as a result of the Recommendation and the CISAC decision.[48]

Thus we can see that not to distinguish between the diverging interests among rights holders benefits the strongest, and weakens the most vulner-

---

[46]   Maybe an extremely proactive international legal initiative could be able to draw back to the bosom of CMS the rights now individually managed by publishers. Such an initiative could be an extended collective licence, a mandatory collective management of the making available right (which still is to properly define) similar to that of international cable retransmission in EU law, or a presumption that every CMS (which also have to be defined) is entitled to enforce copyright in court. One hardly dares to dream of such initiative.

[47]   Following the recommendation, many publishers withdrew from the traditional collective management system the rights they control, and transferred them to specific CMS or their subsidiaries for the exclusive pan-European licensing for musical works on the Internet. The first partnership had been announced regarding rights in the Anglo-American repertoire of EMI publishing, now managed by a joint venture of GEMA and PRS that is called CELAS. The first announcements mentioned that this assignment was exclusive. Due to pressure of the DG COMP, the exclusivity has been abandoned. Soon after, Universal Music Publishing announced its partnership with SACEM; Sony/ATV collaborated with GEMA to build a structure similar to CELAS, but without the participation of PRS: PAECOL; Warner/Chappel made an original constellation (called PEDL) with GEMA, PRS and STIM (the Swedish CMS for musical works), meanwhile SACEM, and BUMA-STEMRA joined the cloud, GEMA seems to have quit it, and SGAE's participation is uncertain. For details on these issues, see ELIAMEP (2009) pp. 34 et seq.

[48]   Case COMP/C-2/38.698. 16 July 2008, OJEC No. C 323, 12. This decision cumulates all critiques made against the refusal to approve Santiago agreements, against the choice made in the IFPI Simulcast decision, as against the Recommendation.

able. One can only hope that future legislative interventions will pursue other aims, preferably the exact opposite.

7.   CONCLUDING REMARKS

The current creation schemes encouraged by the digitisation and the Internet are not that new.[49] Thus, long-standing principles having proved their virtue should not be thrown away together with videotapes and vinyl records. In this respect and under the premise that law protects and enhances creation, 'the investor can only be a derivative owner of authors' rights'.[50] As the following simple truth still holds:

> Of the two of them [creator and exploiter], the only one who is directly or indirectly in contact with customers is the exploiter. The party channelling all the revenue is indeed the exploiter. If the property system does not impose on him a detailed share-out, then he is under no obligation to give an account of the revenue or to share it.[51]

Therefore, if investment issues have to be regarded by law makers, the weak and protection-worth position of creators should not be forgotten. Developments provoked by the Recommendation prove that the failure to protect the creators' side leads to strengthening the stronger, the investors.

Collective management of copyright is the best way to balance the interests of creators, investors (publishers and other commercial users) and the public, considering that creators and the public are similar fellows, not acting as professionals in the virtuous circle of creation and inspiration. They therefore need the most protection. In this respect, the most proper place of publishers is with authors. But it would be inconsequent to continue ignoring the conflicting interests of authors and publishers, and remain passive by observing how publishers are transforming authors' societies into managing subsidiaries of their firms.

In this situation, legislative intervention is only needed to strengthen the position of creators as such in the bosom of CMS and to help these societies to play their pacifying role. That means: mandatory admission of authors whose works belong to the business purpose of a CMS and

---

49   Sharing this opinion, see Gaudrat (2001).
50   Gaudrat (2001) p. 212.
51   Gaudrat (2001) p. 118.

who want to join such a society;[52] mandatory distribution rules between publishers and authors, or ceiling shares for derivative right-holders; mandatory internal collective management governance rules assuring that the interests of creators are sufficiently paid attention to, and the mandatory publication of tariffs, offered repertoires and reciprocal representation agreements.[53]

After the Recommendation of the European Commission, the virtuous blanket licences for the world-wide repertoire seem lost for online use in the musical sector. This, however, should not discourage us to rescue this model for all sectors who escape from this sad conquest of publishers.[54] This could be achieved by the above-mentioned rules, but first of all by an open and dynamic conception of the competition, as proposed by Josef Drexl.[55]

The only novelty[56] brought by the digitisation and the development of the Internet is that professional (or industrial) intermediaries who used to be the only gate keepers for works to be spread are experiencing new competitors: amateur, non professional, non commercial 'broadcasters' providing 'users generated content'. 'Old' copyright law does not consider the financial profit made by users of works in copyright, since in the past the costs of any reproduction (and thus of any broadcasting) were extremely high. Nowadays, most online uses do not have any marginal cost. The acquisition of the licence is the only cost, and the copyright law

---

[52]   Cf. § 6 of the Wahrnehmungsgesetz. See Hilty (2010), p. 143, who maintains that this obligation should concern all kinds of rights managers, in order to avoid that a too strict definition of CMS helps societies managed by publishers to escape this duty.

[53]   After a joint statement on 19 October 2009 following an 'online commerce roundtable' hosted by Neelie Kroes (at that time European Commissioner for Competition), EMI Music Publishing, PRS for Music, SACEM, STIM and Universal Music Publishing, constituted a 'working group on a common framework for rights ownership information' with the aim of developing a common framework for rights ownership information. These major players of the international music licensing and clearing battlefield (joined by Amazon, itunes, and Nokia) meanwhile announced their will to achieve a 'global rights database'. Currently, according to their website http://globalrepertoiredatabase.com, they are still looking for the convenient way to settle the database. Thus, for commercial users, it appears useful that CMS don't wait for this database to work for making their data available.

[54]   See the sector of pictures, achieving a safe success with the help of the EVA network (European Visual Artists), supporting OLA, one-stop-shop for multirepertory and multiterritory licences.

[55]   See Drexl (2007).

[56]   Beside the transnational essence of every online dissemination.

sometimes the only rationale for right holders to reserve some use. The very need for new rules could be found, on the contrary, by taking into account the commercial benefit when defining a copyright infringement rather than charging end users or introducing new protection entitlements such as investment protection rights for online publishers. We cannot continue inculpating end-users only moved by the will to share intellectual goods and at the same time offer a proverbial safe haven to intermediaries making tremendous benefits with such a traffic.[57] It discredits not only the copyright law, but the law in general.

Last but not least, coming back to CMS, if legislators truly wish to intervene, future interventions should help them adapt and evolve in order to allow all stakeholders to find business models which represent a fair reconciliation of all interests.[58] In this respect, first and necessary steps would be to clarify the definition of the making available right,[59] and to rightly distinguish between first right owner and assignees, between creators and investors. This would be smarter than to continue going the easy way, in considering rights holders as a holy whole and CMS as the eternal scapegoat.

BIBLIOGRAPHY

Drexl, Josef (2007), 'Competition in the field of collective management: preferring "creative competition" to allocative efficiency in European copyright law', in Torremans, Paul (ed.) *Copyright Law – A Handbook of Contemporary Research,* Cheltenham, UK and Northampton, MA, USA: Edward Elgar, pp. 255–82.
Dümmling, Albrecht (2003), *Musik hat ihren Wert – 100 Jahre musikalische Verwertungsgesellschaft in Deutschland,* Regensburg: ConBrio Verlag.
ELIAMEP (2009), *Collecting Societies and Cultural Diversity in the Musical Sector,* Study requested by the European Parliament's Committee on Culture and Education, Brussels: European Parliament.
Ficsor, Mihaly (1989), 'Collective Administration of Copyrights and Neighbouring Rights' (Report for the WIPO), Copyright 1989, pp. 309–354.
Gaudrat, Philippe (2001), 'The Eternal Quarrels of a Successful Couple: the Creator and the Investor', RIDA, **190,** pp. 71–243 (French title: 'Les démêlés intemporels d'un couple à succès: le créateur et l'investisseur'), translation into English for the RIDA: Margaret Platt-Hommel.

---

[57] Also supporting (besides other combinations) an 'alternative solution [. . .] under a principle that, wherever commerce is generated through the use of creative content, a share of revenues should flow back into creative production', Kretschmer (2002), p. 156.

[58] On the 'changing roles' of CMS, see Gervais (2010).

[59] Cf. Masouyé (2009), p. 245, in respect of 'RMI, DRM, TPM and Downloading Issues' : 'No adequate rights: no collective management systems!'

Gervais, Daniel (2010), 'Collective Management of Copyright: Theory and Practice in the Digital Age', in Gervais, Daniel (ed.), *Collective Management of Copyright and Related Rights*, Alphen aan den Rijn, The Netherlands: Kluwer Law Internationa, pp.1–28.

Hilty, Reto M. (2010), 'Kollektive Rechtewahrnehmung und Vergütungsregelungen: Harmonisierungsbedarf und -möglichkeiten', in Leistner, Mathias (ed.) *Europäische Perspektive des Geistigen Eigentums,* Tübingen: Mohr Siebeck, pp. 123–66.

Kretschmer, Martin (2002), 'Copyright societies do not administer individual property rights: the incoherence of institutional traditions in Germany and the UK', in Towse, Ruth (ed.), *Copyright in the Cultural Industries,* Cheltenham, UK and Northampton, MA, USA: Edward Elgar, pp. 140–64.

Masouyé, Patrick (2009), 'Copyright is dead. . . Long life to the Right. . . of Users', RIDA, **222,** pp. 188–284.

Melichar, Ferdinand (1991), 'Verleger und Verwertungsgesellschaften', UFITA **117,** pp. 5–19.

Ricolfi, Marco (2007), 'Individual and collective management of copyright in a digital environment', in Torremans, Paul (ed.), *Copyright Law – A Handbook of Contemporary Research,* Cheltenham, UK and Northampton, MA, USA: Edward Elgar, pp. 283–314.

Uchtenhagen, Ulrich, 2005, *The Setting-up of New Copyright Societies – Some Experiences and Reflexions,* Geneva: WIPO.

Vercken, Gilles (1996), *Practical Guide to Copyright for Multimedia Producers,* Brussels: European Commission, Office for Official Publications. Available at: http://bookshop.europa.eu.

7. The emerging U.S. approach to orphan works: a partial fault standard for copyright infringement

Steven A. Hetcher[1]

One conventional manner of characterizing the dichotomy between individualism and collectivism is that individualistic approaches opt for the protection of individual rights over collective welfare interests, if and when they conflict, while collectivist approaches opt for the reverse. This abstract normative framework can be applied across a vast array of particular policy concerns. The one of interest here is the topic of orphan works and their regulation – a growing concern.

Orphan works, defined generally as copyright-protected works for which the owner is unknown or unlocatable, have presented a problem to copyright as long as it has existed. For as soon as works are protected under copyright, the possibility arises of potential uses of these works that do not occur simply due to the inability to locate the owner in order to secure authorization for use of the work.

The Copyright Office claims that the problem of inability to access orphan works is getting worse, due to recent legislation, specifically the recent addition of twenty years to the copyright term under the Copyright Term Extension Act.[2] The Report notes in passing that the problem naturally became worse when the U.S. abandoned the "formalities" in adopting the 1976 Act, as these required for more comprehensive record-keeping.[3] Implicit in the Copyright Office's message is the notion that there is an inherent tension between the sort of moral rights approach taken by most Berne countries and the goal of effectively dealing with orphan works. One important form of collectivism in the domain of

---

[1]   Professor of Law, Vanderbilt Law School. I would like to thank the participants of the ATRIP 2010 Conference who commented on the ideas in this chapter in various fora.
[2]   U.S. Copyright Office Report on Orphan Works, 2 (2006).
[3]   *Id.* at 3.

intellectual property generally and copyright in particular is collectivism in the sense of international harmonization. As the Report makes clear, however, such harmonization may come at a cost – the cost here being the lack of an orderly system to keep track of orphan works.

In response to a growing concern over orphan works, the Copyright Office was asked by Congress to study the problem and propose a solution, which it did with the promulgation of the *Report on Orphan Works*.[4] For a number of years, the Copyright Office has held the Report's proposal for specific legislative amendment high on its agenda.[5]

A second indication that orphan works are becoming more important is the role they have played in the ongoing Google Book Search (GBS) litigation. While Google Books can in some ways be viewed as akin to one of the new wonders of the world, nevertheless, it is estimated that a large number of the 12 million books that Google has digitized are orphan works.[6] Pam Samuelson, who has in the past favored the Google Books Search project as a fair use, has spoken out against the Google Books proposed settlement on the grounds that over time Google will develop a monopoly over access to books.[7] If Samuelson is right, the concern that this raises for orphan books is obvious: namely, that they too will come under the monopoly control of Google. Finally, orphan works are of interest in light of the explosion in user-generated content (UGC). Much user-generated content uses orphan works on the one hand, and much user-generated content is likely to end up as an orphaned work, on the other hand. The number of users and consumers of UGC is massive. How orphan works are regulated will determine whether this collective of users is harmed by the control of orphan works by powerful individual actors such as Google.

In the space afforded here, I will not seek to provide a comprehensive overview of this emerging situation but to instead focus on one,

---

[4] *Id.* at 1.

[5] As stated by David Carson, General Counsel of the Copyright Office, at the Copyright Office road show in Nashville, April 20, 2007.

[6] *See, e.g.,* Jonathan Band, *The Long and Winding Road to the Google Book Settlement,* 27 John Marshall Rev. Intell. Prop. L. 227, 294 (2009) (estimating that 75% of books will remain unclaimed).

[7] *See,* Pamela Samuelson, *Google Book Search and the Future of Books in Cyberspace* (forthcoming; *See also,* Randal C. Picker, *the Google Book Search Settlement: A New Orphan Works Monopoly?* J. Compet. L. & Econ. (2009). In a previous article, I performed an extended doctrinal examination of fair use as applied to Google's copying of books. See Steven Hetcher, *The Half-Fairness of Google's Plan to Make the World's Collection of Books Searchable,* 13 Michigan Telecommunications & Technology Law Review 1 (2006) (concluding that Google Book Service was not a fair use).

particularly interesting development, which is the approach taken to orphan works by the U.S. Copyright Office. While this approach has yet to be implemented into law, if the Copyright Office prevails, the treatment of orphan works under U.S. law will change dramatically. This discussion in turn is relevant to the quest for a collectivist solution to the orphan works problem, for while the Copyright Office claims that its proposal would be in the spirit of the Berne Convention, it is predictable that not all commentators share this view.

The following discussion will first set out the important features of the Copyright Office's *Report on Orphan Works*. I will then argue that the Report provides a preferable alternative solution to the orphan works problem as compared to the solution initially preferred by the parties in the GBS first proposed settlement. Under the proposed terms of this settlement, the private parties to the lawsuit would have essentially controlled the several million orphan works.[8] By contrast, under the approach advocated by the Copyright Office's legislative proposal, there would be significant limitations put on remedies for infringement when users of orphan works first perform "reasonably diligent searches" for the owners.[9]

I will argue that this approach is an implicit move in the direction of fault liability, at least for this corner of copyrightable subject matter. Elsewhere, I have promoted the application of a fault standard to amateur digital content.[10] The topics are related in as much as the more corners of a room that are painted, less open space is left in the room's middle. In other words, the more particular sectors of the copyrightable domain of content appear to be best regulated through a fault standard, the more relevant it is to raise the question as to why this standard should not achieve the sort of dominance it has in tort generally.

In order to take into account the perspectives of various concerned parties, the Copyright Office conducted Roundtables in various venues.[11] In addition, the Copyright Office also placed a notice in the National Register seeking comments. In response, it received over 850 of them.[12]

---

[8] See, *e.g.,* James Grimmelmann, *The Google Book Search Settlement: Ends, Means, and the Future of Books at 10–11, April 2009,* available at http://works.bepress.com/cgi/viewcontenet.cgi?article=1024&context=james_grimmelmann.

[9] Report, at 107.

[10] Steven Hetcher, *The Kids are Alright: Introducing a Fault Liability Standard to Amateur Digital Content,* Florida Law Review (forthcoming).

[11] Report at 19.

[12] *Id.* at 17 ("Virtually every interest group typically involved in copyright policy debates was represented in the comments. . .")

The list of respondents is a who's who list of stakeholders and NGOs.[13] This is a testament to the centrality of the orphan works debate to these actors and thus to meaningful copyright reform. The Copyright Office's response addresses the concern over lack of legal access to orphan works by potential users while also seeking to respect the established rights of owners. Because the Copyright Office's proposed solution to the orphan works problem takes a middle road, it is of course open to criticism from either extreme. At one extreme, some commentators argue that orphan works should be in the public domain, while at the other extreme, some commentators argue that any special treatment for orphan works is contrary to fundamental principles of copyright law.[14] Despite these widely divergent policy preferences, the Copyright Office proposal may, ultimately, be palatable to nearly all parties as a compromise solution.[15]

The Orphan Works Report uses the term "orphan work" to describe a situation in which "the owner of a copyrighted work cannot be identified and located by someone who wishes to make use of the work in a manner that requires permission of the copyright owner."[16] This type of situation can easily lead to market failure. Copyright gives mini-monopolies so that

---

[13]   To name a few: Creative Commons, Electronic Frontier Foundation, Public Knowledge, RIAA, MPAA, PPA and the Authors' Guild, Google, Inc. Report at 77–78 and elsewhere.

[14]   Report, at 89.

[15]   Report, at 2 ("Thus, there is good evidence that the orphan works problem is real and warrants attention, and none of the commentators made any serious argument questioning that conclusion.").

[16]   The Report says its definition is not canonical and encourages others to proffer definitions as well. *Id.* at 34. *See also*, Notice of Inquiry, 70 Fed. Reg. 3739, 3741 (Jan. 26, 2005). Elsewhere in the Report, the definition is given a slightly altered form. The Report notes that it is not an orphan works situation if the potential user is able to communicate with the owner, even if the owner is not responsive. *Id.* It also notes that orphan works are not the same as "out of print" works, although a single work may be both. *Id.* at 34, n. 68. The metaphor of an orphan is somewhat inapt. Orphan children do not have parents anywhere. If you think you have no parents but you are wrong and unbeknownst to you, you do, you will think you are an orphan but you will be wrong. Orphan works on the other hand are not either orphans or not categorically, but rather often it is a question of transaction costs; if a high enough price were paid, ownership could be determined. There may be examples such as old photographs found in an unmarked box in a state historical society, however, that carry no identifying marks and for which there would appear to be no means to track down the creator due to the generic nature of the composition and lack of identifying information. Here it may indeed be the case that no amount of expenditure would allow the users to be located.

people will be directly incentivized to create, such that the public may indirectly benefit from these creations, either through their direct consumption or through their use in the production of other creative works.[17] With orphan works, however, potential users who wish to be law abiding are halted in their tracks because they are unable to locate the owners in order to secure their permission to use the work, or part of the work, either by purchasing it, licensing it, or gaining free access. Thus, the larger, indirect purpose of copyright is ill-served, as potential users will fear the risk of infringement liability and be deterred from what might otherwise be a welfare-producing use of the work. The Copyright Office puts it this way: "Even when the user has made a reasonably diligent effort to find the owner, if the owner is not found, the user faces uncertainty – she cannot determine whether or under what conditions the owner would permit use. Where the proposed use goes beyond an exemption or limitation to copyright, the user cannot reduce the risk of copyright liability for such use, because there is always a possibility, however remote, that a copyright owner could bring an infringement action after that use has begun."[18]

The core problem of orphan works, then, is that the works go unused

---

[17]   As this statement indicates, American copyright is conventionally understood to adhere to an instrumentalist logic. Rights are created, maintained, or extinguished, depending on their causal impact in promoting the goals of copyright. *See generally*, Gillian K. Hatfield, *The Economics of Copyright: An Historical Perspective*, 38 Copyright Law Symposium 1 (1992). While the instrumentalist goals of copyright are often stated in abstract and formulaic terms, Landes and Posner note that a more detailed specification of these goals is more informative and accurate. They contend that it is important to note that more localized or specific economic concerns merit economic analysis as well. William M. Landes & Richard A. Posner, *The Economic Structure Of Intellectual Property Law*, Cambridge, Mass.: Harvard University Press (2003) ("Given the emphasis of the existing scholarly and popular literature concerned with intellectual property, it may come as a surprise to many readers that the economic arguments that we make for intellectual property protection are not based primarily on a belief that without legal protection the incentives to create such property would be inadequate. That belief cannot be defended confidently on the basis of current knowledge. The concerns we highlight have rather to do with such things as optimal management of existing stocks of intellectual property, congestion externalities, search costs, rent seeking, and transactions costs."). A parallel point can be made for the orphan works problem in which the concerns are not confined to the traditional access/incentives discussion but look at more localized factors in detail such as the relative preference for opt-out versus opt-in, in relation to when Google uses unauthorized works. Whether U.S. copyright is at its core utilitarian, non-utilitarian, or a combination, is a matter of longstanding controversy. For purposes of this chapter, I will assume it is the former.

[18]   Report, at 1.

despite the fact that had the owner and potential user been able to bargain, a mutually beneficial, as well as socially beneficial, use would have come about.[19] The Copyright Office explicitly states that the orphan works problem is a threat to the public interest.

> Concerns have been raised that in such a situation, a productive and beneficial use of the work is forestalled – not because the copyright owner has asserted his exclusive rights in the work, or because the user and owner cannot agree on the terms of a license – but merely because the user cannot locate the owner. Many users of copyrighted works have indicated that the risk of liability for copyright infringement, however remote, is enough to prompt them not to make use of the work. Such an outcome is not in the public interest, particularly where the copyright owner is not locatable because he no longer exists or otherwise does not care to restrain the use of his work.[20]

The last sentence of the quoted passage articulates those situations that are particularly troubling, namely, those in which the owner does not exist or does not care if her work is used. These are situations in which the works in question would be unlikely to be the object of a transaction, even if transaction costs were not an impediment. Under conventional copyright economics, creative works are modeled as possessing a public goods structure.[21] The salient feature of public goods is the feature that once created, marginal copies can often be produced at nearly zero cost. This is what is revolutionarily true for digital copies. Thus, other things equal, social welfare will be maximized when the number of consumed copies of a work is maximized. But such maximizing uses will not occur in orphan works situations, as there is no possibility for an agreement due to the inability of the owner and the potential user to interact.

From the perspective of rights under the Copyright Act, there are two major types of situations in which the orphan works problem arises. One

---

[19]   The scope of the orphan works problem is uncertain. Report, at 21. There is scant empirical data but what there is suggests that the problem is probably very significant in terms of the number of works that may be involved. For example, Carnegie Mellon University did a study of the feasibility of obtaining permission to digitize and provide web access for parts of its collection. It discovered that for the works in the study, 22% of the publishers could not be found. Carnegie Mellon University Libraries, Comment 537 to Copyright Office orphan works study.

[20]   Report, at 1.

[21]   Landes & Posner, supra note 3, at 14 ("[IP] is a 'public good' in the economist's sense that consumption of it by one person does not reduce its consumption by another. More accurately, it has public-good characteristics, for we shall show that in some circumstances propertizing intellectual property can prevent overuse or congestion in economically meaningful senses of these terms.").

is where the potential use is of the whole work. Such uses implicate the §106(1) right of reproduction. The other is using the work as a part of some larger derivative work. Such uses implicate the §106(2) derivative works right.[22] The Report creates what is in effect a semi-safe harbor for both types of uses, although the precise specifications of the safe harbor are different for each. If a potential user fulfills certain conditions, namely performs a "reasonably diligent search" for the owner,[23] and gives attribution when possible,[24] then if she uses the work and the owner later "surfaces" or "appears," the user will only be subject to a limited remedy. This remedy is more limited for transformative uses and for noncommercial uses when the user ceases use upon notice by the surfacing owner.

> If a user meets his burden of demonstrating that he performed a reasonably diligent search and provided reasonable attribution to the author and copyright owner, then the recommended amendment would limit the remedies available in that infringement action in two primary ways: First, it would limit monetary relief to only reasonable compensation for the use, with an elimination of any monetary relief where the use was noncommercial and the user ceases the infringement expeditiously upon notice. Second, the proposal would limit the ability of the copyright owner to obtain full injunctive relief in cases where the user has transformed the orphan work into a derivative work like a motion picture or book, preserving the user's ability to continue to exploit that derivative work. In all other cases, the court would be instructed to minimize the harm to the user that an injunction might impose, to protect the user's interests in relying on the orphan works provision in making use of the work.[25]

The quoted passage states that the remedy will be "reasonable compensation." Elsewhere, the Report gives further specification to this general term when it notes that the appropriate remedy is the amount the parties would have agreed to, had they actually bargained prior to the use.[26] Importantly, however, the copy is still an infringement. Thus, under the Orphan Works Report, if the owner once located does not want to bargain, she may refuse and the potential user will be out of luck. The

---

[22] Other copyrights pertain to either whole copies or partial copies; that is, one cannot without authorization display, distribute, perform, or digitally transmit whole copies or parts of copies. 17 U.S.C.§106 (2004).

[23] Report, at 8.

[24] *Id.*

[25] *Id.* at 11.

[26] Though the Report does not discuss it as such, this is plausibly seen as the Copyright Office's attempt to implement Kaldor-Hicks efficiency. In the typical situation, it is the judge who decides what the Kaldor-Hicks outcome would be. This will typically involve a judge making an educated guess.

Report notes in passing, however, that the amount of damages may sometimes be zero.[27] Note the implication that the content industry will be less successful in threatening everyday consumers with lawsuits, as the smaller potential awards will change the calculus leading to settlements.

The Orphan Works Report is clear in its statement in support of protection of author's rights. It states that the hope is that the proposed rule change will lead to more transactions between owners and potential users.[28] This claim is an important part of the Copyright Office's argument, because if this claim is true, then it may be the case that both owners and users benefit from the proposed legislation. Note that while this requirement need not be satisfied under an economic account, as overall welfare may be maximized in a situation in which one party gains at another party's expense, nevertheless, from a pragmatic perspective, it will be much easier to bring about legal change when the interests of all parties are served.[29] Accordingly, the Report's key proposal appears well constructed when viewed in a pragmatic light. The document should, if it is to be politically feasible, not be a huge departure from established rights or politically powerful stakeholders will strongly object because they will be made to suffer a significant harm – when judged from the status quo ex ante – under the proposed rule change.[30]

The fact that the proposal may be politically feasible should not lead theorists to dismiss it, as this palatability should not cause us to lose sight of the fact that important change may come about if the Orphan Works Report is implemented. Most important, potential users will have less risk in using orphan works and so will use them more. As the Report notes repeatedly, in all practical reality, most owners will never surface.[31] This is for a few reasons. With some works, people may not even realize they

---

[27]   Report at 12.

[28]   Report, at 97; Report, at 8 ("First, any system to deal with orphan works should seek primarily to make it more likely that a user can find the relevant owner in the first instance, and negotiate a voluntary agreement over permission and payment, if appropriate, for the intended use of the work."). The Orphan Works Report contends that it does not want the proposal to serve as a shield for those who seek to act in bad faith. *Id.* at 98.

[29]   In a situation in which all parties benefited or were neutral, the conditions for Pareto optimality would be satisfied and there would be no need to resort to a Kaldor-Hicks efficiency criterion.

[30]   Report, at 8. For reasons familiar from behavioral economics, we should expect established rights holders to feel a potential loss of rights acutely, as generally people suffer more when they lose something than they would have suffered in never gaining it in the first place.

[31]   *Id.* at 11.

own it, as the work, or a fractional interest in the work, may have been inherited.[32] Alternatively, the work may be owned by a defunct company. In addition, many uses will go unnoticed. This may be because the use is essentially private. Or a work may be used as part of a larger derivative work and uploaded, for example, to YouTube or some similar site but not readily recognized as constituted in part of the orphan work in question. For many such works, there is a good chance that the owner will never come across the work or have the work called to her attention.

A critic of the Report's approach might conclude that the Copyright Office is promoting piracy in that it supports rule changes that will increase unauthorized uses. The term piracy, however, is heavily loaded. The reality is more nuanced than is suggested by this criticism, as the proposed rule change would also change the normative complexion of these unauthorized uses. First, while still an infringement, and often a willful one, the unauthorized use would nevertheless be in good faith in the sense that it came subsequent to a reasonable search for the owner by the user. This element of good faith – the emergence of reasonableness – renders the unauthorized use less wrongful and thus deserving of a reduced sanction. It is a *grundnorm* of our legal system that lower penalties, other things equal, signify less wrongful acts. Thus, while ostensibly defending established copyrights, the Orphan Works Report is subtly subversive if I am right that its implementation into law would dramatically increase the number of unauthorized uses of these works.

One of the refrains of the Report is that different solutions may be appropriate for different categories of works. For example, different sorts of databases and different sets of best practices may vary by industry. Accordingly, the Copyright Office notes that, "Our recommendation permits, and we encourage, interested parties to develop guidelines for searches in different industry sectors and for different types of works."[33] The Report notes as well that the criterion for a reasonably diligent search will also vary according to the category of work and other factors.[34] The Report attempts to craft a solution that aims to meaningfully address these differences. It rejects the call for a government-run registry of orphan works by arguing that the private sector is better equipped to develop

---

[32] *Id.* at 28.
[33] Report, at 10.
[34] Report, at 9 ("It is not possible at this stage to craft a standard that can be specific to all or even many of these circumstances. Moreover, the resources, techniques and technologies used to investigate the status of a work also differ among industry sectors and change over time, making it hard to specify the steps a user must take with any particularity.").

registries or databases that are customized to the specific challenges presented by particular categories of works.[35]

The Orphan Works Report envisions a world in which there are less orphans due to mechanisms that allow owners and potential users to come together such as through these Registries.[36] Thus, this approach supports the established property rights regime. Nevertheless, many works will not be available in such registries. From the perspective of many potential users, this may be beneficial, as the existence of a Registry presumably will for most users create a duty to check this database as an element, perhaps the most important element, as part of the user's reasonably diligent search. Thus, for the myriad works that are not put in such registries, the potential user may plausibly claim to have conducted a reasonably diligent search, based on evidence that the Registry was fruitlessly searched.

The practical effect overall is to make uses of orphan works lower risk. This is a key point that must be kept in mind. Thus, a new option is added for putative users of orphan works. A user can hope for fair use or alternatively can perform a reasonably diligent search in order to fall within the orphan works safe harbor. This latter option will undoubtedly be more attractive to some creators, as it will provide them with more certainty than will a claim to fair use which is often seen as notoriously open-ended and uncertain in its outcome. As Lawrence Lessig argues, the point is not academic as the unpredictability of the fair use analysis shows up in the marketplace. He gives the example of documentary filmmakers, who are hamstrung in their uses of works, even though these uses are likely fair uses. This is due to the fact that potential programmers of such works require that the works be insured, and insurers are typically unwilling to take the risk of insuring works that contain unauthorized uses and thus would need to rely on a fair use defense in a lawsuit.[37] I share this concern for the unpredictability of fair use analysis but draw a different lesson than does Lessig, who argues for a number of measures to shrink copyright.[38] There is another option to avoid the uncertainty of fair use analysis: create safe harbors that potential users of creative works may sail into

---

[35] Report, at 75.

[36] Report at 74 ("Although most commentators agreed that a mandatory owner registry would violate Berne and would in general be ill-advised, many commentators expressed support for the creation of some sort of *voluntary* owner registry.") (emphasis in original).

[37] Lawrence Lessig, *Free Culture*, New York: Penguin Books 95–9, 186–7, 292 (2003).

[38] Lessig argues for five-year renewable copyright terms with a seventy-five year maximum. Id. at 292.

if they are willing to perform the requisite due diligence as set out in the Orphan Works Report. For example, the type of problem envisioned with Lessig's example of the documentary filmmaker is improved upon under the Orphan Works Report as the filmmaker can do a reasonably diligent search and then use the work if the search is unsuccessful. If it is successful, the filmmaker can attempt to bargain for the use.

One of the striking features of the Orphan Works Report is that it says relatively little about uses of orphan works by private individuals. The focus is instead on public entities, particularly not-for-profit ones, such as museums and archives. From a policy perspective, this makes perfect sense as these types of entities are of special concern to copyright law. Yet, this focus is nevertheless striking as most policy proposals to bring copyright law up to speed with the digital revolution have concerned themselves with the main categories of mass-consumer content such as music, film, software and computer games, or with the impact of new technologies and new laws on the rights or welfare of private individual users. The situations are different for private actors versus public entities. Private individuals generally will not know the law, and typically their copying will be limited to a small number of instances. For museums and archives, the situation is different, as they may hold large numbers of orphan works. In some of the instances discussed in the Report, thousands or millions of works are at issue.[39] These entities are in a better position to know the law. Their behavior can accordingly be expected to respond more readily to the changed incentives introduced by an altered legal, regulatory regime. The stakes will be dramatically higher for public entities, due to the potential liability for a large number of works.[40] These public, not-for-profit entities have some characteristic features that make them difficult orphan works situations. The reason is that for these sorts of entities, the desired works may be, for example, old family photographs or articles from old newspapers. The Orphan Works Report calls these "ephemera."[41] These works are technically copyright protected, yet they are not works that are often even consciously owned or being attempted to be exploited. Nevertheless, archives and museums are still uneasy about using them, which may be

---

[39] Report, at 12.

[40] When we consider this factor for the case of Google, we see how truly gargantuan the stakes are for it. Google could be potentially liable for the infringement of more works than even these major cultural institutions, for literally millions of books. And in addition, because it is a commercial entity, the requirements for getting into the safe harbor will be more onerous. Report, at 22, n. 27.

[41] Report at 26.

prudent as an owner might surface and sue for infringement.[42] Owners surfacing to claim rights is of course more likely given the public character of these institutions.

The notion of ephemera is a little discussed concept in traditional copyright. The Orphan Works Report does not define the concept but instead provides examples.[43] Ephemera may have features of particular interest. They were often not created by artists or writers and the like seeking monetary gain. Accordingly, a rule change that leads to less compensation in cases of infringement will not reduce the incentive to create. It has famously been said that only a blockhead would write for free. In fact, however, millions of people do precisely that. The most widely heralded contemporary examples are blogs and user-generated videos. But it has always been true that people wrote for free. It was not always true, however, that the result of such writing was the grant of a federal copyright. This came about with the passage of the 1976 Copyright Act that grants copyright protection upon fixation rather than publication. This legislative change along with the development of the internet has dramatically increased the number of ephemera. What is different is that in an online world, the cost, not of writing, but of publishing one's writing has been reduced drastically to practically nothing. As economics would predict, a lower cost for publication has increased the amount of publications.[44]

Notice the important role of such works in the production of knowledge. Copyright discussion often focuses on the creative aspects of works. But for museums and archives of certain sorts, it is often *not* the artiness or originality of the works, per se, that gives them their value. For example,

---

[42]   The Report appears to think the goal is to reach a level of "acceptable risk." Report at 26 ("In spite of this uncertainty, however, users occasionally exploit works having indeterminate ownership. This typically occurs only when the user perceives an acceptable risk based on the facts surrounding the work and the user at issue, and almost always after the user has performed some degree of due diligence in attempting to locate the copyright owner based on the limited contextual information available. This appears to be the case for both experienced users of copyrighted works, as well as for members of the public generally.").

[43]   *Id.* at 22.

[44]   People write for free at a scale that has generally been a surprise to commentators. *See generally,* Yochai Benkler, *The Wealth of Networks*, Cambridge, Mass.: Harvard University Press (2006). One would of course need to elaborate the notion of what it means to write for free in a world in which some people appear to write for non-pecuniary but nevertheless real benefits such as reputational enhancement or improved job prospects. Drawing on examples such as Wikipedia, Benkler provides solid arguments for supposing that the revolution in user-generated content is not merely a flash in the pan. *Id.*

photographs and letters from World War II are of value in significant part because of what they can teach us about the underlying events. Nevertheless, under copyright these works are likely protected because copyright law has a low bar for what is copyrightable. A low bar may make sense all things considered but still not maximize locally with regard to ephemera.

It will often be the case that the owners do not even know they are owners. Needless to say, this sort of situation is grist for the orphan works problem; as it will, other things equal, be much more difficult to locate owners who do not even know that they are owners, and hence will take no efforts to be locatable. Say, for example, a World War II veteran died and his children leave his war photos to the state historical society. Unless they are lawyers, they will not realize that when they gave the physical work away, unless acting explicitly to the contrary, they nevertheless retained the copyright in the work. If years later the archive wanted to use some of these works in an exhibit, for it to be law abiding, it would need to secure permission to display these works or to reproduce any of them, say for a catalogue, promotional materials, or even for postcards in the institution's gift shop. Here the worth of the works may be minimal in terms of market value, the owners hard or impossible to track down, and the owners not aware of their ownership, but nevertheless, copyright law may serve as a powerful disincentive for the use, due to the potential for large statutory damages.[45] If authorization is required, most such works would never be used. This example demonstrates how distorted the copyright policy discussion has become when it focuses so heavily on unauthorized copying of works created and promulgated for commercial purposes.

The goal then is to create one set of copyright rules that will protect explicitly commercial works but not overprotect ephemeral works. This means that copyright law must contain a rule that allows for drawing a distinction between these two types of works. Copyright law's traditional means to draw this distinction is with the fair use doctrine. The doctrine would indeed appear capable of distinguishing such cases by means of its multi-factor analysis. As noted above, the complaint against the fair use test is not that it might not work in this instance but that the outcome is sufficiently uncertain. Museums and archives claim that fair use is too shaky a ground upon which to base their potentially large and very public uses of orphan works. Due to the safe harbor it provides, the Orphan Works Report would provide greater certainty, which will work in favor of greater use.

---

45 Report, at 12.

An interesting feature of the Orphan Works Report is that while it is a distinct proposal for dealing with orphan works from how they would be dealt with under fair use doctrine and while the Orphan Works Report explicitly attempts to uncouple its role with regard to orphan works from that of fair use, nevertheless, the Orphan Works Report incorporates a few central elements from fair use analysis, either explicitly or implicitly. Three of the most important factors in fair use analysis are the consideration of superseding versus transformative uses, commercial versus noncommercial uses, and whether the works drawn from are factual versus creative in nature. Curiously, each of these key features of fair use analysis is touched upon in the Report but within an orphan works rubric. The Report echoes fair use doctrine by giving favored treatment to transformative uses. Transformative works are given special treatment with regard to injunctive remedies and the reliance principle. The proposal would limit the ability of the copyright owner to obtain full injunctive relief in cases where the user has transformed the orphan work into a derivative work like a motion picture or book, preserving the user's ability to continue to exploit that derivative work.[46]

The Orphan Works report says little to distinguish creative from more factually based works. Presumably the distinction would count for something here as well. What is typically said in a fair use context is that factual works receive "thin" protection. Thus, a court is more likely to find fair use when such works are concerned. Conventional normative logic would seem to call for the principle of this protection to be generalized apart from a fair use context, as the background First Amendment concerns that animate the distinction in the fair use context do not disappear once fair use is no longer an issue. In other words, works of a factual nature are perhaps less deserving of protection in an orphan works context as well. How this would be operationalized in the orphan works context is that the requirement for a reasonably diligent search will be less stringent if the work is more factual in nature. This intuitively seems right as it, for example, would require less searching prior to use of a casually taken photograph by an everyday camera user as compared to the use of an artistic photograph taken by an established professional photographer such as Ansel Adams. The former is more factual and the latter is more aesthetic.

The Orphan Works report says fairly little about the commercial use consideration but what it does say is important.[47] Most important, com-

---

[46]   Report at 11.

[47]   In fact, the Report's treatment of the issue is brief to the point where one of the few commentators on the topic thus far appears to have misread the

mercial uses may be open to the safe harbor afforded by the proposed legislation. Some commentators had sought to restrict the treatment to non-commercial uses. The Copyright Office rejected this approach.[48] As noted earlier, the commercial aspect matters for purposes of the appropriate remedy limitation. The not-for-profit libraries and archives fought for a rule that would have sharply divided commercial from non-commercial entities. It may be wise to do so as the brunt of owners' objections to unauthorized uses are largely aimed at for-profit uses of their works. Such commercial uses, if permitted under a permissive orphan works rule, would be likely to swamp the size of uses by museums, archives and the like. There are a relatively small number of such institutions and they must receive outside funding in order to operate. By contrast, if orphan works could be incorporated into for-profit business models, it would be reasonable to predict a growth in such uses until a market equilibrium is reached in which all economically viable free uses of such works have been exploited. Thus, commercial use poses a greater threat to owners.

A reason for the not-for-profits to fight for separate treatment is that they arguably have a better case within copyright tradition for claiming special treatment. Libraries get special treatment under section 108 of the Copyright Act.[49] It is reasonable for museums and archives to argue that they are like libraries in that their mission is not to make money but to promote knowledge by serving as cultural repositories.

It is of interest then that the Copyright Office resisted this invitation to draw a bright line rule in favor of a more nuanced approach in which the commercial/non-commercial distinction is relevant but not dispositive. This can be seen as tracking the approach developed in recent case law with respect to fair use, where the trend has been away from making commercial use a determining factor.[50] Nevertheless, noncommercial works

---

Report on the issue. Simon Ting, *The Orphan Works Dilemma and Museums: An Uncomfortable Straight Jacket*, 2 J. Of Intellectual Property Law & Practice 30, 37 (2007).

[48]   The Copyright Office seems correct in refusing to draw a bright line as the commercial, non-commercial distinction can be uncertain. There is no clear bright line, nor does it help when, for example, museums sell reproductions in their gift shops.

[49]   17 U.S.C. § 108 (2004).

[50]   The *Sony* court had placed greater emphasis on the test of commercial use. See, *Sony Corp. of Am. v. Universal City Studios, Inc.*, 464 U.S. 417 (1984). The Campbell court, however, de-emphasized commercial use as dispositive in favor of giving greater importance to the consideration of whether the use was transformative. See *Campbell v. Acuff-Rose Music, Inc.*, 510 U.S. 569 (1994).

do receive privileged treatment by the Orphan Works proposal. The Copyright Office raises the distinction in a few contexts. Most important, as noted above, it propounds a bright line rule whereby noncommercial uses would not be subject to monetary damages.[51]

Some commentators on the Orphan Works Report have complained that it does not guarantee outcomes as a user must still show reasonableness to qualify for the safe harbor.[52] This is the nature of tort liability, however. A fault standard is a different standard from strict liability, but it is still a standard. Noteworthy is the Report's response to this objection. The Copyright Office makes the pragmatic points that assuming the user has done her reasonably diligent search, it is unlikely that the owner will surface and even if she does, the damages are likely to be small.[53]

As I noted at the outset, it is my contention that the U.S. Copyright Office's proposal for legislative change with regard to the treatment of orphan works can be aptly characterized as another instance in which U.S. copyright law is moving in the direction of layering elements of a fault liability regime into what has historically been a domain governed by strict liability. As we saw, the proposal is actually a normative hybrid of sorts in that it has an attribution requirement, which is foreign to U.S. copyright law, but clearly a feature that would make the proposal more palatable, or at least less objectionable, to other Berne countries with copyright regimes built on a moral rights normative foundation.

At numerous places throughout the long Report, the Copyright Office touches on various issues going to the broader topic of international harmonization, that is, a more globally collectivist regulatory approach to orphan works.[54] At one point, however, the Report comes clean in its frank recognition that there is a core moral rights concern that is at odds with the Report's policy prescriptions. As the Report notes, in the world it envisions, it may come to pass that an orphan works owner resurfaces only to discover that a user has used her work in a manner that she finds "offensive."[55] The Report notes, "Several commentators pointed out that if there are no limits on the way that users can use an orphan work, it is

---

[51]   Report at 11.
[52]   Report, at 109 (citing July 26 Roundtable Tr. At 17 "The biggest problem was a reasonable search is you never – you don't know if [what] you've done will satisfy a court and that what you've done really would be considered a reasonable effort search. You don't have the certainty." (Statement of Jonathan Band, Library Copyright Alliance).
[53]   See, *e.g.,* Report at 11.
[54]   Report at 89.
[55]   *Id.*

possible that a user will use it in a way that the author would consider offensive. This might violate the author's moral rights."[56] The Report's response notes in a matter-of-fact manner that "No helpful suggestions were made as to how to solve this problem (other than avoiding an orphan works provision altogether)."[57] What the Copyright Office is saying, in so many words, is that the policy proposal it supports will involve some inevitable tradeoffs and that, as is evident at least in this case, the Copyright Office recognizes the tradeoff but evidently thinks it is worth it. Indeed, it is in light of this that one might better appreciate the proposal's requirement of attribution as a sort of Solomonic compromise between parties who may in the abstract seek greater harmonization with the opportunity for collective solutions involving larger collectives, but come from different normative starting points.

Coming back to the topic of fault liability, it is notable that the Report never makes an explicit mention with respect to any shift in liability standards. Instead, its dominant way of characterizing the proposal is as a change in remedies.[58] Indeed, as discussed above, it is true that there would be an important change in remedies, a huge one, under the proposal. Nevertheless, it is true as well that the sorts of actions that lead to qualifying for the remedy will have changed as well; namely, the user must establish that her use was subsequent to a reasonably diligent search. Thus it is not only the remedy that has changed but also the sort of behavior that may lead to the remedy being awarded. In the past, it was enough that the user used the work without authorization in order to be liable, regardless of whether or not a search for the author – reasonable or otherwise – was conducted. By contrast, what we find now is a form of fault standard, which says in effect that liability for unauthorized use of orphan works is not strict liability but instead takes into account the reasonableness of the copier's behavior with respect to the unauthorized use. It is perhaps understandable that the copyright office downplay this implication of its proposal, given that the law generally prefers to move incrementally. For theoretical purposes, however, it is of value to rightly conceptualize the shift in liability standards implied by the Orphan Works proposal because there may be implications of shifting to a fault standard.

The most apparent implication is that there is a connection between the liability standard and the sorts of damages that may be appropriate.

---

[56] Report, at 89.
[57] *Id.*
[58] *Id.* at 127.

Copyright law in the United States is conceptualized as a tort. In tort, there are three liability standards, not one. The important consideration for present purposes is that punitive damages are generally associated with intentional misconduct or negligent conduct that rises to the level of recklessness, but are not seen as appropriate in the context of fault-based injuries. The connection to copyright is that punitive damages function like statutory damages in copyright. With this in mind, it becomes clearer why the Orphan Works proposal implicitly links together a move toward fault liability with a move away from statutory damages. This factor is particularly significant for amateur digital content, for, as the Report notes, actual damages may be zero, especially in "non-commercial," that is, "amateur" settings.[59]

With regard to the reasonableness test, the Report is not specific as to the formula for the test. It thus begs to be treated as the concept of reasonableness is treated in tort generally, which means that there is no one conventional way but instead deeply contested alternative conceptions from the Hand Test to non-economic conceptions such as corrective justice or civil recourse.[60] What these alternatives share is more important than what divides them: what they share is that it is not enough to show mere causation to establish liability, there must be fault as well. The divergent views come in specifying the nature of the fault. Consider the Hand Test as an exemplar of the manner in which these more general templates may be laid over copyright. With the Hand Test, the B (burden) is a function of the P x L (the loss, discounted by the probability of its occurring); so the smaller the L, the smaller the B. Note that under this test, the lack of real damages in a typical amateur use of unauthorized content is a blessing to the potential defendants, as the smaller the potential injury, the smaller the amount of precaution that is required under a standard Hand Test application.

If we return to the issue raised in the Introduction, the relevance of the individualism/collectivism divide, the preceding discussion has provided

---

[59]   Report at 12.

[60]   See *e.g.,* Jane Stapleton, *Evaluating Goldberg and Zipursky's Civil Recourse Theory*, 75 Fordham L. Rev. 1529, vol. 75, note 48, at 1540 (2006) (citing Benjamin C. Zipursky, *Rights, Wrongs, and Recourse in the Law of Torts*, 51 Vand. L. Rev. 1, note 2, at 5 (1998) (noting that "a private right of action against another person. . .exists only where the defendant has committed a legal wrong against the plaintiff and thus violated her legal right."); Benjamin C. Zipursky, *Rights, Wrongs, and Recourse in the Law of Torts*, 51 Vand. L. Rev. 1, 56 (1998) ("This point applies in the context of every kind of tort. Someone who uses another's property without consent, absent some justification, has trespassed and invaded another's legal rights in his property whether or not she ultimately compensates him.")

some insight into this dichotomy in the context of the regulation of orphan works. If individualism is about giving primacy to individual rights over general welfare, this goal is *not* served by giving greater recognition to the rule of fault in determining liability. A fault standard creates a greater burden for an owner of copyright to sue and so diminishes the value of the right, and in this way the individual interest is diminished in favor of those users for whom it would be particularly unfair to suffer a possible strict liability determination, in light of the fact that it was not reasonably possible for them to contact the owner. Accordingly, the application of a fault liability standard in these circumstances favors the collective mass of everyday users.

As noted, however, one can also use the concept of a collective solution as one that applies across copyright regimes. As we saw, despite the Copyright Office's efforts to paper over the differences, there is a fundamental disconnect between the world envisioned by the Orphan Works Report and the world preferred by the copyright regimes that seek to vindicate author's moral rights, at least as these rights have traditionally been understood. It would appear then that if the U.S. Copyright Office's preferred solution to the orphan works problem is to achieve status as a collective solution across Berne-compliant copyright regimes, compromise is called for in terms of the sorts of moral rights protected and how they must be protected. Specifically, as seen above, resurfacing owners' offense at particular uses may need to be left without redress.

8. The necessity to collectivize copyright – and dangers thereof

Jens Schovsbo[1]

1. INTRODUCTION

My title calls for attention in two directions. Firstly, I will reflect on the claim that copyright "needs" to be collectivized. Secondly, I will describe some of the dangers – and benefits –associated with this. These two aspects are closely interlinked: if one accepts that there is a need to collectivize copyright then probably one would also be willing to accept some level of danger. If on the other hand, there is no clear need to collectivize copyright then why accept the unpleasant by-products of such a process? In this way, the title also indicates that any decisions to further or to restrict "collectivization" of copyright involve a balancing of interests. It is my basic premise that the purpose of such balancing should be to further societal interests at large rather than the interests of special groups be that authors, users or collecting societies. In this regard the collectivization of copyright is an interesting case. It shows how copyright has been and is being used in practice in ways to overcome some of the structural limitations which are built into the copyright system when it comes to mass uses. At the same time, it demonstrates how copyright as part of that process has been transformed from a system based on property rules to a system based *also* on liability rights. And how it has survived. In this way the following may include lessons for other IPRs.

I will focus on the traditional aspects of copyright, i.e., the exclusive rights associated with (individual) authorship of literary and artistic works (in particular music) and on the role of the "author" (i.e. the individual creative person). I do so because these are the areas where collectivization has come the furthest. At the same time, they are the most problematic

[1] Professor, dr.jur., PhD, University of Copenhagen, Centre for Information and Innovation Law (CIIR). Thanks for comments from my colleagues at the University of Copenhagen, Thomas Riis and Peter Roth.

as seen from a traditional copyright perspective. I will concentrate on the collectivization which is related to the *collective rights administration* of (individual) copyright. Issues such as joint authorship, etc., will not be discussed. Nor will clearing houses or similar mechanisms which are only aimed at facilitating contacts between individual "buyers" and "sellers". I will thus only deal with "collective management" which contains what Ficsor (2002) calls "true 'collective' elements" including an organization (a "collecting society") which is capable of licensing the use of copyright-protected works and as part of this function negotiates fees, collects and distributes royalties and monitors the use of the works on behalf of the authors. I will discuss the effects of the process of collectivization and the general consequences of this to copyright law and will not address specific models of rights' administration as such (see for an overview notably Ficsor (2002)).

2. "COLLECTIVIZATION"

First, I will identify copyright's basic norms and describe how this leads to a starting point of individual transactions. Secondly, I will describe how in reality rights are being used collectively and how that changes some of the basic notions of copyright.

2.1 Copyright and Exclusivity

Ideologically, copyright is based on liberalistic and individualistic grounds. The copyright *exclusivity* makes it possible for authors to prevent third parties from copying or making available original works for the duration of protection (normally 70 years after the death of the author). Copyright's exclusivity is thus an example of a "property rule", i.e., a "legal entitlement which cannot be removed without prior bargaining with the author" (Kur and Schovsbo (2009) 2 with references notably to Calabresi & Melamed (1972) 1092). For this reason, publishers and other users must enter into agreements with authors in order to publish music, books, etc. Exclusivity also covers "secondary uses" such as the public performance or the uploading/making available of recorded music and so radio stations, web-casters, etc., also need permission. For works which have been published permission is normally needed from both the author and the publisher.

   The individual character of copyright also lies at the very heart of the basic Continental European and US criterion for deciding the scope of copyright. In order for something to be protected by copyright it must be "original" in the sense that it is the result of a personal, creative effort by a natural person (i.e. the "author"). Some (European) copyright laws take the point even further and see copyright not just as an individual but as a *personal* right and protect also authors' moral rights (e.g. von Lewinski (2010) at pp. 50–54).

Copyright isn't intended to protect authors for their own sake. The purpose of copyright is to benefit society at large and it is for this purpose that copyright grants authors exclusivity. Exclusivity is thought to benefit society by furthering innovation and creativity because it enables authors to include their costs of creativity in the price of their works. This makes it sensible for a rational *homo economicus*-author to create because she will be able to recoup her costs. As seen from an economic perspective, exclusivity is thought to benefit the public because the value of the innovation market made possible by copyright exceeds the societal costs associated with the overprize (monopoly profit) paid by consumers. Copyright is based on the basic assumption that the public benefits in innovation and creativity exceed the private gains of authors. Copyright relies on the market to deliver the reward to the author. This obviously presupposes that the author is able to sell her work and to receive a payment which reflects her costs. To do so, a market-place must exist where authors and users can meet and agree on the terms for the use.

Finally, it's a basic assumption in copyright that the societal benefits arise when the exclusivity is afforded to the "author" (and not to, say, a publisher) and that the author's right corresponds to her contribution to society. The rules on authorship and exclusivity in this way serve to connect the system of benefits to the production of new works. The real link of course is money in the form of payment from a user of the work to the author who without this reward would not – it is the basic copyright claim – have made the work.

2.2   Why Collectivization?

Given the starting points of exclusivity, individuality and personality it may come as a surprise that in reality large portions of copyright such as the rights to receive compensation for secondary uses in connection with public performances, broadcasting of music or photocopying of books, etc., have for many years been exercised collectively through collecting societies (see on the historical development in the music business from the "dark and dingy Parisian theatres" in the 1700s to on-line licensing and the internet (Gervais (2006)). The legal drivers behind these schemes differ (for a full overview, Ficsor (2002) and (2006)). In this chapter the focus is on organizations which have been set up voluntarily by authors (such as composers) who in this way choose to "contract into liability rules . . ." (Mergers (1996)). Sometimes, however, collectivization is the result of specific legislation which may provide for (remuneration) rights which can only be exercised collectively (e.g. EU Satellite and Cable Directive, Article and Council Directive 93/83, art. 9(1), 1993 O.J. (L 248) 15 (EEC)) or of "hybrid models" such as Extended Collective Licenses which rely on a combination of law and contracts (e.g. Riis and Schovsbo (2010)).

2.2.1 Collectivization and liability rules

It's a common feature of collective rights administration of copyrights that it transfers the ability to enter into agreements for the use of protected works from the authors and to the societies which in various ways exercise the exclusive right on behalf of the author. As a result, authors lose the ability to prevent third parties from using their works. In this way, the effects of collectivization can be described as a twist of the base line for the copyright system from a "property rule" (supra 2.1.) and to a *"liability rule"*, i.e., "a legal structure permitting third parties to undertake certain actions without prior permission, provided that they pay compensation for the trespass" (Kur & Schovsbo (2009) 2).

Before the discussion below it's an important point to note that the process of collectivization of copyright and the resulting substitution of the property right with the liability right base line to a very high degree is the result of active choices made by authors to set up collecting societies. As will be demonstrated, *infra 2.2.2.*, this choice is totally rational, given the forms of uses which are covered by exclusivity. Collectivization, therefore, should not just be seen as the choice of a handy way of administering rights. It's also a rejection of the business model identified by copyright law, i.e., the model of individual contracting for the use of individual works.

2.2.2 Why collectivization?

There are two basic arguments for collectivization; an economic and a cultural. These are closely interlinked – the cultural argument, for instance, obviously also presupposes an adequate remuneration of the author – but for the present purposes it makes sense to make a distinction.

The economic argument According to the economic argument collectivization is triggered by a market failure in connection with the identification and negotiation of a large number of individual contracts (generally Handke and Towse (2007)). As seen from this perspective the main point of collectivization is to overcome *transactions costs*. This is done by setting up a transaction mechanism in the form of "collecting societies" which can turn the "useless" individual rights into "useable bundles" (Heller (1998)). In this regard collectivization of copyright has been enormously successful.[2]

The transaction cost argument is based on several assumptions. As seen from a legal perspective the need for collective mechanisms arises because exclusivity also covers secondary uses of a work. If copyright's exclusivity had been "thinner" and, for example, ceased with the transfer of the "property right" in a physical copy of – say – a music CD then collective rights administration would probably not have been needed. The buyer of the CD – for example a radio station – would just have been able to use that copy for its shows. By granting exclusivity also in the "public performance" of the CD, however, copyright exclusivity has created a market which cannot in any rational way be dealt with by individual contracts. This is so because rights for secondary uses are particularly difficult for authors and users to negotiate on an individual basis because the possible uses may not be known at the outset and finding the right price even though the use is known is inherently complicated. As seen from a market point of view, it's also a basic assumption that users need access to large amounts of works. If a radio station wanted to use only one single music-CD it would be feasible to make a contract with the author concerning that CD. Radio stations, however, need access to a large amount of music; indeed to "music" in the abstract.

The combination of a broad scope of exclusivity and a need for access to a multitude of different works mean that users need to contract with many authors and, since this involves transactions costs, an absence of effective transactions mechanisms would either lead to unauthorized use, or to a very limited use, or none at all. This in turn would not benefit the goals of copyright law as the authors would not be compensated and therefore eventually no – or very few – works would be produced – to the detriment of society in general.

As seen from an institutional point of view the transaction-cost argument presupposes a set-up which enables an organization to enter into contracts concerning the use of copyright. This further requires a legal basis either in the form of special provisions in the copyright legislation,

---

[2] CISAC, the International Confederation of Societies of Authors and Composers, according to its website (www.cisac.org) represents 225 authors' societies from 118 countries and indirectly represents more than 2.5 million creators within all the artistic repertoires: music, drama, literature, audio-visual, graphic and visual arts. In 2007, the total amount of royalties collected by CISAC's member societies, on their own national collection territories, came to more than €7.14 billion (64 per cent of which comes from the EU).

or contracts between rights holders and the organization and between the organizations and users. In order for the transactions to take place, it also takes physical structures in the form of an organization to monitor the deals, distribute the fees, and so on. To benefit from economies of scale, benefit societies will have to use standardized contracts and procedures. For works such as music, which can be enjoyed despite differences in languages, the organization finally needs to be international in order to give access also to the music of foreign authors.

Last but not least, the whole set up is based on the basic premise that facilitating access in this way is more beneficial to authors and users than the alternative. From the perspective of the author this means rewards which are higher than those which could have been achieved by individual negotiations and from that of the users' lower fees. It's also part of the story, however, that access to alternative models may be restricted because of the contracts between authors and organizations. This may have lock-in effects. If the transfer of rights to the organization is exclusive then it's very difficult for users to get around the model because authors would have to opt out of the organization in order to be able to make individual contracts. An alternative to collective licensing could also arise because of the development of new technologies, see more *infra* 2.2.4.

The cultural argument The cultural argument emphasizes how collectivization (including the setting up of organizations) serves to protect authors against users to make sure that authors receive their copyright reward. This view sees the societies not only as exchange mechanisms but also – and maybe primarily – as "Authors Guilds" ("Unions"). As seen from this perspective, collectivization is not only a means to make sure that right holders are compensated for the use of their works, but also that their rights are respected as such. As an integrated part of this argument many organizations would see it as being a part of their mission to support a national (or even European) "culture" in a broader sense, for example by grants to members or by prizes (European Parliament Study (2009)). In the same vein Helfer (2006) points out that also a human rights perspective on copyright may support collective rights administration, as such, because it prevents infringement, collects and distributes authors' compensation and makes it possible to maintain the author's individual control over their copyright.

2.2.3 Balancing the interests

It is worth pointing out at the outset that there are obvious *tensions* between the two arguments mentioned above. A very basic tension is that the economic argument only favours collective licensing to the extent that no "better" (i.e. no more efficient) alternatives exist. If more efficient models ever became available then the economic argument for collective licensing would vanish. The economic argument thus only sees collective licensing as an acceptable "second best" solution until something better turns up. The cultural argument, however, sees collective rights administration as having an inherent value of its own such as the "protection of authors" or even "culture". Another basic difference between the two positions is that whereas the economic argument basically seeks to weaken exclusivity by turning the individual rights into manageable bundles, the cultural argument is based on the assertion of exclusivity as an "authors' prize". Similarly, the economic argument is driven by a claim of increased efficiency which points to a constant streamlining of the administration, the use of standard contracts, and so on, (to fully enjoy economies of scale advantages) whereas the cultural argument would often point out that the organizations should also pursue softer and non-economic goals such as "the institutionalisation of a certain amount of solidarity between authors" including the protection for weaker authors such as younger and not particularly popular ones (European Parliament Study (2009) 18).

The traditional *copyright perspective* in the Berne Convention is that copyright is based on a system of exclusivity.[3] In order for member countries to live up to their obligations to give exclusive rights to the public performance or reproduction[4] (or to making works available[5]) it is thus not enough to put into place copyright rules which make sure that rights holders receive compensation for the use of their works by liability rules. Where Berne prescribes for exclusive rights it is required by the states to use exclusivity as the means of remuneration of authors. From this perspective, prima facie, rules which lead to collectivization of exclusive rights are acceptable only if they are voluntary and serve as instruments for the administration of the authors' individual exclusive rights.[6] Mandatory collective models which include compulsory elements

---

[3] Berne Convention Article 9(1): "authors of literary and artistic works protected by this Convention shall have the *exclusive right* of authorizing the reproduction of these works, in any manner or form." The position in TRIPS is similar.

[4] See the Berne Conventions Articles 10 (reproduction) and 11, 11*bis* and 14 (public performance).

[5] WIPO Copyright Treaty Article 8 (WIPO Performances and Phonograms Treaty Articles 10).

[6] The limitations in the Berne Convention (and TRIPS) do not apply to rights which are not provided for as exclusive rights but only as rights to remuneration (such as the resale right, cf. Berne Convention Article 14*ter*). For such rights

and, for instance, prevent authors from exercising their rights individually would fall foul of the Berne Convention, unless especially provided for notably by Article *11bis* which allows for compulsory licensing on broadcast rights. Furthermore, the scope of the limitations which follow from the Berne Convention may be difficult to define very precisely. These difficulties are mostly due to the fact that the three-step-test,[7] which is the basic rule for assessing national limitations in copyright law, is inherently vague and difficult to apply. As seen from a copyright perspective, collective licensing is thus also seen as the *second best* option compared to individual transactions and something to be used only where – as stated by Ficsor – individual exercise of rights "due to the number and other circumstances of uses . . . is impossible or, at least, highly impracticable" (Ficsor (2002) 158). For these reasons one could fear that an overly restrictive interpretation would prevent national legislators from experimenting with new collective models on the fringes of the international rules.[8]

Even though the international copyright rules limit the extent to which collectivization may take place they obviously also allow it to a rather large extent. This, however, does not mean that there are no tensions between the present state of collectivization and copyright. It would thus seem to be obvious that the *process of collectivization* in itself contains elements which tend to erode the individualistic starting point of copyright law. A tension exists between the principles of exclusivity and individuality on which the Berne Convention is built and the logic which is contained in any initiative involving collectivization of the rights. It's important to recognize that this effect is not an incidental by-product of collectivization. It is exactly the idea of collectivization that users *cannot* negotiate individual contracts and that authors *cannot* give permissions on an individual basis.

---

mandatory rules on collective administration are not prevented by the Berne Convention (Ficsor 2006).

[7] The three-step-test originates in the BC article 9(2) but from there it has spread and a related and more general rule is now found in TRIPS Article 13 on "*Limitations and Exceptions*", which reads: "Members shall confine limitations or exceptions to exclusive rights to certain special cases which do not conflict with a normal exploitation of the work and do not unreasonably prejudice the legitimate interests of the right holder."

[8] See as an example of this Riis and Schovsbo 2010 on the Danish rules on Extended Collective Licenses which may be problematic in the light of the three-step-test even though they are wanted by broad circles in Denmark including authors and publishers and they provide for workable solutions to contentious issues such as Orphan Works and compensate authors.

The process of collectivization thus incorporates a logic that is based on an entitlement model more akin to a liability rule than a property rule.

Against this background one could point out that the present state of international copyright law is characterized by being based on a fundamental schism between an ideal world of exclusivity and property rules, which is to a large extent only a mirage and a reality character- ized by liability rules (Kur and Schovsbo (2009)). At the same time, however, one should also recognize that collective administration has long been part of the very fabric of international copyright law. By col- lectivization the exclusivity becomes manageable and this has undoubt- edly paved the way for part of the expansion of copyright to cover situations involving mass uses. If authors were generally unable to exer- cise their rights, for example, of making the work available by wireless means then the pressure to expand copyright to cover such secondary uses would arguably not have been strong. Collectivization of copyright has thus fertilized the ground for an expansion of copyright to areas such as secondary uses in the form of public performance etc. In this way there is (or at least till now, *infra* 2.2.4., has been) a *complementary relationship* between copyright's broad exclusivity and collective rights administration as the one doesn't make sense without the other. A dog- matic view on copyright as a right of "exclusivity" can be accused of overlooking this relationship and for failing to recognize how the use of liability rule elements in copyright has helped make copyright become what it is to day.

2.2.4   Digitization, DRM and collectivization
The technological developments in terms of digitization and the use of Digital Rights' Management systems (DRM) have a great impact on copyright in general and certainly also on collective rights administration.

Firstly, in the digital technologies the expansion of copyright to cover "every copy" (in the EU see the notorious Infosoc.-Directive, European Parliament and Council Directive 2001/29 article 2, 2001 O.J. (L 167) 10 (EC)) has meant that the potential number of (reproduction) rights which have to be dealt with in any technical process of use of works has exploded. Adding to the need to license also the right to communicate to the public the result is what Professor Gervais (2006) calls a "fragmentation" of copyright. This potentially increases the need for collective administration to "de-fragmentize" and "simplify" copyright and the licensing process (Gervais, *ibid*).

Secondly, the new technologies have also opened the door to what may lead to an alternative to collective administration, at least as far as on-line use is concerned. Such systems may not only lead to individual clearing of rights but also to models which are not linked to a particular territory. This latter point is particularly complicated in the EU context where rights administration has traditionally been linked to the individual member countries and where the local collecting societies often see their "cultural" mission as being linked to the national territory of "their" Member State.[9]

Finally, the term "digitization" is normally – and also here – used rather broadly to refer to "technological changes". It's trite to note that these go faster and faster and also that developments take us in unforeseen directions (imagine that Facebook hardly existed 5 years ago). In a world of rapid changes what is needed of the legal structures is the ability to *adapt* to changes. The collecting societies themselves have been developed because of changes in technologies (broadcast, reprography etc.) Collecting societies will no doubt also be part of the changes brought about by the internet, DRM etc. The point to make here is, however, that because the collecting societies have been born in the "old world" there is also a risk that they will oppose changes from emerging technologies merely because they are "new" and different and challenge their business models and traditional ways of thinking. This risk is particularly pertinent because the new technologies would indeed seem to be capable of making individual rights' administration possible to an extent otherwise unheard of. A development towards a more individualized licensing situation would no doubt pose many challenges and new risks such as those related to the identification of authors, to the potential misuse of authors by unfair contracts, or to the "Americanization" of culture. It's one of the challenges, however, to make sure that collecting societies do not use their power to prevent the future developments of new administration models simply because they are not based on the collective structures of the societies (also Ficsor (2006), Gervais (2006) and Handke and Towse (2007)).

3. COLLECTIVIZATION AND INSTITUTIONS

Collective rights' administration comes with institutions for the administration of copyright ("collecting societies"). Collecting societies may be privately owned (by authors) or owned by the state ("public"). For

---

[9] See notably Commission Recommendation of 18 May 2005 on collective cross-border management of copyright and related rights for legitimate online music services, (2005/737/EC) which calls for a practice which "corresponds to the ubiquity of the online environment and which is multi-territorial", *ibid.* point 8.

the discussion it is, however, important to bear in mind that authors' organizations like all other institutions have a vested interest in maintaining a system which is dependent on their services. This has already been hinted at *supra* 2.2.4. It would also be naïve to reject that sometimes these interests would not coincide completely with the interests of users, members (i.e. authors) or "society".

The potential conflicts are the most visible as seen from the economic argument. As mentioned *supra* 2.2.1., this argument sees collective administration and thus the organizations entrusted with this as second-best solutions only. If a better – i.e. more efficient alternative – comes along the economic argument would point to that and dismiss the institutions. The collecting societies therefore obviously see alternative models such as those based on DRM-technologies as threats. One way to respond to such a threat would be to improve the administration to make it even better and more efficient. Another way would be to focus on the cultural aspects. Either way it's important when considering the legal response to collectivization in copyright to recognize the organizations as active players with views and a policy agenda of their own and not just as mindless instruments.

The existence of institutions also brings into play the discussion about the need for external control-mechanisms such as control of the organizations by specialized government agencies such as Copyright Tribunals or ministries. In stark opposition to the individual exercise of copyright, the collective administration through organizations also triggers competition law and this opens a new front for the infusion of economic arguments into copyright, *infra* 5.3.1.

4.   EFFECTS OF COLLECTIVIZATION

To sum up: collectivization has the potential to affect copyright as it is perceived in the Berne Convention and in "traditional copyright" legislation[10] fundamentally. The effects of collectivization can be measured on a number of different levels including:

---

[10]   This notion is admittedly very imprecise. One could possibly argue that the impact is most profound to systems within the *droit d'auteur* tradition. This is so because collectivization in many ways would seem to underline the economic rationales of copyright. On the other hand the "cultural arguments" identified *supra* 2.2.2. would mostly find support in countries belonging to the *droit d'auteur* tradition. The issues are too complicated to pursue within the framework of this chapter.

- the *structural* level;
- the *market* level;
- the *cultural* (value) level; and
- the *policy* level.

The changes on the *structural level* – i.e. from a "property rule to a liability rule" – are the most profound. As it was pointed out *supra* 2.2.1., the shift from "property to liability" is an unavoidable consequence of collectivization which takes place even though the collective models are in full conformity with Berne. These effects challenge copyright's basic understanding of the system as being based on property rules and exclusivity. To some extent, this understanding is clearly false and is the result of a romantic mirage. Copyright in fact is not a monolith based on "property rights" but a patch-work of rules and practices based both on property rules and on liability rules. As seen from a general, normative copyright perspective, however, the changes on the structural level towards liability rules is obviously a threat (it is "dangerous") to the copyright system as it stands today. This perspective is important because the conventions are based on a system built on exclusive rights and this marks room for manoeuvre of national copyright legislation. It's also, however, a dangerous argument because one may confuse the means of copyright – "exclusivity" – with the goals of copyright – "innovation, creativity and recognition of the author". As seen from a policy perspective it's important to bear in mind that exclusivity isn't the purpose of copyright but merely its means. As a matter of policy it's thus not possible to maintain that one should prefer exclusivity to a liability rule as such. One should prefer the entitlement model which maximizes public benefits and that may sometimes be a rule based on exclusivity and sometimes one based on liability. The lessons from copyright may also suggest that the optimum could be a *combination* of property- and liability-based elements. On the structural level collectivization in this way not only poses practical problems, but challenges copyright's own self-image as a system based on property rules.

On the level of the *market* several things happen. First and foremost, collectivization opens access to the use of works which would otherwise have been inaccessible because of transaction costs. This in turn transfers money to authors from users (who receive payment from their users and eventually the end consumers). To this process collectivization is instrumental because it makes copyright work in areas where no individual markets exist, or where such markets would be sub-optimal. At the same time, however, collectivization also changes the position of the parties on the market by strengthening the market power of authors (as represented by their societies). This may sometimes lead to a risk that "authors" misuse their market power for rent seeking or to impose unfair contract terms on users. These risks are basically of a competition law nature. Sometimes, they are regulated by special provisions in the copyright legislation. Normally, however, competition law would also be able to intervene to prevent the abuse (see more on this *infra* 5.3.1.). The balancing act here is thus to make sure that collective administration does not result in an overcompensation of authors (and collecting societies) because of market power at the expense of users and ultimately the society at large.

On the *cultural level* a number of important changes take place when compared to the traditional base line protection envisaged in the Berne Convention and traditional copyright law and their emphasis on copyright as an individual/personal right. On the organizational level the relationship between author and organization is based on contractual grounds and "authors" are here reduced to being mere "members" who must exercise their control on the actual use of their works indirectly, i.e. through the organization by invoking their member rights. This may give rise to a number of problems in making sure that a democratic culture exists in the societies and that members are heard and their views respected etc. These issues have not concerned copyright law much (even though some countries have specific rules – see notably the German Act on Collective Rights Management (*Urheberrechtswahrnehmungsgesetz*[11])). Apart from the transformation from "author" to "member" a transformation also takes place with regard to the object of copyright protection. What is to copyright a "work" which is being protected as the author's "spiritual child" is to the society a "commodity" which is being sold in bulk via blanket licences. This is part of the logic of collectivization (economies of scale). As seen on the cultural level the effect is a co-modification of the work which furthermore erodes the ground under the notion of copyright as an individual/personal right.

On the *policy* level the effect of collectivization is difficult to describe in simple terms. The point to be made here is just that the collecting societies must be expected to pursue their own agenda and that this will not necessarily correspond with what is in the best interest of authors, users or society at large. What is good to the societies is not necessarily good to

---

[11] Gesetz über die Wahrnehmung von Urheberrechten und verwandten Schutzrechten of 9 September 1965, BGBl. I S. 1294 FNA 440-12 as amended lastly by Art. 2 Zweites Urheberrecht-RegelungsG of 26 October 2007 (BGBl. I S. 2513). See for an overview Reinbothe (2006). The law includes obligations for the collecting societies both vis-à-vis members and users including rights for members to have their copyrights administered fairly and for users to be given access to works on equitable conditions. The Act is being supervised by the German Patent Office.

authors or users. The policy risk is, therefore, that the copyright system because of the lobbying of collecting societies pursues a course which is not to the benefit of the policies lying behind copyright law. This caveat is of course relevant also to individual authors or users or representatives of those, so the message here is simply to point out that collecting societies should not be expected to be any different – be that better or worse – than any other member of an interest group. The special thing about the societies, however, is that their interests unlike those of authors and to some extent users have not traditionally been internalized into the international copyright system.

5.   THE DANGERS OF COLLECTIVIZATION

Collectivization implies two set dangers: one from going too far and one from not going far enough. In the following, the focus will be on the first but it's important to bear in mind that the danger of not using the potentials of collective models to their full extent may be grave.

On the basis of the discussions above and in particular on the effects of collectivization the *dangers of going too far in the direction of collectivization* of copyright can be measured from two perspectives: "innovation dangers" and "cultural dangers".

5.1   Innovation Dangers

The innovation dangers notably include *incentive losses* from going from a property model to a liability system. Losses may also be incurred because of monopolization (misuse) or from lock-ins to certain technologies or to collective rights administration models.

As far as dealing with the incentive losses are concerned a first and basic difficulty is to correlate the level of copyright-remuneration to the level of creativity in society. The collecting societies' turnover may give some indication of the level of activity, but as copyright is about incentivizing creativity the crucial point is related to the effects on creativity of the fees raised and not to the fees themselves. This is so even though there would seem to be no doubt that within the areas where no alternative to collective licensing exist more revenue is being raised because of the societies.

If for the present purposes a (positive) correlation is thought to exist, i.e. that authors generally respond to remuneration by being creative and that the level of creativity rises with the level of remuneration, the problem of collective administration would be to consider whether those positive effects are weakened *because* of the collective administration.

Rights organizations not only collect fees but also *distribute* them and sometimes according to other criteria than use. To the extent that fees are distributed on the basis of "cultural reasons", for example to non-popular authors or old or young ones, it could be argued that the level of useful creativity in society is reduced. This would at least seem to be the traditional starting point for copyright. Copyright thus grants exclusive rights in a work no matter the societal benefits of the concrete work in question but simply because it's a "work". Protection is objective and exclusivity is based on the assumption that the protection of "works" in the abstract increases societal benefits. Copyright isn't a prize of the fine arts and protection isn't based on the notion that "this work" should be preferred compared to "that work" or that "this author" should be granted a stronger right compared to "that author". This position is obviously very sensible as copyright thus avoids putting values on the individual works (I for one wouldn't value pop or rock music much but others would disagree).

Authors' societies may of course base their distribution on soft or cultural criteria and decide to, for example, operate funds for older artists or working grants etc. The central *danger* to innovation resulting from collectivization and such activities would seem to be that collectivization may lead to the inclusion of factors and concerns (values) which are *external* when compared to copyright and that this may diminish the positive effects of copyright protection in dynamic efficiency etc. As a consequence of this it isn't possible to extrapolate as a matter of principle the effects on innovation from copyright as such to copyright which has been exposed to collective administration. This point is of particular interest to the competition law assessment. As it will be shown *infra* 5.3.1., competition law normally grants immunity as far as the "existence" of copyright is concerned. The points here indicate that collecting societies should be assessed on the basis of their merits and cannot escape liability simply by claiming to be "part of copyright".

5.2 Cultural Dangers

The cultural dangers are equally hard to measure but relate to the losses of the non-economic values which come about when authors join the society and thereby let go of the individual/personal control which copyright has given them. It's thus correct to point out that copyright is intended to benefit society. But it's equally important that copyright sets out to do so by granting individual rights. According to traditional European copyright thinking these rights are based not only on economic concerns, but also on the protection of the integrity of the authors and their personal and social interests in their works. To measure the "dangers" of collectivization these effects need to be taken into account too.

Copyright's exclusivity doesn't come with an obligation for authors to exercise the rights themselves. Normally, the economic aspects of copyright can be transferred (or at least licensed) to third parties in return for money. Authors do so, of course, all the time and most commercially interesting works make it to the market only because they are put there by producers who have contracted with authors for the publication of their works.

To the extent authors choose to use the rights of exclusivity to enter the market through a collecting society that is no problem as seen from a copyright perspective. On the contrary: authors are as a starting point free to exercise their rights in the way they want to and it's exactly for this reason that copyright should be preferred as a stimulus compared to, for example, state grants or other non-market-based incentives. At the same time, however, it's also clear that in reality authors often have little choice. If one accepts that collectivization occurs because of a market failure regarding certain uses then there simply isn't any individual market for such uses for the author to prefer to the collective marketplace and thus the society. The "choice" therefore is normally reduced to either not having the work used (or at least not receiving a fee) or joining a society. This of course is no real "choice".

Copyright's interest in the contractual and social conditions of authors is generally very limited. Copyright provides the legal framework in the form of rules on exclusivity but leaves it to authors to make the best of it. Some copyright statutes also contain rules on issues such as individual contracts. Generally, however, the rules found in the international copyright treaties do not regulate the aspects of copyright concerning the authors' *exercise* of their rights.

The rules on *droit moral* can be seen as noticeable exceptions to this principle. These rules provide authors with rights, for instance, to be named on the copy of a work. Normally, the moral rights cannot be contracted away and also have to be respected even though rights are being used according to an agreement with a collecting society. The interest in the moral aspects of authorship can be traced back to the natural law justifications of copyright law in continental Europe. Apart from the protection of the metaphysical aspects of authors' moral rights, protection is also, however, based on *social* and even *economic* aspects. The right to be named, for instance, has a social value because it allows an author to be known to society for her views and to be recognized as the author. It's also central for the branding of authors and this in turn may have significant economic value (think of Damien Hirst).

The very idea of protecting an author's broader social and economic interests is therefore not totally unknown to copyright (at least not in the *droit d'auteur*-tradition). This level of protection has not expanded in a way comparable to the economic rights of authors. Despite the fact that a large stream of an author's revenues pass through collecting societies, copyright law does generally not seek to protect the author in her relationship to a collecting society,[12] for example, by granting her a legally based right to be heard, to receive a "fair compensation", or to take part in the decision-making process of the organization. The lack of such *"member rights"* can be explained for the historical reasons indicated above. As seen from a systematic point of view it may also seem strange that copyright should provide for such rights. On the other hand: if one accepts that the protection of moral rights has a social aspect to it and ideally thinks that copyright laws should protect authors and the central aspects of their "creational life", then why shouldn't the possible harmful effects on authors resulting from their relationship to a society interest copyright law? As it will be shown in the following, copyright's lack of interest doesn't mean that authors do not enjoy some "member rights". Their protection, however, is found in *competition law* which basically serves to make sure that societies do not misuse their dominant position vis-à-vis their members. If one accepts, however, that authors should enjoy protection in their capacity of being authors and that such protection should include non-economic issues then this protection system is obviously not satisfactory.

5.3 Balancing

Apart from any internal balancing mechanisms in copyright law the most important external balancing instruments are those found in competition law. Before the final conclusions, it's therefore necessary to cover those aspects as well.

5.3.1 Competition law and collecting societies
The general relationship between IPR and competition law is complicated but it is by now generally accepted that competition law and IPR pursue common goals (i.e. "dynamic efficiency") and also that competition law may serve a "correcting factor" to IPR but only in "special circumstances" such as the misuse of a dominant position involving IPR (e.g. Schovsbo

---

[12] Some countries do, however, provide for protection, e.g. Germany, *supra* footnote 10. The EU Commission's 2005-Recommendations, *supra* footnote 8, also contains provisions on "member rights", see more *infra* 5.3.1.

(2009)). In the following, I'll briefly describe a number of cases involving collecting societies and competition law. Many countries would have addressed some of the competition law issues directly in their copyright statues. Also to those countries the competition rules, however, would often be applicable. In this sense competition law is external not only to the societies, but also to copyright law.

Competition law normally operates two basic prohibitions. The first prohibition concerns agreements between companies which limit competition (the cartel rule). The second type of rules prevents companies from "misusing" a dominant position ("monopolization") (in EU law: Article 102 in the Treaty on the Functioning of the European Union (ex Article 82 of the EC Treaty)). Authors' organizations may give rise to problems in both regards, but for the following I will focus on the issue of misuse of a dominant position and the cases involving collecting societies in the music business and the European cases.[13]

Collecting societies in the music business commit some of competition law's deadliest sins: horizontal price fixing agreements and blanket licensing. In the EU the (national) societies have, furthermore, often limited their licensing to one Member State and only offer access to music by members of other companies by way of reciprocal agreements with those companies. Despite this, collecting societies have been generally accepted by competition law as a necessary evil representing a rational and generally pro-competitive response to a marketplace characterized by "thousands of users, thousands of copyright holders and millions of compositions".[14]

To EU competition law collecting societies have always been considered as being "dominant". Competition law, however, does not ban dominance in itself. It is only if a dominant company *misuses* ("abuses") its market position that competition law intervenes. To EU competition law the basic question in this regard is whether the company "has made use of the opportunities arising out of its dominant position in such a way as to reap trading benefits which it would not have reaped if there

---

[13] From EU law and the cartel rule (Article 101 in the Treaty on the Functioning of the European Union (formerly Article 81 ECT)) see in particular the Decision from the Commission of July 16 2008 relating to a proceeding under Article 81 of the EC Treaty and Article 53 of the EEA Agreement, COMP/ C2/38.698 – CISAC. In this case 24 of CISAC's EU-based societies were found to have engaged in a concerted practice in violation of Article 101 EUT "by coordinating the territorial delineations of the reciprocal representation mandates granted to one another in a way which limits a licence to the domestic territory of each collecting society". The Decision is now pending before the Court of First Instance.

[14] *Broadcast Music Inc. v CBS Inc.* 441 US 1 (1979) 20.

had been normal and sufficiently effective competition".[15] The assessment is normally based on a comparison between the existing market conditions and those that would have existed had the company not behaved the way it did. This starting point is problematic to collecting societies because there is often no alternative market. One therefore instead tries to assess the "reasonableness" of the practice of the societies, for example by benchmarking.[16] This, however, is also a complicated thing because of the "copyright nature" of the companies which requires a distinction between the limits to competition which are part of copyright and the limitations which go beyond and are the result of the market behaviour of the companies. Phrased in the parlance of EU law one could say that the societies are "immune" to competition law as long as their activities can be described as being part of the "existence" of copyright (Schovsbo (2009)). From this also follows that the practice can be attacked if it is only an "exercise" of copyright.[17] As explained *supra* 5.1., these principles only provide limited guidance in practice and do not imply that collecting societies in practice are not subjected to competition law. At the same time, however, the following will show that the copyright dimension to a certain extent has an impact on the way competition law is being applied in these cases.

In EU competition law cases involving collecting societies have erupted both regarding users and members.

Collecting companies vs. users A number of cases involving alleged misuses regarding the relationship between societies and users have been decided over the years. Most cases have dealt with the issue of royalty

---

[15] Case 27/76, Judgment of the Court of 14 February 1978 *United Brands and United Brands Continentaal v Commission*, para. 249.

[16] Case 395/8, Judgment of the Court of 13 July 1989, *Ministère public v Jean-Louis Tournier* para. 46.

[17] E.g. Case 395/8, Judgment of the Court of 13 July 1989, *Ministère public v Jean-Louis Tournier* and the references to the acceptance of practices necessary to "safeguard the interests of the authors, composers and publishers of music" e.g. in paras 31 and 33. See as the latest example Case C-52/07, Judgment of the Court of 11 December 2008, Kanal 5 v. STIM, where the dilemma is spelled out in the following way: "30. In so far as those royalties are intended to remunerate composers of musical works protected by copyright with respect to the television broadcast of those works, it is necessary to take into consideration the particular nature of that right. 31 In that context, it is appropriate to seek an appropriate balance between the interest of composers of music protected by copyright to receive remuneration for the television broadcast of those works and those of the television broadcasting companies to be able to broadcast those works under reasonable conditions."

calculation (see also Handke and Towse (2007) on the complicated economics involved). From the present perspective the most interesting aspect would seem to be the question of to what extent competition law is willing to accept calculation principles which are not based on the actual use of music but on secondary, indirect indicators. This is interesting because a high degree of acceptance could be seen as an acceptance of the logic of collectivization and the transaction cost and economies of scale arguments.

In Tournier from 1989 the EU's Court of Justice ("ECJ"), found that the use of flat-rate royalties is permissible but only "*unless* other methods might be capable of attaining the same *legitimate aim*, namely the protection of the interests of authors, composers and publishers of music, without thereby increasing the costs of managing contracts and monitoring the use of protected musical works".[18] In the most recent case, which dealt with the calculation of royalties for the use of music from a TV-company, the ECJ remarked that the royalties should be determined in a way with "respect to the value of [their] use in trade" (para 36).[19] This meant that as a starting point it was not a misuse according to Article 102 for the company to calculate the royalties on the basis of the revenue of the company and on the amount of music used. The ECJ, however, continued that:

> it is conceivable that, in certain circumstances, the application of such a remuneration model may amount to an abuse, *in particular when another method exists* which enables the use of those works and the audience to be identified and quantified more precisely and that method is capable of achieving the same legitimate aim, which is the protection of the interests of composers and music editors, without however leading to a disproportionate increase in the costs incurred for the management of the contracts and the supervision of the use of musical works protected by copyright (para 40).[20]

Whereas the ECJ thus found that the concrete model used by STIM did not violate competition law, the court in my view with the reference to "another method" also made it clear that the admissibility of the calculation model was based on an assessment which did not just take into

---

[18] Case 395/8, Judgment of the Court of 13 July 1989, *Ministère public v Jean-Louis Tournier* para 45. Italics added.

[19] STIM, *supra* footnote 15.

[20] Italics added. According to para. 48 a discrimination of royalties according to whether the companies concerned are commercial companies or public service undertakings would likely amount to an abuse of the dominant position of the society.

account the existing system but also *alternative* models, *viz.* such which "enable the use of those works and the audience to be identified and quantified more precisely . . ." The court in this way did not provide a *blanco* acceptance of the collective remuneration model used. Instead, it conditioned its acceptance of the practices on there being no better alternative available *presently*. This line of reasoning is completely in line with the economic arguments described *supra* 2.2.2.1. and the position in copyright, *supra* 2.2.3. and thus also only acknowledges collective licensing models as a second-best solution.[21]

The ECJ would, furthermore, seem to take into account also the *cultural line* of argumentation with the remarks that any alternative models would need to protect the "interests of composers and music editors". The next part of the sentence shows, however, that what mostly seem to concern the ECJ are the economic interests and effectiveness of the arrangement (". . ., without however leading to a disproportionate increase in the costs incurred for the management of the contracts and the supervision of the use of musical works protected by copyright").

As seen from an *institutional perspective*, it's finally worth noticing how the ECJ in other parts of the decision clearly seeks to link the acceptable business practices of STIM with the "specific character of *copyright*" (point 30). As has been pointed out *supra* 5.1., the value of this statement is unclear. Not only is the "character of copyright" a somewhat unclear concept (to say the very least) but even if such "characters" could be identified one would still have to make a separate assessment of the business of the collecting society.

In this way the effect of the competition law interference regarding the

---

[21]   Directive 2001/29/EC of The European Parliament and of The Council of 22 May 2001 on the harmonisation of certain aspects of copyright and related rights in the information society imposes in Article 5(2)(b) an obligation on EU-states to make sure that authors receive a "fair compensation" in connection with the limitation which allows for private copying. In her Opinion of May 11 2010 in Case-467/08 the Advocate General Trstenjak found that Member States enjoy a "wide margin of discretion" for implementing the remuneration models which they prefer on the basis of "practical considerations", *ibid.* point 92. Should the ECJ accept this view, a similar principle would likely apply also to collective administration models in general. It is also worth noticing that the Advocate General seems to accept calculation models based on proxies for actual use (i.e. on "presumed private use") only in the absence of practical methods based on the actual private use, *ibid.* This line of reasoning thus is also based on the notion that remuneration models based on something else than the concrete use is accepted as a second-best-solution only. See more on this, Ficsor 2006.

society/user relationship is to keep the societies to the rationale of the economic argument (which is also copyright's): collective rights administration and the resulting licensing mechanisms are accepted but only to the extent that no more efficient individual models are available. Competition law would, therefore, seem to come some way in addressing a number of the dangers associated with the effects of collectivization to copyright on the innovation level and on the policy level.

Collecting societies vs. authors (members)	There have been a number of cases in the EU on misuse of market power by collecting societies in the internal relationship between society and member.[22] These cases are particularly challenging to the societies in their capacity of authors' societies because the basic claim is that the societies have failed to represent the interests of their owners and to protect them against the societies themselves. The cases are also difficult to decide because different authors obviously have different needs. It's part of the logic of being a member of any society or club that one must accept that certain decisions are being made on one's behalf and that one may not agree with all of them. If one is a member of – say – a tennis club and doesn't like the decision made by the board then one may ultimately decide to leave the club and to find another one. Authors, normally, do not have that choice. Even if an alternative society were available there would often not be any way of opting out of *collective rights administration* as such. Authors are locked in if not to a specific society then at least to the system of societies. This situation imposes special obligations on the societies. If, for instance, societies could refuse certain authors from becoming members then they would in fact "punish" the author by denying her access to compensation for the use of her works.

As seen from a competition law perspective, it's interesting to notice how the interests of authors are not limited to having their copyright upheld. Competition law looks upon authors in their capacity as "members" and "commercial entities". This perspective on the author is different from the one in copyright which focuses on the author in her capacity of a creative artist and on her personal/individual rights. Competition law has clearly made the point that authors may need protection in their capacity as "members" and that they have interests in that capacity which go beyond

---

[22]	The latest round of issues has concerned the ability of authors to benefit from the possibilities of cross-border online licensing, see the 2005 Commission Recommendation *supra* footnote 8.

those regulated by traditional copyright. These "member interests" include at the least (from the *CISAC*-decision):[23]

(i)   the cost elements (commission-related deductions, membership fees and associated costs such as pension or cultural deductions);

(ii)   the quality of service (transparency, accountability, royalty payment terms, information, legal protection and enforcement);

(iii) the benefits derived from the membership (such as pension or illness schemes); and

(iv)   the ability to collect the highest proportion of rights due to the authors. (point 134)

As seen from a traditional copyright perspective all of these points are obviously relevant and important. Despite this, copyright could generally not be expected to provide any protection of authors who find these interests to have been violated. The protection which competition law offers author-members is incidental and indirect and is triggered not by an interest in authors but in the societies and their eventual "misuse". Despite this it is submitted that the law works and that authors are better off because of competition law intervention than they would have been without it. In my view copyright should consider how to internalize these concerns. After all the need for authors to join societies to collect their reward is because of the way the copyright system has been constructed. Copyright protection has created a situation where authors have to submit to collective administration. Copyright should also make sure that the system works and that the remuneration ends up with the authors and not the societies.

6.   BALANCING THE INTERESTS: PERSPECTIVES

Collectivization includes dangers to copyright. This is no surprise. Also a system of individual copyright obviously includes dangers and collectivization should normally be seen as a rational response to some of these. The point to take on is then not that collectivization should be generally avoided because of these dangers. Instead policymakers should be *aware* of these dangers and the copyright system should have *mechanisms* in place to deal with them.

---

[23] *Supra* footnote 12. "Member rights" are also part of the Commission's 2005-Recommendation, *supra* footnote 8. These include, e.g., "equitable distribution and deductions", "non-discrimination and representation", and "accountability".

The discussions have shown that in copyright authors (to a certain extent supported by national legislation) have to a large extent opted out of the property rules provided for by law and into collective models based on liability rules. Despite this and as seen from a dogmatic view collective rights administration remains a contentious issue; a "second best" only to be preferred in the absence of individual models. This starting point is problematic. As a matter of principle, copyright should prefer collectivization if this is expected to lead to societal gains; and otherwise not. In finding the right balance, copyright ought to let itself be guided by the *public interests*. As seen from this perspective one cannot prefer property rules to liability rules. Nor can one prefer liability rules to property rules. What matters is what rule provides for the optimum level of creativity, innovation and authors' protection. To find that optimum the development in copyright indicates that a *mixture* of property rules and liability rules may be needed. Copyright also demonstrates how the right mix has to a large extent been found by trial and error. The present system for collective rights administration through authors' societies has developed from below and over many years. For such developments to take place, *flexibility* in the rules is required. At the same time, however, a certain element of *control* and maybe even firmness is required to make sure that the system does not freeze in ways that represent the limitations of an analogous past rather than the options of a digitized future.

The present copyright system would not seem to be ideal for the future developments. In order to be so, copyright should probably change its ways and address collectivization more directly than it does at present. In doing so the law should arguably *encourage* collectivization. At the same time it should seek to *control* and maybe even *restrict* it. Concrete topics for action could include:

- identifying and removing internal barriers to beneficial collectivization. This would mean, in particular, a restrictive use of the three-step-test to initiatives involving collective administration of copyright;
- regulating societies effectively to secure "innovation" interest. This would include both a static perspective relating to the business practices of the societies in connection with fees and distribution, etc. and the dynamic perspectives regarding the use and development of new and more individualized administration models;
- protecting the interests of authors more effectively, e.g. by giving them "member rights" in copyright via-à-vis organisations such as the right to become members, to be heard, and to be protected against misuse.

Defining the right regulatory model is an extremely complicated task. One task in particular is important, however: to make sure that the international copyright legal framework does not stand in the way of beneficial collectivization. As I have argued elsewhere with Annette Kur, international copyright should generally "stand back" to allow for legislative experimentation with regime shifts and one should avoid "canonizing" property rules as the only regulatory model permitted (Kur & Schovsbo (2009) 29). The experiences from the collectivization of copyright have shown that copyright has come a long way in such a direction but also that some work needs to be done. Copyright in this way can serve as an example to other IPRs.

BIBLIOGRAPHY

Calabresi, Guido and A. Douglas Melamed (1972), 'Property rules, liability rules, and inalienability: one view of the cathedral', *Harv. L. Rev.*, **85,** 1089–1128.
European Parliament Study (2009), *Collecting Societies and Cultural Diversity in the Music Sector*, Study from the Directorate General for Internal Policies, IP/B/CULT/IC/2008_136 06/2009 PE 419.110 EN.
Ficsor, Mihály (2002), *Collective Management of Copyright and Related Rights*, Geneva: WIPO.
Ficsor, Mihály (2006), 'Collective management of copyright and related rights in the digital network environment: voluntary, presumption-based, extended, mandatory, possible, inevitable?' in Daniel Gervais (ed.), *Collective Management of Copyright and Related Rights*, Alphen aan den Rijn, The Netherlands: Kluwer Law, pp.37–83.
Gervais, Daniel (2006), The Changing Role of Copyright Collectives in Daniel Gervais (ed.) *Collective Management of Copyright and Related Rights*, Alphen aan den Rijn, The Netherlands: Kluwer Law, pp.3–36.
Gyertyánfy, Peter (2010), 'Collective management of music rights after the CISAG decision', IIC, **1,** 59–89.
Handke, Christian and Ruth Towse (2007), 'Economics of copyright collecting societies', IIC, **8,** 937–57.
Helfer, Laurence R. (2006), 'Collective management of copyright and human rights: an uneasy alliance' in Daniel Gervais (ed.) *Collective Management of Copyright and Related Rights*, Alphen aan den Rijn, The Netherlands: Kluwer Law, 85–113.
Heller, M. A. (1998), 'The tragedy of the anticommons: property in the transition from Marx to markets', *Harv. L. Rev.*, **111,** 621–88.
Kur, Annette and Jens Schovsbo (2009), 'Expropriation or fair game for all? The gradual dismantling of the IP exclusivity paradigm' (Max Planck Institute for Intellectual Property, Competition & Tax Law Research Paper No. 09–14, 2009), available at http://papers.ssrn.com/sol3/papers.cfm?abstract_id=1508330.
Lewinsky, Silke von (2010), *International Copyright Law And Policy,* Oxford: Oxford University Press.

Mergers, R. P. (1996), 'Contracting into liability rules: intellectual property rights and collective rights organisations', *Calif. L. R.,* **84**, 1293–1393.

Reinbothe, Jörg, 'Collective rights management in Germany', in Daniel Gervais (ed.). *Collective Management of Copyright and Related Rights*, Alphen aan den Rijn, The Netherlands: Kluwer Law, 193–226.

Riis, Thomas and Jens Schovsbo (2010), 'Extended collective licenses and the Nordic experience: It's a hybrid but is it a Volvo or a lemon?', forthcoming in *Columbia Journal of Law and the Arts*, **33**(4).

Schovsbo, Jens (2009), 'Fire and water make steam: redefining the role of competition law' in TRIPS, Research Paper, available at http://papers.ssrn.com/sol3/papers.cfm? abstract_id=1339346.

9. Two perspectives on the proposed Google book settlement

John Cross and Fredrik Willem Grosheide

On September 20, 2005, the Author's Guild and three individual authors sued Google, Inc., in a federal district court in New York.[1] The complaint alleges that Google's deal with several major US research libraries, under which Google scans millions of books in those libraries and makes "snippets" of the books available online, constitutes "massive copyright infringement." Plaintiffs sought to have the case certified as a class action. One month later, the Association of American Publishers and individual publishing companies filed a similar case against Google in the same court.[2]

Google's primary defense in both cases is the "fair use" defense provided by US copyright law.[3] Before the court could reach the merits of the claims and defenses, however, the parties in both cases reached a tentative settlement. Numerous perceived flaws in the original proposed settlement led to further negotiations, resulting in the filing of a revised proposed settlement (hereinafter called the "RPS") in November, 2009.[4] The RPS still awaits court approval as of the time this chapter was written.

The RPS has been the subject of widespread discussion and debate among academics, authors, publishers, and the general public. While some of the comments have been generally favorable, most have been critical of one or more aspects of the RPS. Much of the criticism argues the RPS is highly favorable to Google, while unfair to certain rightholders.

---

[1] *The Author's Guild v. Google, Inc.*, No. 05-CV-8136 (S.D.N.Y., filed September 20, 2005).

[2] *McGraw-Hill Cos. v. Google, Inc.*, No. 05-CV-8881 (S.D.N.Y., filed October 29, 2005). These two cases have been effectively merged in the course of the settlement negotiations. Therefore, most of the remaining discussion in this chapter will treat the two cases as one.

[3] The fair use defense is set out in 17 U.S.C. § 107.

[4] The RPS may be found at http://www.googlebooksettlement.com/agreement.html.

This chapter also explores the implications of the RPS. However, unlike most of the commentary to date, its primary focus is not whether the actual terms of the RPS are "fair" to copyright owners and publishers. Nor will the chapter devote all that much attention to the antitrust and competition law issues raised by the terms of the RPS.[5] Instead, this chapter focuses mainly on the policy implications of the RPS. If approved in its current form, the RPS would usher in a new legal model for online distribution of books and other printed works. Many aspects of the RPS resemble the system of collective rights management currently in place for sound recordings and other types of works. At the same time, there are also crucial differences between the RPS system and these rights management organizations. Most fundamentally, the RPS would impose a collective rights management system by judicial fiat rather than by voluntary collaboration among the interested rightholders.

The other novel feature of this chapter is that it evaluates the RPS from two different perspectives: those of the United States and the European Union. Viewing the same issue from these two different perspectives affords unique insights into the various novel and complex issues involved.

Section 1 provides a brief overview of the Google Book project and the RPS. The discussion concentrates almost exclusively on the revised rather than the original settlement agreement. While the original proposal raised even starker policy concerns, that proposal is no longer on the table. In order to understand the evolution of the RPS, it is also necessary to discuss some of the basic rules governing that particularly American device, the class action. These basic class action rules also help explain many of the particular terms of the RPS. Indeed, one feature of the RPS often overlooked in the critical reviews is the inclusion of various protections and limitations that ameliorate some of the potential harm to rightholders and publishers.

Section 2 analyzes the RPS from a United States perspective. First, it explores the effect of the RPS on current rightholders. While the RPS would not, as a practical matter, result in all that great a change in the rights of known rightholders, it has a far more serious impact in the so-called "orphan works" situation, where the rightholder is unknown. This section also explores whether the RPS runs afoul of basic principles of US copyright policy. Finally, the section discusses two particular legal challenges that might be lodged against the RPS, possibly resulting in a court holding the settlement invalid.

Section 3 provides a European perspective on the RPS, focusing in

---

[5] For a brief overview of the gist of these issues, see Section 2.3.1.

particular on foreign authors. It points out that while many European rightholders will be in the class, little consideration was given to these authors in structuring the RPS. Nor did these rightholders receive any significant representation during the process of negotiation. Finally, Section 3 discusses various special issues that arise in connection with applying the RPS in the European Union.

1. OVERVIEW OF THE LITIGATION AND PROPOSED SETTLEMENT

1.1   The Google Book Project

The Google Book litigation has its genesis in Google's campaign to digitize the printed word. In the case of books and other works printed on paper, this effort involves scanning the work and adding it to Google's searchable database. Individuals may then conduct their own word searches of this database to find works that might be relevant to their area of interest. Once a person finds a book in the database, the level of access turns on the book's copyright status. If the work is in the public domain, the person may read or download the entire work. If copyright remains in force in the work, the person may view only a small "snippet" comprising a few lines of the work. Many – but by no means all – books in this latter category are "orphan works": works protected by copyright, but where the owner of the copyright is unknown or cannot be located.

The copyright law implications of this digitization are fairly obvious. Google's act of scanning works still covered by copyright constitutes the making of an unauthorized reproduction in violation of § 106(1) of the Copyright Act.[6] Allowing people to read or download such books

---

[6]   The Google Book Project actually has two separate components. The Google Library Project involves agreements between Google and major research libraries pursuant to which Google will digitalize works currently held in the libraries. The Google Partner Project involves agreements between Google and individual publishers, under which a publisher may submit works for inclusion in the database. Only the Library Project is at issue in the litigation that led to the RPS. The Partner Project has a number of aspects that limit the copyright impact. It depends on the consent of the publisher, who invariably has some sort of license to make copies of and distribute the work. The agreements used in the Partner Project also give the publisher the right to dictate how much of a book will be available in the Google online database. While these aspects do not necessarily prevent all copyright infringements – online distribution could, in theory, violate the agreement between the author and the publisher, *c.f. New York Times Co., Inc.*

is potentially an illegal public display or distribution.[7] Unless Google's acts of copying and making available are (as it claims) protected fair use, its digitization of over ten million books to date would indeed constitute "massive copyright infringement."

1.2   The Proposed Settlement

1.2.1   Basic terms

The RPS is lengthy and complex. Reduced to its essence, it deals with both Google's liability for what it *has* done as well as what Google *may do* in the future. The RPS covers not only entire books, but also "Inserts" and "Partial Inserts," all of which terms are defined in detail in the document. However, some types of printed materials, including sheet music and photographs, maps, and paintings, are not covered by the RPS, leaving those with rights in these sorts of works free to sue Google separately. In fact, a group of photographers has recently filed suit against Google seeking recovery for digitization of their works.[8]

Nor does the RPS cover all books included in the Google Book project. Books in the public domain are, of course, excluded from the RPS. Even if a work is still protected by copyright, the RPS applies only if the following two conditions were satisfied as of January 5, 2009:

1. The work was published or distributed in a bound "hard copy" (that is, in paper book form, as opposed to loose-leaf, CD-ROM, or online distribution) by or under the authorization of the copyright owner, and
2. the work is either

---

v. Tasini, 533 U.S. 483 (2001) (agreement with authors and newspapers authorizing publication in papers did not allow papers to distribute same works electronically) – they may help protect Google against a claim of infringement.

[7]   17 U.S.C. § 106(6) sets out the public display right. The distribution right is set out in 106(3).

[8]   A group of visual artists, including The American Society of Media Photographers, the Graphic Artists Guild, the Picture Archive Council of America, the North American Nature Photography Association, and a few individuals, actually sought to intervene in the main case in early 2009. The trial judge denied their petition, holding not only that the parties did not have a right to intervene, but also that the petition was filed too late. *See The Author's Guild v. Google, Inc.*, 2009 WL 3617732 (upholding initial denial of intervention). In early April of 2010, some of these organizations and others filed a separate action against Google. *American Society of Media Photographers, Inc. v. Google, Inc.*, No. 10-CV-2977 (S.D.N.Y., filed April 7, 2010).

    a.   a "United States Work" (defined in § 101 of the Copyright Act) registered with the United States Copyright Office,[9] or

    b.   a non-United States Work that was either registered with the United States Copyright Office or published in Canada, the United Kingdom, or Australia (even if such publication was not the first worldwide).

Books and inserts failing one or both of these requirements as of January 5, 2009 are completely excluded from the settlement. For example, any book first published after January 5, 2009 is not covered by the RPS. As Section 3 will discuss further, many works published abroad will likewise be excluded. Of course, those with rights in excluded works may eventually band together to strike a very similar deal with Google. Indeed, Google has even provided a mechanism whereby rightholders not covered by the RPS may negotiate directly with Google.[10]

For covered works, the RPS sets a standard measure of liability for Google's past acts. The cut-off date here is May 5, 2009. If Google scanned a covered work without the rightholder's consent on or before that date, the current rightholder is entitled to a lump sum payment. In the case of entire books, that lump sum payment is at least $60 US. Owners of Inserts and Partial Inserts will receive at least $15 US and $5 US, respectively. While Google's total liability under these terms will be at least $45 million US, many have argued that these damage figures are unconscionably low, especially given Google's brazen and widespread infringement.

The terms governing what Google may do in the future are both more

---

[9]   The requirement of registration in this definition probably reflects an erroneous interpretation of United States copyright law. While the US does not make registration a precondition to obtaining a copyright, § 411(a) of the Copyright Act does require a party to attempt to register prior to suing for infringement. For some time, there was considerable doubt whether this requirement was jurisdictional – meaning that a court could not hear the case – or simply a procedural hurdle that a party had to satisfy prior to filing suit. The Supreme Court cleared up this error in *Reed Elsevier, Inc. v. Muchnick*, 130 S.Ct. 1237 (2010). *Reed* involved a class action filed by representatives who had registered their copyrights. However, many members of the class had not sought registration. The Court held that the registration requirement was not jurisdictional, and as all the named plaintiffs had registered, the action could proceed in federal court.

Because of this decision, the RPS could conceivably be amended to cover all works protected by United States Copyright law, regardless of registration. However, it is unlikely that such a change will be made at this late date, especially given that the judge has already tentatively approved the current terms of the RPS.

[10] See http://books.google.com/books-partner-options.

complex and more interesting as a matter of policy. Google would pay a rightholder 63% of all revenues that Google receives from any commercial use of that rightholder's work. Rather than having Google account to each rightholder separately, the RPS provides for the creation of a "Book Rights Registry," which will collect and distribute these royalty payments. This Book Rights Registry is one of the truly novel features of the RPS, and has interesting implications. If the arrangement is approved by the court, Google, in collaboration with the Author's Guild and the Association of American Publishers, will have managed to create, through the judicial process, a sort of collective rights management system for books. The policy implications of this facet of the RPS are explored further in Sections 2 and 3.

If all rightholders were known and could be easily located, this rights management system could operate fairly smoothly. However, a significant majority of the works covered by the RPS are orphan works, where the author cannot easily be found. The original settlement agreement also charged the Book Rights Registry with the task of collecting royalties for these unknown rightholders. After considering significant objections to this arrangement, the parties changed this arrangement in the RPS. The RPS creates a separate and ostensibly independent Unclaimed Works Fiduciary to manage orphan works. Unlike the Book Rights Registry, which is dominated by the commercial publishers, the Unclaimed Works Fiduciary cannot be a publisher.[11] As will be demonstrated below, this change is important, as the Unclaimed Works Fiduciary plays a far more significant role concerning how a work is used than does the Book Rights Registry. The Unclaimed Works Fiduciary also presents more serious policy issues.

1.2.2 Limitations of the RPS

Before turning to the policy implications of the RPS, it is important to identify some of the limitations on the scope of the RPS. Some of these limitations stem from the nature of the class action device. Others are set out in the RPS itself. Because all of these limits directly affect the nature of the collective rights management system established in the RPS, any reasoned evaluation of the RPS must consider them.

Limitations inherent in the class action device   The class action is not unique to the United States. Other nations, most notably Canada, have experimented with the device. Nevertheless, the class action remains one

---

[11]   RPS § 6.2(b)(iii).

of the idiosyncrasies of US procedural law. Certainly no other nation uses class actions so extensively, or in such unusual ways. Due in part to the many myths set out in the popular media, there is a considerable lack of knowledge concerning how class actions actually work. Some criticism of the RPS may actually be a criticism of class actions in general, not anything peculiar to the RPS.

The basic notion of a class action is simple. A class action is a case in which one person (or one group of people[12]) represents both her own personal rights as well as the rights of others similarly situated.[13] Assuming all the requirements are met, the judgment in the case affects all members of the class. If the class prevails, all class members benefit from the judgment.[14] Conversely, if the class loses, all class members are bound. Regardless of the outcome of the litigation, class members are legally barred from pursuing separate lawsuits against the prevailing defendant.

Allowing one person to represent another in litigation is not uncommon. Organizations such as unions and trade associations often represent their members. Similarly, corporations are represented by agents. What distinguishes the class action from these more mundane situations is that the representation is ordinarily involuntary. The class members do not appoint the class representative. Instead, the class representative takes it upon himself to litigate the rights of all the class members.

Such involuntary representation involves serious concerns of fairness and conflict of interest. Accordingly, the law governing class actions has developed numerous safeguards to protect the interests of the absent class members. While a full inventory of these protections is well beyond the scope of this chapter, it is useful to discuss a few of the more important safeguards. Most of these safeguards stem from Federal Rule of Civil Procedure 23, which applies to federal cases like the Google Book litiga-

---

[12]   It is increasingly common for the class to be represented by a small group, rather than one representative. Indeed, the Google Book litigation involves multiple class representatives.

[13]   While most class actions involve a class of plaintiffs, it is also possible to have a class action involving a defendant class. Indeed, the very first class action in the United States federal courts involved a class of plaintiffs suing a class of defendants. Defendant class actions raise additional concerns. Given that the Google Book litigation involves a plaintiff class, the additional issues raised by defendant class actions are beyond the scope of this discussion.

[14]   If the case involves specific relief like an injunction, all members may enforce the injunction. If the case involves individual damages, the court may be required to calculate separate damages awards for all class members. The RPS, by providing for a lump sum payment per work, obviates much of the difficulty of calculating individual damages.

tion, or similar rules in force in the state courts. But the United States Constitution also acts as an ultimate check, providing certain core protections. The Fourteenth Amendment to the United States Constitution prevents government from depriving a person of property without affording due process of law.[15] A person's legal right to recover against another qualifies as "property" under this provision. A judgment denying the person the right to recover on that claim, or limiting the recovery, constitutes a government act "depriving" the person of that property right. Therefore, a court may enter such a judgment only if it provides due process. Due process includes a fair procedure. Moreover, it mandates that a person be afforded the chance to have her claim heard by the tribunal. A judgment that does not meet this minimum due process standard cannot bind the party whose rights were violated.

Due process does not necessarily require that a party be able to litigate her *own* rights. Representational litigation may comport with the due process clause. In the case of involuntary representation, however (that is, where the person does not choose her representative), due process is satisfied only if the representative adequately looks out for the interests of the rightholder. This basic requirement is the cornerstone of most of the limits on class actions in US law. If representation is inadequate, the class member simply is not bound.[16] A person may challenge the adequacy of representation during the pendency of the class action, or even after judgment is entered.[17]

In many respects, the various technical provisions of the class action procedural rules flesh out this basic requirement of adequate representation. Thus, for example, Fed. R. Civ. Pro. 23(a) requires that a class representative be adequate and have a claim that is typical of the class. Rule 23 also establishes various procedural mechanisms to ensure the class action is fair. First, the court must *certify* the case as a class action. Certification involves consideration of a number of factors. Second, the court must appoint the attorney for the class, considering factors such as the attorney's experience in these sorts of cases.[18] Third, even if the class is certified,

---

[15]   The Amendment has also been interpreted to bar government from taking property for public use unless it provides adequate compensation. In many situations, it is important to keep the "deprivation/due process" and "taking/compensation" protections separate. However, because the court in the Google Book case is not appropriating property for use by the public, the additional "takings" protection is not an issue.

[16]   *Hansberry v. Lee*, 311 U.S. 32 (1940).

[17]   *Id.*

[18]   Fed. R. Civ. Pro. 23(g).

class members are likely to receive notice, which gives them the chance to challenge the representative or otherwise look out for their own interests.[19] Fourth, and equally importantly, class members in certain types of class actions – including the type at issue in Google – have the right to "opt out" of the class.[20] A party who opts out of the class is not bound by any judgment or settlement, and can litigate her claims on her own behalf. Fifth, no class action may be settled or dismissed without court approval. Moreover, all class members affected by a proposed settlement must be given notice of the terms, and afforded a chance to object. This explains why the judge in the Google Book case is being asked to approve the settlement, a role judges ordinarily do not play in non-class action cases.

It is important to note that even though a settlement has been reached, the court has not yet certified a class action in the Google Book litigation. Until such certification occurs, the only parties legally bound by any settlement – or indeed any ruling of law or judgment – are the named parties; *i.e.*, Google, the Authors Guild, the Association of American Publishers, and the named individual publisher and author plaintiffs. The Google Book litigation represents an example of the increasingly common practice of a "settlement class action." In these cases, the court simultaneously certifies the class and approves the settlement that would determine the rights of the members of that class. The primary purpose of the class certification is to impose the settlement on the entire class. Of course, because the settlement negotiations precede certification of the class, class members play little, if any, role in negotiating the actual settlement terms. The only safeguards protecting the class are the self-interest of the named parties (who have interests that parallel those of the class members) and the judge's obligation to consider the interests of the class members and the fairness of the settlement prior to approving it. Because of these concerns, the United States Supreme Court indicated in a 1997 decision that settlement class actions should be the exception, not the rule.[21] However,

---

[19]   The Federal Rule distinguishes between three types of class actions, defined in Fed. R. Civ. Pro. 23(b)(1), (b)(2), and (b)(3) respectively. Most class actions fall into the third category. In the first two categories, the court *may* order notice to the class members. In the third category, the court *must* order such notice. This difference reflects that the third category presents greater problems of divergent interests between the representative and the class members.

[20]   The Google plaintiffs seek to have the class certified under the third category described in the prior note. Members of a Fed. R. Civ. Pro. 23(b)(3) class action are entitled to notice, and the right to opt out. In the other two categories, notice and opt-out are not required, but can be ordered by the judge.

[21]   *Anchem Products, Inc. v. Windsor*, 521 U.S. 591 (1977).

because the Court did not ban such class actions per se, the lower courts have continued to use them.

All of the aforementioned safeguards are present in the Google Book litigation and RPS. The court gave class members until January 28, 2010 to object to the proposed settlement. Potential class members, as well as other interested persons and national governments, filed numerous objections and comments. The RPS also preserves the class members' rights to opt out of the settlement and proceed individually against Google. However, whether many individual rightholders will avail themselves of the opportunity to strike out on their own remains to be seen. In the case of orphan works, opt-out seems highly unlikely, as the rightholders may not even be aware of the litigation. Even rightholders who have notice may choose not to opt out. While the damage figure for Google's past scanning seems small on its face, the daunting prospect of bringing an individual infringement action for scanning and posting a snippet of one's work, coupled with Google's plausible fair use defense, may convince most rightholders to remain a part of the settlement.

Additional limitations set out in the RPS The RPS goes beyond the minimum requirements of Fed. R. Civ. Pro. 23 by including additional limitations on the scope of the settlement. First, the RPS only covers claims arising under United States copyright law. This crucial limitation is often overlooked in the commentary. Given the Berne Convention paradigm of parallel national copyrights, which arise automatically without the need to satisfy national formalities, many rightholders will be protected by multiple copyrights in the same work. The RPS only purports to deal with the United States copyright, leaving the others unaffected. Therefore, to the extent Google's actions infringe rights under some other nation's copyright law, a rightholder would be free to sue Google for these other infringements, even if that rightholder participated fully in the RPS with respect to the United States claim. Admittedly, Google's scanning of books is unlikely to infringe foreign copyrights, as such scanning has apparently occurred solely in the United States. However, to the extent that Google allows internet users in other nations to view or download complete or partial works, it may well infringe rights granted by other nations, resulting in significant extra-settlement liability.[22]

---

[22] Most of these actions will probably have to be filed in foreign courts. United States courts typically refuse to exercise jurisdiction over foreign copyright claims. *Voda v. Cordis Corp.*, 476 F.3d. 887 (2007). However, in cases where federal jurisdiction relies solely on the citizenship of the parties, a court may have author-

Second, the RPS expands the basic all-or-nothing opt-out privilege by giving the rightholder a wide array of intermediate options. For example, the owner may accept payment for Google's past acts, but elect to have the book removed from the Google database, preventing any future dissemination. To avail herself of this option, however, a rightholder whose book has already been scanned must direct Google to remove the book on or before March 9, 2012. If the book was digitized after that date, Google indicates it will honor the request only if the request is made before Google scans the book.[23] A rightholder who elects not to remove the book also has a number of options. For books currently in print, Google may only display the work with the rightholder's permission. For works that are out of print, the situation is reversed. Google is free to display out of print books in any manner it chooses unless the rightholder instructs Google not to display the work, or to display it in only a limited manner. The RPS recognizes several different degrees of display, ranging from simple bibliographic information through display of the entire work.

A rightholder who elects to allow display in any fashion also may control the financial terms of access. The rightholder may set any price it chooses for access to and downloading the work. The RPS also explicitly preserves the option of distributing the work for free under a Creative Commons license.[24] This option reflects the concerns of some academic authors, who wanted to maximize availability of their works even though there would be no direct remuneration.

Third, Google's rights under the RPS are non-exclusive. Thus, an individual rightholder who allows Google to display her work may still license the work to others, either on the same terms paid by Google or on different terms. This non-exclusivity provision represents a change from the original settlement proposal. The favored status that the original proposal gave Google raised serious antitrust concerns, which could have led to the agreement's downfall.

As a practical matter, the flexibility afforded to individual rightholders is workable only where the rightholder is known. Orphan works present an altogether different problem. For these works, the Unclaimed Works Fiduciary acts on behalf of the unknown rightholders. In many respects, the UWF retains all of the options available to known authors in its negotiations with Google. Thus, it may remove the work entirely from

---

ity to hear a case under foreign copyright law. *C.f. Baker-Bauman v. Walker*, 2007 WL 1026436 (S.D. Ohio) (deals with a foreign patent claim).

23   RPS § 3.5(a)(iii).
24   RPS § 4.2(a)(i).

the Google database, or allow for full or limited display. However, there is one crucial difference in the options available to individual rightholders and the Unclaimed Works Fiduciary. Unlike individual rightholders, the Unclaimed Works Fiduciary may only negotiate with Google. As will be discussed in Section 2, this limitation poses serious policy concerns.

In its broadest sense, then, the RPS would impose a collective rights management system on a significant chunk of the United States book industry. Individual authors can choose whether to participate in the system through their rights to opt out of the settlement entirely, or to pull one or more works from the Google database. In some ways, the RPS would grant individual rightholders more flexible rights than those present in the music industry rights management systems. Under the RPS, individual rightholders would retain significant control over how their works are used, and how much users are charged. Moreover, unlike in the music industry, the RPS deals only with the US copyright, leaving the rightholder free full control over foreign uses.

Notwithstanding all these limits and protections, however, the RPS still presents a number of serious practical and policy concerns. The next section analyzes some of these problems from a US perspective. Section 3 looks at some of these same concerns from a European vantage point.

2. IMPLICATIONS OF THE PROPOSED SETTLEMENT: A UNITED STATES PERSPECTIVE

2.1 Implications for Known Rightholders

As a purely financial matter, the RPS is not a bad deal for righthold-ers who can be located. Admittedly, a $60 cash payment for previous violations seems quite mean, especially in light of the statutory damages available under US copyright law. On the other hand, the rightholder who accepts the $60 payment is spared the time, trouble, and expense of prosecuting an individual infringement action against Google. Given Google's limited use of the works and its colorable fair use defense, there is no guarantee that the rightholder would fare as well in an individual action. Many, if not most, rightholders are accordingly likely to accept the $60. Nevertheless, any rightholder who insists on looking out for her own interests may opt out of the class action in its entirety, thereby preserving all legal rights.

A rightholder may also accept damages for past harm without waiving her ability to control future distribution. Provided she acts in timely fashion, any rightholder may direct Google to remove her work from the database, thereby preventing any future distribution through Google. Or, the rightholder may allow some distribution through Google, but dictate the terms, including how much of the work may be viewed and the amount charged for access. Many rightholders are likely to authorize readers to view only excerpts, which may encourage the reader to purchase a complete copy of the work through other channels. Finally, regardless of how the work is distributed through Google, the rightowner may also negotiate separate arrangements with other distributors, including both traditional print publishes and online databases. Given that the rightholder may specify the price for access to the work on Google, having the book available in the Google Book system need not undermine these other potential markets.

Financial considerations aside, however, the RPS does present some serious policy concerns. In the case of out of print books, the RPS reverses the default copyright rule on its head. A copyright is a property right. As in the case of trespass to land or use of chattels, someone must obtain the consent of the owner before making a prohibited use of a copyrighted work. The owner is under no obligation to contact the person beforehand to advise that person that he intends to enforce his rights. The RPS, however, would allow Google to display out of print works with impunity, unless the rightholder told Google not to. This provision not only runs counter to basic principles of copyright, but also arguably violates the Berne Convention provision prohibiting formalities as a condition to copyright protection.

A second policy issue is the use of the court system, and in particular the class action device, to create a rights management system for books. At least from a United States perspective, a class action is not a bad way to deal with the question of Google's past acts. The likelihood that many individual rightholders would have sued Google for scanning the entire work, and displaying snippets of such works, seems quite low. If these rightholders are to receive any compensation at all, use of the class action is as good a means of achieving this end as any other. But using the class action to define the future relationship between rightholders and Google is far more problematic. Creation of a rights management system for books is a major step, and should ideally be left either to negotiations among the interested parties – including *all* interested parties, not merely commercial authors and publishers – or the legislative process.

2.2   Implications for Rightholders in Orphan Works

The RPS has more serious problems in its provisions dealing with orphan works. As in the prior section, the core policy concerns of whether copyright should be an opt-in or opt-out system, and whether the courts are the proper forum to resolve these matters, remain. In addition, the actual terms that apply to orphan works create additional problems, both of practicality and core fairness.

The first issue is whether these unknown rightholders will actually ever receive any compensation. The RPS essentially defers this question by placing the onus of locating the rightholders on the Unclaimed Works Fiduciary. But the RPS is conspicuously lacking in any detail concerning the Fiduciary's duty to seek these unknown persons. It is accordingly far from certain that many rightholders in orphan works will receive even the $60 payment provided for by the RPS. Instead, these sums will in all likelihood be distributed to charities, as provided for by the agreement.

Second, and more troubling, the Unclaimed Works Fiduciary is vested with the authority to control future distribution of the work by Google. Given that the rightholder cannot readily be found, the Unclaimed Works Fiduciary will be unable to contact her to determine her true wishes. But the Unclaimed Works Fiduciary still owes that rightholder a fiduciary duty. The safest way for the Fiduciary to protect itself from a claim of breach of duty is to maximize the amount of royalties. And the best way to maximize royalties is to give Google the broadest possible distribution rights. Accordingly, the Unclaimed Works Fiduciary's default position will be to authorize full dissemination of most works.

This default position is even more likely given the RPS's stipulation that the Unclaimed Works Fiduciary may license only to Google. This provision not only gives Google a favored status, but may well run counter to the best interests of the rightholder. For many works, it may be preferable to publish and distribute through specialized channels such as trade or field-specific databases than through a universally accessible and generic source such as Google.

In short, then, the RPS is far less favorable to rightholders in orphan works than to known rightholders. Use of the independent Unclaimed Works Fiduciary may be a step in the right direction. Nevertheless, given that the Fiduciary will almost certainly allow fullest possible distribution of books through the Google system, the system does not ensure that the works will be distributed in a way that maximizes the overall benefit – monetary and reputational alike – to the rightholder.

2.3   Unraveling the Settlement: Possible Legal Challenges

The discussion to this point assumes the court will approve the RPS. Of course, approval is not guaranteed. Given the many objections that have been made to the RPS, the judge would have good reason not to approve the agreement. Indeed, the amount of time that has elapsed since the February, 2010 fairness hearing may suggest the judge is having second thoughts on the matter.

Even if the RPS is approved, however, there is some doubt as to whether the settlement will stand. The RPS, even with its additional limitations, is legally vulnerable on several fronts. This section briefly discusses the two most likely legal challenges.

2.3.1 Antitrust issues

The United States antitrust laws place significant restrictions on a party's ability to develop undue market power, whether by unilateral activity or in collaboration with others.[25] Policed by both the federal government and private parties, the antitrust laws subject violators to civil as well as criminal penalties. Equally important, contracts that violate the antitrust laws are void for illegality. A settlement agreement is merely a form of contract.

In late spring of 2009, the United States Department of Justice (DOJ) launched a formal inquiry into the original proposed settlement in the Google Books litigation. This inquiry focused on the broad privileges that agreement would have afforded Google. The revisions reflected in the RPS respond to many of the DOJ's concerns.

Shortly before the February, 2010 fairness hearing on the RPS, the DOJ issued a statement explaining its views concerning the RPS.[26] While acknowledging that the RPS had resolved many of the antitrust problems with the original, the statement made it clear that the DOJ still had concerns. The primary problem identified in the statement was Google's favored status with the Unclaimed Works Fiduciary. Given that the Fiduciary may only license rights to Google, the DOJ statement suggested the RPS might give Google excessive market power in the digital marketplace.

Whether the DOJ will actually challenge an approved RPS is unclear. Nor is it certain that the DOJ would prevail in such a challenge. First, it is not clear that the market for digital books is separate from that for paper books. Second, even assuming the markets are separate, the RPS does not necessarily give Google undue market power. After all, while the Unclaimed Works Fiduciary may only deal with Google, the RPS does not divest the rightholders of their individual rights. Individual righthold-

---

[25] The primary provisions of the antitrust laws relevant to the ensuing discussion are 15 USC § 1 (dealing with collaboration by two or more people) and § 2 (dealing with unilateral acts).

[26] For a discussion of the DOJ statement, see http://www.justice.gov/opa/pr/2010/February/10-opa-128.html.

ers, to the extent they are or become aware of their rights, remain free to license distribution rights to other sources, including other online sources. However, as it is difficult to predict how many rightholders will exercise this option, as well as whether these other sources would offer meaningful competition to Google, it is impossible to judge whether the RPS affords Google too much market power.

If a successful antitrust claim were to be brought, it would result in invalidation of at least some of the RPS. It is unlikely that the entire agreement would be held illegal. The provisions dealing with known rightholders, for example, would almost certainly remain in force, as those provisions are readily separable from those dealing with orphan works. Similarly, the provisions dealing with damages for past wrongs may be separable. Any declaration of invalidity would accordingly likely affect only the provisions dealing with the Unclaimed Works Fiduciary. It may be that only the particular provision giving Google the exclusive right to negotiate with the Fiduciary would be held invalid. However, if that provision is deemed a key part of the entire orphan works component of the agreement, it is possible that more of the agreement would be invalidated.

2.3.2 Collateral attack based on due process

One common objection to the entire Google Book litigation is that the named plaintiffs represent only a small and discrete segment of the book publishing industry. As discussed above, the named plaintiffs are primarily commercial authors and publishers. Their interests may diverge significantly from those of academic and other authors and publishers, especially when it comes to royalties and related matters. These claims of divergent interests are more than just a cry for fairness. Adequate representation is the sine qua non of a class action. Unless it is present, the case should not proceed as a class action, and the class members should not be bound by the results of the case.

There is a strong likelihood that representation is indeed inadequate in the Google Books litigation. The entire system envisioned by the RPS seems to assume that rightholders want maximum exposure of their works to the general public. That may be the case for many publishers, and for authors of popular novels and general interest books. But academic authors and publishers – and recall, the books in question come from academic libraries – may have different interests altogether. While the RPS does give rightholders the ability to remove their books from the Google database, any agreement that places the onus on the rightholder to demand removal by a set date does not represent the interests of anyone not interested in unfettered distribution.

A finding that representation is inadequate could occur either before the RPS is approved or at a later date. If the trial judge determines that representation is inadequate, he would be forced to deny the requested certification. This would not necessarily result in a complete denial of class action status. While the judge could simply refuse to certify the case at all, a perhaps more likely result would be approval of a class limited to right-holders similar to the named plaintiffs; that is, commercial rightholders and publishers.

The possibility of a ruling of inadequacy at some later date is more intriguing, and potentially more damaging to the settlement. As discussed in the section entitled 'Limitations inherent in class action device' above, adequate representation is required not only by the court procedural rules dealing with class actions, but also by the Due Process clause of the United States Constitution. If representation is constitutionally inadequate,[27] any judgment or settlement cannot bind someone who was not adequately represented.[28] In addition, the trial judge's decision in the certification process that representation was adequate is not binding on these parties. Nor does a person's choice not to opt out of the certified class bar a later challenge based on constitutionally inadequate representation. Because the person was neither a named party not adequately represented in the case, the Due Process prevents that party from being bound by anything the court says or does.

Any member of the class could challenge adequacy after approval of the settlement simply by bringing an infringement action against Google. Google would of course argue claim preclusion based on the court-approved class action settlement. But if the judge in the second case agreed with the plaintiff that representation was not adequate, the plaintiff would be free to litigate the case, and possibly prevail.

These sorts of post hoc challenges could potentially undermine the entire Google Book settlement. The problem from Google's perspective is that it has no sure way to predict which rightholders might be able to succeed on such a claim. If the suit seeks damages for post-settlement distribution of works that Google thought were included in the settlement, Google could be forced to pay significant damages. If a sufficient number of plaintiffs proceed in these post hoc challenges, much of the benefit that Google thought it was deriving from the settlement would be lost.

---

[27] The standard for determining whether representation is adequate differs in the Due Process and Rule 23 analyses. The Due Process standard is easier to satisfy. As just one example, while Rule 23 helps ensure adequate representation by requiring that the representative's claim be typical of the class, Due Process contains no such requirement.

[28] *Hansberry v. Lee*, 311 U.S. 32 (1940).

3. IMPLICATIONS OF THE PROPOSED SETTLEMENT: A EUROPEAN PERSPECTIVE

3.1 Settlement Class

The Google settlement is a global issue. Although the settlement affects only United States copyrights, as a practical matter it affects rightholders (authors and publishers) all over the world. But the American rightholders who purport to represent the class cannot be regarded as representing them all. Moreover, many foreign authors and publishers are generally not permitted membership in the American Authors Guild and the Association of American Publishers.[29]

So, although the settlement only allows Google to use and digitize works within United States territory, the interests of many European rightholders may also be at stake.[30] For, under the significantly narrowed scope of the RPS, rightholders who either registered their copyright with the US Copyright Office or (for non-US works) published their work in the UK, Australia, or Canada by January 5, 2009 are a member of the settlement class, which as a consequence may include European rightholders.[31] But as discussed in Section 2, being a member of the settlement class does not mean at the same time being represented during the approval procedure.

The interests of some non-American rightholders were brought to the floor during the February, 2010 fairness hearing.[32] This was for example the case with some European authors and publishers, which have been heard through the representatives of the French and German governments which submitted an *amicus curiae* brief to the Court. During the court hearing, the representative for the German government underlined that although foreign rightholders to a large extent were excluded from the settlement, their interests could be involved since many foreign authors have rights in works covered by the RPS.

Determining the precise contours of the actually defined settlement class is complicated by the fact that the US Copyright Office registration records are available in an electronic catalogue only from 1978 onwards. Prior

---

[29] See for an overview of Key Supporters, Filers with Reservations and Key Opponents of the settlement http://www.scribd.com/doc/20371700/The-Google-Books-Settlement-Who-Is-Filing-And-What-Are-They-Saying.

[30] European refers to both the European Union and the Council of Europe.

[31] See http://thepublicindex.org/documents/amended_settlement provisionally approved on November 19, 2009 – see www.googlebooksettlement.com/05CV8136_20091119.pdf

[32] 18 February 2010.

registrations need to be searched manually in the Office's Catalogue of Copyright Entries (CCE). In these circumstances, it is difficult to define precisely how many European rightholders are included in the settlement class.

The RPS does not contain clear indications on the fate of European books that were already scanned under the terms of the previous version. It appears that no rightholder whose work was digitized prior to the revision has received any compensation payments from Google, regardless of whether that person's work is included in the RPS. In addition, it has become clear that only rightholders who are part of the settlement class can invoke the *remove* (Section 3.5 (a)) or *exclude* (Section 3.5 (b)) provisions in the settlement. This might put those European rightholders outside the scope of the settlement at a disadvantage in relation to US counterparts. For example, rightholders who are not part of the settlement class must litigate to prevent snippet previews of their works in the United States (and thus clarify the contours of the doctrine of *fair use*) while those in the settlement class can easily prevent snippet previews, as the latter is a display use that can be excluded by the settlement members. On the other hand, rightholders outside the settlement class remain free to litigate the precise scope of *fair use* with Google in the US.

The fact that only members of the indicated countries will be represented on the board of the Books Rights Registry (BRR) raises issues of adequate representation. By the same token, there is no indication that any effort will be made to ensure the Unclaimed Works Fiduciary will make a special effort to consider the interests of rightholders in foreign orphan works.

3.2 Posted Objections

Posted objections to the settlement are of different kinds: from general to specific, from legal to cultural, from the perspective of professionals to that of consumers. Not surprisingly, various objections ventured from Europe concur with those raised from elsewhere.

Many objections were raised during a hearing organized by EU DG Markt between Commissioner Reding and key stakeholders (representatives of the publishing industry, the ICT sector, reproduction rights organizations, libraries, Member States delegates, civil rights and consumer organizations).[33] Generally speaking, the RPS was received with mixed feelings. Libraries welcomed the deal as allowing access to previously

---

[33]   CoEU, Information Note – The Google Book Settlement (GBS) – Impacts from a European perspective, Brussels 24 November 2009, 15109/09. See also

unavailable material and stimulating interest in printed books. However, criticism was voiced by authors, booksellers, publishers and IT industry associations, particularly fearing the monopolization of online access to digitized books. Most stakeholders agreed that the RPS widens the Trans-Atlantic gap with respect to online access to scientific or educational materials and Europe's own cultural heritage. Most of these objections were also raised by representatives of France and Germany during the fairness hearing. A major objection concerned RPS compliance with the international copyright framework. France voiced concerns the RPS might be detrimental to cultural diversity.

A major general objection, raised particularly by European publishers, concerns the violation of a basic principle of copyright law which the settlement implies. European copyright law requires the prior consent of the rightholder before any communication to the public can be made. Is it allowed under existing international copyright law, so it is questioned, to transform the exclusive right basis of national copyright law into an opt-out regime, where permission is supposed to be given unless specifically refused in writing?

Another objection concerns the use (and implications) of the class action device, which is unknown in Europe. To what extent is use of that instrument acceptable under obligations of international copyright law? The kind of compulsory licensing envisioned by the RPS requires a legislative basis under EU copyright law. A related question refers to what extent the named representatives adequately represent some of the affected rightholders and other stakeholders such as librarians and scholars, taking account of the fact that the primary representative – the Authors Guild – consists mainly of literary authors.

A further objection regards the qualification of books that are not commercially available (*i.e.* out of print books and so-called orphan works) under the RPS. These books can be shown in full online without prior authorization. In the RPS the term *commercial availability* is limited to *one or more then-customary channels of trade for purchasers within the United States, Canada, the United Kingdom or Australia.*[34] This is addressed below in section 3.3.

Privacy concerns relate to the potential users of settlement-books. So far, no guarantees have been given that Google will not (or cannot) misuse

---

Communication on copyright in the knowledge economy, COM (2009) 532 of 19 October 2009 and the Communication on Europeana: next steps, August 2009.

[34] See Amended Settlement, 1.31.

its position as the supplier of digitized content to monitor and possibly censor the behavior of its consumers.

A final objection, voiced by the so-called open content-community, (consisting of particularly academic institutions), promotes the deposit of academic publications in open repositoria, preferably under a Creative Commons or similar license.

3.3 Settlement Impact

Impacts of the Google Book settlement taken from a European perspective are at issue in the 2009-Information Note from the Council of the European Union mentioned in footnote 4. Based upon an assessment of the effects of the settlement on copyright, culture and competition in Europe, the document highlights the urgent need to allow similar projects to develop in Europe and welcomes uniform EU rules.

With regard to copyright it is assumed that the narrowed settlement class includes approximately 80% of English language works. Books published in countries of the *copyright tradition* (as opposed to the *droit d'auteur* tradition) will be available in services spawned by the Google Book Search (GBS) services in the US while the other (mostly European and Asian) jurisdictions will remain outside. Rightholders from EU countries other than the UK will have to negotiate individually to become part of GBS.

Since a great number of books available in Europe have never been published in the United States and as a consequence are out of print there, Google made two important concessions to safeguard the copyright of the European publishers in a commitment letter negotiated with EU publishers (the validity of which document has raised some ambiguity).[35] First, European books, which are out of print in the US but are still commercially available in the EU, may not be displayed on GBS without the explicit consent of authors or publishers. In order to determine the out of print status of books, Google will now also consult EU databases that reliably reflect whether books are sold in the EU. In practice this means that EU books sold in EU channels of trade will also be considered as *commercially available* within the terms of the settlement. Second, two non-US representative rightholders will sit on the board of the BRR to represent the interests of non-US rightholders.

As for orphan works, the Settlement will provide Google with a de

---

[35] Commitment letter dated 4 September 2009, addressed to 17 EU publishers.

facto monopoly to use orphan works, which will hinder any competing institutions, particularly digital libraries, in Europe to use them.[36]

With regard to culture it is observed that GBS shows how new business models are evolving to bring more copyright-protected works to an increasing number of users. However, because of the territorial limitation of the RPS, it is also noted that the increased access to digital books, particularly out of print and orphan works, will benefit only users in the United States. It is said therefore to be crucial to step up efforts in Europe to make digitized material from libraries, museums, archives, etc., containing the European cultural heritage, accessible online to EU citizens.

With regard to competition it is said that, since the settlement only operates *inter partes* (Google, authors and publishers), Google competitors cannot avail themselves of the terms of the settlement in their relationship with rightholders. They will have to conclude a similar kind of settlement to obtain similar terms.

Although the RPS has not led any potentially affected parties to file a formal complaint with the Commission against Google, the Commission binds itself to closely monitoring the market developments, including any arrangements deploying the Google book project in the EU.

3.4 Special Issues

A first special issue concerns the EU project Europeana.[37] Europeana stems from the EU's Digital Libraries Initiative (DLI) to make all Europe's cultural resources and scientific records accessible, and to preserve them for future generations. The DLI was launched in 2005 as part of the Commission's i2010 strategy to boost the digital economy. The initiative focuses on two areas: cultural heritage and scientific information. The DLI is part of the Commission's Digital Agenda for Europe.

Europeana is the common access point to the collections of European libraries, archives and museums from all around Europe. It is a so-called aggregator, which means that it does not itself offer any digitized content from its own server, but that it deep-links to the websites of various connected cultural heritage institutions. Books, journals, films, maps, photos, music, etc. will be available for everyone to consult and to use, copyright law permitting. "Copyright law permitting" means that with regard to

---

[36] See for the situation in the Netherlands Google Book Settlement, AMI 2010/2 (March/April 2010), Special Issue.

[37] See www.europeana.eu/portal/aboutus.html; http://tinyurl.com/digitallibraries

digitizing mega-projects and orphan works, the Commission incorporated the opt-in system of existing copyright law. According to Commissioner Reding "(i)f we do not reform our European copyright rules on orphan works and libraries swiftly, digitisation and the development of attractive content will not take place in Europe, but on the other side of the Atlantic."[38]

Obviously, not only orphan works, but also internet-licensing of non-orphan works, pose copyright problems. While the copyright laws of the EU Member States are not fully harmonized, collective management organizations (sometimes many in one Member State) are organized nationally. As a consequence, the Commission warns that "developments in other parts of the world indicate that Europe, and the European way of protecting copyright, could come under substantial competitive pressure if European solutions which ensure legal certainty and a digital level playing field throughout the 27 EU Member States are not rapidly developed."[39]

A second special issue concerns orphan works.[40] Several activities have already been developed in the EU in this respect. The Commission organized two hearings for stakeholders in 2009; the DG INFSO High Level Group on Digital Libraries did considerable preparatory work, and a consultation was conducted on the Green Paper Copyright in the Knowledge Economy.[41] The outcome of all this was consolidated in an impact assessment in March 2010. The impact assessment evaluated six options to deal with the online display of orphan works: (1) to do nothing, (2) a statutory exception, (3)(4)(5) three versions of copyright licenses, or (6) a system of mutual recognition.

Under option 2 Member States would be obliged to enact legislation to provide (i) a system to determine the legal status of orphan works, (ii) an exception allowing for the online display of orphan works across Europe, and (iii) a suitable mechanism of redress for reappearing rightholders. The principle of mutual recognition would thus have the double advantage of identifying a single relevant jurisdiction where a diligent search is most

---

[38] See Ludwig Erhard Lecture 9 July 2009, Brussels http://ec.europa.eu/infor mation_society/topics/reding-lisbon/index_en.htm

[39] Creative Content in a European Digital Single Market: Challenges for the Future. A Reflection Document of DG INFSO and DG Markt, 22 October 2009, p. 7 – http://tinyurl.com/CreativeContentOnline

[40] See Tilman Lueder, The 'orphan works' challenge, 18th Annual Intellectual Property Law and Policy Conference, 2010, Fordham 2010 Intellectual Property Law Institute – www.fordhamipconference.com upon which this part of section 3.4 is based.

[41] See http://tinyurl.com/EChearingorphanworks; EC, Green Paper on Copyright in the Knowledge Economy, Brussels COM (2008) 466/3.

conveniently conducted and of ensuring that the search would not have to be duplicated in all the Member States when their libraries contain the same orphan works or where the orphan works will ultimately be displayed online.

Under option 3 a collecting society is given a mandate to represent the interests of rightholders even if they are not formally registered with the society. Therefore, once a contract allowing a library to use certain books is negotiated with a collecting society, the applicable national law would extend its coverage to all copyright owners beyond the known and registered members of the collecting society (including foreign rightholders). However, the collective licensing does not require that a diligent search for the rightholder is carried out before the orphan work becomes part of the license. Consequently, the principle of mutual recognition of the orphan work status cannot operate under this option because works are not classified as orphans prior to their online display. In Scandinavian countries the issue of orphan works is addressed by extended collective management.

Under option 4 Member States would be obliged to enact legislation to provide (i) a system to determine the legal status of orphan works, (ii) a workable licensing system allowing for the online display of orphan works across the EU, and (iii) a suitable mechanism of redress for reappearing rightholders. Once a diligent search for the rightholder has been conducted in the country of origin or that of the first publication of the book, the result of this search, *i.e.* its orphan work status, is mutually recognized in all EU Member States. The existing VG Wort licensing-project in Germany offers an example of such a workable licensing system, but it is limited to the German territory.

Option 5 obliges the Member States to enact legislation to provide (i) a system to determine the legal status of orphan works, (ii) a workable government authorization allowing for the online display of orphan works across the EU, and (iii) a suitable mechanism of redress for reappearing rightholders. The principle of mutual recognition will have the same advantages as in options 2 and 4. The option is modeled on the Canadian Copyright Law, but the license in Canadian law is limited to the Canadian territory.

Under option 6 Member States would be obliged to enact legislation to provide (i) a system to determine the legal status of orphan works, (ii) a workable rights clearance system allowing for the rapid online display of orphan works in their territories, (iii) a system of mutual recognition for the online display executed in their respective territories, (iv) a suitable mechanism of redress for reappearing rightholders. The option relies on the twofold advantage of the principle of mutual recognition.

After analyzing the respective options, Lueder concludes that the option with the most immediate benefit for the creation of a European Digital Library would be a statutory exception (option 2). This option requires no licensing, although the Member States would be obliged to provide for systems of effective redress in case the legitimate rightholder reappears. However, quite rightly according to Lueder, a statutory exception raises a concern of principle related to the nature of copyright: being unknown does not mean that the rightholder has given up the ownership of his work. As a consequence, Lueder ultimately concludes option 6 is the best compromise solution: mutual recognition of regulatory approaches. First, this leaves the Member States free to apply their national rules on the identification and posting online of orphan works. Second, once the work is identified as an orphan work in a Member State (the country of first publication), the decision is recognized throughout the EU. Third, once an orphan work has been posted lawfully in the country of first publication – under a collective license, a government authorization or a statutory exception – this will be recognized in all other Member States.

4.   CONCLUSION

This chapter has analyzed the proposed settlement in the Google Book litigation from two divergent perspectives: those of the United States and the European Union. The settlement's ambitious plan to impose a rights management system on the book industry will, if approved and upheld in court, have far-reaching implications in both of these systems. However, because the settlement was negotiated primarily with US authors and publishers in mind, it fails to address many of the issues that arise in the European context. Whether these widely disparate interests may ultimately be represented in the settlement remains an open question.

PART IV

Individualism and collectiveness in trademark law

10. Reconciling individualism and collectiveness in trademark merchandising in the United States

Irene Calboli*

1. INTRODUCTION

Trademark merchandising – the use of trademarks on promotional products for profits or simply as advertising – constitutes a ubiquitous phenomenon in today's society.[1] Despite this popularity, however, this booming business technique also constitutes a highly controversial topic and its acceptance under the rule of law still remains unclear in the United States. Not surprisingly, the disagreements surrounding the debate on trademark merchandising reflect the historically opposing views of trademark scholars and practitioners over the scope of trademark protection.[2] Arguing that the

---

* Associate Professor of Law, Marquette University Law School. This chapter summarizes the analysis of the practice of trademark merchandising in the United States that I have originally developed in the article, 'The Case for a "Limited" Protection of Trademark Merchandising', 2011 Ill. L. Rev. 865 (2011). Accordingly, parts of this chapter are adapted from this article. I would like to thank the participants at the 2010 ATRIP Congress "Individualism and Collectiveness in Intellectual Property Law," University of Stockholm School of Law, May 23–26, 2010, and in particular Maggie Chon, John Cross, Rochelle Dreyfuss, Graeme Dinwoodie, Ysolde Gendreau, Annette Kur, David Llewellin, Alberto Musso, Alexander Peukert, Lisa Ramsey, Jerome Reichman, Jan Rosen, Lars Smith, Jens Schovsbo, Peter Yu, and Dafne Zografos for helpful conversation, comments, and suggestions. I also thank Marquette University Law School for research support, and Michael Soule and April Ashby for research and editorial assistance.

[1] See '100 Best Global Brands', *Bus. Wk.*, Sept. 28, 2009, at 50 (reporting that, in 2009, the "top five" brands were: Coca-Cola, IBM, Microsoft, GE, and Nokia). *See also* C. Brinkley, 'Like Our Sunglasses? Try Our Vodka!', Wall St. J., Nov. 8, 2007, at D1 ("We have entered into an age of luxury-brand extension gone wild. Luggage companies make clothes, clothing makers make chocolate, and practically everyone makes watches and perfumes.").

[2] *See* discussion *infra* Section 2.2.

justification for trademark protection has traditionally been based on the premise that trademarks do not exist "in gross" but rather only as indicators of commercial origin, and that trademark rights should be enforced solely to protect consumers against confusion,[3] numerous scholars have opposed the recognition of merchandising because of the "unnatural" expansion of trademark protection and the resulting dangers for market competition.[4] Hence, the business world has commonly treated marks as vital assets and properties per se to be defended against any unauthorized use, also on promotional products.[5] Trademark owners and practitioners have thus traditionally advocated in favor of the legal recognition of trademark merchandising.[6]

Ultimately, the economic changes of the past decades and the unprecedented increase in mass production and distribution of consumer goods have strengthened the position of the business world and reasserted the relevance of trademarks as profitable business assets.[7] As a result, the importance of trademarks has also reached the judiciary and the legislature. During the past decades, multiple judicial rulings and statutory revisions have invariably led to increased trademark protection. In some cases, courts have also granted relief to plaintiffs based merely upon the impairment of the marks per se rather than because of existing confusion among consumers.[8] Not surprisingly, this judicial and legislative favor

---

[3]   Trademark protection has traditionally been justified because marks provide information about the products to which they are affixed, guarantee a predictable quality, and reduce consumer search costs. *See generally* William M. Landes & Richard A. Posner, 'Trademark Law: An Economic Perspective', 30 J.L. & Econ. 265, 265–66 (1987) ("Trademark law . . . can be best explained on the hypothesis that the law is trying to promote economic efficiency."). *See also* Nicholas Economides, 'The Economic Aspects of Trademarks', 78 Trademark Rep. 523 (1988); William P. Kratzke, 'Normative Economic Analysis of Trademark Law', 21 Mem. St. U. L. Rev. 199 (1991).

[4]   *See, e.g.,* Stacey L. Dogan & Mark A. Lemley, 'The Merchandising Right: Fragile Theory or Fait Accompli?', 54 Emory L. J. 461, 481 (2005) [hereinafter Dogan & Lemley, 'Merchandising Right'] ("[G]eneral merchandising right unmoored from confusion conflicts with, rather than promoting, trademarks law's precompetitive goals . . . .").

[5]   *See* Frank I. Schechter, 'The Rational Basis of Trademark Protection', 40 Harv. L. Rev. 813, 818 (1927). "The true functions of the trademark are, then, to identify a product as satisfactory and thereby to stimulate further purchases by the consuming public." *Id.*

[6]   *See* discussion *infra* Part II.B.

[7]   *See* David Kiley, 'Best Global Brands: How the BusinessWeek/Interbrand Top 100 Companies Are Using Their Brands to Fuel Expansion', Bus. Wk., Aug. 7, 2006, at 54.

[8]   *See* discussion *infra* Part II.A.

for strong trademark protection has also translated into favor towards trademark merchandising. Still, while they have favored a de facto legal recognition of trademark merchandising, neither the judiciary nor the legislature has expressly accepted, so far, the validity of this practice in the legal context. Instead, courts have simply adopted a broader interpretation of the traditional standard for trademark infringement – "consumer confusion" – to include confusion "as to the sponsorship" of the marked products to justify trademark enforcement against unauthorized promotional products.[9] Ultimately open-ended and based on a case-by-case approach by the courts, this approach has left ample room for doctrinal opposition and much uncertainty for trademark owners and competitors about the legitimacy of their actions while using trademarks on promotional products.[10]

This chapter argues against this uncertainty and advocates for a solution to reconcile the current uncertainty surrounding the legal treatment of trademark merchandising with business reality and existing trademark rules in the United States. The first section of this chapter summarizes the history and developments of trademark merchandising, and reconstructs the confusing and disconnected debate that characterizes the positions of academics and practitioners on the issue. Highlighting the unsustainable uncertainty of the status quo in this area, the second section of this chapter proposes a solution that carefully balances the increasingly unavoidable recognition of individual merchandising rights in today's society with the need to limit these rights in the interest of market competition and collectiveness in general.

2. THE CONFUSING STATUS QUO ON TRADEMARK MERCHANDISING

2.1 A Brief History and Developments of Merchandising Rights

Historically, the recognition of trademark merchandising in the United States was first addressed by a series of judicial decisions during the 1970s,[11] the most famous of which was issued in 1975 in *Boston*

---

[9] *Id.*

[10] *Id.*

[11] *See, e.g.*, 4 J. Thomas McCarthy, *McCarthy On Trademarks And Unfair Competition* § 24:10–12 (4th edn., Minnesota, USA: Thomson West, 2010) (offering a comprehensive analysis of the positions on trademark merchandising).

Professional Hockey Association v. Dallas Cap & Emblem Manufacturing.[12] In this case, the court enjoined the unauthorized use of a team's logo on clothing simply because consumers "associated" the logo with the team, regardless of any existing "likelihood of confusion" as to the source of the products.[13] Because of this sudden departure from the traditional standard for trademark infringement, however, *Boston Hockey* was not directly followed by other courts at the time.[14] Nevertheless, due to the growing importance of merchandising in the economy, later decisions continued to look favorably upon this practice. In particular, courts progressively expanded the meaning of the traditional standard of "likelihood of confusion" to include "confusion as to sponsorship" of the products,[15] thus accommodating a de facto recognition of merchandising rights.

During the next decade, courts increasingly accepted this concept of confusion at large, even when they denied trademark infringement in the cases at issue.[16] The judiciary continued to apply the new standard during the 1980s as merchandising grew in popularity due to the changes in the economy and the rise of consumer society.[17] Judicial rulings in this area

---

[12]   *Boston Prof'l Hockey Ass'n v. Dallas Cap & Emblem Mfg.*, 510 F.2d 1004, 1011–12 (5th Cir. 1975), *cert. denied*, 423 U.S. 868 (1975). *But see* Dogan & Lemley, 'Merchandising Right', *supra* note 4, at 461 (arguing that the *Boston Hockey* court's reasoning was circular and fallible).

[13]   Trademark (Lanham) Act of 1946, Pub. L. No. 79–489, 60 Stat. 427 (codified as amended at 15 U.S.C. §§ 1051–1141n (2000 & Supp. V 2005)) [hereinafter Lanham Act]. *See* Lanham Act §§ 32, 43, 15 U.S.C. §§ 1114, 1125 (2006).

[14]   *See, e.g.*, *United States v. Giles*, 213 F.3d 1247, 1250 (10th Cir. 2000) (stating that *Boston Hockey* relied "upon a novel and overly broad conception of the rights that a trademark entails"); *Int'l Order of Job's Daughters v. Lindeburg & Co.*, 633 F.2d 912, 919 (9th Cir. 1980) (defining *Boston Hockey* as "an extraordinary extension of the protection . . . afforded trademark owners"); *Ky. Fried Chicken Corp. v. Diversified Packaging Corp.*, 549 F.2d 368, 388 (5th Cir. 1977) (reaffirming likelihood of confusion as requirement for trademark infringement); *Bd. of Governors of Univ. of N.C. v. Helpingstine*, 714 F. Supp. 167, 173 (M.D. NC 1989) (stating that plaintiff "must provide evidence establishing that individuals do make the critical distinction as to sponsorship or endorsement, or direct evidence of actual confusion.").

[15]   *Nat'l Football League Props., Inc. v. Consumer Enters., Inc.*, 327 N.E.2d 242 (Ill. App. 1975). "[T]he buying public has come to associate the trademark with the sponsorship of the NFL or of the particular member team involved." *Id.* at 246.

[16]   *See, e.g.*, *Job's Daughters*, 633 F.2d at 919; Supreme Assembly, *Order of the Rainbow for Girls v. J.H. Ray Jewelry Co.*, 676 F.2d 1079, 1082 (5th Cir. 1982); *Univ. of Pittsburgh v. Champion Prods., Inc.*, 686 F.2d 1040, 1047 (3d Cir. 1982).

[17]   *Univ. of Ga. Athletic Ass'n v. Laite*, 756 F.2d 1535 (11th Circuit 1985); *Boston Athletic Ass'n v. Sullivan*, 867 F.2d 22 (1st Cir. 1989). *But see Helpingstine*, 714 F. Supp. at 173.

turned increasingly favorable to plaintiffs' claims in merchandising cases during those times. In some instances courts even directly relied on *Boston Hockey*'s reasoning and found infringement just because of the "public's knowledge that the trademark . . . originate[d] with the plaintiff."[18] This trend of favorable decisions continued during the 1990s and at the turn of the century following the increasing globalization of trade, the rise of the service economy, and dramatic progress in information technology. Ultimately, the judicial favor toward merchandising has been repeatedly confirmed in recent years.[19] In some instances, courts have even enjoined the sale of unauthorized promotional products reproducing merely the color schemes or slogans (not the logos) associated with plaintiffs – largely sports teams and universities.[20]

In addition to reaching the courts, the growing relevance of trademark merchandising, and of marks in general, has also reached the legislature in the past decades, prompting important changes in trademark policies. The 1988 Trademark Revision Act introduced the concept of "confusion as to the sponsorship" directly into Section 43(a) of the Lanham Act as a qualified action for the infringement of unregistered marks and unfair competition claims when trademark owners believe to be "damaged . . . or likely to be damaged by such act".[21] The 1988 Act also harmonized U.S. trademark law with the majority of other jurisdictions, and established that businesses or individuals could file trademark applications simply

---

[18]   *Laite*, 756 F.2d at 1546 ("'[C]onfusion' need not relate to the origin of the challenged *product*. Rather 'confusion' may relate to the public's knowledge that the *trademark*, which is 'the triggering mechanism' for the sale of the product, originates with the plaintiff.").

[19]   *Audi AG & Volkswagen of America, Inc. v. D'Amato*, 469 F.3d 534 (6th Cir. 2006); *Au-Tomotive Gold, Inc. v. Volkswagen of America, Inc.*, 457 F.3d 1062 (9th Cir. 2006); *Gen. Motors v. Lanard Toys*, 468 F.3d 405 (6th Cir.2006); *Texas Tech Univ. v. John Spiegelberg*, 461 F. Supp. 2d 510 (N.D. Tex. 2006).

[20]   *Bd. of Supervisors for La. State Univ. v. Smack Apparel*, 550 F.3d 465 (5th Cir. 2008); *Univ. of Kansas v. Larry Sinks*, 565 F. Supp. 2d 1216 (D. Kan. 2008). *But see Univ. of Alabama Bd. of Trustees v. New Life Art, Inc.*, 2009 WL 5213713, *1 (N.D. Ala. 2009). *See also* Jeremiah Kline, 'Black and Blue: An Examination of Trademarking University Color Schemes', 16 Sports Law. J. 47, 61 (2009).

[21]   Trademark Law Revision Act of 1988, Pub. L. No. 100-667, 102 Stat. 3935 (Nov. 16, 1988) (*amending* 15 U.S.C. § 1051 et seq.). The 1988 amendment changed the text of Section 43(a) of the Lanham Act to define trademark infringement as any act "likely to cause confusion, mistake, or to deceive as to the affiliation, connection, or association, or as to the origin, sponsorship, or approval of goods, services, or commercial activities by another person" when the trademark owner "believes that he or she is or is likely to be damaged by such act". Lanham Act § 43(a)(1)(A), 15 U.S.C. § 1125(a)(1)(A).

based on the "intent" to use a mark and not necessarily on actual trademark use. Not surprisingly, this change in the trademark statute created the perfect vehicle for trademark owners to preventively secure trademark rights for later uses of the marks on promotional products via trademark licensing and merchandising agreements.[22]

A further push toward the statutory recognition and protection of merchandising finally came from the adoption of the Federal Trademark Dilution Act (FTDA) in 1996.[23] A concept long recognized in American trademark theory and state laws,[24] protection against trademark dilution was introduced into Section 43(c) of the Lanham Act to "expand federal trademark protection beyond the traditional protection against consumer confusion" and protect "famous" marks against the "blurring" of their distinctiveness or the "tarnishment" of their reputation, which could be caused by the unauthorized use of identical or similar marks on unrelated products.[25] As clarified by Congress in the 2006 Trademark Dilution Revision Act (TDRA), these claims could simply rest on a "likelihood" of

---

[22] Lanham Act § 1(b), 15 U.S.C. § 1051(b) (2006). Intent-to-use applications require objective evidence of *bona fide* intended use and applicants are advised to keep detailed documentation of these uses. Trademark Rules of Practice 2.89(d). After filing an intent-to-use application, applicants are given a notice of allowance, provided that no opposition has been filed. Applicants have six months to file a statement of use to obtain trademark registration (extendable to one year automatically and up to three years for good cause). Lanham Act § 1(d), 15 U.S.C. § 1051(d).

[23] Federal Trademark Dilution Act of 1995. Pub. L. No. 104–98, §§ 3(a), 4, 109 Stat. 985, 985–86 (effective Jan. 26, 1996) (codified as amended at 15 U.S.C. §§ 1125, 1127) [hereinafter FTDA]. The FTDA has been amended by the Trademark Dilution Revision Act of 2006. Pub. L. No. 109–312 §§ 2, 3(e), 120 Stat. 1730, 1733 (effective Oct. 6, 2006) [hereinafter TDRA].

[24] *See* Schechter, *supra* note 5, at 818. The first state anti-dilution statute was adopted in Massachusetts in 1947. *See* Robert N. Klieger, 'Trademark Dilution: The Whittling Away of the Rational Basis for Trademark Protection', 58 U. Pitt. L. Rev. 789, 811 (1997). Subsequently, approximately half of the states adopted state anti-dilution statutes prior the adoption of the FTDA. *Id.* at 812.

[25] The FTDA, as amended by the TDRA of 2006, defines "blurring" as an "association arising from the similarity between a mark or trade name and a famous mark that impairs the distinctiveness of the famous mark." Lanham Act § 43(c)(2)(B), 15 U.S.C. § 1125(c)(2)(B) (2006). "Tarnishment" is defined as "an association arising from the similarity between a mark or trade name and a famous mark that harms the reputation of the famous mark." Lanham Act § 43(c)(2)(C), 15 U.S.C. § 1125(c)(2)(C). The FTDA also provides that "a mark is famous if it is widely recognized by the general consuming public of the United States as a designation of source of the goods or services of the mark's owner." 15 U.S.C. §§ 1125, 1125(2)(A).

dilution without the need to prove any "actual" harm to the marks, thus favoring an even stronger protection for famous marks against unauthorized trademark uses.[26]

2.2 The Current Disconnected Debate on Trademark Merchandising

Even if recent decisions and amendments to the trademark statute indicate a de facto acceptance of trademark merchandising in the United States, the debate over the actual legal recognition of this practice remains highly controversial. Contrary to the enthusiasm of the business world, numerous scholars have criticized the judicial favor for merchandising rights as a "fragile theory,"[27] and have severely condemned the tendency of the judiciary to determine infringement solely on the basis of consumer "association" between the marks rather than on consumer confusion, calling it a dangerous anomaly in trademark law.[28]

Specifically, scholars have condemned the "if value, then right"[29] approach that has recently characterized judicial decisions arguing that this direct protection of marks as products or "properties" per se would necessarily result in limiting access to words and symbols – a scarce resource in the business world – and ultimately undermine, if not foreclose, competition in "expressive" or "aesthetically functional" product features to the detriment of the public.[30] While rejecting this "property-value" justification for

---

[26] TDRA of 2006 (codified as amended at 15 U.S.C. §§ 1125, 1127). *See, e.g.,* Jesse A. Hofrichter, 'Tool of the Trademark: Brand Criticism and Free Speech Problems with the Trademark Dilution Revision Act of 2006', 28 Cardozo L. Rev. 1923 (2007).

[27] Dogan & Lemley, 'Merchandising Right', *supra* note 4, at 506.

[28] On the risks of excessive trademark protection, see Ralph S. Brown, 'Advertising and the Public Interest: Legal Protection of Trade Symbols', 57 Yale L. J. 1165, 1206 (1948) *reprinted in* 108 Yale L. J. 1619, 1659 (1999). "In an acquisitive society, the drive for monopoly advantage is a very powerful pressure. Unchecked, it would no doubt patent the wheel, copyright the alphabet, and register the sun and the moon as exclusive trade-marks." *Id. See also, e.g.,* Jessica Litman, 'Breakfast with Batman: The Public Interest in the Advertising Age', 108 Yale L. J. 1717 (1999).

[29] Rochelle Cooper Dreyfuss, 'Expressive Genericity: Trademarks as Language in the Pepsi Generation', 65 Notre Dame L. Rev. 396, 407 (1990) (stating that "[t]he fallacies in the right/value theory can be revealed in a number of ways").

[30] Robert C. Denicola, 'Institutional Publicity Rights: An Analysis of the Merchandising of Famous Trade Symbols', 62 N.C. L. Rev. 603, 613 (1984). "[If] enjoined from using a well-known insignia on T-shirts or caps [defendants are] effectively excluded from the market for such products." *Id. See also* Veronica J. Cherniak, 'Ornamental Use of Trademarks: The Judicial Development and

merchandising, some scholars have also criticized the doctrine of "confusion as to the sponsorship," which they have labeled as "irrelevant confusion"[31] and have criticized as being outside the scope of trademark law.

Generally, scholars have repeatedly underscored that the legal acceptance of trademark merchandising could entail dangerous consequences for market competition. Trademark owners would have the ability to control competition in multiple segments of the market, which in turn would result in inflated product prices, decreased product quality, and ultimately likely market failures.[32] As part of their arguments, these scholars have also severely criticized trademark owners' tendencies to expand trademark portfolios on the basis of "intent-to-use" rather than actual use for securing trademark rights for subsequent licensing and merchandising activities.[33] On the contrary, numerous scholars have observed that the use of disclaimers specifying the "non-affiliation" of unauthorized promotional products with trademark owners could eliminate any risk of confusion, including as to products' sponsorship, on the part of the public, while still allowing competing goods to coexist in the market along with officially authorized products.[34]

Yet, regardless of scholarly concerns, trademark practice has long treated merchandising as a "fait accompli."[35] Firmly convinced that "their" marks belong to their businesses as property, trademark owners

---

Economic Implications of an Exclusive Merchandising Right'. 69 Tul. L. Rev. 1311, 1352–53 (1995). As some trademark owners do not merchandise their marks at all, consumers could be completely foreclosed from access to products displaying certain aesthetically appealing marks." *Id.*

[31]   Mark A. Lemley & Mark P. McKenna, 'Irrelevant Confusion', 62 Stan. L. Rev. 413, 414 (2010). "[S]ponsorship and affiliation confusion has taken on a life of its own, leading courts to declare as infringing a variety of practices that might be confusing in some sense, but that do not affect consumers' decision-making process." *Id.*

[32]   This problem is particularly true for famous marks, which could prevent the use of the same or similar marks with respect to any product, related or unrelated, if a likelihood of dilution is established. Lanham Act § 43(c), 15 U.S.C. § 1125(c) (2008).

[33]   *See* 4 McCarthy, *supra* note 11, § 24:9.50.

[34]   *See, e.g.*, Robert G. Bone, 'Enforcement Costs and Trademark Puzzles', 90 Va. L. Rev. 2099, 2183 (2004) [hereinafter Bone, 'Enforcement Costs'] (noting that disclaimers "can prevent both consumer confusion and the acquisition of monopoly power by official licensees"); Mark A. Lemley, 'The Modern Lanham Act and the Death of Common Sense', 108 Yale L. J. 1687, 1708 (1999) (discussing the "Dallas Cowboys" trademark and dismissing confusion provided that competitor uses "an appropriate disclaimer and makes no false reference to an 'official licensed NFL product'").

[35]   Dogan & Lemley, 'Merchandising Right', *supra* note 4, at 506.

have generally enforced trademark rights as "things," also with respect to their unauthorized use on promotional products. The growing number of decisions accepting the validity of trademark rights in merchandised products has buttressed this tendency by making trademark owners increasingly reliant on positive judicial outcomes.[36] As a result, trademark owners and practitioners have commonly opposed the production and distribution of products bearing identical or similar marks on unrelated and promotional products.[37] Not surprisingly, due to the high costs and fears of litigation, as well as the increasing acceptance of merchandising as a "fait accompli" in the business world, trademark owners and practitioners have largely emerged victorious from these disputes and commonly settled claims by imposing to the acceptance of licensing agreements.[38]

As additional evidence of the established role of merchandising rights in practice, a sizable body of manuals and guides specifically focusing on how to manage trademark portfolios and develop successful merchandising programs has flourished in the past decades.[39] Notably, the emergence of trademarks as "brand builders" in an economy increasingly dominated by advertising has brought a growing number of publications to stress the importance of evaluating whether a mark has "the potential to be used as

---

[36] *See generally Bd. of Supervisors for La. State Univ. v. Smack Apparel Co.*, 550 F.3d 465, 485 (5th Cir. 2008) (noting that, because of "the overwhelming similarity[,] . . . consumers would likely be confused and believe that Smack's t-shirts were sponsored or endorsed by the Universities."); *Univ. of Kansas v. Larry Sinks*, 565 F. Supp. 2d 1216, 1254–55 (D. Kan. 2008) (stating that some of marks displayed on defendant's t-shirts "are overwhelmingly similar to KU's marks"); *Texas Tech Univ. v. Spiegelberg*, 461 F. Supp. 2d 510, 524 (N.D. Tex. 2006) (saying that defendant had "sold unlicensed products with the identical Texas Tech marks since its license was revoked in 2003" and "[t]herefore, Spiegelberg's use of identical marks constitutes trademark dilution").

[37] *See* 2 Barry Kramer & Allen D. Brufsky, *Trademark Law Practice Forms* § 23:1 (Minnesota, USA: Thomson West 2009). Trademark manuals often provide sample forms of cease and desist letters. *See id.* §§ 43:3–4. *See also, e.g., Univ. of Ga. Athletic Ass'n v. Laite*, 756 F.2d 1535, 1543 (11th Cir. 1985) (preventing the use of plaintiff's mark on an unrelated good, beer, because of both "the similarity of design between the two marks and the defendant's intent").

[38] Critically, see James Gibson, 'Risk Aversion and Rights Accretion in Intellectual Property Law', 116 Yale L. J. 882, 913 (2007) (noting that because of the harsh penalties imposed for trademark infringement "[i]t should therefore come as no surprise when trademark users who could mount a decent defense against an infringement claim nevertheless choose to seek a license").

[39] *See, e.g.*, 4 Barry Kramer & Allen, D. Brufsky, *Trademark Law Practice Forms* § 43:14 (Minnesota, USA: Thomson West 2009); Steven H. Bazerman & Jason M. Drangel, Guide to Registering Trademarks § 16 (Maryland, USA: Bazerman & Drangel Aspen Publishers 2009).

a premium or promotion apart from its retail life"[40] as well as directly providing samples of merchandising agreements to trademark practitioners.[41]

Finally, a long established line of reasoning within the United States Patent and Trademark Office (USPTO) has also confirmed the importance of merchandising rights.[42] Following the judicial cases of the 1970s and 1980s, numerous decisions from examining attorneys and rulings from the Trademark Trial Appeal Board (TTAB) have routinely allowed registrations for use on merchandised products and upheld oppositions against trademark registration based on the use of marks on collateral goods under the doctrine of "confusion as to the sponsorship." According to these decisions, "the licensing of commercial trademarks for use on 'collateral' products . . . has become a common practice in recent years."[43] Similar to the courts, however, the USPTO has recognized merchandising only de facto and on a case-by-case basis, thus perpetuating the current uncertainty in this area.

2.3   Negative Consequences of the Confusing Status Quo

As indicated earlier, the current divide between trademark theory and practice over the acceptance and regulation of merchandising rights stems primarily from the diverging views over the scope of trademark protec-

---

[40]   Gregory J. Battersby & Charles W. Grimes, *Law of Merchandise and Character Licensing* § 1:1 (Minnesota, USA: Thomson West 2009) [hereinafter Battersby & Grimes, Merchandising] ("Merchandising now affords small businessmen the opportunity to compete on equal terms with large manufacturers, who historically were the only ones who could afford to invest the substantial sums required by classic marketing techniques.").

[41]   *See generally* Richard Raysman et al., *Intellectual Property Licensing: Forms and Analysis* § 4.11 (New York, USA: Law Journal Press 2009) (providing guidelines in drafting, *inter alia*, clauses for compensation, quality control, ownership, enforcement, and termination of contract).

[42]   *See, e.g., In re 12th Man/Tennessee*, 2008 WL 1897548, *5 (T.T.A.B. 2008); *Chicago Bears Football Club, v. 12th Man/Tennessee LLC*, 2007 WL 683778, *12, (T.T.A.B. 2007); *Baltimore Ravens Limited Partnership and NFL Properties LLC v. 12th Man/Tennessee LLC*, 2007 WL 683781, *11 (T.T.A.B. 2007); *DC Comics v. Pan American Grain Mfg. Co.*, 77 U.S.P.Q.2d 1220 (T.T.A.B. 2005); *Turner Entm't Co. v. Ken Nelson*, 38 U.S.P.Q.2d. 1942 (T.T.A.B. 1996); *General Mills Fun Group, Inc. v. Tuxedo Monopoly, Inc.*, 204 U.S.P.Q. 396 (T.T.A.B. 1979), *aff'd* 648 F.2d 1335, 209 U.S.P.Q. 986 (C.C.P.A. 1981).

[43]   *In re God's Property, Inc.*, 2007 WL 2422992 (T.T.A.B. 2007) (quoting *In re Phillips-Van Heusen Corp.*, 228 U.S.P.Q. 949, 951 (T.T.A.B. 1986)). The TTAB has repeatedly affirmed, for example, that "items of clothing . . . appear to represent a particularly natural area for the 'collateral products' use of commercial trademarks." *Id.*

tion by opponents and supporters of this practice in the United States.[44] Beyond creating theoretical frustrations for scholars and practitioners, however, this divide has also become detrimental for trademark owners and competitors in the market who, absent an official position by the judiciary or the legislature on the issue, continue to lack specific guidance and frequently receive conflicting answers as to the conditions upon which they can legitimately use marks in the course of trade.[45]

Not surprisingly, because of this uncertainty and the "widespread ignorance of the law"[46] that largely defines the business world, trademark owners and competitors have generally adopted the advice – in favor or against merchandising – that best fit their needs depending on the specific circumstances.[47] Yet, as a result, trademark owners have often enforced their rights against unauthorized products, basing their claims on questionable foundations.[48] Trademark owners have also increasingly filed intent-to-use trademark applications for a large number of products, precisely for licensing and merchandising purposes, with dubious effects on market competition.[49] On their side, competitors have repeatedly continued to use third parties' marks without authorization on promotional products, frequently engaging – at times intentionally – in infringing activities, thus triggering additional enforcement and litigation.[50]

Although primarily based on misunderstandings or convenient interpretations of the law, these actions have nonetheless translated into serious adverse effects for the market and the judicial system in the United

---

[44] *See generally* 4 McCarthy, *supra* note 11, §§ 24:7–20 (offering a detailed reconstruction of the various positions on the merchandising debate).

[45] Notably, scholars argue that the line of cases that started with *Job's Daughters* and *Rainbow for Girls*, which rejected trademark owners' claims, is correct and that courts should use those precedents in merchandising cases. *See* Dogan & Lemley, 'Merchandising Right', *supra* note 4, at 477–48 (*quoting Boston Prof'l Hockey Ass'n v. Dallas Cap & Emblem Mfg., Inc.*, 510 F.2d 1004, 1012 (5th Cir. 1975). Yet, practitioners routinely bring lawsuits on the grounds of *Boston Hockey* and similar decisions. Raysman et al., *supra* note 41, § 9.01.

[46] Nathan Isaacs, 'Traffic in Trademarks', 44 Harv. L. Rev. 1210, 1210 (1931).

[47] For a general discussion on the need to control competitors' opportunistic behaviors, see Michael J. Meurer, 'Controlling Opportunistic and Anti-Competitive Intellectual Property Litigation', 44 B.C. L. Rev. 509 (2002–2003).

[48] For an exhaustive list of these cases, see Lemley & McKenna, *supra* note 31, at 422-26.

[49] *See* David S. Ruder, 'New Strategies for Owners of Discontinued Brands', 3 Nw. J. Tech. & Intell. Prop. 61, 74–5 (2004) (suggesting that intent-to-use applications can prevent third parties from considering the use of a trademark, but also warning that the party may be challenged with a claim of bad faith).

[50] *See, e.g.*, 4 McCarthy, *supra* note 11, §§ 24:7–20.

States.[51] In addition, even if the majority of the superfluous claims started by trademark owners usually settle out of court, these claims inevitably add extra costs to the judicial system.[52] In general, they produce high litigation costs and chilling effects on the market. Almost inevitably, these costs are ultimately transferred to consumers through higher product prices, reduced product quality, or reduced product availability altogether.[53] In addition, fears and the costs of litigation often bring competitors to kowtow to aggressive trademark owners and enter into unnecessary licensing agreements simply to avoid any risk of a finding of trademark infringement.[54]

Not all trademark claims against unauthorized promotional products, however, should be considered frivolous or unnecessary. At times, competitors adopt less than legitimate practices against trademark owners in the market and clearly engage in acts of unfair competition, exploiting the uncertainty surrounding the current lack of regulation for merchandising. Furthermore, the assertion by some scholars that competitors could prevent consumer confusion simply by placing disclaimers on unauthorized promotional products[55] has dangerously provided room for counterfeiters to argue that counterfeited promotional products could instead be lawful products as long as they are accompanied by disclaimers to prevent confusion on the part of consumers in the market.[56] Finally, the fact that trademark owners could face claims of trademark abandonment, laches, or acquiescence in infringement actions if they do not react promptly to allegedly unauthorized uses of their marks has also contributed, in general,

---

[51]   *See* Bone, 'Enforcement Costs', *supra* note 34, at 2123.

[52]   For example, although the University of Kansas claimed that an unlicensed t-shirt vendor was infringing Kansas' trademarks on a significant number of t-shirt designs, the court found infringement only on a small number of designs using marks that were "overwhelmingly similar" to plaintiff's marks. *Univ. of Kansas v. Larry Sinks*, 565 F. Supp. 2d 1216, 1254–55 (D. Kan. 2008). *See also Univ. of Alabama Bd. of Trustees v. New Life Art, Inc.*, 2009 WL 5213713, *1 (N.D. Ala. 2009) (denying the university's exclusive rights to the colors of the team uniform).

[53]   *See* Kenneth L. Port, 'Trademark Extortion: The End of Trademark Law', 65 Wash. & Lee. L. Rev. 585, 602–06 (2008) [hereinafter Port, 'Trademark Extortion']. Port also denounces trademark owners' "predation," which creates an atmosphere in which potential market entrants believe they will be sued for trademark infringement. *Id.*

[54]   Gibson, *supra* note 38, at 920

[55]   *See, e.g.*, Bone, 'Enforcement Costs', *supra* note 34, at 2182–83.

[56]   *See Louis Vuitton Malletier v. Burlington Coat Factory Warehouse Corp.*, 2006 U.S. Dist. LEXIS 32884 at *6 (S.D.N.Y. 2006) (holding that plaintiff's counterfeit claims failed because there was not a likelihood of consumer confusion).

to the excessive enforcement and unnecessary licensing agreements that dominate this area.[57]

3. THE CASE FOR A LIMITED PROTECTION OF TRADEMARK MERCHANDISING UNDER CURRENT TRADEMARK RULES

3.1 Flaws of the Current Positions on Trademark Merchandising

In the light of the above, it seems clear that the uncertainty surrounding the merchandising debate must be addressed. A solution should be found to balance business' interests in promotional products with the need to protect the interests of collectiveness and market competition. As repeatedly noted, today's economy relies heavily on merchandising in the United States as well as in most other countries, and cannot afford to perpetuate the current disconnect between theory and practice on this issue. In order to find this solution, however, a more critical analysis of the current debate is first required to address the flaws and the limited legal analysis that has characterized, so far, the positions presented in this area by both opponents and supporters of merchandising.[58]

With respect to scholars' opposition to merchandising rights, for example, scholars have traditionally opposed this practice based on the assertion that trademark law should exclusively, or primarily, protect consumers against confusion. Yet, scholars have frequently neglected to consider that the general scope of trademark law and policy has historically included protecting business goodwill against misappropriation in addition to protecting consumers against confusion.[59] Accordingly, despite scholars' ideological opposition, the judicial and legislative support for trademark merchandising has generally been based on an established

---

[57] The Lanham Act states that a mark is "abandoned" when "use has been discontinued with intent not to resume such use" and "[w]hen any course of conduct of the owner . . . causes the mark to become the generic name for the goods or services . . . ." Lanham Act § 45, 15 U.S.C. § 1127 (2006). Trademark owners who engage in promotional use of their mark must closely protect their mark. In addition, trademark owners must duly enforce their rights to prevent claims of laches and acquiescence. Lanham Act § 19, 15 U.S.C. § 1069.

[58] *See* 4 McCarthy, *supra* note 11, §§ 24:7–20.

[59] *See, e.g., United Drug Co. v. Rectanus Co.*, 248 U.S. 90, 97 (1918). A trademark's "function is simply to designate the goods as the product of a particular trader and to protect his goodwill against the sale of another's product as his; and it is not the subject of property except in connection with an existing business." *Id.*

principle of trademark protection rather than on a "fragile theory."[60] In addition, scholars have often disregarded that infringement in merchandising cases can be found by applying the traditional standard of "consumer confusion" and not necessarily confusion "as to the sponsorship" of the products. Courts have, in fact, repeatedly held that a likelihood of confusion can be "expected" when "sufficiently similar" marks are used on directly competing goods[61] – precisely the case of most unauthorized promotional products. Lastly, no sound reason has emerged from academia to deny that trademark use on merchandised goods represents a valid use of a mark to identify products in the course of trade[62] and thus should not be subjected to the general rules of trademark protection.

Similarly, scholars' arguments about merchandising's negative effects on competition may also seem questionable under a more thorough analysis of the market effects of this practice. Undoubtedly, merchandising marks constitute a limited monopoly and a barrier to entry in the market.

---

[60]   *See* Irene Calboli, 'Trademark Assignment "with Goodwill": A Concept whose Time Has Gone', 57 Fla. L. Rev. 771, 782 (2005). *But see* Robert G. Bone, 'Hunting Goodwill: A History of the Concept of Goodwill in Trademark Law', 86 B.U. L. Rev. 547, 592 (2008).

[61]   *AMF Inc. v. Sleekcraft Boats,* 599 F.2d 341, 348 (9th Cir. 1979). "When the goods produced by the alleged infringer compete for sales with those of the trademark owner, infringement usually will be found if the marks are sufficiently similar that confusion can be expected." *Id. See also Polaroid Corp. v. Polarad Elcs. Corp.* 287 F.2d 492, 495 (2d Cir. 1962) (suggesting that confusion can be expected for similar marks when the products are identical). This direct "presumption" of confusion, and thus infringement, for identical products carrying identical marks is also explicitly stated in Article 16 of the Agreement on Trade-Related Aspects of Intellectual Property Right according to which "[i]n case of the use of an identical sign for identical goods or services, a likelihood of confusion shall be presumed . . ." *See* Agreement on Trade-Related Aspects of Intellectual Property Right, [hereinafter TRIPS], April 15, 1994, Marrakesh Agreement Establishing the World Trade Organization, Annex 1C, *Legal Instruments – General Agreement on Tariffs and Trade – Multilateral Trade Negotiations (The Uruguay Round): Agreement on Trade-Related Aspects of Intellectual Property Rights, Including Trade in Counterfeit Goods* [December 15, 1993].vol. 33, 33 I.L.M. 81 (Washington DC, USA: 1994). Accordingly, this principle should be considered accepted based upon the obligations of the United States as a member of TRIPS, and confusion shall be presumed when the products and the marks at issue are identical, as most often in the case of unauthorized promotional goods. *See* Lanham Act §§ 32, 43, 15 U.S.C. §§ 1114, 1125 (2006).

[62]   *See Univ. of South Carolina v. Univ. of Southern California,* 2010 WL 157220, *2 (C.A. Fed. 2010) (treating merchandising marks as "product marks" while denying the appeal of the University of South Carolina against the TTAB decision to refuse to register the "SC" mark because of direct confusion with the mark from the University of Southern California).

Still, all marks, not solely merchandising marks, are barriers to entry in the market, since the legal recognition of all marks is directly based on an ad hoc "right to exclude" others from using identical or similar signs.[63] Yet, because trademarks also represent the "essence of competition" due to their ability to distinguish products from different ones and to inform the public about the quality of the products that they identify,[64] trademark law and policy have carefully crafted this "right to exclude" by imposing strict limits for acquiring and enforcing trademark rights, as well as specific defenses to safeguard fair competition and non-commercial uses of marks in society.[65] Accordingly, no additional distortions of competition need to result from the use of marks on promotional products compared to the use of marks on "primary" products as long as merchandising marks are protected only when they are used to identify and distinguish products in the marketplace, subject to the rules and limitations provided by current trademark norms.

On their part, trademark owners and practitioners have also adopted a limited analysis of the issue, which has greatly contributed to the current impasse in the merchandising debate. Notably, trademark owners and practitioners have repeatedly ignored that trademark rights find their rationale in guaranteeing the fair functioning of the market both for competitors and consumers rather than protecting trademarks per se.[66] Even more problematically, they have often downplayed the fact that consumer welfare and competition remain the primary scope of trademark law, and that merchandising cannot be considered as a "fait accompli" in practice unless it is carefully subjected to the defenses expressly provided

---

[63] Glynn S. Lunney, Jr., 'Trademark Monopolies', 48 *Emory L.J.* 367, 421 (1999). "In any form, trademark protection grants to a particular individual a bundle of rights . . ." *Id. See also* Brown, *supra* note 28, at 1116; Charlie E. Mueller, 'Sources of Monopoly Power: A Phenomenon Called "Product Differentiation,"' 18 Am. U. L. Rev. 1 (1968).

[64] *See* William M. Landes & Richard A. Posner, *The Economic Structure of Intellectual Property Law*, 184 (Cambridge, MA, USA: Belknap Press of Harvard University Press, 2003).

[65] *See* Robert P. Merges et al., *Intellectual Property in the New Technological Age* 890–947 (5th edn., Maryland, USA: Aspen Publishers 2010) (discussing various defenses in trademark law).

[66] *See* Daniel McClure, 'Trademarks and Unfair Competition: A Critical History of Legal Thought', 69 Trademark Rep. 305, 329 (1978). "The result of the realist attacks brought about changes in the rhetoric of judges and commentators . . . . The property justification of protection was replaced by arguments in favor of protecting business good will and values resulting from use." *Id.* As a result of these changes, "[p]rotecting the public from confusion and deception became a more prominent rationale than protecting property." *Id.*

to prevent the abuse of trademark rights to the detriment of competitors and consumers.[67]

Finally, trademark owners and practitioners have also generally minimized the importance of trademark defenses and the dangers that unlimited merchandising rights could entail for society in terms of appropriation of words and symbols and negative effects for competition.[68] As a result, this perception has brought trademark owners to increasingly value marks "in gross" and frequently forget that infringement claims with respect to promotional products cannot be based on the simple desire to control marks per se but rather must be based on actual trademark use and likelihood of consumer confusion.[69] Even if rent-seeking attempts are commonly part of trademark owners' behaviors with respect to merchandising products, courts have repeatedly stated that trademarks do not exist "in gross," and have denied relief when marks were abandoned or products were not competing.[70]

3.2   Calling for a Limited Protection of Merchandising Rights

In light of the above, considering the economic relevance of merchandising and the negative consequences of absolute merchandising rights, the most sensible solution to address the divide that still reigns in this area in the United States seems to be to explicitly apply to the marks that are used to identify promotional products the same rules that apply to marks in general.[71] Contrary to common criticism, this protection of merchandising

---

[67]   Generally, on trademark fair use, and the problems related to its actual implementation and effectiveness, see William McGeveran, 'Rethinking Trademark Fair Use', 94 Iowa L. Rev. 49, 54 (2008) (providing a comprehensive review of the problems currently affecting the application of fair use exceptions in trademark law).

[68]   *See, e.g.*, Lunney, *supra* note 63, at 485 (noting that copying and competition are the exception, rather than the rule, in a property-based trademark regime).

[69]   Port, *Trademark Extortion*, *supra* note 53, at 555–56 (noting that "[t]he Supreme Court has continuously held that the trademark right is 'not in gross' and not a copyright or a patent, but that any rights to trademarks are appurtenant to the related business").

[70]   *See, e.g.*, *Emergency One, Inc. v. American FireEagle, Ltd.*, 228 F.3d 531 (4th Cir. 2000); *Silverman v. CBS Inc.*, 870 F.2d 40 (2d Cir. 1989); *Int'l Order of Job's Daughters v. Lindeburg & Co.*, 633 F.2d 912 (9th Cir. 1980); *Supreme Assembly, Order of Rainbow for Girls v. J.H. Ray Jewelry Co., 676 F.2d 1079 (5th Cir. 1982)*; *Univ. of Pittsburgh v. Champion Prods., Inc.*, 686 F.2d 1040 (3d Cir. 1982); *DeBeers LV Trademark, Ltd. v. DeBeers Diamond Syndicate, Inc.*, 440 F. Supp. 2d 349 (S.D.N.Y. 2006).

[71]   *See* discussion *supra* Section 1.

marks would not further restrict competition in the marketplace. Instead, it would finally provide a precise guideline for the validity of this practice, while confining the recognition of merchandising rights within the existing norms for trademark enforcement, defenses, and fair use.[72]

Undoubtedly, to directly acknowledge the validity of merchandising rights under the above premises would immediately solve the major downfall of the current dispute – the uncertainty that intrinsically defines this area would end and competitors would be provided with a precise standard when enforcing or using trademarks for promotional products.[73] This clear but limited acceptance of merchandising rights would also provide a compromising solution to the present controversy between trademark theory and practice. As repeatedly noted, although courts have increasingly recognized merchandising de facto and enjoined unauthorized trademark uses on merchandised goods, they have left room for inconsistency and have not specifically addressed the application of trademark defenses and fair uses in merchandising cases.[74]

Equally importantly, while accepting that trademark use on promotional products can legitimately represent "trademark use,"[75] the proposed solution also subjects and limits trademark protection for marks used on promotional goods to the requirement that trademark owners use their marks in the course of trade to distinguish and identify the products

---

[72] *See generally* 4 McCarthy, *supra* note 11, § 24:17-20 (suggesting that a trademark owner's rights in markets in which it may explore in the future should be limited by the perception of consumers).

[73] *See* discussion *supra* Section 1.

[74] To date courts do not seem to have extensively elaborated, however, on trademark defenses and fair use doctrines in this context. Theoretically, courts have confirmed the application of defenses and fair use to trademark merchandising, but have generally found or denied infringement based on likelihood of confusion, and accepted or denied dilution claims based on blurring or tarnishment. *See, e.g., Rainbow for Girls*, 676 F.2d at 1082 (providing no discussion of trademark defenses); *Univ. of Pittsburgh*, 686 F.2d at 1044 (focusing primarily the doctrine of laches); *Boston Prof'l Hockey Ass'n v. Dallas Cap & Emblem Mfg.*, 510 F.2d 1004, 1013 (5th Cir. 1975), *cert. denied*, 423 U.S. 868 (1975) (undertaking a brief discussion of functionality). Still, the effective judicial application of defenses and fair use will prove fundamental to prevent chilling effects in trademark practice and guarantee a lasting solution in this area.

[75] The general premise for trademark protection is that marks are either in use or are intended to be in use. Lanham Act § 1, 15 U.S.C. § 1051. *See, e.g.*, Stacey L. Dogan & Mark A. Lemley, 'Grounding Trademark Law through Trademark Use', 92 Iowa L. Rev. 1668 (2007) [hereinafter Dogan & Lemley, 'Trademark Use']. *Cf.* Graeme B. Dinwoodie & Mark D. Janis, 'Confusion over Use: Contextualism in Trademark Law', 92 Iowa L. Rev. 1597 (2007).

for which protection is sought.[76] Following the general principles of trademark law, merchandising marks would thus be explicitly protected only against confusingly similar marks with respect to competing or related products[77] and not with respect to unrelated goods or services, unless the marks at issue are famous and a likelihood of dilution – blurring or tarnishment – could be found.[78] Ultimately, in the case of both famous and ordinary marks, this protection would not apply when third parties are not using the same or similar marks in commerce but for other purposes, as repeatedly affirmed by the majority of the courts.[79]

Granting merchandising rights legal status when marks are used to identify products that are offered for sale would also clearly subject this practice to the defenses and fair uses currently set forth by the law for all marks.[80] Trademark rights in promotional products would thus be explicitly limited by existing statutory defenses and trademark owners would not be able to enforce their rights upon evidence of abandonment, laches, and acquiescence.[81] Likewise, merchandising rights would be directly subjected to the defenses of descriptive and nominative fair use, including comparative advertising, parody and satire, as repeatedly affirmed by the courts[82] and recently confirmed by Congress for famous marks under the TDRA.[83]

Finally, since most merchandising activities are carried out under

---

[76]   *Univ. of South Carolina v. Univ. of Southern California*, 2010 WL 157220, *2 (C.A. Fed. 2010) (treating merchandising marks as "product marks" and finding the respective "SC" logos of the Universities of South Carolina and Southern California confusingly similar).

[77]   Lanham Act §§ 32(1)(a), 43(a)(1)(A), 15 U.S.C. §§ 1114(1)(a), 1125(a)(1)(A) (2006).

[78]   Lanham Act § 43(c), 15 U.S.C. § 1125(c).

[79]   *See generally* 1-800 *Contacts, Inc. v. WhenU.com, Inc.*, 414 F.3d 400 (2d Cir. 2005) (stating that infringement does not apply if defendants are not using the mark to identify product source). *See* Dogan & Lemley, 'Trademark Use', *supra* note 75, at 1675-90.

[80]   *See* Merges et al., *supra* note 65, at 890–947; 6 J. Thomas McCarthy, *McCarthy on Trademarks and Unfair Competition* § 31 (4th edn., Minnesota, USA: Thomson West 2010).

[81]   Lanham Act §§ 19, 45, 15 U.S.C. §§ 1069, 1127 (2006).

[82]   Courts have generally accepted parody as fair use. *See Mattel, Inc. v. MCA Records, Inc.*, 296 F.3d 894 (9th Cir. 2002). Courts have also created the doctrine of "nominative fair use" to protect the unauthorized use of a mark to describe competitors' products to the extent necessary and truthfully. *See New Kids on the Block v. News Am. Publ'g*, 971 F.2d 302 (9th Cir. 1992). For the relationship between trademark law and the First Amendment, see *Cliffs Notes, Inc. v. Bantam Doubleday Dell Pub. Group, Inc.*, 886 F.2d 490 (2d Cir. 1989).

[83]   Lanham Act § 43(c)(3), 15 U.S.C. § 1125(c)(3).

licensing agreements, accepting the validity of merchandising rights would also subject the validity of this practice to the general requirements provided for trademark licensing – "quality control" and "consistent product quality"[84] – lest trademark owners could face claims of naked licensing and ultimately findings of abandonment and trademark cancellations.[85] Even though courts seem to have adopted a formalistic reading of this requirement and have increasingly focused on consumers' deception rather than on "quality control"[86] while assessing the validity of licensing agreements in practice, these requirements would additionally cabin the extent of merchandising protection to those promotional products whose quality is, at least in principle, guaranteed by trademark owners.[87] To the contrary, trademark rights could be forfeited, and competitors would be able to freely use identical or similar marks for any product in the market.

3.3 Reconciling Individualism and Collectiveness in Trademark Merchandising

Consistent with the historical rationale of trademark law, any solution to solve the existing impasse should also balance the consideration of trademark owners' individual interests with those of collectiveness, consumers, and market competition. As repeatedly mentioned, to recognize the validity of merchandising rights when the marks are used to identify products in the market would precisely satisfy this need while also bringing a much required legal response to a long-established business reality, still within existing trademark rules.[88] In particular, while this solution

---

[84] Lanham Act §§ 5, 45, 15 U.S.C. §§ 1055, 1127.

[85] Lanham Act § 14(3), 15 U.S.C. § 1064(3) (2006). *See, e.g.*, *Barcamerica Int'l USA Trust v. Tyfield Imps., Inc.*, 289 F.3d 589 (9th Cir. 2002).

[86] *See generally Nitro Leisure Prods., L.L.C. v. Acushnet Co.*, 341 F.3d 1356, 1370 (Fed. Cir. 2003) (consistent quality means the product is of "'the same character and source . . . as other goods previously purchased bearing the mark'"); *Taco Cabana Int'l, Inc. v. Two Pesos, Inc.*, 932 F.2d 1113, 1121 (5th Cir. 1991) (consistent quality means "no actual decline in quality standards"), *aff'd*, 505 U.S. 763 (1992).

[87] *See, e.g.*, *Univ. of Pittsburgh v. Champion Prods., Inc.*, 686 F.2d 1040, 1047 (3d Cir. 1982).

[88] As repeatedly noted, scholars have generally opposed the creation of an ad hoc merchandising right. "Most cases of consumer confusion can be solved without a merchandising right." Dogan & Lemley, 'Merchandising Right', *supra* note 4, at 506. By recognizing the right of trademark owners to use marks to identify their promotional products directly or under licensing, this chapter ultimately agrees with this position since trademark protection would not be based on an ad hoc new right but on existing trademark rules and defenses.

would unlikely eliminate all trademark owners' attempts to control their marks, it would nonetheless provide competitors with a more sound basis to refuse unnecessary licensing by clarifying which trademark uses do not require trademark owners' consent because products are not related or due to existing defenses.[89]

In addition, contrary to common criticism, explicitly recognizing merchandising rights under the general trademark rules would not necessarily imply increased costs for market competition. As already noted by some scholars,[90] although protecting merchandising would most likely result in slightly higher product prices compared to a system without merchandising rights, the "fairly elastic demand"[91] for promotional products in the market could ultimately offset these costs, both because licensees need to cover production costs and may choose alternative marks if royalties are excessive, and because consumers may switch to alternative products, or boycott promotional goods altogether, if prices become too high.[92] As a result, contrary to scholars' argument that protecting merchandising would amount to a monopoly on ornamental product features, this limited recognition of merchandising would simply permit trademark owners to use their marks to identify products for sale, while leaving consumers free to choose among similar promotional products available in the market.[93]

---

[89]   *See* Rebecca Tushnet, 'Why the Customer Isn't Always Right: Producer-Based Limits on Rights Accretion in Trademark', 116 Yale L.J. Pocket Part 352 (2007), *available at* http://yalelawjournal.org/2007/04/25/tushnet.html. *See, e.g.,* *Univ. of Alabama Bd. of Trustees v. New Life Art, Inc.*, 2009 WL 5213713, *1 (N.D. Ala. 2009) (denying infringement when an artist uses the color of a team's uniform to depict historically accurately football scenes); *MasterCard Int'l, Inc. v. Nader 2000 Primary Committee*, 70 U.S.P.Q.2d 1046 (S.D.N.Y. 2004) (where Ralph Nader parodied the MasterCard "priceless" slogan for political purposes).

[90]   Denicola, *supra* note 30, at 634.

[91]   *Id.*

[92]   *Id.*

[93]   For example, should a consumer find that the price of the RED SOX sweat-shirt she would like to purchase is "too high" compared to "similar" goods, she may decide to purchase, instead, a sweat-shirt with the logo of another baseball team (probably not the YANKEES), or a sweat-shirt with the logo of a football team, like the GREEN BAY PACKERS, or with the logo of her university. Or, she could decide to purchase a sweatshirt with the NIKE logo, or with a different logo or design altogether. In other words, the consumers could choose among similar, although not identical, products, since the logo on the sweat-shirt does not represent the product per se, but only indicates the affiliation of that sweat-shirt with the team, institution, or company which is identified by the logo. Thus, despite scholars' reluctance to accept this reality, recognizing the validity of trademark rights in these products would not deprive consumers of alternative choices of similar products identified by other marks.

Notably, rather than negatively impacting the market, directly recognizing merchandising rights could even benefit consumers by increasing the number of comparable products available to the public in the market. In particular, when prohibited to use third parties' marks on their t-shirts, mugs, or keychains because of likely consumer confusion or dilution, producers of these goods could choose between entering into a licensing agreement with trademark owners, or using an alternative design for their products, which could either use the same mark under an established defense – parody, nominative fair use, etc. – or a totally different and original work. Accordingly, consumers could have access to a larger number of similar promotional products marketed under the control of trademark owners, or be provided with additional product choices with alternative designs to the overall benefit of market competition and societal creativeness.[94]

Based upon these premises, it seems indisputable that to recognize, and to cabin merchandising rights under the existing trademark rules would provide the most sensible compromise to the current impasse. Generally, notwithstanding their diverging positions over the extent of trademark protection, trademark scholars, trademark owners, and practitioners should agree that the ultimate function of trademark law is to prevent commercial misconduct in the market, and detriment both to consumers and competitors.[95] As this chapter has demonstrated, protecting merchandising rights when marks are used to identify promotional products offered for sale against confusingly similar goods, or against diluting uses of the marks, would not unnaturally expand trademark protection. Instead, this limited recognition of trademark merchandising would straightforwardly apply existing trademark principles following the general spirit of trademark law: protecting consumers against confusion and business goodwill against misappropriation and unfair competition.

Despite the reluctance of merchandising opponents to accept modern trademark reality, the role of marks has undergone a profound evolution in the past century following the changes in economic production and distribution.[96] The rise of trademark merchandising is a direct reflection

---

[94] *See* Landes & Posner, *supra* note 3, at 270 (stating that protection of trademarks is essential to create an incentive for owners to invest resources and create new marks).

[95] *See generally* 1 J. Thomas McCarthy, *McCarthy on Trademarks and Unfair Competition* § 2 (4th edn., Minnesota, USA: Thomson West 2010) (analyzing the policy rationales of trademark law).

[96] Thomas D. Drescher, 'The Transformation and Evolution of Trademark – From Signals to Symbols to Myth', 82 Trademark Rep. 301, 321-38 (1992); Mark P. McKenna, 'Trademark Use and the Problem of Source', 2009 U. Ill. L. Rev 773,

of this process and this practice should be directly recognized and given legal status. Still, the belief that marks are merely business assets under the absolute control of trademark owners remains erroneous, and the rationale for protecting trademark rights in promotional products should continue to focus on safeguarding market competition and consumers.[97] Accordingly, while courts should forbid confusing or truly diluting trademark uses in promotional products, non-confusing unauthorized products using famous marks for parodies and otherwise established fair uses should be allowed to the benefit of the market and collectiveness in general.

4.   CONCLUSION

Trademark merchandising unquestionably constitutes a widely used business technique in today's economy to establish brand image and customer affiliation. Still, the legal status of this practice continues to be unclear and highly disputed in the United States. Although courts and legislators have progressively accepted merchandising rights de facto, ambiguity continues to dominate judicial outcomes and no sufficient guidelines have been elaborated so far as to the application of trademark defenses and fair use in this area. The time has come to address this ambiguity and grant trademark merchandising explicit, but limited, protection when marks are used to identify and distinguish promotional products that are offered for sale. Contrary to criticism, this protection would not distort competition or negatively impact consumers. Instead, it would only protect merchandising marks provided that marks are used in the course of trade, and within the existing norms for infringement and dilution, subjected to the application of existing trademark defenses and fair use doctrines. Ultimately, as long as the courts apply trademark principles correctly, this protection could prevent abusive enforcement and unnecessary legal actions, thus fostering fairness in competition and preventing consumer confusion.

---

821 (2009); Lynn M. Lopucki, 'Toward a Trademark-Based Liability System', 49 UCLA L. Rev. 1099 (2002).
    [97]   Landes & Posner, *supra* note 3, at 184.

11. The competitive significance of collective trademarks

Alexander Peukert*

1. INTRODUCTION

This chapter deals with the protection of collective trademarks under European Union (EU) and German law. It was triggered by the remarkable statement of the ECJ in its 2009 *L'Oréal* decision, according to which the protected functions of a trademark include not only the essential function to guarantee the origin of goods or services, but also its other functions, "in particular that of guaranteeing the quality of goods or services and those of communication, investment or advertising".[1] The aim is to explore whether the expansionist functional paradigm of *L'Oréal* also applies to collective marks or whether the ownership structure and competitive significance of this type of trademark requires a different treatment compared to individual trademarks.[2]

The peculiarity of collective marks is their ownership structure. The holder of the right is not an individual market participant, but an association of producers of goods or suppliers of services. The members of the association entitled to use the collective mark may bring an action for infringement only if the association, as the proprietor, agrees.[3] Thus, collective marks are owned by one legal person, but they may be lawfully used

---

*   Dr. iur., Professor of Law, Chair for Civil Law, Commercial Law and Intellectual Property Law, Goethe University Frankfurt/Main, Cluster of Excellence Normative Orders, http://www.jura.uni-frankfurt.de/peukert/.

[1]   ECJ Case C-487/07 *L'Oréal/Bellure* [2009] ECR I-05185 para. 58; similar Fezer, Karl-Heinz (2009), *Markenrecht*, 4th edn., Munich, Germany: C.H. Beck, Einl D MarkenG para. 1-20.

[2]   See generally Peukert, Alexander (2011), 'Individual, multiple and collective ownership of intellectual property rights – Which impact on exclusivity?', in Kur, Annette and Mizaras, Vytautas (eds), *The Structure of Intellectual Property Law*, Aldershot, UK and Brookfield, US: Edward Elgar, 195–225.

[3]   Art. 66(1), 72 Council Regulation (EC) No. 207/2009 of 26 February 2009 on the Community trademark (codified version), OJ L 78/1 (in the following: Reg.

and enforced by a plurality of persons. Three sub-categories of collective trademarks can be discerned:

- *Conventional* collective marks that are capable of distinguishing the goods or services of the members of an association from those of other undertakings according to their origin from a given enterprise – e.g. "FLEUROP";[4]
- Collective *guarantee* marks that distinguish goods or services not according to their origin, but according to their quality – e.g. "Urlaub auf dem Bauernhof" (Vacation on the farm);[5]
- Collective *geographical indication (GI)* marks designating the geographical origin of goods or services – e.g. "Bayerisches Bier" (Bavarian beer).[6]

2.   THREE TYPES OF COLLECTIVE TRADEMARKS

2.1   Conventional Collective Trademarks

Conventional collective trademarks serve to distinguish the goods or services not of individual undertakings, but those of the members of an association from those of outsiders or other groups.[7] Acknowledging the classical distinctive function, but at the same time the particular ownership structure of collective marks, EU and German trademark law set out that the general law of trademarks applies, unless the special rules on

---

207/2009); Sec. 97, 98, 101 German Trademark Act (*Markengesetz*), available at http://www.gesetze-im-internet.de/markeng/.

⁴   Community Trademark No. 001286491, available at http://oami.europa.eu/CTMOnline/RequestManager/en_SearchBasic_NoReg.

⁵   See RAL (2010), Gütezeichenübersicht, RAL-RG 163/1, Urlaub auf dem Bauernhof, available at http://www.ral-guete.de/fileadmin/lib/pdf/guete/Guetezeichenuebersicht_Juni_2010.pdf; The DLG Quality Marker in Rural Tourism (Landtourismus) (2010), available at http://www.landtourismus.de/446.html

⁶   Community Trademark No. 000226621, available at http://oami.europa.eu/CTMOnline/RequestManager/en_SearchBasic_NoReg; Schennen (2007), in Eisenführ, Günther and Schennen, Detlef, *Gemeinschaftsmarkenverordnung*, 2nd edn., Cologne, Berlin, Munich, Germany: Carl Heymanns Verlag, Art. 64 para. 5.

⁷   Art. 66(1) s. 1 Reg. 207/2009; Sec. 97(1) German Trademark Act; German Federal Court of Justice, Case I ZB 32/93, *Gewerblicher Rechtsschutz und Urheberrecht (GRUR)*, 1996, 270; Wüst, Birgit and Jansen, Manuel (2009), in Ekey, Friedrich L. et al. (eds), *Markenrecht, Band 1*, 2nd ed., Heidelberg, Germany: C.F. Müller Verlag, § 97 para. 12-17.

collective trademarks provide otherwise.[8] And indeed, these rules deviate from general trademark law, bearing also on the protected functions of collective marks.

According to Article 7*bis* paragraph 2 of the Paris Convention, each country shall be the judge of the particular conditions under which a collective mark shall be protected, and that country may refuse protection if the mark is contrary to the public interest.[9] Similarly, Article 15 of the EU trademark directive[10] proclaims that Member States whose laws authorize the registration of collective marks may provide that such marks shall not be registered, or shall be declared invalid, *on grounds additional* to those specified for individual marks. In this regard, the directive does not refer to additional reasons of public policy like the Paris Convention, but to the functions of collective marks. National law may prohibit the registration of collective marks *"where the function of those marks so requires"*. The directive thus explicitly ties the specific limits of protection of collective marks to their legally relevant functions.

To understand this nexus between functions and limits, one has to take a closer look at the content of these additional grounds to refuse protection. As explained, collective marks differ from individual marks in that they are held by associations rather than by individual undertakings. The association is established and organized by a *private agreement* among the members. This internal regulation governs the use of the collective mark, i.e., who is entitled to use the sign and under which conditions.[11]

The additional grounds for a refusal of protection of collective marks mentioned in the Paris Convention and the EU Trademark Directive also address this *internal agreement* and not – as in the case of individual marks – the sign as such. First, EU and German trademark law require that the regulation of the association be submitted in the course of application. The document must specify *inter alia* the object of the association, the persons authorized to use the mark, the conditions for membership, and the conditions of use of the mark.[12] Anyone may inspect the

---

[8] See Art. 66(3) Reg. 207/2009; Sec. 97(2) German Trademark Act.

[9] Paris Convention for the Protection of Industrial Property as amended on 28 September 1979, available at http://www.wipo.int/treaties/en/ip/paris/.

[10] Directive 2008/95/EC of the European Parliament and of the Council of 22 October 2008 to approximate the laws of the Member States relating to trademarks (Codified version), OJ L 299/25 (in the following: Dir. 2008/95).

[11] Art. 70 Reg. 207/2009; Ingerl, Reinhard and Rohnke, Christian (2010), *Markengesetz*, 3rd edn., Munich, Germany: C.H. Beck, § 97 para. 13.

[12] Art. 67 Reg. 207/2009; Rule 43 Commission Regulation (EC) No 2868/95 of 13 December 1995 implementing Council Regulation (EC) No 40/94 on the Community trademark, OJ L 303/1; Sec. 102 German Trademark Act.

regulations.[13] The aim of this registration requirement is transparency. Second, if the internal *regulation* governing the use of the collective mark – again not the sign as such – is contrary to public policy or to accepted principles of morality, the application shall be refused, unless the applicant amends the regulation in such a way that the ground for refusal ceases to exist.[14] Under EU law, any person, group or body may submit written observations related to these aspects in the course of the registration procedure.[15]

In addressing the agreement of competitors to establish a collective trademark, these rules reflect *competition concerns*, which are not apparent if an individual undertaking registers a trademark.[16] The guidelines on the applicability of EU competition law to horizontal cooperation agreements explain why such commercialization arrangements deserve scrutiny even if they fall short of joint selling.[17] First, joint commercialization provides a clear opportunity for exchanges of sensitive commercial information particularly on marketing strategy and pricing. Second, depending on the cost structure of the commercialization, a significant input to the parties' final costs may be common. As a result, the actual scope for price competition at the final sales level may be limited. Joint commercialization agreements such as regulations governing the use of a collective mark can thus fall under the prohibition of agreements in restraint of competition

---

[13] Sec. 102(4) German Trademark Act. See e.g. the bylaws, etc. of Fleurop-Interflora Association, Community Trademark No. 001286491, available at http://oami.europa.eu/CTMOnline/RequestManager/en_DetailedTrademarkInformation_NoReg.

[14] Compare Art. 67, 68 Reg. 207/2009 with Art. 7(1)(f) Reg. 207/2009 or Art. 3(1)(f) Dir. 2008/95 (*"trademarks* which are contrary to public policy or to accepted principles of morality"*).

[15] Art. 69 Reg. 207/2009.

[16] European Commission (1980), Proposal for a council regulation on the Community trademark of 27 November 1980, COM (80) 635, final, *Gewerblicher Rechtsschutz und Urheberrecht Internationaler Teil (GRUR Int.)*, 1981, 86, 97; Ingerl, Reinhard and Rohnke, Christian (2010), *Markengesetz*, 3rd edn., Munich, Germany: C.H. Beck, § 103 para. 2; Wüst/Jansen (2009), in Ekey, Friedrich L. et al (eds.), *Markenrecht, Band 1*, 2nd ed., Heidelberg, Germany: C.F. Müller Verlag, § 104 para. 8; contra Kober-Dehm (2009), in Ströbele, Paul et al. (eds.), *Markengesetz*, 9th edn., Cologne, Berlin, Munich, Germany: Carl Heymanns Verlag, § 102 para. 11, § 103 para. 5; Gruber (2007), in von Schultz, Detlef (ed.), *Kommentar zum Markenrecht*, 2nd edn., Frankfurt am Main, Germany: Verlag Recht und Wirtschaft, § 103 paras. 4, 14 (restraints of competition only to be inquired by the competition authorities).

[17] European Commission (2001), Guidelines on the applicability of Article 81 of the EC Treaty to horizontal cooperation agreements, OJ C 3/2, paras. 139 et seq.

if they either allow the exchange of sensitive commercial information, or if they influence a significant part of the parties' final cost.[18] However, only if the regulation of the association contains clauses obviously in violation of competition law, will the trademark office refuse to register. Not only is an inquiry into the economic and competitive pros and cons of such a joint commercialization not feasible for a trademark office, but the more limited wording of "public policy" signals that only agreements that clearly restrain competition warrant a refusal of registration of the collective mark.[19]

By requiring transparency and ex officio examination, trademark law denies its benefits to those co-operations between competitors that not only establish a collective mark, but moreover fix prices, limit or streamline production or divide markets. In its decision to declare the latter kind of clause – market division – illegal, the German Federal Court of Justice asked whether such a regulation of the usage of a collective mark is necessary to achieve the legally protected functions of the mark. The court rejected the argument that a division of markets was necessary to guarantee a high quality of the product – in this case bread for toasting – because at the time of the decision in 1991, German trademark law protected only the function of the trademark to indicate the origin of the product, not its quality.[20]

This case confirms that the ownership structure, scope and purpose of collective marks are interrelated. The more legally protected functions of a collective mark are accepted, the broader the exclusive right becomes and the harder it is to integrate competition-related concerns into trademark law.

2.2 Collective Guarantee Marks

This interrelation can also be observed with regard to the second category of collective marks: collective *guarantee* marks. The German Trademark Act refers to these marks by stating that also such signs may be registered as a collective mark that are capable of distinguishing the goods or services of the members of the association from those of other undertakings not

---

[18] Art. 101 Treaty on the Functioning of the European Union, OJ 2010 C 83/47; European Commission (2001), Guidelines on the applicability of Article 81 of the EC Treaty to horizontal cooperation agreements, OJ C 3/2, paras. 146, 177.
[19] Ingerl, Reinhard and Rohnke, Christian (2010), *Markengesetz*, 3rd edn., Munich, Germany: C.H. Beck, § 103 para. 2.
[20] German Federal Court of Justice, Case KVR 1/90, *Gewerblicher Rechtsschutz und Urheberrecht (GRUR)*, 1991, 782, 785.

only according to their origin, but also according to their *"nature, quality or other properties"*.[21]

Generally, trademarks consisting exclusively of signs designating the quality, value or other characteristics of the goods or service are not protectable because they are not capable of distinguishing the goods or services of one undertaking from those of other undertakings.[22] They simply indicate a certain quality, for example that you will spend your vacation at an actual farm with a distinct agricultural character if you make a reservation at a host advertising with the sign "Vacation on the farm".[23] Protection is available, however, if an association of businesses – in our example farmers – and not an individual undertaking applies for a collective guarantee mark. It is argued that in this situation, the sign is again capable of distinguishing goods in the sense that the sign indicates that the good or service originates from an undertaking that in turn belongs to a specific association that in turn guarantees a certain level of quality.[24] Thus, collective guarantee marks convey additional information compared to conventional collective marks. They not only distinguish and guarantee origin, but also quality. Jurisdictions like Germany that protect this type of collective marks automatically acknowledge the quality function of those signs.[25] Accordingly, collective guarantee marks have more and broader protected functions than conventional collective marks.

Both categories also differ with regard to their competitive significance. To be able to use a collective mark like FLEUROP, designating a widespread floral delivery network, may already be important. Access to collective guarantee marks can be even decisive. If the respective sign – for example "Vacation on the farm" – enjoys a high reputation with consumers, it is considerably more difficult to promote holidays in the countryside without the sign, even if your service objectively equates the quality of competitive offers using the sign.[26] It may even be virtually impossible to

---

[21]   Sec. 97(1) German Trademark Act; Entwurf eines Gesetzes zur Reform des Markenrechts, 14 January 1994, *Bundestags-Drucksache* 12/6581, 108.

[22]   Art. 3(1)(c) Dir. 2008/95; Art. 7(1)(c) Reg. 207/2009; Sec. 8(2) No. 2 German Trademark Act.

[23]   See supra, note 5.

[24]   Ingerl, Reinhard and Rohnke, Christian (2010), *Markengesetz*, 3rd edn., Munich, Germany: C.H. Beck, § 100 para. 3.

[25]   German Federal Court of Justice, Case I ZB 11/75, *Gewerblicher Rechtsschutz und Urheberrecht (GRUR)*, 1977, 488, 489; Helm, Horst (1999), 'Die Unterscheidungsfunktion der Kollektivmarke nach neuem Markenrecht', *Wettbewerb in Recht und Praxis (WRP)*, 41–5.

[26]   See Frankfurt Court of Appeals, Case 6 U (Kart) 122/84, *Wettbewerb in Recht und Praxis (WRP)*, 1986, 98, 102; Bundeskartellamt, Case W 190/66,

market products without the guarantee mark if industry standards refer to the *sign* and not to an objective minimum quality as such.

As the German system of handling collective guarantee marks illustrates, their anti-competitive potential is also stronger than that of conventional collective marks. If a group of let's say organizers of rural tourism wants to acquire a German guarantee mark, they cannot develop the sign and the quality standard on their own and simply submit an application to the German trademark office. Instead, the trademark office requires a certificate from the "German Institute for Quality Protection and Labeling". This institute is a non-profit association, its membership being composed of industry and consumer associations, government and administrative bodies.[27] Its history dates back to the early 20th century. The "Institute for Quality Protection and Labeling" was established in 1925 as the *"Reichs-Ausschuss für Lieferbedingungen"* – RAL – which is still the abbreviation used today.[28] At that time, the German government and industry tried to respond to post-World War I depression and inflation by collectivizing and cartelizing industries.[29] Irrespective of this corporatist history and structure, RAL guarantees that the quality sign identifies an objective standard, and that the association applying for the sign is actually able to control this standard. Only after RAL has issued its certificate may the quality association (*Gütegemeinschaft*) apply for a collective guarantee mark.[30] From that time on, however, it is only the association and in the end its members who decide on amendments of the standard and the conditions to use the sign. In some industry and product sectors, these associations have only very few members. For example, the "Quality Association

---

Wirtschaft und Wettbewerb (WuW), 1968, 222; Düsseldorf Court of Appeals, Case U (Kart) 16/88, *Wirtschaft und Wettbewerb (WuW)*, 1991, 642.

[27] See Fezer, Karl-Heinz (2009), *Markenrecht*, 4th edn., Munich, Germany: C.H. Beck, § 97 paras. 19-22; Bundeskartellamt (1968), 'Tätigkeitsbericht', *Bundestags-Drucksache* V/4236, 53; Bechtold, in Bechtold, Rainer (2010), *Kartellgesetz, Gesetz gegen Wettbewerbsbeschränkungen*, 6th. ed., Munich, Germany: C.H. Beck, § 20 para. 106.

[28] See RAL (2010), 'RAL – Eine historische Rückblende', available at http://www.ral-guete.de/fileadmin/lib/pdf/guete/Die%20Institution%20RAL_Eine%20historische%20Rueckblende.pdf.

[29] See Böhm, Franz (1933/2010), *Wettbewerb und Monopolkampf*, Baden-Baden, Germany: Nomos; Eucken, Walter (1952/2004), *Grundsätze der Wirtschaftspolitik*, 7th edn., Tübingen, Germany: Mohr Siebeck, 55 et seq.

[30] For a list of German guarantee marks see RAL (2010), Gütezeichenübersicht, available at http://www.ral-guete.de/fileadmin/lib/pdf/guete/Guetezeichenuebersicht_Juni_2010.pdf.

for Fabric Expansion Joints" is comprised of the *four* leading German manufacturers of these goods.[31]

Whereas the anti-competitive potential of such a structure is obvious, quality associations are not in and of themselves illegal cartels. Product standardization can increase efficiency. The same is true for guarantee marks indicating that a product complies with a standard because such a sign reduces search and transaction costs.[32] According to the European Commission guidelines on horizontal agreements, an agreement among competitors to develop a quality mark to denote the fact that a product or service meets certain minimum technical specifications does not violate EU competition law as long as participation in standard setting is unrestricted and transparent, and the standardization agreement does not set an obligation to comply with the standard. If the parties, however, agreed only to manufacture products conforming to the new standard, the agreement would limit technical development and prevent the parties from selling different products. Such an agreement would likely infringe EU competition law.[33]

But even if the regulation is generally in line with competition law, the problem remains that newcomers must have a fair opportunity to join the club. Recall our four manufacturers of fabric expansion joints: they will not be particularly happy if a foreign company applies for membership because it intends to extend its activities to Germany and use the German guarantee mark for that purpose. In view of the difficulties that new market participants might face in such a situation, the French Intellectual Property Code requires that the usage of a certification mark is open to any person who meets the quality standards.[34] Similarly, the German Act Against Restraints of Competition provides that "quality mark associa-

---

[31]   See Quality association for fabric expansion joints, http://www.qafej.org/.

[32]   Wiebe,   Andreas   (1993),   'Wettbewerbs-   und   zivilrechtliche Rahmenbedingungen der Vergabe und Verwendung von Gütezeichen', *Wettbewerb in Recht und Praxis (WRP)*, 74, 77.

[33]   European Commission (2001), Guidelines on the applicability of Article 81 of the EC Treaty to horizontal cooperation agreements, OJ C 3/2, para. 177. On German competition law see Bundeskartellamt (1958), 'Tätigkeitsbericht', *Bundestags-Drucksache* III/1000, 39; Bundeskartellamt (1964), 'Tätigkeitsbericht', *Bundestags-Drucksache* IV/3752, 21; Bundeskartellamt (1968), 'Tätigkeitsbericht', *Bundestags-Drucksache* V 4236, 52; Bundeskartellamt (1993/1994), 'Tätigkeitsbericht', *Bundestags-Drucksache* 13/1660, 33-34; Wiebe, Andreas (1993), 'Wettbewerbs- und zivilrechtliche Rahmenbedingungen der Vergabe und Verwendung von Gütezeichen', *Wettbewerb in Recht und Praxis (WRP)*, 74, 84.

[34]   Art. L715-2(3) Code de la Propriété Intellectuelle (CPI), available at http://www.celog.fr/cpi/.

tions shall not refuse to admit an undertaking if such refusal constitutes an objectively unjustified unequal treatment and would place the undertaking at an unfair competitive disadvantage".[35] The purpose of this rule is to ensure that if competition law accepts collective measures to standardize and commercialize quality in the first place, access to these associations and signs has to remain open on non-discriminatory terms.[36]

In applying this rule, German courts have acknowledged the competitive significance of guarantee marks. If the product of a newcomer complies with the objective quality standard, there is generally no reason to refuse an application to become a member. Additional requirements have to be justified in light of the functions of the guarantee mark and the ability of the association to control the quality and the usage of the sign.[37] It is, for example, unjustified and thus illegal to refuse membership because the applicant is a foreign company or produces abroad,[38] if the requirements regarding the minimum standard can only be met by certain undertakings,[39] or if they relate to personnel or the technical equipment of the applicant.[40] Last but not least, membership fees must not be so high as to effectively exclude new members. In one case, a quality association of producers of condoms holding a combined market share of 70% demanded the payment of 50,000 euros from a new company with a market share of only 1%. The association argued that its members had invested heavily to promote the collective guarantee mark and that newcomers must not profit from this high reputation without donating respectively. The German Federal Cartel Authority (*Bundeskartellamt*) rejected this argument. It reasoned that a new market participant must

---

[35] Sec. 20(6) German Act against Restraints of Competition (*Gesetz gegen Wettbewerbsbeschränkungen*); available in English at http://www.bundeskartellamt.de/wEnglisch/download/pdf/GWB/0911_GWB_7_Novelle_E.pdf.

[36] Bundeskartellamt, Case W 190/66, *Wirtschaft und Wettbewerb (WUW)*, 1968, 223.

[37] Düsseldorf Court of Appeals, Case U (Kart) 16/88, *Wirtschaft und Wettbewerb (WuW)*, 1991, 642; Cologne District Court, Case 28 O 495/06, *Wirtschaft und Wettbewerb Entscheidungssammlung (WuW/E)*, DE-R 2090-2092; Emmerich, Volker (2008), *Kartellrecht*, 11th edn., Munich, Germany: C.H. Beck, p. 420; Bechtold, in Bechtold, Rainer (2010), *Kartellgesetz, Gesetz gegen Wettbewerbsbeschränkungen*, 6th. edn., Munich, Germany: C.H. Beck, § 20 paras. 108-110.

[38] Bundeskartellamt, Case W 190/66, *Wirtschaft und Wettbewerb (WUW)*, 1968, 223.

[39] Wiebe, Andreas (1993), 'Wettbewerbs- und zivilrechtliche Rahmenbedingungen der Vergabe und Verwendung von Gütezeichen', *Wettbewerb in Recht und Praxis (WRP)*, 74, 87.

[40] Bundeskartellamt (1993/1994), 'Tätigkeitsbericht', *Bundestags-Drucksache* 13/1660, 33-34.

not be forced to contribute to past investments of its competitors that had helped them to gain a large market share.[41]

This case should ring a bell. It refers again to the functions of collective marks. Would the result be different if the association relied upon the "investment" function of the trademark according to the *L'Oréal* decision of the ECJ?

2.3   Collective Geographical Indication Marks

The third and final sub-category of collective marks concerns signs which may serve, in trade, to designate the geographical origin of the goods or services of the members of the association – our example was "Bavarian Beer". These collective geographical indication (GI) marks are available both in Germany[42] and under the EU trademark regulation.[43] As with signs that only identify the quality of a good or service, signs designating the geographical origin of goods or services are generally not protectable.[44] Again, this is different if the geographical indication is registered as a collective mark. The sign is then understood to convey the information that the undertaking using the sign belongs to an association from that geographical area.

Such collective GI marks can imply even more market power than collective guarantee marks. Consider how difficult it is to sell hard cheese if you may not use the term "Parmesan" or anything similar because it is reserved for members of the Italian consortium "Parmigiano Reggiano". In spite of the fact that the term "Parmesan" has become customary in German to a certain extent, both the ECJ and German courts have held that "Parmesan" has to be produced in the Parma region of Italy according to the respective product specifications.[45] If the local consortium were a closed group, it would effectively hold an exclusive right to market this kind of cheese.

---

[41]   Bundeskartellamt, Case 592232-W-76/82, *Wirtschaft und Wettbewerb (WUW)*, 1985, 835 et seq.

[42]   Sec. 99 German Trademark Act; Entwurf eines Gesetzes zur Reform des Markenrechts, 14 January 1994, *Bundestags-Drucksache* 12/6581, 109; Hacker, Franz et al. (2006), 'Das Verhältnis zwischen Marken und geographischen Herkunftsangaben (Q 191)', *Gewerblicher Rechtsschutz und Urheberrecht Internationaler Teil (GRUR Int.)*, 697; see also Art. 15(2) s. 1 Dir. 2008/95.

[43]   Art. 66(2) Reg. 207/2009.

[44]   Art. 3(1)(c) Dir. 2008/95; Art. 7(1)(c) Reg. 207/2009; Sec. 8(2) no. 2 German Trademark Act.

[45]   See ECJ Case C-132/05 *Commission/Germany* [2008] ECR I-957, paras. 46 et seq.; Berlin Court of Appeals (Kammergericht), Case 5 U 97/08, *BeckRS*, 2010, 18302; Heath, Christopher (2008), 'Parmigiano Reggiano by Another Name –

To counter this anti-competitive potential, collective GI marks are subject to additional requirements and limitations under EU and German trademark law. First, if the collective mark consists of an indication of geographical origin, the regulations governing use of the mark *must* provide that any person whose goods or services originate in the area concerned and fulfil the conditions for use set out in the respective regulations shall be authorized to become a member of the association.[46] Thus, the right to access the association and to use the GI on non-discriminatory terms is a necessary feature of the agreement between the local producers. Second, such a mark shall not entitle the proprietor to prohibit a third party from using the geographical indication, if that is done in accordance with honest practices in industrial or commercial matters. In particular, a collective GI mark may not be invoked against a third party who is entitled to use the geographical indication.[47] With these provisions, the protection of collective marks is streamlined with the protection of geographical indications. According to the latter, any person whose goods or services originate in the respective area, for example the Parma region, may lawfully use and claim protection for the respective GI, for example "Parmesan".[48] Under the special rules on collective GI marks, this right to use the indication is also valid against a collective GI mark in the same sign, even if the local manufacturer is not yet a member of the association owning the collective mark. It is thereby ensured that GIs may not be turned into exclusive rights beyond what is possible under general GI protection schemes. Seen from this perspective, the protection of collective GI marks is more akin to unfair competition law than to exclusive rights in individual trademarks.

3.   CONCLUSION

In sum, one can observe a correlation between the competitive impact of collective marks on the one hand, and additional requirements for and

---

The ECJ's Parmesan Decision', *International Review of Intellectual Property and Competition Law (IIC)*, 951.

[46]   Art. 67(2) s. 2 Reg. 207/2009; Sec. 102(3) German Trademark Act.

[47]   Art. 15(2) s. 2 Dir. 2008/95; Art. 66(2) s. 2 Reg. 207/2009; Sec. 100(1) German Trademark Act ("in addition to the limits of protection according to Sec. 23. . ."); German Federal Court of Justice, Case I ZR 207/00, *Gewerblicher Rechtsschutz und Urheberrecht (GRUR)*, 2003, 242.

[48]   See Art. 10(2), 9 (3) Paris Convention; Art. 5(1) s. 3 Council Regulation (EC) No. 510/2006 of 20 March 2006 on the protection of geographical indications and designations of origin for agricultural products and foodstuffs, OJ L 93/12.

limits of protection on the other. The more important it is to lawfully use the sign, the thinner is trademark protection. The reason is that trademark law should not support the formation of cartels. For the most part, this is achieved via safeguards built into trademark law.

Part of this subtle balance concerns the question of which functions of a collective mark enjoy legal protection. Recall the two examples where this nexus between function and limits was particularly striking. May an association holding a conventional collective mark allocate geographical markets in order to better guarantee that the bread bearing the sign is always fresh?[49] Is a newcomer obliged to contribute to prior investments of the association in the reputation of the collective guarantee mark?[50] As was shown, German courts and competition authorities have answered these questions in the negative. They denied that conventional collective marks have a legally protected guarantee function, and that guarantee marks serve to protect the investment in the goodwill.

In the aftermath of the ECJ's decision in *L'Oréal*, it has become doubtful whether this restrictive reading can be upheld. Henceforth, the protected functions of a trademark also include that of guaranteeing the quality and of communication, investment or advertising.[51] This requires a new assessment of questions like these: if trademark law protects the investment in the goodwill of the mark, can the association not require newcomers to contribute to these efforts? If the purpose of trademark law is to establish a specific form of sales promotion or commercial strategy – so the wording in the ECJ's *Google* decision[52] – is an association owning a collective mark not entitled to completely collectivize sales efforts?

No question that competition law will remain applicable. As all other IP rights, rights in collective trademarks are not immune to external limits set by competition law.[53] But this is not my point. My point is that the functional expansion of trademark law has the potential to erase or at least weaken *internal* limits within trademark law as illustrated with regard to collective marks. As also explained, these limitations are there for good reason. In contrast, the ECJ has not given any reason to substantiate its

---

[49]   Supra note 20.
[50]   Supra note 41.
[51]   ECJ Case C-487/07 *L'Oréal/Bellure* [2009] ECR I-05185 para. 58.
[52]   ECJ Joined Cases C-236/08 to C-238/08 *Google v Louis Vuitton* [2010] ECR 0000 paras. 91-98.
[53]   ECJ Joined Cases C-241/91 P and C-242/91 P *RTE and ITP v Commission* (*'Magill'*) [1995] ECR I-743; ECJ Case C-418/01 *IMS Health v NDC Health* [2004] ECR I-05039.

functional activism. Not to forget that this jurisprudence relates to *individual* and not to *collective* marks. The latter are subject to the general law of trademarks only in so far as the special rules do not provide otherwise. From these special provisions one can derive that the underlying objective of protection of collective marks is not identical with that of individual trademarks. Thus, conventional collective marks indicate origin – and nothing else. A specific quality is only designated by collective guarantee marks. These are available under German and other countries' trademark laws, but not under the EU Trademark Regulation. A proposal for an EU collective guarantee mark did not come into effect.[54] Courts are bound to this legislative decision. They are therefore barred to ascribe a protected guarantee function to conventional EU collective marks – an expansion of protection which would increase the anti-competitive potential of collective commercialization. At least in this regard, the *L'Oréal* doctrine cannot apply to EU collective marks.[55]

The other allegedly protected functions of trademarks – communication, investment, advertising, etc. – should also be applied *to individual marks only*.[56] Member States are not obliged to protect collective trademarks in the first place. If they do, the Trademark Directive expressly refers to the fact that collective marks have specific, distinct functions.[57] If the ECJ's jurisprudence were applied to national collective marks, this would increase the probability of conflicts between trademark and competition law. Up to now, concerns relating to competition have been part of trademark law. To shift these solutions to competition law would require new market participants to show that competition law has to step in due to exceptional circumstances.

---

[54] See European Commission (1980), Proposal for a council regulation on the Community trademark of 27 November 1980, COM (80) 635, final, *Gewerblicher Rechtsschutz und Urheberrecht Internationaler Teil (GRUR Int.)*, 1981, 86, 97; Art. 86-96 of the Amended Proposal for a Council Regulation on the Community Trademark, COM (84) 470, final, OJ C 230/1, p. 43; Schennen (2007), in Eisenführ, Günther and Schennen, Detlef, *Gemeinschaftsmarkenverordnung*, 2nd edn., Cologne, Berlin, Munich, Germany: Carl Heymanns Verlag, Art. 64 para. 11.

[55] Contra Fezer, Karl-Heinz (2009), *Markenrecht*, 4th edn., Munich, Germany: C.H. Beck, § 97 para. 2.

[56] Contra Fezer, Karl-Heinz (2009), *Markenrecht*, 4th edn., Munich, Germany: C.H. Beck, § 97 para. 2.

[57] See Art. 15(1) Trademark Directive 2008/95; European Commission (1980), Proposal for a first directive to approximate the laws of the Member States relating to trademarks of 27 November 1980, COM (80) 635, final, *Gewerblicher Rechtsschutz und Urheberrecht Internationaler Teil (GRUR Int.)*, 1981, 30, 32.

There are reasons to be sceptical about this development. Trademark law has to remain an instrument that ensures that competition is *not* distorted.[58] It must not be rededicated in a way that makes it easier to collectively employ exclusive rights for strategic, anti-competitive purposes.

---

[58]   See Art. 3 Treaty on European Union and Protocol No 27 on the internal market and competition, OJ C 83/1 of 30 March 2010.

12. Multinationals' global governance on the Internet

Hong Xue*

> When you cross the border, the game will be same but the rules will be different.
> (An advertisement at Stockholm-Arlanda Airport)

Multinational corporations have been governing the world indirectly through lobbying and other means. Businesses are seen actively involved in not only technological standard-setting but law-making. All through the formation process of the TRIPS Agreement, the pharmaceutical industry, software industry, music industry, Hollywood and international brands industry had monitored the agenda-setting, negotiation contents and final result to secure their intellectual property interests.[1] Nothing has been changed at the time of the Anti-Counterfeit Trade Agreement. When the draft text was kept from the public, the United States Trade Representative (USTR) stated that it had "consulted with an array of experts from various IP and tech industries."[2] The trustworthy insiders who had the privilege to access the draft were from leading businesses (Google, eBay, Sony, Time Warner, etc.), the Industry Trade Advisory Committee on Intellectual Property Rights (Motion Picture Association of America, Inc., International Intellectual Property Alliance, International, Recording Industry Association of America, Entertainment Software Association, etc.) and the Industry Trade Advisory Committee on Information and Communications Technologies, Services, and Electronic Commerce (Software and Information Industry Association, Verizon Communications Inc., etc.).[3]

---

* Hong Xue, Ph.D of Law, Professor of Law, Director of Institute for the Internet Policy & Law, Beijing Normal University, China. The chapter is based on the presentation made at ATRIP 2010 Congress held in Stockholm University.
1 See Peter Drahos, *Information Feudalism: Who Owns the Knowledge Economy?*, 2003 New Press (New York), pp. 109–149.
2 "White House shares the ACTA Internet text with 42 Washington insiders, under non disclosure agreements", available at http://keionline.org/node/660.
3 Ibid.

Businesses have been very successful in the traditional government avenues to consolidate and optimize their intellectual property interests. But the international regimes in the traditional government model do not change the territorial nature of intellectual property rights. National laws and enforcement measures can be harmonized or flattened but not unified. A global business has to face different rules in different countries. Global laws, per se, do not exist in the international arena. It is the Internet that provides multinationals with a brand new opportunity to set up their direct global governance on intellectual property rights. Governance may have broad meaning to cover the governance of affairs of any institution, including non-governmental ones.[4] However, global governance on the global network, although truthfully beneficial to global businesses, has the caveat of further unbalancing the intellectual property regime.

The Internet enables a small number of multinational companies to quickly capture a large share of the world market and to dominate human life.[5] For most of us, the Internet only means a few services we use daily for work, entertainment and social life. For example, we search on Google, connect with friends on Facebook, blog on Twitter, and post videos on Youtube. When we use these services, we inevitably subscribe to their service terms or rules. The Internet is so inherently global that any set of rules adopted by the most powerful businesses will reign by default and undeniably exert a social-economic impact around the world.[6]

Multinationals are more ambitious than governing their subscribers. They are making global "norms" to govern the people at large. The binding effect of these global norms is not incomparable to national or international laws in the traditional sense. These business measures contain all four major components of Internet governance, namely scope,

---

[4]   *See* Jovan Kurbalija, *An Introduction to Internet Governance*, 2008 DiploFoundation (Geneva) and National Internet Exchange of India (New Dehli), p. 9.

[5]   A new breed of micro-multinationals, starting as dispersed virtual businesses with employees, clients and resources located in various countries, are growing into super businesses like Google or Facebook. *See* "How Startups Go Global", available at http://money.cnn.com/2006/06/28/magazines/business2/star tupsgoglobal.biz2/index.htm.

[6]   For example, Google, in February 2010, introduced its social network service "Buzz", which constructed lists of people to follow and be followed based on their email address books and activities on Gmail, a widely used e-mail service offered by Google. The default setting of Buzz aroused privacy uproars. In response, Google had to make a public apology and several privacy-related changes to its service. Google Buzz is available at http://www.google.com/buzz.

instruments, process and actors.[7] In the era of the Internet, multinationals directly set up the de facto global governance to reshape the international regimes on intellectual property and other legal issues such as privacy and network neutrality.[8]

Through examining two on-going global governance cases on intellectual property issues, this chapter discloses the conspicuous caveats of business direct governance that cannot be effectively regulated by state authorities. After researching the theory and practices of Internet governance, the chapter attempts to explore whether the new multi-stakeholder model would develop into a more balanced regime to address intellectual property issues globally.

1. GOOGLE BOOK PROJECT

Google Book Project was initially launched in 2004 to build up an online archive of millions of out-of-print books.[9] It has already scanned at least 7 million books, using cameras able to convert up to 1,000 pages an hour. Google has established partnerships with a number of the world's biggest libraries, including those of Harvard and Stanford and the Bodleian in Oxford.

In September 2005, the Authors Guild and three of its members sued Google on behalf of all owners of U.S. copyright interests in books in the collection of the University of Michigan Library.[10] Five major trade

---

[7]   See Bertrand de la Chapella, "Towards Multi-Stakeholder Governance – The Internet Governance Forum as Laboratory", in *Power of Ideas: Internet Governance in a Global Multi-stakeholder Environment*, edited by Wolfgang Kleinwaechter, 2007 Marketing for Deutschland GmbH (Berlin), pp. 256–59.

[8]   At the beginning of August 2010, the reports concerned the consumers that Google and Verizon, two leading players in Internet service and content, were nearing an agreement that could allow Verizon to speed some online content, such as Youtube owned by Google, to Internet users more quickly if the content's creators were willing to pay for the privilege. The deal was immediately criticized because "the fate of the Internet is too large a matter to be decided by negotiations involving two companies, even companies as big as Verizon and Google." *See* "Google and Verizon Near Deal on Web Pay Tiers", *New York Times*, August 4, 2010, available at http://www.nytimes.com/2010/08/05/technology/05secret.html?pagewanted=1&_r=3&hp.

[9]   Google Book Project is available at http://books.google.com.

[10]   *Authors Guild, Inc. v. Google, Inc.*, Case No. 05 CV 8136 (S.D.N.Y. Sept. 20, 2005). The Authors Guild charged Google with copyright infringement for scanning books from the Michigan library with the intent of indexing their contents and making snippets available in response to queries made by users of its

publishers brought a similar suit a month later. In October 2008, Google, the Authors Guild, and the Association of American Publishers (AAP) announced that they had reached an agreement to settle the combined lawsuit under which Google would pay $45 million to compensate rights holders for works it had already scanned at a rate of $60 per book and $15 per insert.[11] The most important part of the proposed settlement was, however, the license the settling class would give Google to commercialize all in-copyright, but out-of-print books. This included selling copies of the books to individual consumers, licensing access to an institutional subscription database of millions of out-of-print books, and serving ads next to book contents. Under the agreement, Google promised to pay 63% of the proceeds to a newly established Book Rights Registry, which would be charged with locating rights holders and paying them for Google's uses of their books.[12]

On November 19, 2009, the Court granted preliminary approval of the Amended Settlement,[13] which only covers the owners of copyrights in books and inserts published in the UK, Canada, and Australia, and owners of rights in books and inserts registered with the U.S. Copyright Office.[14] On February 18, 2010, Judge Denny Chin held a fairness hearing on the proposed Amended Settlement. The final ruling is yet to be released.

Google states that its project is to organize the world's information and make it universally accessible and useful.[15] But Google's ambition

---

search engine. Google claimed that this scanning was fair use because it facilitated greater access to books and Google offered links to libraries from which the books could be checked out and to bookstores from which the books could be purchased.

[11]   Settlement Agreement, *Authors Guild, Inc. v. Google, Inc.*, No. 05 CV 8136 (Oct. 28, 2008), is available at http://www.googlebooksettlement.com/intl/en/Settlement-Agreement.pdf. Inserts refer to e.g. book chapters, short stories, and forewords.

[12]   Ibid.

[13]   Under the United States' Civil Procedure Rules, class action lawsuits can only be settled if the presiding judge holds a hearing and determines that the proposed settlement is fair, reasonable, and adequate to the class on whose behalf it is being proffered.

[14]   The original Agreement consisted of all persons who owned a U.S. copyright interest in one or more books or inserts (i.e. all owners of copyrights in books and inserts in the world). The preliminary approval of the Amended Settlement Agreement is available at http://static.googleusercontent.com/external_content/untrusted_dlcp/www.googlebooksettlement.com/zh-CN//05CV8136_20091119.pdf.

[15]   "The Future of Google Books" is available at http://books.google.com/googlebooks/agreement/#6.

prompts growing opposition from authors and legal experts for a couple of persuasive reasons. Google was criticized for grabbing the power to control and commercialize the books of the whole world, irrespective of the fact that most right owners are unknown, unnoticed or unwilling. The whole project capitalizes on unpermitted digitization, display and commercialization of copyright works. The project has the potential to monopolize gross knowledge of a body of out-of-print works, particularly orphan works.[16] The United States Department of Justice recommended against approval of the settlement for the concerns of violation of competition law.[17]

Most important of all, Google attempt to create a mass-scale de facto licensing via the Amended Settlement Agreement to not only uphold Google's unpermitted acts that occurred but to set out forward-looking norms to handle the books of the whole world. Although approval of a settlement that only involved Google paying $60 per book for its past scanning of in-copyright books may be feasible because of its limited coverage and impact, a settlement that would grant Google a license to commercialize all in-copyright but out-of-print books, even though Google never claimed, is quite different. The forward-looking commercial aspects of the settlement use the current legitimate dispute between the parties about scanning-to-provide-snippets to remake the market for e-books.[18] The sweeping impact should not be undermined.

Google Book Project typically presents a case of business global governance based on market dominant position. Irrespective of approval of the Amended Settlement Agreement by the court, Google is determined to proceed to digitize all the books in the world and put them in use under its own rules. Any right owner from any part of the world who did not utterly oppose the Project or sue Google in the relevant jurisdiction would automatically be subject to Google's default rules, such as $60 per book or 63 % of the proceeds.

Forward-looking and opt-out features make Google Book Project similar to legal norms, which are characteristic of normativity, generality and enforceability. So far Google has been insisting on an opt-out rather

---

[16] *See* Pamela Samuelson, "Is the Proposed Google Book Settlement 'Fair'?", available at http://www.ischool.berkeley.edu/~pam.

[17] The Statement of Interest by the Department of Justice Regarding the Proposed Settlement, *Authors Guild, Inc. v. Google, Inc.*, Case No. 05 CV 8136 (DC) (S.D.N.Y. Feb. 4, 2010) is available at http://thepublicindex.org/docs/amended_settlement/usa.pdf.

[18] *See* Pamela Samuelson, "Is the Proposed Google Book Settlement 'Fair'?", available at http://www.ischool.berkeley.edu/~pam.

than an opt-in regime. In an opt-in regime, authors and publishers could decide whether to allow Google to commercialize their out-of-print books. However, in an opt-out regime, Google can presume right owners' consent effortlessly and costlessly, but right owners have to assume the burden of "opting-out." In case of legal suits, the financial burden to opt out will not be insignificant.

Although it is pending whether the American court will approve Google's Amended Settlement Agreement, it is clear that no law or country can stop Google from continuing the project under its own "default" norms and rules.[19] Google's global opt-out regime is different from any business model or contractual relationship. Google is not collectively "managing" but "governing" copyright globally. Management has to base on existing contracts but governance is based on enforcement of norms and rules. Even if Google's project may have a positive effect on knowledge access and dissemination, it is questionable whether a commercial entity in market dominance and having the potential of global monopoly should become the de facto global knowledge shepherd. Google's norm-setting practice signals a dangerous tendency of business global governance for commercial interests rather than public interest. Although TRIPS Agreement and other intergovernmental legal arrangements have their shortcomings, it is even worse to let a for-profit entity, without a check-and-balance mechanism and due process, to set out the norms to rule the world.

2. ICANN'S TRADEMARK PROTECTION MEASURES

Internet Corporation for Assigned Names and Numbers (ICANN) in its 12-year history has developed into a unique organization on the Internet. As a not-for-profit organization incorporated under the law of the State of California in the United States, ICANN oversees or coordinates the management, allocation and operation of a domain name system, Internet protocol addresses and root servers. In its early days, ICANN had attempted to play a pure and limited role of technical coordination. However, its

---

[19] At the end of 2009, a French court ruled that the Google Books project violates the country's copyright laws. The decision came after a three-year battle between Google and a group of powerful French publishers, including the prestigious Le Seuil publishing house. *See* "French Court Shuts Down Google Books Project", *Los Angeles Times*, December 19, 2010, available at http://articles.latimes.com/2009/dec/19/world/la-fg-france-google19-2009dec19.

unique oversight over critical Internet resources inevitably involves important public policy issues.[20] To ensure all the Internet resources are accessible and interconnected around the world, ICANN maintains a single, coherent and globalized system to keep all identifiers on the Internet unique and resolvable. The special function of universal resolvability makes all of ICANN's policy globally impactful and implementable.

Some of ICANN's policies have already had or are going to have significant impact on the global intellectual property regime. Although ICANN is not an intergovernmental organization established by any international treaty, ICANN's policies that are implemented through the resources and technical setting on the globally accessible network can be more ubiquitous and effective than treaties concluded and enforced by sovereign states.

As a result, multinationals discover the new opportunity in ICANN's policy to globalize their intellectual property assets without the burden of lobbying in the lengthy and hard international negotiation process and struggling with the territorial enforcement mechanisms in different jurisdictions. If ICANN can set up globalized uniform measures to safegurard intellectual property rights, corporation giants get a new channel to extend the global governance.

When ICANN plans to introduce new gTLDs, the intellectual property industry pushes for deployment of an extensive and forceful enforcement mechanism. Although ICANN has the so-called multi-stakeholder bottom-up decision-making process, in which ICANN's Board of Directors make the final decisions on various policy issues based on the consensus of relevant stakeholder groups, the intellectual property industry was able to muscle its way to make intellectual property an overarching issue after the policy development process for new gTLDs was completed.[21] In March 2009, the ICANN Board resolved to form an Implementation Recommendation Team (IRT) to seek solutions to address the trademark owners' concerns over trademark abuse, consumer confusion and heavier enforcement burden for trademark owners. IRT members were principally "from the organizations and persons that proposed such solutions in the public comment period on the first draft Applicant Guidebook (for new

---

[20]   ICANN's mission statement, available on its website at http://icann.org/en/participate/what-icann-do.html, has been changed many times. The current version deliberately blurred its powers, functions and status to avoid controversies.

[21]   In October 2007, the Generic Names Supporting Organization (GNSO) completed its policy development work and approved a set of recommendations. The Board of Directors adopted the policy at ICANN's Paris meeting in June 2008.

gTLDs)." [22] Noticeably, all these organizations and persons proposed that ICANN should extend the global protection and enforcement measures for trademarks. Intellectual property constituency (IPC) that represents intellectual property interests within ICANN took the lead,[23] and IRT members largely had the same mindset.[24]

IRT openly stated, in its Final Report, its series of recommendations on trademark protection reflecting "the views of business and trademark interests in general."[25] But IRT's extensive and forceful recommendations generated strong criticisms from the other stakeholder groups in ICANN and the general public.

IRT recommended the creation of a Globally Protected Marks List to provide protection to "globally protected marks" at the top and second levels of domains. However, the notion of "globally protected marks" is self-contradictory.[26] More importantly, there are no globally protected marks that exist in any international intellectual property law, and ICANN has absolutely no authority to create such international law to eliminate the territorial nature of trademark rights. What was recommended by IRT is to push ICANN to set up de facto global governance not only for trademark enforcement, but also for trademark rights per se. ICANN should not engage in such a trademark protection regime

---

[22]   ICANN Board Resolution is available at http://www.icann.org/en/minutes/resolutions-06mar09.htm#07.

[23]   IPC is a component of the Generic Names Supporting Organization (GNSO), which is a main policy-making body of ICANN and comprises four main groups: registries, registrars, commercial users and non-commercial users of the Internet.

[24]   On March 13, 2009, WIPO's Arbitration and Mediation Center dispatched a letter to ICANN regarding the protection of trademarks on new gTLDs. That letter is available at http://www.wipo.int/export/sites/www/amc/en/docs/icann130309.pdf.

[25]   The IRT Final Report is available at http://www.icann.org/en/topics/new-gtlds/irt-final-report-trademark-protection-29may09-en.pdf. The recommendations are in the following five aspects, i.e.: IP Clearinghouse, Globally Protected Marks List and associated Rights Protection Mechanisms, and standardized pre-launch rights protection mechanisms; Uniform Rapid Suspension System; Post-delegation dispute resolution mechanisms; Whois requirements for new TLDs; and Use of algorithm in string confusion review during initial evaluation.

[26]   IRT defined that "globally protected marks" meant the marks that had been registered in a number of countries across all five ICANN Regions, i.e., North America, Europe, Latin America, Asia Pacific and Africa. However, such arbitrary criteria to decide whether a trademark has become globally protected are legally baseless.

that would go beyond existing international intellectual property law and inherent the territorial limit of trademark rights.[27]

According to ICANN's policy decision, each applied-for gTLD string is to be preliminarily compared against existing TLDs, Reserved Names and other applied-for strings to prevent user confusion and loss of confidence in the DNS.[28] During Initial Evaluation of new gTLD applications, only visual similarity check is involved. IRT, however, recommended a revision to the string confusion review to include consideration of the aural and commercial impression (meaning) created by the string. IRT's recommendation would help trademark owners to exclude the other competitors over the same or similar new gTLD string applications. In the case of non-Latin script TLDs (such as in Chinese, Cyrillic or Arabic), IRT's recommendation would significantly unreasonably prejudice non-Latin script applicants. Extension of string evaluation to aural or meaning similarity would unavoidably be subjective and arbitrary. Legal protection for a trademark in translation or transliteration must be subject to the complicated legal analysis and judgment based on special law by the competent authority in the respective territory.[29] ICANN has neither the authority nor capacity to do this in the Initial Evaluation process. If taking into account those famous marks that consist of generic terms, the IRT proposal would seem absurd. A trademark owner for "BOSS" does not have any right to exclude the others from using the meaning of the term in a language that is completely different from Latin script. In addition, the "meaning" (commercial impression) criterion has never been applied to the existing Latin TLDs, for example, ".biz" was not precluded for being "meaningfully similar" to ".com." ICANN should not impose the double standards to the non Latin TLDs merely for protection of the interests of trademark owners.

---

[27]   More comments and analyses on IRT Final Report are available at http://wiki.iipl.org.cn/?cat=4.

[28]   ICANN New Generic Top-Level Domains (gTLDs) Draft Applicant Guidebook (Version 4) is available at http://www.icann.org/en/topics/new-gtlds/draft-rfp-redline-28may10-en.pdf. ICANN reserves a list of names, such as ICANN, IETF, who is and www, from any use for new gTLD strings.

[29]   Article 6*bis* of Paris Convention provides, the countries of the Union to undertake, ex officio if their legislation so permits, or at the request of an interested party, to refuse or to cancel the registration, and to prohibit the use, of a trademark which constitutes a reproduction, an imitation, or **a translation**, liable to create confusion, of a mark **considered by the competent authority of the country** of registration or use to be well known in that country as being already the mark of a person entitled to the benefits of this Convention and used for identical or similar goods. (Emphases added)

Although some of IRT's recommendations were modified to a certain extent, most of the mechanisms it proposed were adopted by ICANN.[30] When ICANN published its amended new gTLD policy,[31] IRT's legacy could be clearly recognized. For example, the new gTLD registry operator is required to comply with Trademark Post-Delegation Dispute Resolution Policy (PDDRP), under which a trademark owner (of either registered or unregistered marks) may claim against a gTLD registry operator that one or more of its marks have been infringed by domain name registrations under the corresponding gTLD. Once the claim is supported, the registry operator may be required to "monitor registrations not related to the names at issue in the PDDRP proceeding"; or in extraordinary circumstances where the registry operator acted with malice, may be subject to termination of a registry agreement.[32] In addition to the highly subjective and ambiguous criteria for judgment of malice of a registry operator, application of the procedure would impute an indirect liability on gTLD registry operators to force them to police the domain names registered in their system. This will not only stretch the capacity of a new gTLD registry operator, but may have a serious chilling effect to drive a registry operator to monitor and supervise the content of the websites for which the domain names are used, as well as the domain name strings per se for proof of their innocence in operation or use of the pertinent gTLD.

ICANN is not an inter-governmental treaty organization, and its policy-making does not follow the treaty negotiation process. If ICANN's so-called multi-stakeholder bottom-up consensus-based decision-making process is functioning well, ICANN would not become a barrier-free forum for assertors of intellectual property globalization. However, ICANN's ever-growing trademark measures show that the intellectual property industry can actually dominate and manipulate the decision-making process to globalize their rights and enforcement for their rights. More seriously, the group that represents intellectual property interests

---

[30] A Special Trademark Issues (STI) group was formed in October 2009 to make recommendations for a Uniform Rapid Suspension System and a Trademark Clearinghouse. STI Report was published in December 2009. STI Report is available at http://www.icann.org/en/announcements/announcement-2-17dec09-en.htm.

[31] ICANN published the Draft Applicant Guidebook (Version 4) in May 2010 and incorporated trademark protection measures, including improvements to the Uniform Rapid Suspension, the Trademark Clearinghouse, and the Post-Delegation Dispute Resolution Proposal (PDDRP).

[32] The latest version of Trademark Post-Delegation Dispute Resolution Procedure (PDDRP) was published in May 2010 and is available at http://icann.org/en/topics/new-gtlds/pddrp-clean-28may10-en.pdf.

and masterminds those trademark measures is almost solely composed of legal professionals from North America or Europe,[33] which explains why the terminologies, concepts and rules adopted in ICANN trademark policy show clear traits of American laws.[34] If developed countries' high standards of protection and enforcement for intellectual property are globalized through ICANN's policy and uniformly applied to the whole world, developing countries would be more marginalized in the information society and knowledge economy.

ICANN's policy, including trademark measures, seriously impacts public interests. But ICANN's accountability and transparency are still in question.[35] Since ICANN is a not-for-profit organization registered in California, literally only the United States can claim jurisdiction over it. ICANN concluded the Affirmation of Commitments (AoC) with the United States Department of Commerce in September 2009 to "institutionalize and memorialize the technical coordination of the Internet's domain name and addressing system, globally by a private sector led organization."[36] But AoC does not provide direct supervision power to the United States government. Therefore, any person or entity who believes that he/it has been materially affected by any ICANN policy and the policy contradicts law or public interest can only resort to the American courts. ICANN has been involved in a number of lawsuits.[37] But these sporadic legal actions cannot regularly and substantially supervise ICANN's policies and decisions.

---

[33] The composition of Intellectual Property Constituency (IPC) in ICANN's GNSO, available at http://gnso.icann.org/intellectual-property/, reveals that all of its officers and GNSO Council Representatives are from either North America or Europe, which largely matches the geographical distribution of its members. In 11 years of history, only 4 people from Latin America and 1 person from Asia Pacific were ever elected to be IPC officers.

[34] For example, the Report produced by the Special Trademark Issues (STI) group directly cited Rule 56 of United States Federal Rules of Civil Procedure on summary judgment as the standard of evaluation of Uniform Rapid Suspension, even though summary judgments are not common in civil proceedings of all jurisdictions. The proposal adopts a completely American-centered approach. *See* "Comments on Proposal of GNSO Selected Trademark Issues Review Team", available at http://wiki.iipl.org.cn/?m=200911.

[35] ICANN has a series of internal accountability mechanisms, such as ombudsman, reconsideration and independent review. But they are non-effective and rarely used.

[36] Affirmation of Commitments is available at http://www.icann.org/en/documents/affirmation-of-commitments-30sep09-en.htm.

[37] The documents from lawsuits and similar legal proceedings related to ICANN are available at http://www.icann.org/en/general/litigation.htm.

3. MULTI-STAKEHOLDER INTELLECTUAL PROPERTY GOVERNANCE ON THE INTERNET

Super multinationals have developed global business, but there is no globalized uniform legal system to meet their business need. The private global governance regimes on intellectual property developed by businesses concisely address this issue. Notwithstanding their contribution to economic development, multinationals are profit-driven organizations that care for investors/owners' private interests. Global governance that merely caters to certain business models or intellectual property interests can go against public interest by excluding competition, suffocating innovation and damaging the interests of consumers. The reality that the economy is globalized but polity is still national means that global multinationals are largely unregulated, particularly in respect of competition, consumer protection and intellectual property issues, and will keep increasing their power at the expense of public interest. The situation on the Internet is particularly serious, which is illustrated by both Google Book Project and ICANN's intellectual property measures. Fortunately, instead of becoming a wild frontier that is solely subject to jungle rules, Internet governance is developing into a process of organizational innovation and mutual adaptation between society and technology around the world in pursuit of the objective of ensuring the openness and neutrality of the Internet.[38]

In 2001, The United Nations General Assembly Resolution endorsed the holding of the World Summit on the Information Society (WSIS) for a global discussion on digital revolution and digital divide.[39] WSIS was in two phases. The first phase took place in Geneva in December 2003 and the second phase took place in Tunis in November 2005. WSIS acknowledges that the Internet has evolved into a global facility available to the public and its governance should constitute a core issue of the Information Society agenda. The primary outcome of WSIS is two principal documents, namely the Declaration of Principles and Tunis Agenda for the Information Society, and a new forum for global policy dialogue – called the Internet Governance Forum (IGF).

WSIS Declaration of Principles reflects a global consensus on a range

---

[38]   *See* Council of Europe "Resolution on Internet Governance and Critical Internet Resources", available at http://www.coe.int/t/informationsociety/docu ments/internetcriticalresources_en.pdf.

[39]   *See* "Resolution Adopted by the General Assembly 56/183 on World Summit on the Information Society", available at http://www.itu.int/wsis/docs/ background/resolutions/56_183_unga_2002.pdf.

of global policy issues on governance of the Internet. It establishes guiding principles on the conduct of governance processes, that is, the international management of the Internet should be multilateral, transparent and democratic, with the full involvement of "governments, the private sector, civil society and international organizations."[40] It holds that international Internet governance issues should be addressed in a coordinated manner, and that governance should ensure an equitable distribution of resources, facilitate access for all and ensure a stable and secure functioning of the Internet, taking into account multilingualism.[41] The Tunis Agenda for the Information Society, as a follow-up, attaches great importance to multi-stakeholder implementation at the international governance level. It defines multi-stakeholder governance as a process to enable governments, the private sector and civil society, in their respective roles, to develop and apply shared principles, norms, rules, decision-making procedures, and programs that shape the evolution and use of the Internet.[42]

The WSIS principles are briefly summarized as transparency, inclusive participation and coordination.[43] These principles provide, for the first time, a baseline set of tools the international community could use to promote holistic collective learning about and improvements in Internet governance.

The principles provide valuable measurements for the current international or global governance regimes regarding the Internet. For example, completely contrary to the WSIS principles, the ACTA negotiation process has been opaque, exclusive and one-sided, in which negotiation parties are by invitations only, draft texts were kept secret from the public for almost four years and only large businesses can access and participate in drafting.[44]

---

40   *See* WSIS Declaration of Principles, paragraph 48, available at http://www.itu.int/wsis/docs/geneva/official/dop.html.

41   *See* WSIS Declaration of Principles, paragraphs 48 & 50, available at http://www.itu.int/wsis/docs/geneva/official/dop.html

42   *See* the Recommendations of the Tunis Agenda in regards to Internet Governance, paragraphs 34 & 108, available at http://www.itu.int/wsis/docs2/tunis/off/6rev1.html. The document mentioned the term "multi-stakeholder" in 16 paragraphs, namely paragraphs 27, 37, 41, 67, 72, 73, 78, 80, 83, 97, 98, 101, 102, 105, 108 & 110 respectively.

43   *See*, William J. Drake, "Encouraging Implementation of the WSIS Principles on Internet Governance Procedures", in *Power of Ideas: Internet Governance in a Global Multi-stakeholder Environment*, edited by Wolfgang Kleinwaechter, 2007 Marketing for Deutschland GmbH (Berlin), pp.271–3.

44   ACTA is currently being negotiated by Australia, Canada, the EU (and its 27 Member States), Japan, Korea, Mexico, Morocco, New Zealand, Singapore,

Business direct governance is obviously at odds with the WSIS principles, particularly on multi-stakeholder equal participation. Intellectual property governance inherently involves multiple stakeholders, including actual creators/inventors, medias/intermediaries, commercial exploiters, users and regulatory authorities. The rules, norms and procedures for intellectual property subsistence, ownership, exploitation and enforcement inevitably affect all the stakeholders involved. Without uniform regulation and effective supervision at the international level, the governing regimes set up by multinationals exclusively and imposed on the other stakeholders can easily optimize business interests and disregard external effects on other stakeholders. Given that multinationals are largely developed country based, business governance also worsens the North-South digital divide. WSIS principles exactly reflect the caveat of business direct governance and provide guidance for good global governance.

Under the WSIS principles, the private sector can play its respective roles[45] but should coordinate with other stakeholders and observe the principles of public interest.[46] Taking Google Book Project, for example, since Google's acts have involved important public policy issues that affect the people at large, Google should not make and enforce the rules, norms and procedures on maintaining and commercializing an enormous body of human knowledge unilaterally and exclusively, without public consultation, participation from the other stakeholders and supervision from regulatory authorities.

However, multi-stakeholder governance by WSIS principles is in its infancy. Its implementation is still an experiment. According to Tunis Agenda for the Information Society, IGF was convened by the UN Secretary-General in 2006 to discuss public policy issues related to key elements of Internet governance in order to foster the sustainability, robustness, security, stability and development of the Internet.[47] Since 2006,

---

Switzerland, and the United States. The official version of the current ACTA draft was not published until 20 April 2010.

[45]   WSIS Principles states that the management of the Internet encompasses both technical and public policy issues and should involve all stakeholders. In this respect it is recognized that the private sector has had and should continue to have an important role in the development of the Internet, both in the technical and economic fields.

[46]   They include but are not limited to equitable distribution of resources, facilitation of access for all and safeguarding a stable and secure functioning of the Internet.

[47]   *See* the Recommendations of the Tunis Agenda in regards to Internet Governance, paragraph 72, available at http://www.itu.int/wsis/docs2/tunis/off/6rev1.html.

IGF had organized four meetings in Athens, Rio de Janeiro, Hyderabad and Sharm El Sheikh respectively. As a global multi-stakeholder policy dialogue forum, IGF's working function has been multilateral, multi-stakeholder, democratic and transparent. Key issues on Internet governance, such as openness, access, diversity, security and management of critical Internet resources, were discussed by thousands of participants from various stakeholder groups. Multi-stakeholderism seems to be functioning well at IGF. But IGF has no oversight power and only constitutes a non-binding process without decisions being made.[48] It is questionable whether discussions at IGF can truthfully impact on business direct governance on intellectual property or other critical issues. In the case of Google Book Project, there are a lot of questions pending answers, such as how to engage Google in the relevant discussions at IGF, how to make such a super business more subscribed to WSIS principles, and why Google would care about the IGF process at all. When IGF is a non-binding soft process and WSIS principles are a soft reference without compliance assessment, why would multinationals take them seriously and behave accordingly themselves? Although multi-stakeholdersim is the right direction, there is a very long way to go before its realization.

On the other hand, there is real danger for the multi-stakeholder process to be manipulated or even hijacked by multinationals, in which other stakeholders are merely used as window dressing but their presence justifies business governance. IGF is only a dialogue forum, so it is a risk-free environment for multi-stakeholder participation and discussions. Once a multi-stakeholder process is adopted for decision-making, multinationals can win in the power struggle and stakeholders' conflicts. ICANN's IRT process concisely reflects the reality that multinationals' resources, coverage and influence far dwarfed the other stakeholder groups, particularly civil society.[49] Therefore, multi-stakeholdersim has been strongly criticized for only succeeding in giving political space and respectability to mega-corporates and helping spread the unbridled corporate power even more.[50]

---

[48] *See* the Recommendations of the Tunis Agenda in regards to Internet Governance, paragraph 77, available at http://www.itu.int/wsis/docs2/tunis/off/6rev1.html.

[49] In case of ICANN, large businesses have representation in full time professional jobs and ensure a devotion to the needs and views of those represented; civil society, on the other hand, largely consists of idealistic volunteers who have their own full jobs and can only use their spare time for policy debate and delivery.

[50] *See* Parminder Jeet Singh's comments in Email Archival of Internet Governance Caucus, at http://lists.cpsr.org/lists/arc/governance.

Exclusion of businesses from multi-stakeholder regimes or abandonment of multi-stakeholderism, however, cannot be the solution. Multinationals have been successfully and strongly lobbying the government to influence the policy and law making processes, and are proactively developing a direct governance regime to advantage and to consolidate their business interests. Leaving them alone means a more profit-driven and public-interest-ignored future on the Internet. Therefore, the critical task is to balance the power of the private sector, rather than increasing it, through proper configuration of multi-stakeholder structures, dynamics across and within stakeholder groups and the development of concrete implementation procedures. A business group is not hegemonic. The diversity within the group is significant. With respect to intellectual property issues specifically, businesses in the North and South may have different propositions, small-and-medium-size businesses and multinationals may not share common interests, and businesses in different fields may have conflicting interests on intellectual property exploitation and enforcement. Inclusion of business groups in a multi-stakeholder regime can, to some extent, confine multinationals to the commonly-accepted principles and practices, particularly addressing intellectual property issues "in a coordinated manner."[51]

The growing importance of IGF prevents multinationals from carelessly setting aside its process and outputs. Under the mandate, IGF not only provides an open forum for discussion, but also creates a venue for all stakeholders to collaborate towards developing public policy for the Internet, through a process by which they would identify emerging issues, bring them to the attention of the relevant bodies and the general public, and, where appropriate, make recommendations.[52] The global community's increased acceptance and endorsement of the multi-stakeholder model shows that IGF's promotion and assessment of embodiment of WSIS principles in Internet governance would have an impact on multinationals' development path and business model. In the long run, IGF can develop into a global watchdog to assess Internet governance entities' WSIS principles adherence in performances, including discussion and decision-making on global intellectual property issues, and deliver corresponding advices or recommendations for improvement.[53]

---

[51] *See* paragraph 50 of WSIS Declaration of Principles and paragraph 71 of Recommendations of the Tunis Agenda in regards to Internet Governance.

[52] *See* the Recommendations of the Tunis Agenda in regards to Internet Governance, paragraph 72, available at http://www.itu.int/wsis/docs2/tunis/off/6rev1.html.

[53] In accordance with the Recommendations of the Tunis Agenda in regards to Internet Governance, United Nations General Assembly (UNGA) will make an

Furthermore, IGF's spin-off effect should not be undermined. WSIS principles have been taken forward by other international initiatives, such as the Code of Good Practice on Information, Participation and Transparency in Internet Governance, to which all the stakeholders and internet governance entities are encouraged to subscribe.[54] The Code states that entities concerned with Internet governance, irrespective of their diverse role and character, share a broad commitment to transparency and information-sharing, multi-stakeholder participation and open discussion and decision-making. The Code emphasizes Internet governance entities' duty to include within their deliberations countries and people that are under-represented. The Code provides a valuable reference for global intellectual property governance.

4. CONCLUSION

The Internet provides a globalized media for intellectual creations to be consumed and exploited. Traditional intergovernmental international regimes cannot quench multinationals' thirst for globalized uniform intellectual property arrangements to optimize their interests via the global network. As a result, business direct governance was established by multinationals. However, a private global governance regime that blurs the territorial nature of intellectual property rights can worsen the imbalance of commercial interests and public interest. Furthermore, governance on the Internet that is completely dominated by economic powers is contradictory to the inherent multi-stakeholder characteristic of intellectual

---

overall review of the implementation of WSIS outcomes in 2015. United Nations Secretary-General is examining the desirability of the continuation of the IGF, in formal consultation with Forum participants, as its five-year initial mandate draws to an end in the Vilnius meeting on 14–17 September 2010, and will make recommendations to the United Nations Membership in this regard. One proposal for enhancement of IGF recommended setting up a database collecting internet governance best practices. Such a database might serve as a reference output, while at the same time avoiding more authoritative measures. *See* "Internet Governance 2010: Future of the IGF, Competition among Institutions", available at http://www.ip-watch.org/weblog/2010/01/15/internet-governance-2010-future-of-the-igf-competition-among-institutions/.

[54] The Code of Good Practice, available at http://www.intgovcode.org/images/c/c1/COGP_IG_Version_1.1_June2010.pdf, was jointly initiated by Association for Progressive Communications, Council of Europe and United Nations Economic Commission for Europe. Its first version incorporates feedback gathered from multiple stakeholders and internet governance entities at the IGF held in Sharm el-Sheikh in December 2009.

property protection. The international community has established principles in Internet governance entities, processes and conducts. WSIS principles, particularly multi-stakeholderism, clearly denounce unilateralism of business governance and multinationals' dominance and decisiveness in the governance process. With the guiding principles being gradually accepted and implemented, intellectual property can be governed in a fairer and more balanced manner across the globe.

13. Trademark take-over or *sui generis* regimes: absolute merchandising rights in sports

Katja Weckström*

1. INTRODUCTION

> In a constitutional state, committed to liberal values, the intervention of the legislator in the market forces of free competition requires a specific justification. Economically speaking, this justification rests on the consideration that, without any such intervention, a market failure would ensue after a certain period of time.[1]

When considering justifications, there are two possibilities. We can consider the justification for each individual right in intellectual property, i.e., copyright, design, geographical indication or trademark, separately. Legislatures tend to do so when balancing incentives for intervention against those for non-intervention.[2] Alternatively, we could consider the market position conferred by IP rights in general in a particular field, before considering whether market intervention is justified via a particular form of IP protection.

The latter, i.e., horizontal intellectual property law issues are seldom considered.[3] A natural consequence of this is that horizontal issues related to the rest of the legal system are also ignored, or considered from only one perspective; e.g. trademarks are balanced against freedom of expression concerns. I argue that it is here, when protection crosses over the interface

---

* Lecturer, LL.D. Candidate University of Turku Faculty of Law. The author would like to thank John Cross, Graeme Dinwoodie, Shuba Gosh, Annette Kur for comments on previous drafts of this article.
[1] Hilty, Reto M., 'The Law Against Unfair Competition and Its Interfaces', pp. 1–2 in Hilty, Reto M. & Henning-Bodewig, Frauke, *Law Against Unfair Competition – Towards a New Paradigm in Europe?*, Springer-Verlag Berlin (2007) pp. 1–52.
[2] Hilty, at 26, see supra note 1.
[3] Hilty, at 51, see supra note 1.

between IP rights,[4] where the system is most vulnerable to over-protection and thus, where we should ask the question whether a justification for protection still exists.

This is not to say that we would have to resort to examination in search of a violation akin to competition law.[5] Instead we can operate within one IP framework, but shift the emphasis from the rights holder to a broader unfair competition[6] perspective. The threshold for our consideration is whether *market failure* will ensue if protection is removed, bearing in mind that *market change* does not equal market failure. Hence, a legitimate justification exceeds the *private interest*, and has consequences, where preserving a balance between market forces amounts to a *public interest*.

For example, the sports industry can be placed in a legal framework. It is likely uncontested that sports serve important, e.g. educational, public health, social, cultural and recreational, functions. Together the legal protection of sports as well as the infra- and governance structures that facilitate the public access to, practice and dissemination of sports clearly serve legitimate societal interests.[7]

---

[4]   The example of trademark protection combined with exclusive broadcasting rights is used here. Monopoly rights positions may also follow from combined trademark protection and publicity rights (sports video games), database protection (protecting sports results, statistics against use in fantasy sports), unfair competition (non-confusing slavish imitation); free riding, copyright (fan fiction); tarnishment, defamation (fan sleuth fiction or games), criminal law (ambush marketing); contract law (exclusive visibility deals).

[5]   True competition law issues may naturally arise, when considering for instance whether sports leagues constitute illegal collusion, or whether they abuse a dominant position in relation to their teams or players. For an analysis from this perspective see Brandon L. Grusd (1999), *The Antitrust Implications of Professional Sports' League-Wide Licensing*, 1 Va. J. Sports & L. 1.

[6]   Unfair competition here is a broad and general concept asking *whether* a use can be considered unfair as an exception to the general rule of freedom of competition. It is not intended to reference unfair competition laws in some civil law traditions used to extend trademark protection in new areas. It is also not necessarily synonymous with the opposite, i.e. that unfair competition counterbalances and restricts trademark protection as the concept could be considered in the UK (if searching for an equivalent in name, not function). See Dworkin, G. (2010), 'Unfair competition: is it time for European harmonisation?', in David Vaver and Lionel Bently (eds), Intellectual Property in the New Millennium: Essays in Honour of William R. Cornish, Paperback Edition, (Gerald Dworkin) at pp.176-177. See also Helen Norman, 'Blowing the Whistle on Trade Mark Use?' [2004] I.P.Q., No.1, 1-34, at 2.

[7]   White Paper on Sport, COM (2007) 391, 11 July 2007 at 1-2. Commission Communication Developing the European Dimension in Sport, COM (2011) 12, 18 January 2011 at Ch. 4.2, p. 11.

Like any regulation that facilitates attainment of a specific societal interest its justification ultimately comes down to a question of balancing and degree, when pitted against other interests in society.[8] Therefore, the law tends to phrase the question as one of proportionality[9] of adopted means to the end sought, the relative weight of competing interests and the effect of regulation for the benefit of some interests on the overall attainment of the competing values.[10] While the benefit may ultimately be private its protection must serve a greater public interest.

Conversely, protection of purely private interests to the detriment of other private or public interests tends to be treated as unfair, protectionist or as favoritism without legal foundation and is specifically targeted under national,[11] regional[12] and international[13] law.[14] Thus, the sports industry faces legal pressure at these junctions, where leagues/teams abuse the rights of players, where financial interests de-root the activity from its (local) educational, public health moorings, and when community (cultural) interests are routinely trumped by private profit-making.[15]

---

[8]   See Stephen Weatherhill, The Influence of EU Law on Sports Governance in Simon Gardiner, Richard Parrish, Robert C.R. Siekmann (Eds.), EU, Sport, Law and Policy: Regulation, Re-Regulation and Representation, T.M.C. Asser Press, 2009 at 79 arguing that whether the EU has competence to intervene is at heart a constitutional matter.

[9]   Annex 1 to the Commission Staff Working Document SEC (2007) 935, 11 July 2007 at Ch. 2.1.5 referring to established guidelines from cases Case 36/74, *Walgrave v Union Cycliste Internationale*, ECR 1405 [1974] at 4 and 9, Case 13/76 *Donà v Mantero* ECR 1333 [1976] at 12 and 15, Case C-415/93 *URBSFA v Bosman* ECR I-4921 [1995] at 73 and 76 and Case C-176/96, *Lehtonen* ECR I-2681 at 34 that distinguish between "purely sporting interests" and "reasons of economic nature" and Case C-519/04 *Meca Medina* ECR I-6691 [2006] at 42 which further requires a legitimate objective, that the measure is inherent in the pursuit of that objective and proportionate to the ends sought.

[10]   Case C-519/04 *Meca Medina* ECR I-6691 [2006] at 42. Commission Communication Developing the European Dimension in Sport at Ch. 3.2 at 8-9 and Ch. 4.2 at 11. See generally e.g. Articles 50-54 EU Charter of Fundamental Rights Official Journal C303 Volume 50 14 December 2007, 2007/C 303/01 and Explanations relating to the Charter of Fundamental Rights, Official Journal C 303 Volume 50, 14 December 2007, 2007/C 303/02 at C 303/23.

[11]   E.g. rules on public procurement, competition or positions for Ombudsmen to protect the generally disadvantaged.

[12]   E.g. EU rules on the free movement of goods, services, capital and people.

[13]   E.g. the GATT and WTO rules targeting taxes, tariffs, subsidies and other protectionist measures.

[14]   Weatherhill at 80.

[15]   Henrik Erik Meier, Emergence, Dynamics and Impact of European Sport Policy in Simon Gardiner, Richard Parrish, Robert C.R. Siekmann (Eds.), EU,

In essence, while law has long recognized the need for consideration of the unique features of the sports industry, it declines to exempt it entirely from the application of other more general rules of law and to equate private self-governance in practice to private self-governance at law.[16]

One extension of trademark rights, i.e. the[17] sports merchandising right is discussed and compared to protection already offered under trademark law in an attempt to define "what more" is at issue, when arguing for extension of protection. After all, it is argued, protection cannot be tested for legitimacy or balanced against countervailing interests, unless it is clear what protection or non-protection adds to the market. Unlike most scholarship[18] on the merchandising right this chapter *does not* ask or *argue for or against* the merchandising right as a justified *theoretical* construct. The practical starting point presumes that the right exists[19] on formally valid[20] grounds and therefore the question becomes, when it applies.[21] A consequence of this approach is that the article does not ask, when the merchandising right is not justified (negative statement).[22] Instead, *it seeks tools to*

Sport, Law and Policy: Regulation, Re-Regulation and Representation, T.M.C. Asser Press, 2009, at 8-9.

[16]   Commission Communication at 3.2 at 8-9 and 4.2 at 11. Weatherhill at 79, Melchior Wathelet, Sport Governance and EU Legal Order: Present and Future at 58-59 and 68-69; and Richard Parrish, Introduction in Simon Gardiner, Richard Parrish, Robert C.R. Siekmann (Eds.) EU, Sport, Law and Policy: Regulation, Re-Regulation and Representation, T.M.C. Asser Press, 2009 at 2.

[17]   Arguing for a more nuanced approach to the question of protection in its old and new manifestations. See supra note 4.

[18]   For an overview of academic discussion on the topic see infra note 19 and J. Thomas McCarthy, McCarthy on Trademarks and Unfair Competition ss 24:10-12 (4th Ed. 2011).

[19]   Trademark merchandising is big business. Grusd at 6. Stacey Dogan and Mark Lemley, The Merchandising Right: Fragile Theory or Fait Accompli? 54 Emory L.J. 461 (2005), at 461; Irene Calboli, The Case for A Limited Protection of Trademark Merchandising, 2011 U. Ill. L. Rev. 865 at 872; Joseph P. Liu, Sports Merchandising, Publicity Rights, and the Missing Role of the Sports Fan, 5 B.C.L. Rev. 493 [2011] at 495-496.

[20]   Validity here stems from legislative action that follows constitutional *procedure* and therefore the result is formally valid. Arguments against normative justification of the legislative decision are considered as constraints on this right, i.e. when considering its legitimate scope and application.

[21]   See Bruce Proctor, Unauthorised Use of Trade Marks: A Trade Mark Proprietor's Perspective in Jeremy Phillips (Ed.) Trademarks At the Limit, Edward Elgar 2006 at 212-214 and 219 arguing that only some unauthorised uses that amount to 'a taking' or are intuitively 'unfair' (albeit most) should be preventable.

[22]   This chapter does not for example discuss so called ambush marketing and whether or not it can be prevented.

distinguish when there exist legitimate interests for extension of protection (positive statement) from the point of view of a functioning market. These tools may serve and inform the decision-making process both in courts and legislature, ideally turning an all-or-nothing political question into justified and proportionate judgment applicable to the circumstances at hand.

Part 2 defines the practical context, the market consequences and the legal manifestation of the sport merchandising right with the example of protection for the Olympic Symbol in the Nairobi Treaty. It focuses on the international level,[23] since *global absolute protection* generally is stronger than more extensive (additional) national protection. Its purpose is to define *the minimum level* of protection for sports merchandising. Part 3 sketches trademark protection with a focus on *the maximum level*[24] of protection for renowned marks in relation to product categories and geographical scope. It is presumed that sports merchandises have *registered marks* that are well known, reputed, famous or renowned in the traditional trademark law sense in their *primary areas of business*, and that it is where this right ends, because of *countervailing societal interests* that the sports merchandising right begins (the floor of the merchandising right).[25] Part 4 continues discussion of the maximum level of protection from the point of view of *limits on the use* of a protected trademark. It is presumed that these limits reflect some of the *same societal interests*[26] at stake, when considering

---

[23] At this level, it is safe to presume that the right is formally valid, since it has been accepted by 49 states outside the Western world, where the extensive protection of trademarks is usually questioned. Western nations protect sports franchises more extensively both in scope and application than the Nairobi Treaty.

[24] It is not argued here that there is a fixed and clear maximum level of protection. Like any legislation there is disagreement on some aspects of protection. The discussion focuses on the agreed upon normative framework and takes the rulings of the EUCJ as the authoritative statements of the content of the law that they are. It is not argued that the statements are clear, all-encompassing or uncontroversial or that there is not more to trademark law than meets the eye. For the purposes of this chapter it is important to show that there is *some agreement* on what is protected and what is not, although there would be ample opportunity to criticize the EUCJ for inconsistency. The aim of sections 3 and 4 is to show that there is *some logic* after all to the protection of trademarks although there is much confusion and controversy on the optimal protection of trademarks.

[25] It could be argued that the rights are paralell and overlapping and therefore, it is not possible to view them as separate blocks. It is argued here that if we allow this type of fluidity to restrict the evaluation of whether protection is justified, protection may never be scrutinzed. *Theroretical* scrutiny is contingent on defining the right and what indeed is considered worthy of protection.

[26] Opinion of the Advocate General in Case C-228/03 *The Gillette Company and Gillette Group Finland Oy v LA-Laboratories Ltd Oy*, 9.12.2004, at 54-55.

protection for merchandising. Thus, it is argued that the concept of "honest practices in industrial and commercial matters" can be utilized as a threshold (the ceiling of the merchandising right) to consideration of legitimacy of extended protection for merchandising, or alternatively, restriction of various forms of marketing. Part 5 combines these interests and concludes with a tailored test for evaluating whether increased protection is legitimate from the point of view of a functioning market.

2. THE PROTECTION OF THE OLYMPIC SYMBOL – THE PINNACLE OF SPORT MERCHANDISING

The most traditional form of sports merchandising; strong trademark right combined with exclusive broadcasting rights for the Olympic Games, is used as an example of how increasing protection affects the market for competitive sports. This example is used to bring forth the market reality from which global rights emerge, but also the strength of legitimate social interests of the protection of sports in global culture.[27] The aim of this section is to find some normative and theoretical contours for the elusive concept of sports merchandising.[28]

The protection of the Olympic symbol shows the market reality, which follows from extreme trademark protection. The trademark itself becomes a commodity[29] that is bought and sold; the cornerstone of a profitable business.[30] Consequently, *any unauthorized use* of the mark *affects* the owner's exclusive *right to control the use* of the mark from which follows that absolute protection is warranted.[31] The right in question is commonly referred to as

---

[27] White Paper on Sports at 2–3.

[28] Calboli discusses how the concept, despite its controversial nature, has escaped definition in both linguistic and normative terms at 871–872.

[29] Sonia Katyal, Trademark Intersectionality, 57 UCLALR 1601 (2010) at 1620. Mark Lemley and Mark McKenna, Irrelevant Confusion, 62 Stan. L. Rev. 413 (2010), at 437.

[30] Stacey Dogan and Mark Lemley, The Merchandising Right: Fragile Theory or Fait Accompli? 54 Emory L.J. 461 (2005) at 461–463.

[31] There are several reasons and theories underlying this conclusion. Logically, however, it is the fact that competing/concurrent use affects the control of a valuable commodity that lies at the heart of the discussion. Critics of the merchandising right argue that *effect on the market*, not on the trademark owners' ability to control 'their' mark, should be decisive. Spyros M. Maniatis discusses the right-based rationale of trademark protection as property: "A right over some object means that the right holder can determine the object's destiny, therefore rights endow the right holder with power, yet rights themselves do not stem from that power". . . . "The marketplace is constantly changing, creating new arenas of appro-

Figure 13.1   The Olympic symbol

the *sports merchandising right*. Following this line of reasoning the commodity in question, in our case the Olympic symbol, needs to be defined.[32] The Olympic symbol consists of five interlaced rings: blue, yellow, black, green and red, arranged in that order from left to right (see Figure 13.1 above).

It consists of the Olympic rings alone, whether delineated in a single color or in different colors. Article 1 of the Nairobi Treaty on the Protection of the Olympic Symbol obligates to refuse or invalidate the registration of a mark and to prohibit by appropriate measures the use, as a mark or other sign for commercial purposes of any sign consisting of or containing the Olympic Symbol, as defined in the Charter of the International Olympic Committee, except with the authorization of the International Olympic Committee.[33]

The form of trademark protection set forth in the Nairobi Treaty translates into a market position of the trademark holder, i.e., the International Olympic Committee that at least to some extent is related to marketing revenue. Table 13.1 shows the Olympic marketing revenue.

Every trademark owner enjoys an unabridged monopoly on trademark licensing, since compulsory licensing of trademarks is prohibited by Article 21 of the TRIPS Agreement.[34] The absolute right to the Olympic

---

priation where the exclusionary property role of trademarks as a regulatory tool needs to be justified. Otherwise, trade mark law will succumb to the fallacy that whatever has value is also worth protecting – or that what is worth copying is also worth protecting – and will become a tool in the hands of competing actors rather than a relational and justified system of protection." internal references omitted. Spyros M. Maniatis, *Trademark Rights – A Justification Based on Property*, [2002] I.P.Q., No.2 123 at 126 and 128.

[32]   Property theory, however strongly advocating for preserving private property, recognizes that the property right is really a bundle of rights that can vary depending on market values and laws. Harold Demsetz, Toward a Theory of Property Rights, 57 Am. Econ. Rev. Pap. & Proc. 347-358 (1967) at 347-348. William P. Landes and Richard Posner, The Economic Structure of Intellectual Property Law, Harvard University Press, 2003 at 11.

[33]   Nairobi Treaty on the Protection of the Olympic Symbol adopted in Nairobi September 26, 1981.

[34]   Under EU law a trademark owner cannot erect artificial barriers to trade by way of trademark licensing (Case C-10/89 HAG AF [1990] ECR I-3711, para

Table 13.1   Olympic marketing revenue

Source[1]	1993–1996	1997–2000	2001–2004	2005–2008
	US$	US$	US$	US$
Broadcast	1 251 000 000	1 845 000 000	2 232 000 000	2 570 000 000
TOP Programme[2]	279 000 000	579 000 000	663 000 000	866 000 000
Domestic Sponsorship	534 000 000	655 000 000	796 000 000	1 555 000 000
Ticketing	451 000 000	625 000 000	411 000 000	274 000 000
Licensing	115 000 000	66 000 000	87 000 000	185 000 000
Total	2 630 000 000	3 770 000 000	4 189 000 000	5 450 000 000

Notes:
[1.] Olympic Marketing Fact File, p. 6, available at http://www.olympic.org/Documents/ FactFile25_11.pdf, "Olympic Marketing Revenue: The Past Four Quadrenniums". All figures in the chart above have been rounded to the nearest US$1 million. N.B. Does not include NOC domestic commercial programme revenues." "The Olympic Partners (TOP) programme is the worldwide sponsorship programme managed by the IOC.
[2.] The TOP programme provides each Olympic partner with exclusive global marketing rights and opportunities within a designated product or service category. The global marketing rights include partnerships with the IOC, all active NOCs [National Olympic Committees] and their Olympic teams, and the two OCOGs and the Games of each quadrennium." Olympic Marketing File, p. 11. See supra note 5.

symbol trademark arguably facilitates the revenue incurred by licensing, including the TOP Program, as well as domestic sponsorship. The TOP program is the worldwide sponsorship program managed by the IOC. It provides each Olympic partner with exclusive global marketing rights and opportunities within a designated product or service category. The global marketing rights include partnerships with the International Olympic Committee, all active National Olympic Committees and their Olympic teams, and the two Organizing Committees of the Olympic Games and the Games of each quadrennial.

Table 13.2[35] shows the evolution of the TOP program, a program that was at least in part enabled by the merchandising right conferred by the Nairobi Treaty.

The economic value of all or next to all sponsorship lies in the ensured right of visibility guarded by the exclusive right to broadcast the Olympic

---

13). However, no entity can decide whether to license or to whom other than the trademark owner.

[35]   Olympic Marketing Fact File p. 11, available at http://www.olympic.org/ Documents/FactFile 25_11.pdf

Table 13.2   Evolution of the TOP program

Quadrennium	Games	Partners	NOCs	Revenue
				US$
1985–1988	Calgary/Seoul	9	159	96 million
1989–1992	Albertville/Barcelona	12	169	172 million
1993–1996	Lillehammer/Atlanta	10	197	279 million
1997–2000	Nagano/Sydney	11	199	579 million
2001–2004	Salt Lake/Athens	11	202	663 million
2005–2008	Torino/Beijing	12	205	866 million

Games. National broadcasting companies have to buy at a price set by the seller, who enjoys an absolute monopoly. The content is also controlled exclusively by the IOC, and it is this part of the broadcasting monopoly that is most closely enabling the trademark monopoly.[36] Thus, the broadcasting monopoly inevitably benefits the trademark monopoly and vice versa.

The determination of whether the merchandising right in a trademark acquired through the Nairobi treaty is justified should not be possible without considering the underlying broadcasting monopoly. Likewise, the question of whether imminent market failure would ensue lest trademarks or broadcasting rights are protected cannot be determined in isolation.

The Olympics are unique, and the question of whether such strong protection is justified is not easily determined. Due to the event's symbolic value the protection is likely based upon moral values rather than economic ones. Accurately so, not everything has to be justified with economic values.[37] The Olympics seem to protect a public rather than a

---

[36]   Kitch argues that intellectual property rights and especially trademark rights do not confer a monopoly on their holder. Nevertheless, he notes that there are circumstances under which intellectual property rights, namely patents, can confer a monopoly on their holder. For the purpose of determining whether a monopoly exists, it is relevant to consider the market share of the actor in question. Since the IOC, in our case, is the only actor on the market, and enjoys exclusive rights to broadcast and exclusive rights to trademark licensing, it is safe to assume that the IOC in fact enjoys an economic monopoly. Kitch, Edmund, 'Elementary and Persistent Errors in the Economic Analysis of Intellectual Property Rights', 53 Vand.L.Rev.1727 (2000) at 1729–1730 and 1734.

[37]   Case C-228/03 *The Gillette Company and Gillette Group Finland Oy v LA-Laboratories Ltd Oy* [2005] ECR I-2337 at 35. Opinion of Advocate General Tizzano in Case C-228/03 *The Gillette Company and Gillette Group Finland Oy v LA-Laboratories Ltd Oy,* 9.12.2004, at 64–72.

purely private interest, and in the late 1970s, the venture seemed to be losing money and on-site spectators, due to expensive tickets. Yet, the cost involved in arranging the Olympic Games were continually increasing with the requirement of state-of-the-art facilities for an increasing number of Olympic sports from an ever-greater number of nations. Thus, market failure was arguably foreseeable. Speculation on past events and the prevailing market situation at a historic point in time is, however, not fruitful. It suffices here to say that the argument for absolute control of the mark for commercial exploitation can be considered warranted both morally, economically and legally.

The example of the Olympics can be particularly useful, when considering whether other sports events or activities should enjoy similar trademark protection. The Nairobi Treaty shows us, that despite its strength, the protection was tailored quite narrowly. It included only one trademark, the Olympic rings and only in their traditional interlaced formation. The protection given included colors or black and white.[38] The word marks Olympics, Olympic Games, Olympiad are outside the area of protection both as part of a figure mark and as word marks as such.[39] The IOC has had to apply for, and enjoys traditional trademark protection for any other trademarks than the Olympic Rings. What might also be of relevance is the public nature of the international venture, as well as the representative nature of the IOC.

Thus, in considering whether trademark protection is justified, we need to consider whether;

1) protection is justified from a moral, legal or economic standpoint, that serves
   a.   public or
   b.   private interest, and
2) non-protection would lead to market failure
   a.   using a holistic approach[40] not restricted to one field of IP
   b.   with a trademark-centric[41] view with emphasis on unfair competition.

---

[38]   Nairobi Treaty, see supra note 33.

[39]   These word marks may enjoy protection similar to that conferred by the Nairobi Treaty under national law, see for example the Amateur Sports Act, 36 U.S.C. 380, as interpreted by the Supreme Court in *San Fransisco Arts and Athletics Inc. v. US Olympic Committee*, 483 US 522 (1987).

[40]   Hilty, at 47 and 51, see supra note 1.

[41]   It is true that the *trademark* takes a central position in trademark infringement analysis and consequently that the trademark owner's interests are pro-

What does 'absolute' protection entail? Is protection absolute in geographical scope, across all product categories, covering non-commercial uses or even as broad as an exclusive 'right to authorize use' translating into a *right to prevent all unauthorized marketing that interferes with the exclusive right of authorization?* We focus next on building a context in which such consideration may take place. We begin by reviewing the different forms of trademark protection and their evolution within contemporary EU trademark law. Next, the limits on the effect of the trademark right in EU trademark law are discussed.

3. WELL-KNOWN MARKS, FAMOUS MARKS AND ORDINARY TRADEMARK INFRINGEMENT

This section focuses on what forms of protection are available to marks that may constitute a commodity in themselves. It is presumed that a merchandising right stems from one or several marks registered for the primary sports-related activity that enjoy a certain amount of fame. Therefore, it is also presumed that they would qualify for extended protection under trademark or unfair competition laws and these rights would be exercised to the fullest. This presumption rests on the fact that the mark has to have value in order to successfully serve as a commodity. Value is based on consumer recognition, i.e. fame that makes the mark a desirable asset to other commercial actors than the trademark owner.[42]

---

tected. After all the civil law statutes confer negative rights to one party only: the trademark owner. In recent years, this statutory construction has been read by many courts to equal near absolute protection of the trademark *owner's interests*. I argue that this does not constitute the true premise of trademark law. The trademark owner's interests are protected only to the extent conferred by statute. We have learned from settled EU trademark case law that it is limited to instances when the trademark's ability to guarantee the origin of goods or services, that is the ability to distinguish the trademark owner's goods from the goods of another, is threatened. When there is no threat, there is no protection. Thus, while the trademark is at the heart of the analysis both trademark and unfair competition law interests and issues are raised. To avoid the misleading term proprietor, I would like to call the court's approach trademark centric. On the history of the competing interests in trademark law, see Kur, Annette, 'Well-Known Marks, Highly Renowned Marks and Marks Having a (High) Reputation: What's It All About?' IIC 1992, 218–231, at 218–219. Hereinafter Kur (1992).

[42] Whether the trademark owner is the gate-keeper to a valuable forum, which attracts others for visibility of their own marks, is not important at this juncture, where it is asked when and to what extent *trademark protection* is normatively

It is therefore necessary to define at least to some extent the different avenues for protection and their limits under current international and EU trademark law. The cases are approached from the point of view of a national judge, indicating the extent of protection and possible difficulties surrounding interpretation in practice.[43] The aim is not to criticize the cases, but to *sketch a conceptual and normative framework* in which the modes of protection and legal reasoning operate.[44]

3.1   Protection for Well-Known Marks

Paris Convention Article 6*bis*
Marks: *Well-Known Marks*
(1) The countries of the Union undertake, ex officio if their legislation so permits, or at the request of an interested party, to refuse or to cancel the registration, and to prohibit the use, of a trademark which constitutes a reproduction, an imitation, or a translation, liable to create confusion, of a mark considered by the competent authority of the country of registration or use to be well known in that country as being

---

justified. It becomes relevant when asking when and to what extent *merchandising protection* is morally, economically or legally justified.

[43]   It is presumed here that whether or not there is *inner logic* to EU trademark law that the interpretation of judicial decisions is far from straightforward or clear. The thorough *contextual discussion* of EUCJ cases is therefore not trivial, but could serve a purpose for national judges that are not necessarily familiar with the intricacies of EU trademark law. Normative constraint is however exercised, which strictly limits the discussion to the attempts of the EUCJ to create a *new* normative framework for EU trademark law. It follows that this new framework is not interpreted in light of old national doctrines. Informed by traditional trademark law and its historical and contemporary development the contextual approach employed here, however, searches for similar limits in the new places that the EUCJ indicates that they exist. For a critique of the case-law of the EUCJ on limitations, see Tobias Cohen Jehoram, Constant van Nispen and Tony Huydecoper, European Trademark Law, Community Trademark Law and Harmonized National Trademark Law, Wolters Kluwer, 2010 at 384–389.

[44]   The cases are read as authoritative statements of the law that presumably follow certain *normative logic*. It is not the purpose of this article to test the justification of normative logic against e.g. national doctrines or general principles of trademark law. It is argued that the general principles of EU trademark law take form when reading the cases together. While it is not a complete picture of how such principles operate in EU trademark law, it nevertheless constitutes a *legitimate basis* for which the EUCJ can build on. There are signs that the EUCJ views the concept of 'honest practices in industrial and commercial matters' as a broader concept that defines and restricts the concept of the essential function of trademarks. Case C-17/06 *Céline SARL v Céline SA* [2007] ECR I-07041 and Case C-558/08 *Portakabin v. Primakabin* [2010] ECR I-0000.

already the mark of a person entitled to the benefits of this Convention and used for identical or similar goods. These provisions shall also apply when the essential part of the mark constitutes a reproduction of any such well-known mark or an imitation liable to create confusion therewith.

International protection for non-registered trademarks is conferred only on marks that can be considered internationally well-known. Although the trademark owner is not required to have registered or used[45] the mark on goods in the relevant country, protection can be granted based on the trademark being well-known in the country in question. Article 16(2) of the TRIPS Agreement extended protection to services. Determination of whether a mark is well-known, should take into account the knowledge of the trademark in the relevant sector of the public, including knowledge that has been obtained as a result of promotion of the trademark.[46] The latter focus on advertising is of course essential, since the mark generally has not been used in the traditional trademark sense, in the country in question.

A joint recommendation concerning the provisions on the protection of well-known trademarks was adopted by the Assembly of the Paris Union and the General Assembly of the World Intellectual Property Organization (WIPO) in 1999.[47] A group of experts on international trademark law recommended a flexible approach according to which any circumstances indicating that a mark is well-known may be taken into account.[48] Factors that may be relevant are:

---

[45] Kelbrick, Roshana, 'The Term Well-Known in South African Trademark Legislation: Some Comparative Interpretations', XXXVIII CILSA 2005 p. 435–52, at 436.

[46] Article 16(2) of the Agreement on Trade-Related Aspects of Intellectual Property Rights (The TRIPS Agreement) is Annex 1C of the Marrakesh Agreement Establishing the World Trade Organization, signed in Marrakesh, Morocco on 15 April 1994.

[47] Joint Recommendation Concerning Provisions on the Protection of Well-Known Marks, adopted by the Assembly of the Paris Union and the General Assembly of the World Intellectual Property Organization at the Thirty-Fourth Series of Meetings of the Assemblies of the Member States of WIPO, September 20 to 29, 1999.

[48] The Joint Recommendation is treated as a soft law document. Some commentators argue for attaching a legal obligation onto member states due to general adherence to the recommendation. See Study on the Overall Functioning of the European Trade Mark System presented by the Max Planck Institute for Intellectual Property and Competition Law, Munich, on 15 February 2011, available at http://ec.europa.eu/internal_market/ indprop/tm/index_en.htm and Martin Senftleben, The Trademark Tower of Babel, 40 IIC 1/2009 45–77 at 51–53.

a) the degree of knowledge or recognition of the mark in the relevant sector of the public; b) the duration, extent and geographical area of any use of the mark; c) the duration, extent and geographical area of any promotion of the mark, including advertising or publicity and the presentation, at fairs or exhibitions, of the goods and services to which the mark applies; d) the duration and geographical area of any registrations, and/or any applications for registrations, of the mark, to the extent that they reflect use or recognition of the mark; e) the record of successful enforcement of rights in the mark, in particular, the extent to which the mark has been recognized as well known by competent authorities; and f) the value associated with the mark.[49]

A confusingly similar application for identical or similar goods or services is generally refused *ex officio*, but can also be triggered by an application by the trademark owner with reference to Article 6 *bis* of the Paris Convention. Most countries today have incorporated Article 6 *bis* into their national laws.[50] The same is true for the EU Trademark Directive, which incorporates the provision in Article 4(2)(d).[51] Protection does not extend to dissimilar products, unless otherwise provided by national unfair competition law,[52] a field which, unlike trademark law, is not harmonized in the European Union.[53]

Do defenses[54] apply, when well-known marks are in question? In South

---

[49]   Joint Recommendation, see supra note 47, at p. 6.

[50]   Kur (1992) at 219 see supra note 41.

[51]   Directive 89/104/EEC of 21 December 1988 to approximate the laws of the Member States relating to trade marks, OJ L 40, 11.2.1989, p.1–7. Directive 2008/95/EC of the European Parliament and of the Council of 22 October 2008 to approximate the laws of the Member States relating to trade marks, OJ L 299/25, p. 25–33 (Trademark Directive).

[52]   Article 16(3) of the TRIPS Agreement loosened the similarity requirement to allow for protection of well-known marks against use on dissimilar goods or services, when there is a connection between the uses and that connection damages the interests of the well-known marks holder. This provision should not be confused with protection for famous marks on the national level.

[53]   Kur, Annette, 'Fundamental Concerns in the harmonization of (European) trademark law', at 169, in Dinwoodie, Graeme & Janis, Mark (Eds.), *Trademark Law and Theory A Handbook of Contemporary Research*, Cheltenham, Edward Elgar Publishing, 2008, at 151–176. Hereinafter Kur (2008).

[54]   Defences are treated differently in civil and common law systems. First, a typical civil law trademark statute confers negative rights to the trademark owner, but hardly any to the defendant. Defendants' rights are implicitly taken into account in statutory interpretation. Second, it is counterintuitive to make conclusions based on facts (inductive reasoning) in a system based on reasoning that deduces the law from general principles. Traditionally only common law systems explicitly and exhaustively include available defences in the statutory text. Legal concepts and tests thus naturally develop in common law to further

Africa two decisions have held in favor[55] of BMW against re-sale and repair services, where the court concluded that defenses do not apply

---

refine the decision-making process and enable categorical statements about the law. With each brick that is laid there is no way back, without overruling prior precedent. The more refined the rules the more certainty exists in the legal system. In contrast, civil law systems usually list only causes of action and some limits on the acquired rights in the statutory text. The acquired right is subject to numerous implicit limitations, when tested against the general principles of law operating in the legal system as a whole. Unlike, the common law where a single decision may lay the groundwork for a categorical exclusion, the "stare decisis" of a civil law decision is which general principles interacted and how in the case at hand. Categorical conclusions may be drawn from a decision, but this is not always the case. A civil law court may affirm several valid interpretations of a general principle. Because of the authoritative influence of general principles of law within the civil law system, and the near impossibility of overruling such general statements, the court treads carefully in relatively new, *contested* areas of law. Once the debate has raged and a body of lower level decisions has developed the question of law is ripe for inclusion in the network of general principles. A systemic consequence of the civil law system is that an affirmative statement of validity carries no *e contrario*–value. The acceptance of an approach thus carries precedential value, while the rejection of another approach does not preclude the valid use of it in another setting. All decisions are presumptively consistent with the general principles of law and an interpretation to the contrary is invalid. Certainty within the system is maintained by way of repetition, thus, rather than overruling prior rulings, the EUCJ has a tendency to reaffirm parts of its rulings that support coherence and ignore or recast statements that have subsequently proven inconsistent with the general theoretical framework of law. Case C-228/03 *The Gillette Company and Gillette Group Finland Oy v LA-Laboratories Ltd Oy* [2005] ECR I-2337 at 47 arguably recasting Case C 337/95 *Parfums Christian Dior* [1997] ECR I-6013, and Case C-63/97 *Bayerische Motorenwerke AG (BMW) and BMW Nederland BV v. Deenik* [1999] ECR I-905, in favor of a more flexible ruling despite explicit reference to the 'consistent' practice of the court in all three cases at 41. See also Triton et al. on the EUCJ subsequent treatment of the ruling in the BABY-DRY-case at 273.

[55] It is certainly possible that the court was influenced by *how* the marks were used indeed it seems the court determined that the marks were protectable trademarks based on how the defendant had used them. Since the *cases are used as an example* of how extended protection of *unregistered marks* is or can be interpreted in practice (not theory), it is of great interest that the court did not have to reach this conclusion based on the evidence before it. See Roshana Kelbrick, New Trademark Infringement Provisions: How Have the Courts Interpreted Them? (2007) 19 SA Merc LJ 86, at 95. Indeed, the defendants were found to infringe the *registered* trademarks of BMW. Courts are often asked to rule on infringement, dilution and unfair competition based on the same conduct by the defendant. However, the case only turns on dilution (renowned registered marks) or unfair competition (here well-known unregistered marks), when confusion cannot be shown. These cases are rare and therefore thorough *assessment* of these claims is *not common*.

against well-known marks protected under Article 6 *bis* of the Paris Convention. The marks E30, E36 and E46, were not registered, but widely used by BMW in South Africa and abroad.[56] *Kelbrick* criticizes this interpretation, since well-known marks protection "was introduced to protect the interests of traders who had not yet expanded to a particular market, not to avoid the legitimate defenses available to persons who have used the trademarks of others".[57] BMW was present on the South African market and held several registrations. The E-codes, however, had not been registered. In most countries such a case would be decided under unfair competition law or even trademark law, where the burden is on the plaintiff to prove rights in the mark. If rights are established the plaintiff must prove that infringement has occurred. Use of a mark for descriptive purposes, i.e., to describe the goods or services or their qualities, characteristics or nature, is exempt from uses that the trademark owner can prevent. By claiming protection under Article 6 *bis*, BMW were only required to prove the marks well-known to enjoy absolute protection.

This interpretation of well-known marks protection is not in line with its purpose or common interpretation.[58] First, as most protection on the international level, Article 6 *bis* is focused on protection against uses in bad faith. A use for descriptive purposes is generally accepted, thus, such

---

It could be argued that some cases involving well-known or famous marks are so clearly unfair and therefore it may explain a seemingly odd (theoretically and doctrinally) outcome. The purpose here, to which the cases are used, is to *test the soundness of the outcomes in light of the provisions and their purpose*. The odder the outcome in light of theoretical and legislative background of the protection (yet viewed as routine) the more justified stricter scrutiny would seem, irrespective of whether protection extends to the factual setting or not. The practical example is used to depict the situation in which it is before the national judge and allows a discussion searching for practical tools that could aid in reaching an outcome consistent with the normative basis of the type of protection. The approach starts from the grass-root (case-specific setting on national level) instead of the top (legislative history on the international level).

[56]   Some countries require registration, some use, for conferring rights in a trademark. Others protect both non-registered, i.e. used, and registered marks. Yet, others confer only 6*bis* protection to unregistered marks. Regardless of initial requirements for protection most countries require at least some use of the mark in commerce for the maintenance of rights in a mark. Dinwoodie, Graeme & Janis, Mark, *Use, Intent to Use and Registration in the USA*, at 313–314, and Klein, Sheldon H. & Norton, N Christopher, *The Role of Trade Mark Use in US Infringement, Unfair Competition and Dilution Proceedings* at 330, in Phillips, Jeremy & Simon, Ilanah (Eds.), Trade Mark Use (2005). Kur (1992), at 219 see supra note 41.

[57]   Kelbrick at p. 95, see supra note 45.

[58]   Kelbrick, at p.95 criticizing the decisions and at 86–87, discussing the different origins of the two types of protection.

a use is one in good faith. Second, a typical scenario where Article 6 *bis* applies is when a mark of global fame has not been used in the country where protection is sought. The South African case, where the fast-food restaurant McDonald's successfully claimed Paris 6 *bis* protection against earlier fast food restaurants that had taken advantage of the international embargo, is a case in point.[59] Third, protection for non-registered mark is only exceptionally regulated by international law; in fact Article 6 *bis* is such an exception. To interpret it to cover all situations where unregistered marks are used and to allow one element for protection i.e. fame, to conquer all, would amount to creating an international unfair competition law out of an exception. Such an interpretation is not plausible.[60]

The EUCJ has not considered a case relating to well-known marks protection within the meaning of Article 6 *bis* of the Paris Convention, Article 16(2) of the TRIPS Agreement or Article 8(2)(c) of the Community Trademark Regulation (CTMR).[61] The EU General Court (EUGC) has heard one case, where Article 8(2)(c) CTMR was at issue. The court made reference to the Joint Recommendation Concerning the Provisions on the Protection of Well-known Trademarks adopted by the Assembly of the Paris Union and the General Assembly of the WIPO and, in light of the recommended standards, found the evidence put for it insufficient.[62]

According to the 70 reported decisions on CTMR Article 8(2)(c) by the Board of Appeal at the Office of Harmonization in the Internal Market (OHIM), only one succeeded on the basis of CTMR Article 8(2)(c), that is, for being well known within the meaning of Article 6 *bis* of the Paris Convention.[63] Some mark holders have satisfactorily proven well-known status before the Opposition Division.[64] The otherwise successful cases, but whose claim for well-known mark protection was rejected, show the

---

[59] *McDonald's Corporation v. Dax Prop CC & Another; McDonald's Corporation v. Joburgers Drive-Inn Restaurant (Pty) Ltd & Another; McDonald's Corporation v. Joburgers Drive-Inn Restaurant (Pty) Ltd & Another and Dax Prop CC & Another*, 1997 1 SA 1 (A). Kelbrick at p. 438–39, see supra note 45.

[60] Note cases before the OHIM and the South African example, where plaintiffs assert protection for unregistered marks based on Article 6 bis PC.

[61] Council Regulation 40/94 of 20 December 1994 on the Community Trademark.

[62] T-420/03, *El Corte Ingles, SA v. Office for Harmonisation in the Internal Market*, 17.6.2008 at para.80.

[63] *Old Blue S.p.A. v. S.A. Confiserie Leonidas*, Decision of the Fourth Board of Appeal 19.5.2009 at para 33. The owner of the well-known mark was successful in showing renown for goods, but not for services.

[64] Harri Salmi, Petteri Häkkänen, Rainer Oesch, Marja Tommila, *Tavaramerkki*, Helsinki, Talentum (2008) at 400.

wide-ranged confusion on the topic. Protection was claimed for registered marks,[65] for use on dissimilar goods,[66] and when the marks were neither famous nor similar.[67] The fame of one mark cannot be transferred to another in order to receive broader protection.[68] Conversely, well-known marks protection is unnecessary, when likelihood of confusion has been shown.[69] This last holding seems to support the interpretation that Article 6 *bis* was intended to protect trademark owners whose marks did not already enjoy protection in the territory in question. However, as also noticed by the Board of Appeal, the question of renown[70] of (all relevant)

---

[65]   *TorreFaccao Camelo, LDA. v. Japan Tobacco Inc.*, Decision of the Second Board of Appeal 22.2.2006 at para 33; *Ragdoll Limited v. Triunfo Produtos Alimentares, S.A.*, Decision of the Second Board of Appeal 2.7.2004 at para 46–47.

[66]   *Losberger GmbH v. Hanhwa Polydreamer Co., Ltd*, Decision of the Fourth Board of Appeal 18.5.2009 at para 29; *Isabella Productiones S.A. v. Factoria de Informacion, S.A.*, Decision of the Second Board of Appeal 11.3.2008 at para 39; *Elleni Holding B.V. v. SIGLA, S.A.*, Decision of the Fourth Board of Appeal 16.8.2007 at para 39–41; *Formula One Licensing B.V. v. Produits Petroliers Organisation S.A.*, Decision of the First Board of Appeal 17.12.2002 at para 38–39, 43.

[67]   *Formula One Licensing B.V. v. Produits Petroliers Organisation S.A.*, Decision of the First Board of Appeal 17.12.2002 at para 38–39, 43.

[68]   *Erika Schindler v. Georges RECH S.A.*, Decision of the Fourth Board of Appeal 26.9.2006 at para 37.

[69]   *Colgate- Palmolive Company v. Sangi Co., Ltd.*, Decision of the Third Board of Appeal 14.9.2001 at para 18-20; *Elleni Holding B.V. v. SIGLA, S.A.*, Decision of the Fourth Board of Appeal 16.8.2007 at para 39-41.

[70]   National unfair competition or trademark laws had long recognized the special nature of renowned marks and the need for their protection under different doctrines, such as Frank Schechter's theory (Frank Schechter, The Rational Basis for Trademark Protection, 40 Harv. L. Rev. 813 (1927)) recognizing absolute protection against dilution by blurring, the Kodak-doctrine, the Rat Poison-doctrine, Abstandslehre (theory of distance) or the action for passing-off in the UK. The difference between these doctrines is whether harm to a renowned mark is a question of law or question of fact, and even if protection follows as a matter of law, what procedural, factual or evidentiary constraints there are on enforcing the right in practice. See Cornish (2004) at 87 footnote 42: "In passing off and unfair competition, the comparison is between the actual trading practices of claimant and defendant at the date when action commences. At least comparison is not with the claimant's mark as *registered*, which is the basic test in EU law." (emphasis original). See Michael Lehmann, Unfair Use of and Damage to the Reputation of Well-Known Marks, Names and Indications of Source in Germany. Some Aspects of Law and Economics, IIC 1986, 17(6) 746-767 at 766 "the principle of free competition and its corollary theory of freedom to imitate cannot generally provide justification for *the selection* of a trademark or company name as near as possible to famous marks or names, on the contrary, this establishes a well-founded presumption that *an attempt is being made to tap another's marketing efforts* without authorization for the promotion of one's own competition. After all, in the area

marks is a vital aspect of the assessment of likelihood of confusion and is thus a necessary part of the global assessment.[71] Providing well-known status is beneficial for proving renown; however, proving renown does not necessarily amount to protection for unregistered marks.[72]

3.2   Protection for Famous Marks

3.2.1   Introduction

Unlike protection for well-known marks, the protection for famous marks focuses on national or regional protection for registered marks.[73] Although wording similar to famous marks protection can be found in Article 16(3) of the TRIPS Agreement, there is no international minimum standard that requires member states to provide for additional protection for famous marks within their national laws.[74] The EU Trademark

---

of creating designations and their accompanying advertising, the observance of a creative distance is demanded. . . in the field of designations, there is namely enough latitude for individual creative efforts." (Author's emphasis) Thus, while national examples on protecting (or not) renowned marks are abundant they are by no means one and the same; nor could these national doctrines be interpreted as *reached consensus* on protection for renowned marks as a rule rather than exception. Cornish 2004, at 87 discussing how the EUCJ forced change to the UK view "[b]ut rule it is, at least for the present." See also Ilanah Simon Fhima, Dilution by Blurring: A Conceptual Roadmap, [2010] I.P.Q.: No. 1, 44-87 at 84 concluding thoughts on theoretical approaches to dilution by blurring.

The language of the Trademark Directive was 'new', since it is not clearly traceable to any of these doctrines. See J. Thomas McCarthy, Dilution of a trademark: European and United States law compared 159 174 in David Vaver and Lionel Bently (eds), Intellectual Property in the New Millennium: Essays in Honour of William R. Cornish, Paperback Edition 2010 at 160. The EUCJ has since confirmed that the protection is 'new' in the sense that it is something different from previous national or international forms of protection.

[71]   *Societe des Produits de Nestle S.A. v. Mars Incorporated*, Decision of the Third Board of Appeal 31.10.2001 at para 21–23, 25, 28–29.

[72]   *Societe des Produits de Nestle S.A. v Mars Incorporated*, Decision of the Third Board of Appeal, 31.10.2001 at 21–23, 25, 28–29.

[73]   Kur (1992), at 223, see supra note 41.

[74]   Article 16(3) of the TRIPS Agreement reads: "Article 6*bis* of the Paris Convention (1967) shall apply, *mutatis mutandis*, to goods or services which are not similar to those in respect of which a trademark is registered, provided that use of that trademark in relation to those goods or services would indicate a connection between those goods or services and the owner of the registered trademark and provided that the interests of the owner of the registered trademark are likely to be damaged by such use." The wording extends the protection for well-known marks from identical or similar goods to goods that are not similar. Unlike protection for famous marks, Article 16(3) of TRIPS requires likelihood of

Directive first introduced additional protection for famous marks on the international level by harmonizing the trademark laws of the EU member states. Protection was two-fold.[75] The concept of likelihood of confusion, which is required for a showing of traditional trademark infringement, was extended to include likelihood of association between the marks in Article 5.1(b) of the Trademark Directive. Second, a new form of protection altogether was introduced in Article 5.2. The case-law of the EUCJ has thus naturally considered the protection of famous marks under both the provision for "ordinary" trademark infringement, as well as, under the "famous marks" provision of Article 5.2.

Article 5 of the Trademark Directive, in relevant part, reads as follows:

(1) The registered trade mark shall confer on the proprietor exclusive rights therein. The proprietor shall be entitled to prevent all third parties not having his consent from using in the course of trade:
   a. any sign which is identical with the trade mark in relation to goods or services which are identical with those for which the trade mark is registered;
   b. any sign where, because of its identity with, or similarity to, the trade mark and the identity or similarity of the goods or services covered by the trade mark and the sign, there exists a likelihood of confusion on the part of the public, which includes the likelihood of association between the sign and the trade mark.

(2) Any Member State may also provide that the proprietor shall be entitled to prevent all third parties not having his consent from using in the course of trade any sign which is identical with, or similar to, the trade mark in relation to goods or services which are not similar to those for which the trade mark is registered, where the latter has a reputation in the Member State and where use of that sign without due cause takes unfair advantage of, or is detrimental to, the distinctive character or the repute of the trade mark.

(3) The following, inter alia, may be prohibited under paragraphs 1 and 2:
   a. affixing the sign to the goods or to the packaging thereof;
   b. offering the goods, or putting them on the market or stocking them for these purposes under that sign, or offering or supplying services thereunder;
   c. importing or exporting the goods under the sign;
   d. using the sign on business papers and in advertising.

---

confusion on the part of the public to be shown. Such a showing is not necessary for the famous marks protection.

[75] As noted in the 10th recital of the preamble of the Trademark Directive the use of an identical mark for identical goods or services triggers a presumption of infringement. Protection under Article 5.1(a) thus allows for strengthened protection for both ordinary and famous marks in the case of double-identity. As we will see in this chapter, this protection is not absolute, but subject to the exceptions in Article 6 of the Trademark Directive.

(5) Paragraphs 1 to 4 shall not affect provisions in any Member State relating to the protection against the use of a sign other than for the purposes of distinguishing goods or services, where use of that sign without due cause takes unfair advantage of, or is detrimental to, the distinctive character or the repute of the trade mark.

Reputed marks may receive protection under Article 5.1 a), Article 5.1 b) and Article 5.2 of the EU Trademark Directive, although renown may influence the scope of protection or not.[76] However, even when a presumption of infringement is triggered under Article 5.1 a) and the reputation of the mark is considered as an aggravated factor, the protection is not absolute, as the EUCJ stated in its Grand Chamber –ruling in *Céline SARL v. Céline SA*.[77] The use can still be permissible under Article 6 of the EU Trademark Directive. Prior to considering the limits on the trademark holder's right, it is necessary to review the prerequisites for protection, and most importantly how fame influences the assessment.

3.2.2 Consumer understanding

In *Adidas v. Fitnessworld* the EUCJ considered the effect of a finding of fact that the public views the defendant's sign not as a trademark, but as an embellishment, on the trademark proprietor's ability to invoke Article 5.2 of the Directive. Adidas sought to prevent the use by Fitnessworld of two stripes on athletic wear in the Netherlands, where it arguably was clear that the defendant's use was not likely to confuse the general public. The Hoge Raad referred the following question to the European Court of Justice:

If the sign alleged to be infringing is viewed purely as an embellishment by the relevant section of the public, what importance must be attached to that circumstance in connection with the question concerning the similarity between the mark and the sign?

Although the use was made on the same or similar products, and the wording of Article 5.2 only refers to use on dissimilar products, it is settled

---

[76] Ordinary marks may also receive protection under Article 5(1)(a) and 5(1)(b) and these forms of protection, as noted above, do not turn on renown, like the protection under Article 5.2. There are limits to protection under all articles that apply whether or not the mark is renowned. In the context of sports merchandising (extending protection outside the primary sports activity) it is here presumed that the form of protection presumes some ability to capitalize on the *renown of primary registered marks* outside the services where the trademark owner primarily does business.

[77] Case C-17/06 *Céline SARL v Céline SA*, [2007] ECR I-07041, at 32.

case law that a trademark holder, nonetheless, may rely on Article 5.2.[78] The EUCJ stated that the fact that a mark is generally viewed as an embellishment will not, of itself, prevent the later mark from being infringing.[79] However, if the national court makes the finding of fact that the relevant section of the public views the mark *purely* as an embellishment, the requisite link between the marks is absent, and therefore there can be no dilution of the earlier mark.[80]

In a later case based on similar facts it was asked if it makes any difference whether the signs which are to be held available are seen by the relevant public as being signs used to distinguish goods or merely to embellish them?[81] The EUCJ rejected the principle of a need to leave free, based on the German concept "Freihaltebedürfnis". It is settled case law that a general need to leave free is not an individual element that must be considered in the overall assessment of infringement, likelihood of confusion or detriment or harm under Article 5 of the EU Trademark Directive.[82] Unlike its previous ruling, the court held that the fact that the public views the mark purely as an embellishment cannot prevent a finding of infringement, when the "sign is so similar to the registered trade mark that the relevant public is likely to perceive that the goods come from the same undertaking or, as the case may be, from economically-linked undertakings".[83] When considering whether the capacity of the trademark to indicate origin is endangered, the degree of similarity between the marks and the degree of fame of the earlier mark is relevant.

---

[78]   Case C-487/07, *L'oréal SA, Lancôme parfums et beauté & Cie SNC and Laboratoire Garnier & Cie v. Bellure NV, Malaika Investments Ltd and Starion International Ltd*, unreported 18.6.2009, at 35 referring to Case C-292/00 *Davidoff* [2003] ECR I-389, paragraph 30; *Adidas-Salomon and Adidas Benelux*, paragraphs 18 to 22; and *Adidas and Adidas Benelux*, paragraph 37.

[79]   Case C-408/01 *Adidas-Salomon AG and Adidas Benelux BV v Fitnessworld Trading Ltd.*, [2003] ECR I-12537 at 39.

[80]   Case C-408/01 *Adidas-Salomon AG and Adidas Benelux BV v Fitnessworld Trading Ltd.*, [2003] ECR I-12537 at 40.

[81]   Case C-102/07 *Adidas AG, Adidas Benelux BV v. Marca Mode CV, C&A Nederland CV, H&M Hennes & Mauritz Netherlands BV and Vendex KBB Nederland BV*, [2008] ECR I-02439.

[82]   Advocate General Ruiz-Jarabo Colomer discussed the incompatibility of this German concept with EU law at length in his opinion in Case C-102/07 *Adidas AG, Adidas Benelux BV v. Marca Mode CV, C&A Nederland CV, H&M Hennes & Mauritz Netherlands BV and Vendex KBB Nederland BV* delivered on January 16th, 2008, at 33–45.

[83]   Case C-102/07 *Adidas AG, Adidas Benelux BV v. Marca Mode CV, C&A Nederland CV, H&M Hennes & Mauritz Netherlands BV and Vendex KBB Nederland BV*, [2008] ECR I-02439, at 34.

The more the mark is well known, the greater the number of operators who will want to use similar signs. The presence on the market of a large quantity of goods covered by similar signs might adversely affect the trade mark in so far as it could reduce the distinctive character of the mark and jeopardise its essential function, which is to ensure that consumers know where the goods concerned come from.[84]

This conclusion is also apparent from the court's ruling in *Budweiser*,[85] where the court, clarifying *Arsenal*,[86] discusses the type of uses that constitutes infringement:

[The required link is established], in particular, where the use of that sign allegedly made by the third party is such as to create the impression that there is a material link in trade between the third party's goods and the undertaking from which the goods originate. It must be established whether the consumers targeted, including those who are confronted with the goods after they have left the third party's point of sale, are likely to interpret the sign, as it is used by the third party, as designating or tending to designate the undertaking from which the third party's goods originate.[87]

3.2.3 The required link

A link in the mind of the public is necessary for a finding of infringement. However, such a link is not in and of itself, sufficient to establish harm.[88] Whether the requisite link exists is to be determined by an overall assessment, taking account of all relevant factors in the case at hand.[89] The EUCJ has reiterated some factors that are relevant to the inquiry as well as how these factors operate, in relation to marks of different degree of distinctiveness and repute. First, the degree of similarity between the marks

---

[84] Case C-102/07 *Adidas AG, Adidas Benelux BV v. Marca Mode CV, C&A Nederland CV, H&M Hennes & Mauritz Netherlands BV and Vendex KBB Nederalnd BV*, [2008] ECR I-02439, at 36.

[85] Case C-245/02 *Anheuser-Busch Inc. v Budějovický Budvar, národní podnik* [2004] ECR I-10989.

[86] Case C-206/01 *Arsenal Football Club plc v Matthew Reed* [2002] ECR I-10273.

[87] Case C-245/02 *Anheuser-Busch Inc. v Budějovický Budvar, národní podnik* [2004] ECR I-10989 at 60.

[88] Case C-252/07, *Intel Corporation Inc. v. CPM United Kingdom Ltd.* [2008] ECR I-08823, at 31–32 and C- 487/07, *L'oréal SA, Lancôme parfums et beauté & Cie SNC and Laboratoire Garnier & Cie v. Bellure NV, Malaika Investments Ltd and Starion International Ltd*, unreported 18.6.2009, at 37.

[89] Case C-408/01 *Adidas-Salomon AG and Adidas Benelux BV v Fitnessworld Trading Ltd.*, [2003] ECR I-12537 at 30. C-102/07 *Adidas AG, Adidas Benelux BV v. Marca Mode CV, C&A Nederland CV, H&M Hennes & Mauritz Netherlands BV and Vendex KBB Nederalnd BV*, [2008] ECR I-02439, at 42. C-252/07, *Intel Corporation Inc. v. CPM United Kingdom Ltd.* [2008] ECR I-08823, at 41.

is relevant, and the more similar the marks, the higher the likelihood that the later mark evokes an image of the famous mark. The mere similarity of the marks, however, is not sufficient to form the requisite link within the mind of the consumer.[90]

Second, the nature of the goods or services for which the conflicting marks were registered is clearly relevant, as similar marks are frequently registered in different categories. The degree of closeness or dissimilarity between those goods or services, as well as whether the marks operate in the same or different sections of the public are relevant considerations. The courts notes that even a famous mark can be unknown to consumers in a different sector. Naturally, a famous mark can also be known outside the goods or services for which it has registered trademarks.[91]

Third, the strength of the earlier mark's reputation may lead to protection in clearly different fields; and fourth, the degree of the earlier mark's distinctive character is a viable factor. The higher the natural or acquired distinctiveness of the mark, the higher the likelihood that it evokes the image of the famous mark. A famous mark that has been registered due to acquired distinctiveness enjoys protection under Article 5.2. The degree of distinctiveness is, however, proportionate to the uniqueness of the mark. Thus, it is relevant whether the mark in question is unique or essentially unique.[92] Lastly, in the event that likelihood of confusion on the part of the public is shown the necessary link has been established. Protection, however, is not contingent on such a showing.[93]

In conclusion, the fame or distinctiveness of the mark cannot in and of itself, establish the necessary link. However, the more immediately and strongly the famous mark is brought to mind by the later mark, the greater the likelihood that the current or future use of the later mark is taking unfair advantage of, or is detrimental to, the distinctive character or the repute of the earlier mark[94] Similarly, the more distinctive and famous the mark, the easier it will be to accept that detriment has been caused to it.[95]

---

[90]   Case C-252/07, *Intel Corporation Inc. v. CPM United Kingdom Ltd.* [2008] ECR I-08823, at 42 and 44–45.

[91]   Case C-252/07, *Intel Corporation Inc. v. CPM United Kingdom Ltd.* [2008] ECR I-08823, at 46–50.

[92]   Case C-252/07, *Intel Corporation Inc. v. CPM United Kingdom Ltd.* [2008] ECR I-08823, at 51–56.

[93]   Case C-252/07, *Intel Corporation Inc. v. CPM United Kingdom Ltd.* [2008] ECR I-08823, at 57–58.

[94]   Case C-252/07, *Intel Corporation Inc. v. CPM United Kingdom Ltd.* [2008] ECR I-08823, at 64, 67, 69.

[95]   Case C-375/97, *General Motors Corporation v. Yplon SA*, 14.9.1999, at 30.

3.2.4 Types of harm

What types of harm are relevant for the purposes of Article 5.2? There are three distinct types of harm, which on their own may constitute infringement.[96] First, detriment to the distinctive character of the mark is caused by a use that leads to "dispersion of the identity and hold upon the public mind of the earlier mark". Such is the case when a mark that has once triggered an immediate association to the goods or services for which it is registered, and due to the use by a third party no longer does so.[97] Second, detriment to the repute of the mark is caused when an identical or similar sign is used so that the trademark's power of attraction is reduced. This situation is more likely to arise when the goods or services offered by the third party possess a negative characteristic or quality.[98] Third, the concept of taking unfair advantage of the distinctive character or the repute of the trade mark relates to the advantage taken by the third party as a result of the use of the identical or similar sign. In particular, it covers cases where there is clear exploitation on the coat-tails of a mark with a reputation.[99]

4. LIMITS ON THE TRADEMARK RIGHT

4.1 Trademark Use in Europe

During the past years a debate has raged of whether trademark law only applies to uses that can be considered "trademark use". The debate originated in the United States, and thus asked the question whether

---

[96] Case C-252/07, *Intel Corporation Inc. v. CPM United Kingdom Ltd.*, [2008] ECR I-08823, at 28 and Case C- 487/07, *L'oréal SA, Lancôme parfums et beauté & Cie SNC and Laboratoire Garnier & Cie v. Bellure NV, Malaika Investments Ltd and Starion International Ltd*, unreported 18.6.2009, at 42.

[97] Case C-252/07, *Intel Corporation Inc. v. CPM United Kingdom Ltd.*, [2008] ECR I-08823, at 31-32 and Case C- 487/07, *L'oréal SA, Lancôme parfums et beauté & Cie SNC and Laboratoire Garnier & Cie v. Bellure NV, Malaika Investments Ltd and Starion International Ltd*, unreported 18.6.2009, at 39. The use can also be referred to as "dilution", "whittling away" or "blurring".

[98] Case C-487/07, *L'oréal SA, Lancôme parfums et beauté & Cie SNC and Laboratoire Garnier & Cie v. Bellure NV, Malaika Investments Ltd and Starion International Ltd*, unreported 18.6.2009, at 40. The use can also be referred to as "tarnishment" or "degradation".

[99] Case C-487/07, *L'oréal SA, Lancôme parfums et beauté & Cie SNC and Laboratoire Garnier & Cie v. Bellure NV, Malaika Investments Ltd and Starion International Ltd*, unreported 18.6.2009, at 41 and 49. The use can also be referred to as "parasitism" or "free-riding".

"non-trademark uses" constituted an absolute defense to trademark infringement.[100] An inquiry framed as a defense would as a matter of law presume a lack of detriment to the mark in those certain types of cases, thus in effect turning the trademark use requirement into a question of fact. What is then the meaning and significance of trade mark use in European trade mark law?

Exactly *what theoretical significance and weight* should in infringement analysis be placed on whether or not the defendant is in fact engaging in trademark use or other use remains unclear. Is trademark use a *factual phenomenon*, i.e. a type of use, *or a legal concept*, i.e. a positive or negative delimiting tool of trademark law? *I argue below that 'trademark use', as legal concept in EU trademark law, does not refer to 'use in fact' or uses that are outside trademark law in theory or in practice. Instead it is a tool of theoretical inclusion that does not address whether the right is legitimately exercised against practical uses or not.*[101] This argument is based on an interpretation of EUCJ case law in tune with civil law interpretation and general principles of EU law. The fact that the EUCJ views the question of trademark use so differently than the prevailing Anglo-American debate alters the perspective employed in this section. First, the case law of the EUCJ is interpreted at face value in light of jurisdictional, procedural and factual constraints. Second, a search for a *functional equivalent* to a trademark use requirement in EU trademark law is conducted. It is argued that one can be found in the case law of the EUCJ interpreting Article 6. Third, it is argued that the duty to act fairly in light of the legitimate interests of trademark owners and the test for 'honest practices in industrial and commercial matters' may serve as a functional equivalent to the Anglo-American limiting doctrine and a defense in the non-procedural, but factual meaning of the word that takes the form of a balancing test between the legitimate interests of trademark owners against the legitimate interests of third parties.[102] A balancing test

---

[100]   See discussion supra note 54.

[101]   This point is abstract and its mirror-image may result in inclusion or exclusion of certain types of uses. The theoretical difference in approach is essential in understanding why categorical inclusion or exclusion of uses based on type are frowned upon by the EUCJ.

[102]   One could approach the nominative fair use or trademark use debate and seek to interpret EUCJ case law in light of how they are understood in the Anglo-American world. One could focus on how the EUCJ has interpreted concepts such as 'use as a trademark', 'use for goods or services', 'use in the course of trade'. This chapter follows a different approach, because, it is argued, the cases decided by the EUCJ give an incomplete picture of the law and principles cannot be deduced based on *e contrario* conclusions or attempts to distinguish the cases based on facts. The approach chosen in this chapter is based on civil law interpretation

may sit easier with a civil law court than a categorical exclusion that would upset the presumption underlying EU trademark law; that the trademark owner can rely on the exclusive right.[103]

The legal concept "trademark use" can be understood in several ways and in all its meanings has both positive and negative dimensions.[104] In fact, in contemporary trademark law, trade mark use is not one concept, but many and to a large extent undefined, if not indefinable.[105] Nonetheless, for the purpose of framing the discussion we will pursue this topic based on two general understandings of trademark use.[106]

---

and *e contrario*-conclusions from the court's statements are therefore avoided. It is not here argued that the EUCJ has not talked about 'trademark use' (quite the opposite, it has been repeatedly asked and has therefore answered), the argument is broader; the Court's statements are reviewed for inner normative logic that is not necessarily premised on how a legal or factual concept is viewed in a foreign legal system. The discussion focuses on placing the statements of the court in a general legal context, not on distilling the law by distinguishing the statements in the cases from each other. The court is not necessarily consistent in that regard, instead the EUCJ may alter meanings of statements and dislocate them from the factual context as they have done in e.g. BMW-Gillette, Arsenal-Adam Opel (see Norman at 31 arguing that the EUCJ went too far in Arsenal), and Adam Opel-BMW.

[103] The concept of honest practices in civil and commercial matters has been recognized in Art. 7 case law (considering the trademark owner's legitimate interests) of the EUCJ and in the interpretation of the Directive on comparative advertising and is thus not a concept defined to the limited circumstances of Art. 6. In fact it is argued that it could be viewed as a general test for fairness and freedom of competition.

[104] See Bojan Pretnar, 'Use and Non-Use in Trade Mark Law' 15–20 and 21–23, in *Trade Mark Use*, Eds. Jeremy Phillips and Ilanah Simon, Oxford, Oxford University Press, 2005. See also Graeme B Dinwoodie and Mark D Janis, 'Intent to Use and Registration in the United States' in *Trade Mark Use*, Eds. Jeremy Phillips and Ilanah Simon, Oxford, Oxford University Press, 2005 at 314 and 326–7, and Stacey Dogan and Mark Lemley in *Grounding Trademark Law through Trademark Use* (http://ssrn.com/abstract =961470 February 2007) at 6.

[105] Bojan Pretnar, at 27, see supra note 104.

[106] Each contributor to the discussion seems to have a slightly different take on trade mark use as a theoretical phenomenon. Many look at trademark use in relation to a specific legal question; what is required to acquire a distinctive character (Arnaud Folliard-Monguiral, 'Distinctive Character Acquired through Use: The Law and the Case Law' and Anna Carboni, 'Distinctive Character Acquired through Use: Establishing the Facts' in *Trade Mark Use*, Eds. Jeremy Phillips and Ilanah Simon, Oxford, Oxford University Press, 2005.); drawing the line to functional use; (Thomas Hays, 'Distinguishing Use versus Functional Use: Three dimensional Marks' in *Trade Mark Use*, Eds. Jeremy Phillips and Ilanah Simon, Oxford University Press, 2005.); drawing the line to denominative use (Neil J Wilkof, 'Third Party Use of Trade Marks' and Massimo Sterpi, 'Trade Mark Use and Denominative Trade Marks' in *Trade Mark Use*, Eds. Jeremy Phillips and

First, one could view trademark use as a requirement for obtaining and maintaining the trademark right. The trademark owner is required to use the mark as a trademark.[107] The negative[108] dimension of this understanding of trademark use is that non-use or failure to use the trademark as a trademark will result in the revocation or unenforceability of the rights in the mark.[109] Second, one could view trademark use by another as a type of infringement. A third party may not affix another's trademark to his goods, or market his products with the aid of another's mark.[110] The negative dimension of this type of trademark use asks if other uses than trademark uses are infringing. Put the other way; are uses that do not fall within the statutory or common law definition of trademark use, automatically outside the purview of the trademark owner's right and thus inherently lawful?

Although a trademark-use requirement might initially seem desirable to combat overprotection of trademark owners, the introduction of

---

Ilanah Simon, Oxford University Press, 2005.); or looking at trade mark use on the Internet (Spyros Maniatis, 'Trade Mark Use on the Internet' in *Trade Mark Use*, Eds. Jeremy Phillips and Ilanah Simon, Oxford University Press, 2005.). While chosen scope, labels, juxtapositions and categorizations differ, the substantive law recognized as relevant for the discussion on trade mark use covers the two general categories outlined below. Attempts to theorize on the problems surrounding trade mark use have been made by tying the concept to the user (Bojan Pretnar discussing the trademark owner's use in 'Use and Non-Use in Trade Mark Law' and from the perspective of third parties, Jennifer Davies, 'The Need to Leave Free for Others to Use and the Trade Mark Common' in *Trade Mark Use*, Eds. Jeremy Phillips and Ilanah Simon, Oxford, Oxford University Press, 2005.); or to the context of acquisition and enforcement of rights as opposed to infringement analysis (Bojan Pretnar, *Use and Non-Use in Trade Mark Law*). Stacey Dogan and Mark Lemley in *Grounding Trademark Law through Trademark Use* (http://ssrn.com/abstract =961470 February 2007) look at the historical emphasis on the concept of trademark use in infringement analysis through the lens of the distinction between indirect and direct infringement. Graeme B Dinwoodie and Mark D Janis in 'Use, Intent to Use and Registration in the United States' in *Trade Mark Use*, Eds. Jeremy Phillips and Ilanah Simon, Oxford, Oxford University Press, 2005, discuss the significance of the temporal dimension to the concept of trademark use in US trademark law. Most authors recognize the other dimensions of the concept, but choose to focus on a certain aspect of it.

[107] Article 10 of the Directive.

[108] Note how the terms positive and negative may quickly become confusing, since trademark statutes are framed to confer negative rights. The starting point is that this negative right is the basis for the articulation of the positive dimension, and its opposite, limitations on the right, the negative dimension of the concept of trademark use.

[109] Articles 11 and 12 of the Directive.

[110] Article 5(3) of the Directive.

an all-encompassing concept carries with it several difficulties.[111] Most notable are the difficulties in defining the elusive concept of trademark use.[112] Another obstacle to introducing a trademark use requirement into trademark law is its capability of serving as a limiting tool in practice. To this day, even proponents of the trademark use doctrine have encountered severe obstacles in devising a theory of trademark use that could easily remove non-trademark uses from infringement analysis.[113] For example, the solution put forth by the Third Circuit Court of Appeals in the United States in *Lendingtree* has been criticized for requiring a more intrusive inquiry than likelihood of confusion – analysis, and most importantly, for shifting the burden of proof to the defendant.[114]

It is necessary, therefore, to distinguish the discussions about the importance of trademark use in trademark law, from discussions advocating the introduction of a threshold requirement of trademark use to trademark law. The latter discussion merges with the former, when discussing the historical and current importance of the requirement of trademark use for maintenance of rights. A contested addition to contemporary trademark law is, however, at issue when advocating for a *trademark use requirement in infringement analysis.*

All the same, there is both a practical and theoretical aspect to this debate. It has been argued that certain uses inherently trigger different questions of trademark law, and should be removed from traditional infringement analysis.[115] The EUCJ has refused to make trademark use a threshold question in infringement analysis in practice.[116] The federal courts in the United States are divided on the issue whether such a

---

[111] Stacey Dogan and Mark Lemley in *Grounding Trademark Law through Trademark Use* (http://ssrn.com/abstract =961470 February 2007) at 5–6. Graeme Dinwoodie and Mark Janis 'Confusion over Use: Contextualism in Trademark Law' (August 31, 2006) U Iowa Legal Studies Research Paper No. 06-06 Available at SSRN: http://ssrn.com/abstract=927996.

[112] Graeme Dinwoodie and Mark Janis, 'Lessons from the Trademark Use Debate', 92 Iowa L. R. 1703, 1713 (2007).

[113] Stacey Dogan and Mark Lemley in *Grounding Trademark Law through Trademark Use* (http://ssrn.com/abstract =961470 February 2007)

[114] *Century 21 Real Estate Corporation v. Lendingtree Inc.,* 425 F.3d 211, 76 U.S.P.Q.2d 1769, 217 (2005). For a more general discussion and critique of the nominative fair use defence, see Thomas McCarthy, Trademarks and Unfair Competition § 24:124.

[115] *Century 21 Real Estate Corporation v. Lendingtree Inc.,* 425 F.3d 211, 76 U.S.P.Q.2d 1769, 217 (2005), Case C-C-206/01 *Arsenal Football Club plc v Matthew Reed* [2002] ECR I-10273.

[116] Case C-C-206/01 *Arsenal Football Club plc v Matthew Reed* [2002] ECR I-10273; Case C-C-408/01 *Adidas-Salomon AG and Adidas Benelux BV v*

categorical exclusion is possible outside the statutory fair use defense.[117] Others see the limits of a trademark use requirement in practice, and would like to emphasize its doctrinal significance in certain circumstances, and thus place conceptual safeguards in trademark law to allow the type of use in question to presumptively weigh heavier in infringement analysis in certain categories of use.[118] It seems that there is consensus among courts and commentators that some weight must be given to the type of use in question.[119] Exactly what theoretical significance and weight should infringement analysis be placed on (whether or not the defendant is in fact engaging in trademark use or other use) remains unclear. For our purposes, the trademark use debate is interesting.

The next section proceeds with the following questions in mind: How are the issues raised in the trademark-use debate considered in sports merchandising? Should we subject the merchandising right to questions of fair dealing and fair use? And should we do so ex ante in tailoring the right or ex post in devising defenses or implicit limitations to the exclusive right?

Fitnessworld Trading Ltd., [2003] ECR I-12537; Case C-C-48/05 *Adam Opel AG v Autec AG* [2007] ECR I- 01017.

[117]   *Century 21 Real Estate Corporation v. Lendingtree Inc.*, 425 F.3d 211, 76 U.S.P.Q.2d 1769, 217 (2005) (The 3rd Circuit recognizing a nominative fair use defence); and *New Kids on the Block v. News America Publishing, Inc.*, 971 F.2d 302, 23 U.S.P.Q.2d 1534 (1992); *Playboy Enterprises, Inc. v. Welles* 279 F.3d 796, 61 U.S.P.Q2d 1508 (2002) and *Cairns v. Franklin Mint Company*, 292 F.3d 1139, 63 U.S.P.Q.2d 1279 (2002), (The 9th Circuit recognizing nominative use as a protectable type of fair use), and *Chambers v. Time Warner, Inc.*, 282 F.3d 147, 61 U.S.P.Q.2d 1761 (2002) (The 2nd Circuit holding that likelihood of confusion analysis is the relevant test) and *Pebble Beach Company v. Tour 18 I Limited*, 155 F.3d 526, 48 U.S.P.Q.2d 1065 (1998) (The 5th Circuit holding that likelihood of confusion analysis is the relevant test); and *Interactive Products Corporation v. A2Z Mobile Office Solutions* 326 F.3d 687, 66 U.S.P.Q.2d 1321 (2003); *PACCAR Inc. v. Telescan Technologies*, 319 F.3d 243, 65 U.S.P.Q.2d 1761 (2003) (the 6th Circuit holding that likelihood of confusion analysis is the relevant test).

[118]   Stacey Dogan and Mark Lemley in Grounding Trademark Law through Trademark Use (http://ssrn.com/abstract =961470 February 2007) at 5–6 and 38.

[119]   Case C-C-206/01 *Arsenal Football Club plc v Matthew Reed* [2002] ECR I-10273; Case C-C-408/01 *Adidas-Salomon AG and Adidas Benelux BV v Fitnessworld Trading Ltd.* [2003] ECR I-12537; Case C-C-48/05 *Adam Opel AG v Autec AG* [2007] ECR I-01017. Stacey Dogan and Mark Lemley in *Grounding Trademark Law through Trademark Use* (http://ssrn.com/abstract =961470 February 2007) at 5–6 and 38; and Graeme Dinwoodie and Mark Janis 'Confusion over Use: Contextualism in Trademark Law' (August 31, 2006) U Iowa Legal Studies Research Paper No. 06-06. Available at SSRN: http://ssrn.com/abstract=927996 at 10, see also 5–7.

4.2 Defenses under Article 6 of the Directive

4.2.1 *Arsenal v. Reed*

The exclusive right conferred under Article 5 of the Trademark Directive is limited – or its effects are limited – by Article 6 of the Trademark Directive that reads as follows:

> Article 6
> Limitation of the effects of a trade mark
> 1. The trade mark shall not entitle the proprietor to prohibit a third party from using, in the course of trade,
>   (a) his own name or address;
>   (b) indications concerning the kind, quality, quantity, intended purpose, value, geographical origin, the time of production of goods or of rendering of the service, or other characteristics of goods or services;
>   (c) the trade mark where it is necessary to indicate the intended purpose of a product or service, in particular as accessories or spare parts;
>   provided he uses them in accordance with honest practices in industrial or commercial matters.

The EUCJ has specifically refused to adopt a trademark use requirement into infringement analysis, as the concept is defined and understood in the United Kingdom, into Community trademark law.[120] First, the court rejected such a requirement in *Arsenal v. Reed*, where a question was referred by an English court on the interpretation of Art. 5(1)(a), that is, an identical mark was used on identical goods.[121] Mr. Reed sold scarves bearing the Arsenal word mark and logo at a stall outside the team's stadium. His stall visibly displayed a sign stating that the goods were not official Arsenal merchandise, thus removing any possible confusion on the part of the public.[122] The High Court referred the following question to the European Court of Justice:

---

[120] Case C-206/01 *Arsenal Football Club plc v Matthew Reed* [2002] ECR I-10273 at 62; Case C-408/01 *Adidas-Salomon AG and Adidas Benelux BV v Fitnessworld Trading Ltd.*, [2003] ECR I-12537 at 39-40. See Ilanah Simon, *Embellishment: Trade Mark Use Triumph or Decorative Disaster*, E.I.P.R. 2006 28(6), 321-328 at 321.

[121] Case C-206/01 *Arsenal Football Club plc v Matthew Reed* [2002] ECR I-10273 at 62.

[122] The claims of initial interest confusion or post-sale confusion are sidestepped here, since they are attempts at extending the underlying argument of absolute property that is discussed below. These doctrines originate in the United States and are for reasons explained above, ill-suited in the context of understanding the approach of the EUCJ. For a thorough account on United States' case law

Where a trade mark is validly registered and
(a)   a third party uses in the course of trade a sign identical with that trade mark in relation to goods which are identical with those for which the trade mark is registered; and
(b)   the third party has no defense to infringement by virtue of Article 6(1) of the Directive
does the third party have a defense to infringement on the ground that the use complained of does not indicate trade origin (that is, a connection in the course of trade between the goods and the trademark proprietor)?[123]

In its answer the court adopted a trademark-centric approach, relying on protecting the essential function of the trademarks to guarantee to consumers the origin of the goods.[124] The court places great weight on the fact that the case is one of double identity, and notes the 10th recital of the preamble of the Directive, which offers near absolute protection at the core of trademark protection.[125] In this regard, the court notes that only uses for purely descriptive purposes are permissible and other uses fall within the scope of trademark protection that the trademark owner consequently is entitled to prevent.[126]

First, the court focuses on the essential function of the trademark reiterating the basis for trademark protection:

> Trade mark rights constitute an *essential element in the system of undistorted competition* which the Treaty is intended to establish and maintain. In such a system, undertakings must be able to attract and retain customers by the quality of their goods or services, which is made possible only by distinctive signs allowing them to be identified.[127]

---

on initial interest and post-sale confusion and its critique see Mark Lemley and Mark McKenna, 'Irrelevant Confusion', 62 *Stan L. Rev.* 413 (2010).
    [123]   Case C-206/01 *Arsenal Football Club plc v Matthew Reed* [2002] ECR I-10273 at 27.
    [124]   Case C-206/01 *Arsenal Football Club plc v Matthew Reed* [2002] ECR I-10273 at 47-48. The concept of "essential function" was introduced and developed in the free movement of goods case law of the court. On the one hand, "companies must be able to attract and retain customers by the quality of their goods and services" (Case C-10/89 *HAG AF* [1990] ECR I-3711, para 13). On the other hand, trademark protection is limited to guaranteeing "the identity of origin of the marked goods or services to the consumer or end user by enabling him, without any possibility of confusion, to distinguish the goods or services from others which have another origin" (Case 102/77 *Hoffman la Roche* [1978] ECR 1139, para 7).
    [125]   Case C-206/01 *Arsenal Football Club plc v Matthew Reed* [2002] ECR I-10273 at 51.
    [126]   Case C-206/01 *Arsenal Football Club plc v Matthew Reed* [2002] ECR I-10273 at 54.
    [127]   See, *inter alia*, Case C-10/89 *HAG GF* [1990] ECR I-3711, paragraph 13,

In that context, the essential function of a trade mark is to *guarantee* the identity of *origin* of the marked goods or services to the consumer or end user by enabling him, without any possibility of confusion, to distinguish the goods or services from others which have another origin. For the trade mark to be able to *fulfill its essential role* in the system of undistorted competition which the Treaty seeks to establish and maintain, it must offer a *guarantee* that all the goods or services bearing it have been *manufactured or supplied under the control of a single undertaking* which is *responsible for* their *quality*"[128]

Second, the court emphasizes that the case involves the truest form of trademark infringement, use of an identical mark on identical goods. International treaties starting with the Paris Convention have traditionally considered a use of an identical mark on identical goods as one at the heart of trademark protection. The TRIPS Agreement as well as the Trademark Directive also reflects the same "hierarchy" of protection, evolving from a presumption of infringement, through a presumption of a right to exclude to a more balanced assessment of detriment or harm. Substituting the trademark centric approach with a trademark use analysis would arguably amount to changing the traditional premise of trademark law. The presumption of trademark protection in these circumstances would unavoidably be watered down by such an open-ended exception.[129]

Third, the court noted that certain permissible uses, namely use for descriptive purposes were already exempted in Article 6 of the Trademark Directive.[130] The EUCJ, perhaps constrained by the conceptual framework of the case and conceptual unfamiliarity with the question posed, seemed somewhat sidetracked on this point.[131] It would seem that the

---

and Case C-517/99 *Merz & Krell* [2001] ECR I-6959, paragraph 21. Cited by the court in C-206/01 *Arsenal Football Club plc v Matthew Reed* [2002] ECR I-10273 at 46. Author's emphasis.

[128] See, *inter alia*, Case 102/77 *Hoffman-La Roche* [1978] ECR 1139, paragraph 7, and Case C-299/99 *Philips* [2002] ECR I-0000, paragraph 30. Cited by the court in C-206/01 *Arsenal Football Club plc v Matthew Reed* [2002] ECR I-10273 at 47. Author's emphasis.

[129] Note how the European Court of Justice rather shifts the inquiry from Article 5 analysis to the interpretation of Article 6, where an open-ended, presumptively neutral test would serve the same purpose. Reviving a dormant clause with a flexible test creates a counterweight in practice, but does not affect the viability of the right in traditional cases. See discussion in section 5 infra.

[130] Case C-206/01 *Arsenal Football Club plc v Matthew Reed* [2002] ECR I-10273 at 54.

[131] At this juncture the court's approach to trademark law was truly proprietor-centric: assessing the impact of the use on the interests of the trademark owner without regard to the merits of any countervailing interest on the part of the defendant.

court ruled that protection of trademarks in cases of double identity is absolute unless the use is for purely descriptive purposes.[132] However, such a strict reading of the case would render the concept of the essential function both meaningless and unnecessary. It would also imply that all uses of identical marks on identical goods, including non-commercial uses would constitute trademark infringement and that all available defenses are exhaustively listed in the Trademark Directive.[133] As the court has noted in subsequent case law the wording of the Directive allows for member states to introduce exceptions to trademark rights.[134]

Lastly, it should be noted that the court did not say that the type of use is irrelevant for the purposes of determining infringement; it is merely not decisive of whether the provisions of trademark law apply.[135] The

---

[132]   Case C-206/01 *Arsenal Football Club plc v Matthew Reed* [2002] ECR I-10273 at 55–61.

[133]   Exceptions and limitations could be understood in a strict or broad sense. In the strict sense, the Trademark Directive clearly caps the possibility of exceptions to registrability (e.g. refusing registration of certain types of trademarks) and level of protection (e.g. what meaning is to be given to the wording of Article 5.1 and 5.2), or allowing for national or global exhaustion contrary to Article 7, derogations that would in effect frustrate the harmonization of the elements vital for achieving free movement of goods and services in the EU. Exceptions and limitations in the broad sense i.e. limiting the effect of trademark rights outside the competitive relationship or against uses for purposes other than for distinguished products or services, are not, it is argued, exhaustively considered in the Trademark Directive. This raises issues both of normative harmonization and competence. See to this effect Han Illrich, 'Harmony and Unity of European Intellectual Property Protection', 20–47 in David Vaver and Lionel Bently (eds), *Intellctual Property in the New Millenium: Essays in Honour of William R. Cornish*, 2004 at 42, arguing that even far-reaching harmonization does not provide for general competence of the EU to legislate *autonomously*. Nevertheless, the Trademark Directive may set requirements for such exceptions, i.e. that they take account of the legitimate interests of trademark owners. See also Article 17 TRIPS Agreement.

[134]   Article 15(2) of the Directive and Article 17 of the TRIPS Agreement, Agreement on Trade-Related Aspects of Intellectual Property Rights, Annex 1 C of the Agreement Establishing the World Trade Organization, signed in Marrakesh April 15, 1994, entered into force January 1, 1995. See also joined Cases C-108/97 and C-109/97, *Windsurfing Chiemsee Produktions- und Vertriebs GmbH (WSC) and Boots- und Segelzubehör v. Walter Huber, Franz Attenberger* [1999] ECR I-02779 at 27, Case C-23/01 *Robelco v. Robeco Groep* [2002] ECR I-10913 at 31 and 34. Case C-245/02 *Anheuser-Busch Inc. v Budějovický Budvar, národní podnik* [2004] ECR I-10989 at 64 and 76.

[135]   One could argue the opposite, since the court states in Case C-206/01 *Arsenal Football Club plc v Matthew Reed* [2002] ECR I-10273 at 61 "Once it has been found that, in the present case, the use of the sign in question by the third

court views the concept of use from the perspective of the type of uses a trademark owner is entitled to prohibit.[136] The court moves on to focus on whether the use is one 1) "in the course of trade", 2) of an identical mark, 3) on identical goods and services and 4) whether it is liable to harm the essential function of the trademark by creating a link between the defendant and the trademark owner in the mind of the consumer.[137]

4.2.2 *Adam Opel v. Autec*

In *Adam Opel v. Autec*, the EUCJ once again refused to follow the suggestion of the Advocate General to introduce a trademark use -requirement into European Union trademark law.[138] Instead, the EUCJ reiterated the trademark-centric approach, when answering the following question put to it by a German State District court:

> Does the use of a trademark registered for 'toys' constitute use as a trademark for the purposes of Article 5 (1) (a), if the manufacturer of a toy model car copies a real car in scale, including the corresponding trademark, and markets it?

Article 5(1)(a), as was the case in Arsenal, concerns uses of an identical mark on identical goods. Autec manufactured remote-controlled cars and had affixed the Opel trademark on the front grill of its Opel Astra V8

---

party is liable to affect the guarantee of origin and that the trademark owner must be able to prevent this, it is immaterial that in the context of that use the sign is perceived as a badge of support for or loyalty or affiliation to the proprietor of the mark." In the context of the opinion, I would place the emphasis on the first part of the sentence. The test announced by the court is the relevant one, not the one presented to it by the UK court. Similarly to rejecting trademark use as a threshold requirement to a finding of infringement, the European Court of Justice closes the back door. Non-trademark uses cannot be categorically excluded at any stage of infringement analysis. An *e contrario*-conclusion, that the use of a mark as a badge of loyalty is never relevant in infringement analysis, is not consistent with civil law interpretation. To this effect see also Case C-245/02 *Anheuser-Busch Inc. v Budějovický Budvar, národní podnik* [2004] ECR I-10989 at 61 stating that the national court must assess whether a link is present "in light of the specific circumstances of the use of the sign allegedly made by the third party."

[136] Case C-206/01 *Arsenal Football Club plc v Matthew Reed* [2002] ECR I-10273 at 38. "Article 5 (3) gives a non-exhaustive list of the kinds of use which the proprietor may prohibit under Article 5(1). Other provisions of the Directive, such as Article 6, define certain limitations on the effects of the trademark."

[137] Case C-206/01 *Arsenal Football Club plc v Matthew Reed* [2002] ECR I-10273 at 40 and 56.

[138] Opinion of Advocate General Ruiz-Jarabo Colomer in Case C-48/05 *Adam Opel AG v Autec AG* dated March 7, 2006.

Coupe replica.[139] It was clear that the defendant had clearly marked both the packaging and transmitter with its own trademark "cartronic®" and trade name "AUTEC®".[140]

The court first concluded that the use was clearly one "in the course of trade" and that an identical mark was affixed on identical goods, since Opel had registered its trademark for toys.[141] In those circumstances the use must be one that the trademark owner is entitled to prohibit under Article 5(1)(a).[142] This time the court however explained its approach further:

> It should, however, be remembered that, in accordance with case-law of the Court of Justice the exclusive right under Article 5 (1) of the directive was conferred in order to enable the trade mark proprietor to protect his specific interests as proprietor, that is, to ensure that the trade mark can fulfill its functions and that, *therefore, the exercise of that right must be reserved to cases in which a third party's use of the sign affects or is liable to affect the functions of the trade mark, in particular its essential function of guaranteeing to consumers the origin of goods.*
>
> Therefore, the affixing by a third party of a sign identical to a trademark registered for toys to scale models of vehicles cannot be prohibited under Article 5(1) (a) of the directive unless it affects or is liable to affect the functions of that trade mark.[143]

The factual situation was similar to the case in *Adidas v. Fitnessworld*, where the referring court indicated that the relevant public in Germany *does not* view Autec's products as originating with Opel.[144] The EUCJ once again held that such a finding of fact would mandate the conclusion that the use at issue does not affect the essential function of the Opel logo as a trademark registered for toys.[145]

On its own motion the EUCJ also assessed the situation in relation to Art. 5(2) of the Directive and concluded that the use in question constitutes a use that the trademark owner is entitled to prohibit, if the national

---

[139]   Case C-48/05 *Adam Opel AG v Autec AG* [2007] ECR I- 01017, at 5-6.

[140]   Case C-48/05 *Adam Opel AG v Autec AG* [2007] ECR I- 01017, at 7.

[141]   Case C-48/05 *Adam Opel AG v Autec AG* [2007] ECR I- 01017, at 18-20.

[142]   Case C-48/05 *Adam Opel AG v Autec AG* [2007] ECR I- 01017, at 20.

[143]   Case C-48/05 *Adam Opel AG v Autec AG* [2007] ECR I- 01017, at 21-22. Author's emphasis.

[144]   On remand the national court did hold the use fair. See press release of the German Federal Supreme Court Nr. 9/2010 on January 15, 2010 available at http://juris.bundesgerichtshof.de/cgi-bin/rechtsprechung/document.py?Gericht=b gh&Art=pm&Datum=2010&Sort=3&nr=50551&pos=1&anz=10

[145]   Case C-48/05 *Adam Opel AG v Autec AG* [2007] ECR I- 01017, at 24.

court finds that the use without due cause takes unfair advantage of, or is detrimental to, the distinctive character or repute of the mark.[146]

The second question at issue in *Adam Opel v. Autec* was whether the use in question could be considered an indication of the intended purpose of the toys, which would constitute a permissible use under Article 6(1)(b) of the Directive, or a use of the trademark designed to indicate the intended purpose of the toys, which would constitute a permissible use under Article 6(1)(c). The EUCJ clearly rejected a broad reading of Article 6(1) (c) and held that the affixing of a trademark to scale models is not necessary to indicate the intended purpose of the toy itself.[147] The EUCJ reached the same conclusion regarding the use in question, in relation to Article 6(1)(b); the use of a trademark registered for (*note!*) motor vehicles, on scale models, in order to faithfully replicate the original, is not intended to provide an indication as to a characteristic of the replica within the meaning of Article 6(1)(b).[148]

The EUCJ was, however, more open to a broad reading of Article 6(1)(b) and with reference to its prior ruling in *Windsurfing Chiemsee*[149] concluded that although "the provision is primarily designed to prevent the proprietor of a trade mark from prohibiting competitors from using one or more descriptive terms forming part of his trade mark in order to indicate certain characteristics of their products. . ., its wording is in no way specific to such a situation."[150] Uses for other than purely descriptive purposes can therefore not be categorically excluded.[151] The relevant test for other uses is whether the use is made in accordance with honest practices in industrial and commercial matters.[152]

4.2.3 *Gillette v. Parason Flexor*

The EUCJ has repeatedly held that "the condition requiring use of the trade mark to be made in accordance with honest practices. . . must be regarded as constituting in substance the expression of a duty to act fairly

---

[146]   Case C-48/05 *Adam Opel AG v Autec AG* [2007] ECR I- 01017, at 31–37.

[147]   Case C-48/05 *Adam Opel AG v Autec AG* [2007] ECR I- 01017, at 39.

[148]   Case C-48/05 *Adam Opel AG v Autec AG* [2007] ECR I- 01017, at 44.

[149]   Joined Cases C-108/97 and C-109/97, *Windsurfing Chiemsee Produktions- und Vertriebs GmbH (WSC) and Boots- und Segelzubehör v. Walter Huber, Franz Attenberger* [1999] ECR I-02779 at 28.

[150]   Case C-48/05 *Adam Opel AG v Autec AG* [2007] ECR I- 01017, at 42.

[151]   Case C-48/05 *Adam Opel AG v Autec AG* [2007] ECR I- 01017, at 43.

[152]   Case C-48/05 *Adam Opel AG v Autec AG* [2007] ECR I- 01017, at 43.

[153]   *Korkein käräjäoikeus* [Supreme Court], KKO 2006:17, *Gillette Company and Gillette Group of Finland v. LA Laboratories*, Feb. 22, 2006, paragraph 2. Author's translation.

Note: Above is the packaging used by the defendant, which triggered the lawsuit by Gillette. The sticker directly translated reads: "This blade FITS all Parason FLEXOR* and all Gillette SENSOR* HANDLES. *registered trademarks"[153]

Figure 13.2   Packaging used by the defendant in Gillette v. Parason Flexor

in relation to the legitimate interests of the trade mark owner."[154] In *Gillette v. Parason Flexor* where the defendant used red stickers on the packaging of razor blades stating that the razor blades are compatible with all handles produced by Parason Flexor (the defendant) and Gillette (the plaintiff), the court indicated that the use would be fair.[155] See Figure 13.2.

The EUCJ first tackled a question relating to the peculiar wording of Article 6(1)(c) and the meaning of the fragment "in particular as accessories or spare parts" to the overall interpretation of the provision.[156] The

---

[154]   Case C-63/97 *Bayerische Motorenwerke AG (BMW) and BMW Nederland BV v. Deenik* [1999] ECR I-905 at paragraph 61, See also C- 100/02 *Gerolsteiner Brunnen GmbH & Co. v Putsch GmbH* [2004] ECR I-691 at 24 and Advocate General Ruiz-Jarabo Colomer in C-48/05 *Adam Opel AG v Autec AG* at 55.

[155]   Case C-228/03 *The Gillette Company and Gillette Group Finland Oy v LA-Laboratories Ltd Oy* [2005] ECR I-2337 at 14, 33–36 and 38. The national court subsequently held the use fair. KKO 2006:17.

[156]   The wording stems from a legislative compromise. Some member states have traditionally included a special exception for spare parts in their trademark laws with the underlying presumption that the trademark owner can prevent most uses.

court rejected a reading of the provision that would assess the permissibility of references regarding accessories or spare parts differently than other permissible uses, and instead interpreted the provision as only citing an example of a permissible use.[157] The focus of the provision lies on the necessity of the use of another's trade mark and whether or not the mark "is being used by a third party in order to provide the public with comprehensible and complete information as to the intended purpose of the product".[158]

Only uses in accordance with honest practices in industrial and commercial matters can be necessary and permissible under Article 6(1)(b). As guidelines to the national court the EUCJ produced four categories of uses that *do not* constitute use in accordance with honest practices under the Directive:

1) the use of a trademark is done in a manner that it may give an impression that there is a commercial connection between the parties;[159]
2) the use of a trademark affects the value of the trademark by taking unfair advantage of its distinctive character or repute;[160]
3) the use of a trademark discredits or denigrates the trademark or;[161]
4) the third party presents its product as an imitation or replica of the product bearing the trademark of which it is not the owner.[162]

Based on the facts before it, the national court determines whether the use should be considered honest. At this juncture, it should be borne in mind that the mere fact that the third party uses the trademark to convey its message does not "mean that it is presenting that product as being of the same quality as, or having equivalent properties to, those of the product

---

[157] Case C-228/03 *The Gillette Company and Gillette Group Finland Oy v LA-Laboratories Ltd Oy* [2005] ECR I-2337 at 23 (1) and (2) and 32.

[158] Case C-228/03 *The Gillette Company and Gillette Group Finland Oy v LA-Laboratories Ltd Oy* [2005] ECR I-2337 at 31 and 33-34.

[159] Case C-228/03 *The Gillette Company and Gillette Group Finland Oy v LA-Laboratories Ltd Oy* [2005] ECR I-2337 at 42 citing C-63/97 *Bayerische Motorenwerke AG (BMW) and BMW Nederland BV v. Deenik* [1999] ECR I-905 at 51.

[160] Case C-228/03 *The Gillette Company and Gillette Group Finland Oy v LA-Laboratories Ltd Oy* [2005] ECR I-2337 at 43 citing C-63/97 *Bayerische Motorenwerke AG (BMW) and BMW Nederland BV v. Deenik* [1999] ECR I-905 at 52.

[161] Case C-228/03 *The Gillette Company and Gillette Group Finland Oy v LA-Laboratories Ltd Oy* [2005] ECR I-2337 at 44.

[162] Case C-228/03 *The Gillette Company and Gillette Group Finland Oy v LA-Laboratories Ltd Oy* [2005] ECR I-2337 at 45.

bearing the trademark."[163] Such a conclusion would in practice nullify the wording of Article 6. Instead, the national court *should assess* the use by assessing the overall presentation of the product marketed, in particular:

1) the circumstances in which the trade mark is displayed;
2) the circumstances in which distinction is made between the trade mark and the defendant's mark and;
3) the effort made by the defendant to ensure that consumers can distinguish its products from the trade mark owner's products.[164]

In assessing and determining honesty, the national court *must* take into account any evidence, or lack thereof, of an attempt to represent the products as being of the same quality or having equivalent properties to the trademark owner's product.[165] The overall conclusions and the court's choice of terminology show that the balancing test should weigh in favor of the plaintiff in case of clear evidence of passing off, while it should equally clearly weigh in favor of the defendant, when such evidence is absent.[166] The type of use is only indirectly relevant in that some uses are less likely than others to cause consumers to make a connection between the origins of the products. A typical non-trademark use thus inherently weighs less on the balancing scale than a trademark use, which if entailing use of an identical mark on identical goods, mandates a finding of infringement. In contrast, under Article 5.2 the court is obliged to consider whether the defendant has used the mark without due cause. The type of use employed is clearly relevant in this inquiry.

4.2.4 Practical implications

It has been argued that the approach of the EUCJ in the *Gillette* case creates an unreasonable margin of uncertainty, a grey area, which is inconsistent with the basic presumption of trademark law that the trademark owner can rely on his right.[167] The EUCJ rejected this argument by asserting that the maintenance of the delicate balance between equally weighty

---

[163] Case C-228/03 *The Gillette Company and Gillette Group Finland Oy v LA-Laboratories Ltd Oy* [2005] ECR I-2337 at 47.

[164] Case C-228/03 *The Gillette Company and Gillette Group Finland Oy v LA-Laboratories Ltd Oy* [2005] ECR I-2337 at 46.

[165] Case C-228/03 *The Gillette Company and Gillette Group Finland Oy v LA-Laboratories Ltd Oy* [2005] ECR I-2337 at 48.

[166] Case C-228/03 *The Gillette Company and Gillette Group Finland Oy v LA-Laboratories Ltd Oy* [2005] ECR I-2337 at 29, 48-49.

[167] Gilette in Case C-228/03 *The Gillette Company and Gillette Group Finland Oy v LA-Laboratories Ltd Oy* [2005] ECR I-2337.

societal interests required *in casu* balancing in Article 6 cases.[168] The Court referred to Advocate General Tizzano's opinion, where the inadvisability of extending the presumption of validity of the trademark owner's right to cases brought under Article 6 of the Directive was discussed in more detail.[169]

When discussing the requirement of "necessity" and the standard to which the third-party use should be held, Advocate General Tizzano noted that his proposed solution does produce a large grey area in the law. He, like the court, defined necessity as "the sole means of providing full information to consumers about the characteristics of ones product" and rejected Gillette's literal reading of Article 6(1)(c) indicating a requirement of showing economic necessity to access the market. Advocate General Tizzano further opined that the fact that the Trademark Directive concerns only trademark owners' rights cannot result in all other interests being excluded from the interpretation of its provisions; Article 6 in particular *implicitly* refers to those competing interests.[170] Together these interests serve to protect a functioning marketplace in which consumers are not confused and are able to benefit from the full extent of competition on the market.[171]

Therefore, the focus of Article 6(1)(c) analysis should not be on the necessity of the use, instead the evaluation of third-party conduct should focus on whether it is in accordance with honest practices in commercial matters. Thus, the court's ruling should not be construed as in practice creating a safe harbor for third party uses either. The use should be evaluated in relation to the circumstances and manner of use and the factual question of whether the use constitutes the sole means available to inform consumers, is but an element of the overall analysis seeking to determine whether the use is honest.[172] Consequently, by focusing on the practical necessity of the use, the test of Article 6 adequately protects the legitimate

---

[168] Case C-228/03 *The Gillette Company and Gillette Group Finland Oy v LA-Laboratories Ltd Oy* [2005] ECR I-2337 at 29, 35 and 39.

[169] Case C-228/03 *The Gillette Company and Gillette Group Finland Oy v LA-Laboratories Ltd Oy* [2005] ECR I-2337 at 35 Opinion of Advocate General Tizzano in C-228/03 *The Gillette Company and Gillette Group Finland Oy v LA-Laboratories Ltd Oy*, 9.12.2004, at 64–72.

[170] Opinion of Advocate General Tizzano in Case C-228/03 *The Gillette Company and Gillette Group Finland Oy v LA-Laboratories Ltd Oy*, 9.12.2004, at 54–5.

[171] Opinion of Advocate General Tizzano in Case C-228/03 *The Gillette Company and Gillette Group Finland Oy v LA-Laboratories Ltd Oy*, 9.12.2004, at 56.

[172] Case C-228/03 The *Gillette Company and Gillette Group Finland Oy v LA-Laboratories Ltd Oy* [2005] ECR I-2337 at 35 and Opinion of Advocate General

interests of the trademark owner.[173] Meanwhile, the harmful chilling effect of an abstract necessity standard is avoided.[174]

In its Grand Chamber-ruling in the *Céline* case the EUCJ finally clearly opined on the relationship between the rights conferred by Article 5 and Article 6.[175] The case involved the use of an identical mark on identical goods and the trademark owner thus asserted its right under Article 5(1)(a) of the Directive. First, the court dealt with the issue of when the use of a trade name constitutes a use that the trademark owner is entitled to prohibit, but the second issue is central for our purposes.[176]

If the use of a trade name is deemed one that falls under Article 5(1)(a), and a presumption of infringement thus is triggered, how is a national court to deal with the inherent conflict with Article 6(1)(a), which entitles a trader to use its name while trading honestly? The court concluded that Article 6(1)(a) can operate as a bar to a use, which falls under Article 5(1)(a), when the third party uses its name according to honest business practices.[177] Consequently, a finding of infringement is not automatic, but instead the national court must assess the use according to the test put forth in the *Budweiser* case.

> . . . in assessing whether the condition of honest practice is satisfied, account must be taken first of the extent to which the third party's name is understood by the relevant public, or at least a significant section of the public, as indicating a link between the third party's goods or services and the trade-mark proprietor or a person authorised to use the trade mark, and secondly of the extent

---

Tizzano in Case C-228/03 *The Gillette Company and Gillette Group Finland Oy v LA-Laboratories Ltd Oy*, 9.12.2004, at 70.

[173] Case C-228/03 *The Gillette Company and Gillette Group Finland Oy v LA-Laboratories Ltd Oy* [2005] ECR I-2337 at 35 and Opinion of Advocate General Tizzano in Case C-228/03 *The Gillette Company and Gillette Group Finland Oy v LA-Laboratories Ltd Oy*, 9.12.2004, at 68.

[174] Case C-228/03 *The Gillette Company and Gillette Group Finland Oy v LA-Laboratories Ltd Oy* [2005] ECR I-2337 at 35 and Opinion of Advocate General Tizzano in Case C-228/03 *The Gillette Company and Gillette Group Finland Oy v LA-Laboratories Ltd Oy*, 9.12.2004, at 69.

[175] Case C-17/06 *Céline SARL v Céline SA* [2007] ECR I-07041.

[176] Case C-17/06 *Céline SARL v Céline SA* [2007] ECR I-07041, at 13–28. The court concluded that the purpose of trade names is to identify a company, and when a trade name is used in this manner, it cannot be considered as being used "in relation to goods or services" within the meaning of Article 5(1). However, when a trade name is used in such a way that a link is established between the sign which constitutes the trade name and the goods marketed by it, the use may be prohibited by the trademark owner. Such a use is presumptively liable to harm the essential function of the trade mark to indicate the origin of goods.

[177] Case C-17/06 *Céline SARL v Céline SA* [2007] ECR I-07041, at 36.

to which the third party ought to have been aware of that. Another factor to be taken into account when making the assessment is whether the trade mark concerned enjoys a certain reputation in the Member State in which it is registered and its protection is sought, from which the third party might profit in marketing his goods or services."[178]

Introducing a new consumer-centered test to replace a clear presumption certainly seems to open up a can of worms for trademark owners. Can trademark owners still rely on their exclusive right in trademark law or has it lost its value? Has the case law of the EUCJ introduced a test that is too uncertain and unpredictable and requires costly and burdensome litigation in national courts? On the other hand, a general test that decides when trademark rights are implicitly restricted by other market considerations might provide for the flexible tool needed to weed out uses that do not impact the trademark owner's legitimate interests.

Although the outcome of the test arguably is uncertain, its existence creates certainty since it signals to trademark owners and third parties alike that the test does not favor or disfavor either party, but is tied to a presumptively neutral standard of *honesty in commercial matters*. Ideally the test curbs attempts to maximize the benefits of exclusion by asserting trademark rights in instances where harm to the essential function of the trademark is unlikely. The scope of trademark law thus presumptively remains tied to preventing free-riding in competitive business relationships and only applies to uses traditionally considered non-competitive, in exceptional circumstances.

5. CONCLUSION

The above analysis shows that the EUCJ has resisted the temptation to grant an absolute right *to use* the trademark to the trademark owner. The traditional emphasis remains; the trademark owner has the right to prevent only certain uses.[179] Even in instances, like *Arsenal*, where the economic, practical and perhaps even moral[180] arguments might have

---

[178]   Case C-17/06 *Céline SARL v Céline SA* [2007] ECR I-07041, at 34 and Case C-245/02 *Anheuser-Busch Inc. v Budějovický Budvar, národní podnik* [2004] ECR I-10989 at 60 and 83.

[179]   Max Schoenthal, 'Major events and reporting right', in Ian Blackshaw, Steve Cornelius and Robert Siekman (eds), *TV Rights and Sport Legal Aspects,* T.M.C. Asser Press, 2009 at 65–69 discussing the competing interests in public access to sports events and exclusive broadcasting rights.

[180]   By moral here, I refer to the concept of fairness in commerce. It is usually seen as morally wrong to trade on the reputation of another. This concept of moral

supported such a finding, the court displayed *theoretical unease* with granting an absolute sports merchandising right. Accurately, so. Even the most protected events' trademark, the Olympic Symbol, is subject to many implicit fair uses.[181] The Olympic symbol is widely used in all media- and news-reporting or for descriptive reference to the Olympic Games. Media- and news-reporting is not exempted in Article 6 of the Trademark Directive, nor are descriptive uses for all purposes. The broadest categorical exclusion of uses from application of the Trademark Directive, lies in the statement of the EUCJ, which limits the trademark owner's right to prevent uses that affect the functions and most importantly the essential function of the trademark to indicate origin.

> It should, however, be remembered that, in accordance with the case-law of the Court of Justice, the exclusive right under Article 5(1) of the directive was conferred in order to enable the trade mark proprietor to protect his specific interests as proprietor, that is, to ensure that the trade mark can fulfil its functions and that, therefore, the exercise of that right must be reserved to cases in which a third party's use of the sign affects or is liable to affect the functions of the trade mark, in particular its essential function of guaranteeing to consumers the origin of the goods.[182]

Another traditional interpretation of Article 5 has been to limit uses that the trademark owner may prevent to "uses as a trademark".[183] This restriction, implicitly referring to various uses traditionally considered outside the purview of trademark protection is, however important, constantly under pressure.[184] Unlike uses that fall under Article 6 of the Trademark Directive, and thus are tested for honest practices in commercial matters, there is no test for weeding out honest or fair uses. Instead, the built-in presumptions favor the trademark owner, especially where the alleged infringer is a business and there is use in the course of trade.

Before considering an extension of protection of rights in sports merchandising, one should consider the extent to which the trademark owners

---

unfairness is broader than legal concepts such as "unfair practices in industrial and commercial matters", "free-riding" or "unfair competition".

[181]   Hilty, at 33, see supra note 1. See also Kur (1992), at 229, see supra note 41, on the criteria for such protection.

[182]   (*Arsenal Football Club*, paragraph 51; Case C-245/02 *Anheuser-Busch* [2004] ECR I-10989, paragraph 59) as cited by the court in *Adam Opel v. Autec* [2007] ECR I- 01017, at 21

[183]   Kur (2008), at 165–70 see supra note 53. See also supra 4.1. on the concept of trademark use.

[184]   Kur (2008), at 172, and 176, referring explicitly to the dangers that expanding EU trademark law pose to commercial speech. See supra note 53.

in question already enjoy protection under the well-known marks and famous marks doctrines. As the *Arsenal* case shows, protection can be quite extensive. Similarly, a sport franchise also enjoys protection via contractual arrangements, thus achieving a stronger market position than the regular trademark owner that is otherwise constrained by competition law. In reference to the example of the Olympic symbol, it is necessary to consider *the scope* of protection when protection – under the two-tier test put forth above – is considered justified. The Arsenal franchise argued rights not only in their Gunners-logo, or combination mark, but in the word mark ARSENAL as well. Not even the word mark OLYMPICS receives absolute protection.[185] Nevertheless, the venture seems successful. However, the societal cost of overprotection in scope of an (already) absolute right is naturally great, since implicitly and traditionally fair uses, which naturally challenge any absolute right, may in practice fall peril to extra-judicial enforcement efforts.

It is thus evident that sports franchises would not pass the *justification-test* to enjoy absolute rights to all uses of all their marks, and join the *sui generis*-regime where the Olympics reign alone. They nevertheless continue to enjoy strong trademark protection in addition to protection under other laws. A more nuanced approach to assessing whether sports merchandising rights are justified from a market (legal and economic) perspective may allow use to consider rights and positions created by multiple IP rights.

In each case, at the outskirts of trademark law, we should, I argue, apply the justification-test. The concept of *use as a trademark* or *trademark* use could serve as an indicator of when the use should be presumed infringing or fair. This would give a voice to uses that have traditionally, albeit implicitly, been considered outside trademark law.

Thus, in considering whether trademark protection is justified, we need to consider whether:

1) protection is justified from a moral, legal or economic standpoint, that serves
   a. public or
   b. private interest, and
2) non-protection would lead to market failure
   c. using a holistic approach[186] not restricted to one field of IP

---

[185]   The Nairobi Treaty, see supra notes 33 and 39. Note that national laws may confer a wider monopoly to the use of trademarks that refer to the Olympics.

[186]   Hilty, at 47 and 51, see supra note 1.

    d.   with a trademark-centric[187] view with emphasis on unfair competition.

Our holistic approach to the protection of the Olympic Symbol shows that the practice of sports merchandising can be legally defined and, consequently, new forms of protection can be tested for legitimacy. We can benefit from a more nuanced approach to IP rights in sports. For example, when considering trademark protection and (1) protecting publicity rights as applied to sports video games; (2) database protection protecting sports results and statistics in fantasy sports; (3) unfair competition and copyright protection for fan fiction; (4) protection for privacy and against defamation in fan sleuth fiction or games; (5) criminal law applied to so-called ambush marketing or; (6) contract law protecting exclusive visibility deals. Similarly, courts may benefit from subjecting claims for extended protection to the neutral test, asking whether the defendant uses the trademark in accordance with honest practices in industrial and commercial matters.

In addition, there are several actors in the on-line world that would benefit from legal rules that are based on a holistic perspective rather than one based on each field of IP separately. Using the justification test, while understanding protection to mean not affording IP rights but protection against market failure, may allow us to create *sui generis* regimes on-line that are designed to foster competition, and weed out unfair competition and dishonest commercial practices.

---

[187]   See supra note 41.

PART V

Teaching and research in IP law – individual
and collective aspects

14. Virtual teachers: a copyright paradox?

Laura Carlson and Sanna Wolk

Modern teaching methods and materials invoke IT to a significant extent, with digital learning platforms and networks used by both teachers and students in turn also affecting learning environments. The development of e-learning has brought issues of the employer's prerogative, intellectual property rights, as well as the protection of privacy, more and more into the legal foreground. Many institutions of higher education today are interested in creating digital and sound recordings of lectures – creating quite simply a "virtual teacher." The recording of lectures naturally is an invaluable tool for helping students master the knowledge conveyed orally by teachers. However, the actual lecture often is encompassed by copyright protection, and such forms of recordings facilitate an increased dissemination and broadened use of the result of the intellectual work and academic research; at the same time, this can be experienced as a violation of privacy by many teachers. The modern methods for recording and disseminating a teacher's oral performance can quite simply result in conflicting interests, and alternative education methods involving virtual learning have led to controversy among faculty and teachers. From the perspective of teachers, the recording of lectures can both be disturbing for the actual lecture as well as the fact that a teacher's future influence on the result and its dissemination is decreased. From the perspective of the university as employer, the recording can be seen as a good way through which to develop teaching and attract students to the university.

Tensions arise at the interstice of individualism and collectiveness with respect to the use of virtual teachers. On the intellectual property side, extremely individually based rights with respect to copyright of the materials and the actual "performance" or digitally captured lecture are being sought after by both teachers and institutions of higher education, with the issue becoming whether the needs of the many outweigh the needs of the few. Moral rights weigh heavily here. On the employment law side, two sets of tensions arise at this interstice, the first naturally between employers and employees. The second set arises due to the collective nature of the

Swedish (and Nordic) labor and employment law model.[1] This chapter explores aspects of these different layers of tension.

1.   INTELLECTUAL PROPERTY RIGHTS AND OWNERSHIP

Intellectual property rights, for example copyrighted works, designs, trademarks and patents, are often developed by employed persons. The point of departure in Swedish intellectual property law is that the creator is placed in the foreground, irrespective of whether he or she has an employee status. The fundamental principle which applies here is that any person who has actually created the work covered by proprietary rights, or which can be protected by intellectual property law, becomes the holder of that right. This means that a proprietary right emerges in relation to the person who has created the (intellectual property) product necessary for protection under intellectual property law to apply.

An employee-creator thus has the same right to his or her intellectual property product as other types of creators. This fundamental principle is well established in the field of intellectual property law. Since the right arises in the first place in relation to employees, the employer may only receive a derivative right from the employee in order to exploit the product and obtain protection under intellectual property law. The employer's right to control intellectual property working results cannot thus be obtained directly through the employment relationship, but must be acquired by means of a separate agreement. Such transfers of rights may be effected either under applicable law,[2] by means of agreement, or, in some cases, based on the implicit terms and conditions of employment.

However, as regards university teachers' intellectual property rights, these normally belong to the employed teacher, and not the university. As

---

[1]   The terms "labor law" and "employment law" fall within the same Swedish term, *arbetsrätt*. This Swedish term is sometimes further categorized as collective labor law (*kollektiv arbetsrätt*) and individual labor law (*individuell arbetsrätt*), referred to in this chapter as labor law and employment law, respectively.

[2]   *See further* the Act (1949:345) on the Right to Employee's Inventions, Sec. 40a of the Act (1960:729) on Copyright in Literary and Artistic Works and Sec. 3(2) of the Act (1992:1685) on the Protection of Circuit Designs used in Semi-conductors. See also Art. 14(3) of the Regulation (EC) No 6/2002 on Community Designs, *cf.* Art. 11(4) of the Regulation (EC) No 2100/94 on Community Plant Variety Rights.

regards inventions, this is set out as a statutory exemption in Sec. 1(2) of the Act on the Right to Employee Inventions, and academics are personally entitled to their inventions resulting from work at the university.[3] In Sweden there is, however, no statutory exemption for teachers with respect to copyrights. Instead, a right mirroring, to a certain extent, the exemption created by the Act on the Right to Employee inventions has been created by custom, discussed more in depth below.

2. EMPLOYMENT LAW GENERALLY

To fully examine the complexity of the issues arising in the Swedish context with respect to virtual teachers, an understanding of the Swedish (and basically Nordic[4]) labor and employment law model is necessary. One of the distinctive and main features of this model is self-regulation, with both employers and employees often organized on several levels. There are 4.1 million employees in Sweden, which has a population of almost 9.4 million as of 2010. Approximately one-third of all employees work in the public sector, while two-thirds work in the private sector.[5] In the field of higher education, the vast majority of employees at all Swedish universities and university colleges are public employees, as there are no private universities in Sweden.

This aspect of self-regulation has strong historic roots. The development of labor and employment law in Sweden can be seen as comprising three stages, the first beginning at the turn of the twentieth century. The Swedish

---

[3]   Many European countries, however, at the end of the 20th and beginning of the 21st century have extended the employers' rights to employee inventions to the university area. Nowadays universities as employers may have a right to inventions made by professors and other academic staff researching at universities. *See further* von Falck and Schmaltz (2005), *University Inventions:* 'Classification and Remuneration in Germany, the Netherlands, France, the UK, the U.S. and Japan', IIC pp. 912–927 and Stallberg (2007), 'The Legal Status of Academic Employees' Inventions in Britain and Germany and its Consequences for R&D Agreements', Intellectual Property Quarterly pp. 489–530.

[4]   The Swedish model of industrial relations (*den svenska arbetsrättsmodellen*) falls within the "Nordic model," perceived of as a third alternative to the more liberal, deregulated models found in countries such as the United Kingdom, and the more regulated models such as in Germany. For a further presentation of the Swedish labor model, labor law and employment law in English, *see* Eklund, Sigeman and Carlson (2008), *Swedish Labor and Employment Law: Cases and Materials*, Stockholm, Sweden, Iustus Förlag.

[5]   These statistics are available at Statistics Sweden, www.scb.se in both Swedish and English.

model was put into place by the December Compromise (*decemberkompromissen*) of 1906 between the Swedish Employers' Confederation (now the Confederation of Swedish Enterprise) and the umbrella blue-collar worker union, LO. With this compromise in the form of an agreement between the social partners, the procedure of resolving labor market problems internally within the labor market was affixed, and the social partners kept the state at bay. The Act (1949:345) on the Right to Employee Inventions was passed during this first phase in 1949, a marked exception to the neutrality policy of the state with respect to legislation governing the labor market. The second phase in the development came with the codification of labor and employment law in the 1970s, with the third phase characterized by Sweden's EU membership beginning in 1995. The first phase was marked by the absence of individual employment agreements, with collective agreements being the rule. The second phase saw an increase in use of individual employment agreements, which cannot, however, conflict with the rights granted in the collective agreement in the sector. The third phase can be seen as characterized by a greater emphasis on individual employee rights than that which has occurred before historically, this new approach a result in part of the requirements of EU law.

As one of the most salient features of the Swedish model is the underlying premise that the state should be neutral with respect to the social partners, the employer and employee organizations, the perception being that legislation is an unwanted intrusion in the labor market, the legislation historically was (and still often is) quasi-mandatory, as seen by the Act on the Right to Employee Inventions described above, giving the parties (most often only the social partners) the opportunity to opt out of statutory requirements through agreements, usually collective agreements at the central levels.

3.   DEVELOPMENTS IN TEACHING MATERIALS AND METHODS

A similar development can also be seen in the field of education. An important task for universities is conveying knowledge, information and culture. Historically, this has occurred through scheduled and instructor-led teaching in the form of lectures, seminars and laboratories with a large quantity of educational materials produced at higher educational institutions. This material often is the object of copyright protection. It can, for example, be copyrightable works such as educational books, articles, lectures, PowerPoint-presentations and compendiums. Historically, the reproduction and distribution of teaching materials could be fairly easily controlled by the teacher as excessive work was required to reproduce with, for example, printing presses, typewriters, mimeograph machines and even with respect to the older photocopying machines. However, teachers, in the form of scholars, have the additional task of producing and selecting the knowledge that is to be transmitted.

Modern technology has made the reproduction and mass distribution of teaching materials instantaneous. And just as this has affected the actual creation of teaching materials, the breakthrough of modern information and communication technologies in society has led to a highly tangible demand for virtual educational forms. More and more courses have consequently come to be Internet based. A mutual characteristic of these courses is that lectures, advising and other communications occur with the help of web-based technologies in digital environments such as the Internet, as well as other specifically formulated teaching environments. Also social media (for example blogging, Facebook, twitter, Linkedin etc.) is fast-becoming an integral part of the education landscape.

4. VIRTUAL TEACHERS' COPYRIGHT

Just as there is no general statutory regulation on employee copyrights, neither is there any specific regulation in the Swedish Copyright Act (1960:729) regarding the rights of teachers to teaching materials. There has quite simply not been any reason to specifically regulate the rights of researchers and teachers before. However, the copyright to teaching materials generated at higher educational institutions in Sweden normally belongs to those persons active there as instructors and researchers, constituting a deviation from the general copyright solutions achieved in employment agreements. The other Nordic countries also have a right based on custom for teachers and researchers with respect to copyright-protected materials. In other countries, the copyright also remains as a rule with the teacher or researcher, respectively. This is explained by the fact that traditionally, a teacher's copyright has been of significance in the publication of research results and the production of teaching books. This is reflected in the legislation and regulation by contract in other countries, and many have a "teachers' exemption" that includes articles, dissertations, teaching books, etc. But with the digital developments, this also has begun to follow restrictions in the rights of university teachers. For example, in the United States, the Technology, Education, and Copyright Harmonization Act" (Teach Act) was passed in 2002, regulating materials for distance learning, particularly over the Internet.

The copyright to the intellectual production of teachers in Sweden is regulated by custom (*sedvana*).[6] The primary rule is that any copyright with respect to teaching materials is to accrue to the teacher, based on reasons of academic freedom and creativity under the copyright "teachers' exemption", an exemption based on a long tradition predating modern technology, with roots in the academic freedom. Traditionally, the teachers' employment relationship is characterized by a broad freedom in employment with a right to self-determination and autonomy in teaching (with origins arguably stemming from classical Greece). The unique nature of the employment of teachers can be viewed as being of benefit to both creativity and research.

The digitalization of our educational environments entails that new ways to utilize copyright-protected works continuously arise, not in the least with university courses. The development of e-learning furthermore entails that higher educational institutions in the capacity of employer become all the more interested in their employed teachers' copyright protected works, such as PowerPoint-presentations and web-published compendiums. Certain educational facilities have even adopted specific guidelines for managing the copyright to the teachers' educational materials. Higher educational institutions are also more and more interested in producing film and sound recordings of lectures, in order to allow those students who so wish to be able to follow lectures live or later as a recording placed in the course's web-based educational environment or at iTUNES U. Higher educational institutions quite simply wish to have "virtual teachers". The employment law starting point is that the employer, through its prerogative within a relatively broad framework, decides on the employee's actual work tasks, as well as the manner, place and hours for the work's performance.

However, despite the fact that higher educational institutions are the employer with the right to lead and distribute work, it has historically been the case that teachers have been given rather free hands to teach in the manner that the teacher (and not the higher educational institute) has considered to be best, through the choices of course literature, the scheduling of teaching, as well as the choices of educational forms and grading forms. This "package" has not been seen as work results belonging to the higher educational institutions, as it is strongly tied personally to the teacher and falls within the framework for the copyright teachers' exemption. Teaching in digital environments and the virtual teacher, however, place these issues at their extreme.

---

[6] *See* for example, Wolk (2008), *Arbetstagares immaterialrätter,* Stockholm, Sweden, Norstedts pp. 205–227 and also by the same author (2003), *Lärarundantaget i omvandling* in NIR 2003 p. 415 and therein cited sources.

Instead, the copyright to the intellectual production of teachers is regulated by the teachers' exemption, arguably created to balance the tasks of the universities to accumulate, preserve and disseminate knowledge against those of the teacher to produce and select the knowledge to be accumulated, preserved and disseminated. This can be seen as the first set of tensions in that the teacher's moral rights are intimately intertwined with the production and selection of knowledge, academic freedom, and the university's trampling in this territory by capturing this process digitally can result in the teacher being "frozen" in time and consequently, out of context with a potential subsequent result being deemed to no longer master the current knowledge in the field.

Another aspect of virtual teachers that raises the issue of individualism versus collectiveness is whether a teacher can be "forced" to a digitalization of a lecture by his or her employer, and the subsequent issues of privacy, and whether intellectual property rights should accrue to the teacher due to reasons of personal integrity. In a situation where a teacher is hired with the explicit understanding that the digitalization of lectures is to occur, the employer has the right to insist on such digitalization as part of the individual employment contract. However, the vast majority of teachers today in Sweden have been hired under collective agreements that have not addressed this issue. Rights of privacy also come into play with the digitalization of lectures, particularly where safeguards with respect to copying and dissemination have not been used. Knowledge in most areas in which any type of research is being conducted can become obsolete, entailing that the capturing of a lecture digitally can have the effect of the teacher appearing out-of-date, not that the digital copy is based on an old lecture.

The third set of tensions arises with the fact that the copyright teachers' exemption can most closely be described as an unwritten legal rule constituting the current state of the law on the question as to a teacher's educational materials. Where the boundaries for this custom lie in practice, however, can differ somewhat between different universities, as these might have developed their own local custom. A growing trend can be traced, however, with different educational institutions deviating from this main rule. For example, several universities now state that their policy is that such rights are to accrue to the university and not to the teacher. This diversity in approach can only be understood against the Swedish labor and employment model as described above, where the social partners are left to resolve the majority of issues arising in the labor market, including employment terms and conditions for individual employees (particularly in the public sector) thus giving a freedom to set new customs as well as incurring a risk that employee rights can vary from workplace to workplace. This can be seen as the third set of tensions between individualism and collectiveness and the use of virtual teachers brings this lack of systemic statutory approach to the forefront. The question of who has the rights to any digitalization of a lecture is not explicitly addressed on a national level.

5.   CONCLUDING COMMENTS

The flexibility that is a product of the technological development entails that education as offered by universities and similar institutions can quite simply be made accessible to a wider circle now. This is, however, an accessibility that requires the consent of the copyright holder, in other words, the teacher. Nevertheless, the technological development has opened new and simpler avenues for recording the lectures of teachers at institutions of higher education, and today it is very common that universities record lectures.

Universities play key roles in shaping national and international copyright policies and in protecting and promoting access to knowledge. Today there are different approaches. Certain educational facilities have adopted specific guidelines for managing the copyright to the teachers' educational materials and how this material should be available digitally. Some universities have even adopted guidelines regarding recordings of lectures and how these films should be made available to the public on the Internet.

When handling teachers' copyrighted works, a central question is whether the employer should be allowed to make recordings of its teachers' performances and therewith locally change the copyright custom and thereby depart from the copyright teachers' exemption at universities. A related issue is how higher educational institutions could use these recordings; should they be placed on the course's website or on iTUNES U? Academic freedom is another aspect of e-learning.

Nevertheless, the current state of change in the role and position of education speaks for a future restriction in the right of teachers as to their copyright-protected lectures and other teaching materials. The debate on the right, for example to lectures in the university system is strongly polarized between the traditional rule giving teachers complete control over how and to what extent copyright-protected work results are to be published and exploited, against the view that the right to a teacher's copyright-protected work result should accrue to the university in line with applicable other sectors of the labor market. This debate is sharpened by the potential exposure that can result when a recorded lecture is disseminated, which can be perceived as a violation of privacy. There is, however, a strong need for universities to push teaching forward, and compelling reasons speak for a revision of the copyright custom in the area of higher education to meet the need for assuring the transfer of knowledge. The use of new technology affects the work environment of teachers and the study environment of students. There are both opportunities and risks associated with education in digital environments. Therefore there is reason to commence a discussion about a new approach of legally regulating the rights to the recording of lectures.

Any eventual legislation in this area ought to have as an overarching objective to ensure that education and research at institutions of higher learning is stimulating and leads to further development. If this situation is to be regulated at all, a suitable solution could be a statutory regulation that allows the recording of a lecture, and even its dissemination, but with the possibility for the copyright holder, proposed here as the teacher, to receive financial compensation. This regulation would, however, retain the feature of allowing for derogations by agreement, and the parties should be able to contract as to this issue. Such a regulation would not consequently directly take into consideration the holder's personal interests, which may be deemed to be more important than the issue of financial compensation. This right to personal integrity is to be respected, and perhaps not always is sufficiently so with today's regulations that attempt to incorporate the holder's personal interests. This protection of "personal integrity" ought to be strengthened by a regulation giving teachers the right to stop the dissemination of recordings that for different reasons no longer represent the current research in a field.[7]

---

[7] *Cf.* Art. 6*bis* of the Berne Convention for the Protection of Literary and Artistic Works (1886).

15. The education sector and copyright issues in the digital age: a perspective from Africa*

Adejoke Oyewunmi

1. INTRODUCTION

The impact of digital technology, particularly the Internet on copyright, has attracted the attention of stakeholders in the copyright sector for well over a decade now. Whether this technology is perceived as a threat to protection or welcomed as an opportunity for access depends largely on the position of the stakeholder concerned, whether creator/copyright owner, or user, and the interest which is sought to be advanced.

Whatever the case may be, it is trite that intellectual property laws, including those relating to copyright, endeavour to balance two fundamental, though seemingly competing interests. The first is the securing of private interests, through the protection of ownership and investment rights in eligible copyright works, while the second is the protection of public interest to access these works. These underlying interests and the need for balance are both accorded recognition in international human rights instruments which, while acknowledging the right of everyone to take part in the cultural life and to enjoy the benefits of scientific progress and its applications, equally provide that everyone has a right to the moral and material interest resulting from any scientific, literary or artistic production of which he is the author.[1]

---

* Adejoke O. Oyewunmi, LL.B. (Ife), LL.M. (Lagos), LL.M.I.P. (PiercelawUSA), Senior Lecturer, Faculty of Law, University of Lagos, former Visiting Researcher, Max Planck Institute for Intellectual Property, Competition and Tax Law, Munich, Germany (April-December, 2009).

[1] Article 27 of the Universal Declaration of Human Rights 1948 (UDHR) and Article 15 of the International Covenant on Economic, Social and Cultural Rights of 1966 (ICESCR). On its part, the US Constitution states the basis for copyright and patent legislation as "to promote the Progress of Science and the useful Arts, by securing for limited Times, to Authors and Inventors, the exclusive Right to

Copyright laws try to achieve this balance by, on one hand, conferring certain exclusive economic and moral rights on copyright owners, while, however, limiting the full exercise of these rights in the interest of the public, through provisions such as limited duration of rights and appropriate limitations and exceptions to exclusive rights. The issue of balance is therefore central to the copyright regime.

The emergence of digital technology on the technological landscape has, however, impacted the delicate copyright balance in a variety of ways, which impact is well documented in a number of works that are available on the subject.[2] On the one hand, digital technology and the emergence of electronic networks present an opportunity to advance public interest by promoting the ideals of scholarship and research, because they facilitate access to the available repository of knowledge and information. These electronic networks are imbued with peculiar characteristics, including ease of transmission and possibility of simultaneous use by multiple persons, as well as unprecedented search and link capacities.[3] These attributes have rendered irrelevant geographical boundaries and territorial limitations to access and, if properly harnessed, can help to overcome the knowledge divide that exists between developed and the less developed countries.

On the other hand, however, digital technology poses new and peculiar challenges to copyright owners with regard to loss of control over the use and exploitation of their works in cyberspace. Such uncontrolled exploitation may threaten the economic and moral rights of copyright owners, and thereby discourage investment of time and effort in creative enterprise, to the disadvantage of society at large.

Not surprisingly, the impact of digitalisation on copyright has elicited some responses in the international arena, as well as under some national and regional systems. This chapter aims to contribute to the discourse from the African perspective, by examining some emerging developments relating to digitalisation in Nigerian universities, and the copyright issues raised by this development.[4] The work also examines, on a comparative

---

their respective Writings and Discoveries." See Article 1, Section 8, Clause 8 of the Constitution of the United States of America.

[2]   Ruth L. Okediji, (2009) "The Regulation of Creativity under the WIPO Internet Treaties", Vol 77, Fordham Law Rev., 2379; Pamela Samuelson, "Digital Media and the Changing Face of Intellectual Property Law", [1990] Rutgers Computer & Technology Law Journal, 323–40.; and Peter S. Menell, (2002–2003) "Envisioning Copyright's Digital Future", 46 N.Y. Law School Law Review 63.

[3]   See Samuelson, op. cit. at 324-329, while identifying some of the peculiar characteristics of digital technology which impact the copyright system.

[4]   The second part of this work focuses on the impact of digital technology on Nigeria's vibrant entertainment industry, and is upcoming.

basis with Ghanaian copyright legislation, emerging legal and institutional responses to the impact of digital technology on the copyright sector, and highlights the need to balance protection of copyright with the safeguarding of access to works for permitted purposes.

2. THE LEGAL FRAMEWORK FOR THE PROTECTION OF COPYRIGHT IN NIGERIA

As with many other branches of the law, the Nigerian copyright regime owes its origins to English law, specifically, the English Copyright Act of 1911, which was extended to apply to the Protectorates of Northern and Southern Nigeria in 1912.[5] This Act remained in force until the promulgation of the first indigenous copyright legislation in 1970,[6] which repealed the English Act. The 1970 Act was itself repealed by the 1988 Copyright Act, and this Act remains in force, subject to the two amendments made to it in 1992 and 1999, [7] and supplemented by a number of regulations.

Under the Copyright Act, six categories of works are eligible for copyright protection. The first three categories comprise creative works, namely literary works, musical works and artistic works. [8] Beyond these three categories of creative works, the Act also extends protection to entrepreneurial rights arising from activities connected with primary exploitation of the creative works, namely sound recording, cinematograph films and broadcasts. [9]

The types of works which fall under each category are further defined in Section 39 of the Act. In particular, literary works are defined as including, irrespective of literary quality, computer program and compilations.[10] Although protected immediately upon fixation, without the need for registration, literary, artistic and musical works must comply

---

[5]   This was by Order-in-Council No 912 of 1912.

[6]   Copyright Act (No 61) of 1970.

[7]   Copyright (Amendment) Act No. 98 of 1992, and the Copyright (Amendment) Act No. 42 of 1999. The amended Act is to be found in Cap C28, Laws of the Federation of Nigeria, 2004, and is hereinafter, described as "the Act".

[8]   See Section 1(1) of the Act.

[9]   Ibid.

[10]   Others are novels, stories and poetical works; plays, stage directions, film scenarios and broadcasting scripts; choreographic works; encyclopedias, dictionaries, directories and anthologies; letters, reports and memoranda; lectures, addresses and sermons; and law reports (excluding decisions of courts). For the definition of other categories of works, see Section 39 of the Act.

with the twin requirements of originality,[11] fixation,[12] and connecting factors.[13]

Exclusive rights conferred by copyright include the rights of reproduction, publication, performance, adaptation and translation of the work.[14] Also, the making of cinematograph films or records in respect of the work, its distribution to the public for commercial purposes by way of rentals, leases, hire, loan or similar arrangement, as well as the broadcasting or communication of the work to the public by a loudspeaker or any other similar device are all within the scope of the exclusive rights conferred on the author.[15]

The issue of ownership of copyright is dealt with by section 9 of the Act, which provides as a general rule, that the first owner of copyright in a work, including works made in the course of employment, or pursuant to a commission, is the author of the work, unless otherwise stipulated in a written agreement.[16] For works which are made by or under the direction or control of government, however, copyright shall vest initially in the government and not in the author.[17]

As a form of property, copyright is freely assignable and transmissible,

---

[11] To fulfil the originality requirement, the Act requires that sufficient effort must have been expended on making the work to give it an original character – Section 1(2)(a) of the Act.

[12] Fixation means that the work must have been fixed in a definite medium of expression now known or later to be developed, from which it can be perceived, reproduced or otherwise communicated either directly or with the aid of any machine or device. See Section 1(2)(b) of the Act.

[13] This connection may be by virtue of the status of the author or the first place of publication of the work. To this end, the Act stipulates that a work may be qualified by virtue of the author's being a citizen of, or domiciled in Nigeria, or a citizen of, or domiciled in a country that is a party to an obligation in a treaty or other international agreement to which Nigeria is a party . A work may also become qualified if first published in Nigeria. See sections 2-4 of the Act.

[14] See generally, Sections 5-7 of the Act.

[15] Ibid. In addition, performers' rights and expressions of folklore, are also protected – see sections 23 and 28 of the Act.

[16] Section 9(2) of the Act, as well as the case of *Joseph Ikhuoria v. Campaign Services Ltd. & Anor.* [1986] FHCR 308. Section 9(3) further creates an exception to the general rule in cases involving literary, artistic or musical works made by the author in the course of his employment by the proprietor of a newspaper, magazine or similar periodical under a contract of service or apprenticeship. Here, the proprietor shall, in the absence of any agreement to the contrary, be the first owner of copyright in the work, for purposes of publication of the work in any newspaper, magazine or similar periodical. However, in all other respects, the author shall be the first owner of copyright in the work.

[17] Section 9(5) of the Act

by licence, assignment or other means.[18] Thus, each of the exclusive rights as provided for in respect of the various categories of works may be exploited by the author, or transferred by licence or assignment, either individually or collectively.[19] Such transfer or transmission of copyright may also be limited in ways prescribed by the agreement of the parties

Liability for infringement arises where any person, without the licence or authorisation of the owner of copyright does, or causes any other person to do, an act controlled by copyright; or imports or causes to be imported, exhibits in public, or distributes an infringing copy of a work.[20] Also, making, or having in one's possession, plates, master tapes, machines, equipment or contrivances used for the purpose of making infringing copies of a work, as well as permitting a place of public entertainment or of business to be used for a performance in the public of an infringing work, are all actionable.[21] The doing of these acts for the purpose of sale, hire, trade or business constitutes a criminal offence, punishable by the payment of a fine, and/or a term of imprisonment.[22] The Act further criminalises the sale, hire, renting, and importation of works which contravene the anti-piracy devices prescribed by the Commission, as well as the importation or possession of machines or equipment for their production.[23]

Very importantly, and in line with international standards, the Act recognises exceptions from copyright control in respect of the exclusive rights conferred on copyright owners in appropriate circumstances deemed necessary to safeguard public interest. Such exceptions include acts by way of fair dealing for purposes of research, use in an educational institution, private use, criticism or review, the reporting of current events, parody, etc.[24]

Two major rights are also protected as neighbouring rights under the Act.[25] These are the rights of performers to exclusively control, in relation to their performances, the performing, recording, broadcasting live, reproduction in material form or adapting of the performance;[26] as well

---

[18]   See generally section 10 of the Act.
[19]   See Sections 5-7 of the Act, which describe the nature of the rights conferred by copyright.
[20]   Section 14 of the Act.
[21]   Ibid.
[22]   See section 18 of the Act.
[23]   Section 18A of the Act.
[24]   See 2nd Schedule to the Copyright Act.
[25]   See Part II of the Act.
[26]   Performance in this context extends to dramatic performances, which includes dance and mimes, musical performances, as well as recitations of literary

as expressions of folklore, against reproduction, communication to the public, adaptation or other means of exploitation which is either for commercial purposes, or for purposes outside their traditional or customary context.[27]

With regard to copyright administration, the Copyright Commission is entrusted with responsibility concerning all matters relating to copyright in Nigeria. [28] The duties of the Commission include responsibility for monitoring Nigeria's position in relation to international conventions and advising government thereon; enlightening the public on matters relating to copyright; and maintenance of an effective data bank on authors and their works.[29] The Commission is further empowered to grant compulsory licences,[30] appoint copyright inspectors, [31] approve collecting societies, [32] and to make regulations for administering copyright.[33]

3. DIGITALISATION AND INTERNET ACCESS IN THE AFRICAN SCENARIO

A survey of the rate of penetration of digital online technology globally indicates that though unevenly spread, the impact of the technology has continued to be felt in an increasing number of countries and localities. For obvious reasons of availability of the necessary infrastructural and technical wherewithal, the developed countries such as the USA, Canada and the European countries, enjoy the highest levels of penetration and use. As at the end of June 2010, an estimated 77.4% of the population in North America, and 58.4% in Europe enjoyed access to the Internet, as compared to only 10.9% in Africa.[34]

Notwithstanding this wide disparity, however, there are encouraging statistics of growth in access and use within the continent, although the rate varies between countries. In this regard, the period between 2000 and 2010 reveals an impressive users' growth rate of 2,357.3% in Africa, thus

---

works. See section 23 of the Act.

27 Section 28 of the Act.
28 See generally Part III of the Act .
29 See section 30(3).
30 Section 30A.
31 Section 32A.
32 Section 32B.
33 Section 37(4)
34 Internet World Stats, World Internet Usage Statistics News and World Population Stats, available online at http://www.internetworldstats.com/stats. htm, last visited 30th August, 2010.

placing the continent in the first position as the continent with the fastest growing rate of Internet access in the world. [35]

Within Africa, Nigeria reportedly had, as at 2009, close to 24 million Internet users, representing 16.1% of the population.[36] Nigeria enjoys a rising profile as the country with the largest number of Internet users, ahead of Egypt, Morocco and South Africa.[37] The country has thus come a long way from the position in the year 2000 when it had only about two hundred thousand Internet users, and came way behind South Africa's over two million users. [38] At that time, Nigeria had only a few dial-up e-mail providers and Internet service providers (ISPs) operating on slow links, and the country was labelled as "one of the slumbering giants of the African Internet world."[39] Since that period, the infrastructure for digital access has been strengthened. In particular, the deregulation of the telecommunications sector and consequent licensing of four GSM networks between 2001 and 2002 has, among other benefits, revolutionalised digital access. It has also been hailed as marking Nigeria's transition from an era of inefficient monopoly operation characterised by slow Internet links, poor service and high cost, to an improved, competitive system affording choices for Internet applications and services.[40]

Even as investments continue to be made in international submarine cables, to supplement the existing cable connecting West Africa to the world,[41] efforts are also being made to promote individual ownership of computers. In this regard, the putting in place of a number of schemes

---

[35]   Followed by the Middle East, with 1,825.3% and Latin America and the Caribbean, with 1,032.8%. See Ibid.

[36]   See Internet World Stats, supra note 34. As at 2010, the latest data estimates reveal that over 43 million people now use the Internet in Nigeria, representing 28.9% of the country's estimated population of about 152 million people. Ibid.

[37]   Ibid.

[38]   Ibid.

[39]   See the Telecoms, Internet and Broadcast in Africa (Balancing Act) website at http://balancingact-africa.com/country_profile.php?id=24, viewed 31st July, 2009.

[40]   Ibid. See further, Ike Mowete, (2007), "Nigeria Telecommunications Sector Performance Review A Supply Side Analysis of Policy Outcomes", online at http://www.researchictafrica.net/new/images/uploads/RIA_SPR_Nigeria_07.pdf, viewed 19th September, 2009.

[41]   The old cable is called South Atlantic Telecommunications Cable Number 3/West African Submarine Cable, or SAT-3. Other cables that are in the pipeline are Glo 1, which is owned by Nigerian mobile phone service provider, Globacom Ltd and West Africa Cable System, being led by the MTN Group. On its part, France Telecom is leading a separate submarine cable project – LION 2 on the Eastern coast of Africa. See the Silicon valley news report of 30th August 2010,

to facilitate the acquisition of personal computers, by government bodies and a number of organisations is also promoting access to the hardware for digital access. At the University of Lagos, for example, the "Laptop for all Staff and Students Project" was launched on the 8th of September, 2009, as a flexible personal computer acquisition programme in which computer companies like Zinox Technologies and Hewlett Packard collaborate with the university to facilitate the purchase of computers and laptops by staff and students, based on a convenient instalment payment plan.[42] Additionally, some universities, including OAU, Ile-Ife, Lagos, Nsukka and Jos provide free Internet access for their staff.

Another possibility is the use of mobile phones to gain Internet access. In this regard, telecom service providers in Nigeria, including MTN, Globacom and Zain all have comprehensive user packages for their customers, which include Internet access and browsing opportunities.[43] For the vast majority, however, Internet access is made possible through the ever-present cybercafés which exist, and continue to spring up in most neighbourhoods especially in the urban centres and within and around educational institutions.[44]

As access increases, awareness of the potentials of the Internet as a communication tool, as well as a source of information and entertainment also continues to rise.

4. DIGITAL TECHNOLOGY AND THE NIGERIAN EDUCATIONAL SECTOR

One sector where awareness of the potential of the Internet has gained considerable ground in Nigeria is the educational sector. At present, most universities in the country have established websites where vital information about the institution, including its staff, available courses, and other important information about the university can be obtained. University

---

titled "New Cables Tie West Africa Closer to Internet", online at http://www.siliconvalley.com/news/ci_15941224

[42] See the University of Lagos website at http://www.unilag.edu.ng/index.php?page=news_viewdetail&id=356, last viewed 22nd November, 2009.

[43] See for example, the Zain website at http://www.ng.zain.com/Extras/ZainMobileInternet/tabid/129/Default.aspx, as well as the MTN Nigeria website at mtnonline.com.

[44] See Ike Mowete, op. cit. finding that the highest concentration of Internet use is in the urban centres, like Lagos, Port-Harcourt, Kano, Ibadan etc.

websites are also widely used to publish examination results, disseminate news about admission, academic activities, and other information to staff, students and the public at large.[45]

More importantly, like their counterparts in developed countries, academic libraries in Nigeria are increasingly tapping into the possibilities presented by digital technology, as they move beyond the limitations of physical libraries to a new technological paradigm. Thus, beyond exclusive reliance on books, journals and other physical resources, which are stored, accessed and used in a physical location during specified opening hours, many universities in Nigeria now provide access to online resources. Here, limitations of time and geographical boundaries are unknown, thereby affording access to users outside of fixed hours and locations.

In this regard, it is gratifying to note the efforts of the Nigerian Universities Commission (NUC) in elevating digital technology to its rightful place in the educational sector.[46] The Commission has embarked on a National Virtual Library Project, as one of the several strategies devised to bolster the quality of teaching and learning in Nigerian schools.[47] The successful completion of the project, and its utilisation by staff and students of the country's universities will help to overcome the limitations of physical libraries, including inadequate number of up-to date books and materials, and other restrictions. To this end, resources in the virtual library collection include electronic books, journals, films, videos and maps, and this is with a view to ensuring that there is made available the highest and latest publications in diverse fields to facilitate teaching, research and learning.[48]

The effort of the NUC is being complemented by a number of universities who are also actively making efforts to provide access to digital libraries and other online resources, to facilitate access to academic resources in diverse areas of science, art, law, health sciences, etc. Examples include the Universities

---

[45]   See for example, the University of Calabar, at http://www.unicaledu.com/, University of Ibadan, http://www.ui.edu.ng/, Obafemi Awolowo University at http://www.oauife.edu.ng/, and University of Maiduguri at http://www.unimaid.edu.ng/, to mention just a few.

[46]   The NUC is a parastatal under the Federal Ministry of Education, responsible for regulating Nigerian universities, including the approval of new academic programmes, quality assurance, etc. See the NUC website at http://www.nuc.edu.ng/

[47]   See the NUC virtual library website at http://www.nigerianvirtuallibrary.com/

[48]   Ibid.

of Lagos, [49] Abuja,[50] Jos, [51] and Ahmadu Bello University, Zaria.[52] Not unexpectedly, however, high costs of accessing commercial databases of academic works remain challenging due to budget limitations. This makes the identification and provision of linkages to reliable academic resources in the digital commons a more accessible and viable option, effort being taken, however, to respect the stipulated terms of access and use of such works.[53]

A further option is to emulate the initiative being undertaken by some university libraries in Nigeria to meet the need for local content in the digital environment. At the University of Nigeria, Nsukka, for example, the MTN digital library, which also has portals for e-learning,[54] has embarked on a digitisation project, involving its literary resources, including student theses and dissertations, as well as published works of university staff. [55] The same also applies to the Universities of Jos,[56] and Lagos.[57] These efforts, particularly those targeting staff research output have the potential to contribute to the promotion of access to locally relevant intellectual resources for teaching and research purposes.

5.   BENEFITS AND CHALLENGES OF DIGITALISATION FOR COPYRIGHT OWNERS

Among other benefits, digitalisation provides opportunities for scholars and researchers to project their works by utilising online resources to

---

[49]   Based on personal experience as a member of staff of the university, as well as interviews of management staff of the university. See also the University of Lagos Library website at http://library.unilag.edu.ng/.

[50]   See the Website of the University Library at http://www.uniabujalibrary. net/eresources.html.

[51]   See the Library website at http://www.unijos.edu.ng/library/?q=Services.

[52]   See the website of the Kashim Ibrahim Library of the Ahmadu Bello University, Zaria, online at http://www.abu.edu.ng/library/eresources.html.

[53]   For example, Usman Dan Fodio University Library, Sokoto identifies and provides direct links to websites hosting digital resources obtained from the digital commons. See its website at http://www.udusok.edu.ng/onlineresourses/index.html

[54]   The e-learning portal lists courses and programmes that are available electronically on its website at http://www.unn.edu.ng/moodle/

[55]   See the UNN Library website at http://www.unn.edu.ng/library/content/ view/122/178/, last visited 15th May, 2010. An interview with Dr C. O. Omekwu, UNN University Librarian was also conducted. See further, Omekwu C.O., "University Libraries in an Environment of Change and Transformation" online at http://unnlib.blogspot.com/.

[56]   See the Library website at http://www.unijos.edu.ng/library/?q=Libresources.

[57]   Interview with Dr Adediji, Librarian, University of Lagos.

disseminate their scholarly works to the public. Some, who are authors of academic texts that are listed in electronic bookshops, welcome the opportunity to widen their customer base, with positive socio-economic consequences (in terms of foreign exchange earnings and higher sales that this entails). Beyond monetary compensation, such online listing also helps to project the author internationally and thereby widen his renown.

Current initiatives to digitise local works, including books, journals, projects and other resources will further expand the scope of online resources, and more importantly, increase local content of research output in diverse sectors. In this regard, the possibility of the involvement of private sector players also needs to be taken into account, particularly where such players brings in focus, efficiency and consistency which results in high output.

The obvious challenge for this sector, as commercial, profit-oriented entities, however, is that they cannot afford, like government institutions, to make the digitised works freely available. They will therefore need to explore ways of securing such digitised works from unauthorised exploitation which may pose as threats to their investments. Like their counterparts elsewhere in the developed world, an option is to resort to measures for protection and control, including appropriate digital rights management systems which adequately safeguard the work. Such systems will require a legal framework to provide the necessary safeguards against the circumvention of such systems. It is in this regard that the role of a suitable legal framework to safeguard intellectual property rights in the digitised resources, including legal protection against circumvention of technological devices for unlawful purposes, becomes relevant.

On the other hand, however, even as digitalisation provides opportunities to permeate boundaries limiting access to educational and teaching resources, there is, however, paradoxically, the risk of an increasing digital divide due to poor capacity to access the necessary educational resources. This is the inevitable outcome of a tendency towards commodification of knowledge, and the resort to technological protection measures to safeguard access to works, unless and until the terms of access, usually involving pecuniary considerations, have been duly met. This is unlike the physical environment where a work may be freely accessed for permitted purposes like research, education, etc., from libraries and other sources, without payment.

The role of the copyright regime in balancing the competing interests of protection and access therefore becomes relevant and topical. The bottom line is that as stakeholders in the Nigerian educational sector become partakers of the online digital environment as creators, entrepreneurs and users, and as awareness increases and digital technology gradually becomes an indispensable tool for education and research, there is a greater need to bring to the fore legal issues pertaining to ownership, permitted uses and legal protection of digitised content.

In this regard, it needs to be appreciated that uploading and electronic distribution of works raises a number of fundamental copyright issues, including the ownership of copyrights in the works concerned. In the case of academic works of staff and students, it is not right to assume that ownership is automatically vested in the university, as the employer of the staff. This is because, unlike what obtains in some other jurisdictions, Nigerian law is clear that even in cases involving creation of works in the course of employment, the first owner of copyright is the employee or creator of the work, unless there is a contrary agreement.[58]

It is also not unusual for authors of literary research works, including members of the academia, to transfer exclusive rights of publication and reproduction to the publishers of the journal or book where the work has been accepted for publication. Digitisation and online publication of such works in the university depository ought therefore to be preceded by the necessary copyright contracts, to avoid unnecessary exposure to the possibility of litigation. Finally, the scope of the fair dealing exception in the digital environment needs to be clarified.

On the part of student dissertations, while some are silent on the issue, others may require the insertion of a declaration by students in their dissertation consenting to the reproduction or digitalisation of the dissertation. This presumably serves as the contractual clause authorising the exercise of the exclusive right of reproduction of the copyright work by the university librarian. Where the reproduction is used for teaching or research purposes, the clause is superfluous, as such use is a permitted use under the exceptions and limitations provisions of the Nigerian Copyright Act.[59] In the unlikely event, however, that the work is used for purposes outside of the permitted categories, the validity of the clause may need to

---

[58] See Section 9 of the Nigerian Copyright Act. The Nigerian position in this regard may be contrasted with that of the United Kingdom, Australia and the United States of America, where the presumption is that ownership of copyright for works created in the course of employment is vested in the employer. See, respectively, Section 11 of the U.K. Copyrights, Designs and Patents Act of 1988, (as amended), Section 35(3) of the copyright Act, 1968 of Australia, and Section 201(b) of the United States Copyright Act, 17 U.S.C. respectively.

[59] See the 2nd Schedule to the Nigerian Copyright Act, which in Par. H exempts from copyright control any use made of a work in an approved educational institution, for the educational purposes of that institution. The major hitch here, however, is the requirement that such work must be destroyed at the end of twelve months.

be determined. This is because, in one's view, considering the imbalance of power between the student and the university, there is the question of whether such declaration satisfies the requirement of voluntariness in contract law. In other words, the principle of undue influence may give rise to a presumption of an element of indirect coercion which renders the "consent" involuntary, and leads to the possibility to avoid the contract.[60]

To deal with some of these emerging concerns, the putting in place of a copyright policy by universities and other institutions of higher learning in Nigeria, either independently, or as part of a broader intellectual property policy becomes imperative. The relevant terms of such policies should be brought to the attention of staff and students at the commencement of the employment or studentship relationship, and incorporated by reference in the employment contracts or the admission letters as the case may be. In this regard, there is a need for consultation and collaboration between the regulatory authorities in the copyright and educational sector, notably the Nigerian Copyright Commission, on the one hand, and the National Universities Commission, (NUC) and the National Information Technology Development Agency, on the other.[61]

Beyond ownership of copyright, the issue of digitisation of rights also needs to be clarified. In this regard, both the economic and moral rights of owners of online works need to be reasonably safeguarded. In particular, due to the fact that developments in digital technology and the Internet now make new forms of electronic delivery possible, there is a need to ascertain who, as between the author and the publisher, has the right to authorise the digitisation of affected works. This requires that within or outside the education sector, parties need to be guided on the need for publishing contracts to include a specific contractual clause dealing with this contingency.[62]

Lessons may be learned from other jurisdictions, where such issues have given rise to litigation to determine the respective rights and obligations of parties. A case in point is the case of *The New York Times, Co. v. Tasini*[63]

---

[60]   This, however, is more likely to be more of an academic argument.

[61]   The role of NITDA is discussed below, in section 7 of the chapter.

[62]   This in no way detracts from the goal of digitalisation of academic works in the universities or the possibility of establishing its own digital commons, as rights can be voluntarily surrendered in such cases, in line with the established culture of wide dissemination of research favoured by the academia. On the other hand, however, it is also necessary to note that, especially in the patent arena, the possibility of securing intellectual property rights in university research is also starting to gain some ground, with the establishment of University intellectual property centres/offices.

[63]   533 U.S. 483(2001).

where litigation was initiated by some freelance authors in respect of articles they contributed to three print periodicals. Without the freelancer's consent, agreements were reached between the periodicals' publishers and two computer database companies to place copies of the freelancers' articles (along with all other articles from the periodicals in which the freelancers' work appeared) into three electronic databases. In this medium, the articles could be retrieved by users in isolation, clear of the context of the original print publication. The authors alleged that their copyrights had been infringed by the inclusion of their articles in the databases. The publishers, in response, relied on the privilege of reproduction and distribution accorded them by Section 201(c) of the US Copyright Act.[64] The Court, however, held in favour of the authors, finding that the sale and electronic re-publication of the materials without any additional payment or negotiation of electronic rights with the authors constituted copyright infringement. It was further held that the reproduction involved a new use, for which the original authors were entitled to receive royalties.

In the case of *Greenberg v. National Geographic Society*,[65] the Court of first instance had also held that the reproduction of freelance photographers' work in a searchable CD-ROM collection of past magazine editions involved a new use, for which the original authors were entitled to receive royalties. However, this decision was reversed on appeal.[66] The appellate court held that there was no infringement of copyrights as the photographs had been reproduced in the exact same context as they originally appeared, thus merely constituting digital reproductions of the original printed pages. The reproduction was held to qualify as a "revision" under Section 201(c) of the Copyright Act, to which the appellants, as assignees were entitled.

These conflicting decisions reflect the uncertainty which could arise with regard to the issue of digitisation of works. Although the US courts distinguished the earlier case of *The New York Times, Co. v. Tasini* from the *Greenberg v. National Geographic*,[67] it may be better to make for certainty by providing clear provisions in the Copyright Act dealing with the

---

[64] 17 U.S.C. S 201(c).
[65] 244 F.3d 1267.
[66] 11th Circuit, June 30, 2008, No. 05-16964, online at http://jolt.law.harvard.edu/digest/copyright/greenberg-v-national-geographic-society
[67] The distinction was on the basis that in the *Tasini* case, the databases reproduced and distributed articles standing alone and not in context, not "as part of that particular collective work" to which the author contributed, "as part of . . . any revision" thereof, or "as part of . . . any later collective work in the same series" within the meaning of Section 201(c) of the Copyright Act.

issue of electronic rights. This will help parties to such contracts avert their minds to this concern, and at the inception of the contract, make provisions to deal with the contingency.

Also, in the US case of *Random House Inc. V. Rosetta Books LLC*, [68] the plaintiff sought to restrain the defendants from selling in digital format, eight specific works in respect of which the authors of the works had previously granted the right to "print, publish and sell the works in book form" to the plaintiffs. The defendants, on the other hand, claimed that it was not infringing upon the rights those authors gave to the plaintiff, because the licensing agreements between the publisher and the author did not include a grant of digital or electronic rights. The Court rejected the plaintiff's argument that an "e-book" was simply a "form" of a book, and therefore within the coverage of appellant's licenses. It therefore upheld the defendant's claim, and held that the right to "print, publish and sell the works in book form" in the contracts at issue did not include the right to publish the works in the format that has come to be known as the "e-book." [69] In doing this, the court deemed as relevant, fact-finding regarding, inter alia, the "evolving" technical processes and uses of an e-book, and the reasonable expectations of the contracting parties "cognizant of the customs, practices, usages and terminology as generally understood in the . . . trade or business" at the time of contracting.[70]

Taking a cue from a case such as this, Nigerian publishers and authors need to be aware of their options in relation to the grant or acquisition of electronic rights alongside traditional print publication rights. Normally, publishers tend to seek maximum flexibility to exploit works in whatever ways they can. However, authors also need to be able to maximise opportunities to profit from the exploitation of the work and by safeguarding their right to fair remuneration. Thus, publishing contracts need to deal with book publication rights as well as electronic publishing rights (online and offline, the latter relating to reproduction of the work in digital format through audio tapes of readings of the work). On its part, the statutory framework needs to clearly include, among the repertoire of rights of copyright owners, specific exploitation rights relating to, and peculiar to, the digital environment.

In this changing scenario, it must, however, be reiterated that the issue of balance remains critical, and it is thus in the interests of users and the

---

[68]   150 F. Supp. 2d 613, 614-15 (S.D.N.Y. 2001)

[69]   Defined by the court as a digital book that can be read on a computer screen or electronic device.

[70]   Upheld on appeal. See *Random House Inc. V. Rosetta Books LLC*, 283 F.3d 490 (2d Cir. 2002). See also *Tasini v. New York Times*, supra.

public generally that exceptions and limitations to copyright, which are recognised in the traditional era, need to, as far as possible, be migrated to the digital arena. A worrisome development, in this regard, is the reported institution of action against an Argentinean university professor for copyright infringement. [71] The action was in respect of the translation to the local Spanish language, and online posting of the works of a French philosopher.[72] The posting was allegedly made in an attempt to make the works of foreign philosophers available to Spanish students, but it drew the ire of the publisher of the author of the work, who has reportedly instituted criminal action against the professor. This case brings to light the concerns of user communities, especially in developing countries where most students can ill afford the cost of accessing foreign materials needed for their educational pursuits. The action presents a strong case to make clear provisions exempting educational uses from copyright control in the digital environment. At any rate, the fear that such free access may interfere with the reasonable exploitation of the work in the author's market hardly applies to poor countries where the average student and even lecturer can ill afford the cost of accessing these materials, in the absence of institutional subscriptions.

The next section will examine the extent to which Nigerian law as presently is, responds to these emerging issues and the need for balance. In this regard, a comparison will be made to other copyright laws elsewhere, notably in Ghana, one of Nigeria's neighbours on the West Coast of Africa.

6. THE ONLINE ENVIRONMENT AND THE LEGAL FRAMEWORK FOR THE PROTECTION OF COPYRIGHT IN NIGERIA

This final section will comparatively focus on three main issues: the online dissemination of works and the scope of exclusive rights under Nigerian law vis-à-vis what obtains under Ghanaian and other laws; anti-circumvention measures and rights management systems; and exceptions and limitations to copyright. Finally, emerging legislative developments in Nigeria will be highlighted.

---

[71] See Intellectual Property Watch news report of 12th May, 2009, online at http://www.ip-watch.org/weblog/2009/05/12/argentina-copyright-case, viewed on 12th May, 2009.
[72] See Intellectual Property Watch news report of 12th May, 2009, online at http://www.ip-watch.org/weblog/2009/05/12/argentina-copyright-case, viewed on 12th May, 2009.

6.1   Online Dissemination of Copyright Works and the Scope of Exclusive Rights in the Digital Environment

As mentioned above, exclusive rights conferred by copyright under Nigerian law include the rights of reproduction, publication, performance, adaptation and translation of the work.[73] Also, the making of cinematograph films or records in respect of the work, its distribution to the public for commercial purposes by way of rentals, leases, hire, loan or similar arrangement, as well as the broadcasting or communication of the work to the public by a loudspeaker or any other similar device are all within the scope of the exclusive rights conferred on the author.[74]

With regard to online dissemination of works, however, there is the question of whether existing rights accommodate the uploading, downloading and dissemination of works in the digital environment. In other words, do acts connected with Internet transmission fall within the existing exclusive rights conferred by the Nigerian Copyright Act on a copyright owner? If yes, is it accommodated under a particular category, or a combination of two or more different rights? On the other hand, if the response is no, how best can these new rights be guaranteed under the copyright regime?

An examination of the meaning and scope of existing exclusive rights which may possibly cover Internet digital transmissions may be helpful in proffering a solution. In this regard, possible options include under Section 5(1)(a)(vi), which provides for the right to distribution, and section 5(1)(a)(vii), which provides for the right of communication to the public.

The distribution right refers to the right "to distribute . . . copies of the work by way of rentals, leases, hire, loan *or similar arrangement*". The limited forms of distribution specified, however, restrict what might otherwise have been a broad right of distribution. This is because according to the *ejusdem generis* rule of interpretation, where specifications of particular things belonging to the same genus precede a general word, the latter word is confined in its meaning to things belonging to the same genus, and does not include things belonging to a different genus.[75] The words "similar arrangement" must therefore be *ejusdem generis* the specified methods, i.e. rentals, leases, hire, loan, and transmission over digital interactive networks appears to stretch this rule of interpretation rather too far.

On its part, there is a right of communication to the public by "a loud-

---

[73]   See generally, Sections 5–7 of the Nigerian Copyright Act, Cap C28, Laws of the Federation of Nigeria, 2004.

[74]   Ibid. In addition, performers' rights and expressions of folklore, are also protected – see sections 23 and 28 of the Act.

[75]   See *Lake v. Simmons*, [1927] A.C. 487, per Sumner L.J. at 507.

speaker or any other similar device."[76] The right is defined to include, in addition to any live performance or delivery, any mode of visual or acoustic presentation, but does not include a broadcast or re-broadcast.[77] Close as this right may have been in the context of digital online transmissions, it is, however, again limited by its restriction of modes of communication to that by "a loudspeaker or any other similar device." Clearly, digital online transmission cannot, by any stretch of the imagination, be described as a similar device to loudspeakers, and so the right of communication also appears somewhat defective to accommodate digital transmissions.

It is therefore far from clear under the current law in Nigeria that an interactive transmission or other form of making available through interactive network constitutes a distribution or communication within the meaning of the Act. At any rate, to make for certainty, one is of the view that a better course would be to clarify the position beyond doubt by including a specific right which covers digital transmissions. Available examples in this regard include the express inclusion of a new right of communication to the public, as contemplated by the WIPO Copyright Treaty,[78] and implemented under a number of national legislations, including that of Australia,[79] and Japan.[80] Coming closer to home, there is also the example of the copyright law of Ghana, which has recently been

---

[76]   Section 5 (1)(a) (vii) of the Act.

[77]   Section 39 of the Act.

[78]   The WIPO Copyright Treaty (WCT) along with the WIPO Performances and Phonograms Treaty (WPPT) are commonly referred to as the "Internet Treaties", and entered into force on March 6, 2002, and May 20, 2002 respectively. As at August 19, 2009, the WCT had 70 Contracting Parties. African countries who are now parties to the treaty include Burkina Faso (1999), Guinea (2002), Togo (2003), Botswana (2004), as well as Ghana and the Republic of Benin, (both in 2006). The treaty provides for a right of communication to be conferred on authors of literary and artistic works to authorise any communication to the public of their works, by wire or wireless means, including the making available to the public of works in a way that the members of the public may access the work from a place and at a time individually chosen by them. See Article 8 of the WCT.

[79]   The right of communication is defined under Australian law as to "make available online or electronically transmit (whether over a path, or combination of paths, provided by a material substance or otherwise) a work or other subject matter. See Section 10(1) of the Australian Copyright Amendment (Digital Agenda) Act No 110 of 2000, as amended by Act No 63 of 2002.

[80]   In Japan, the author of a copyright law is conferred with the exclusive right to make the public transmission of his work (including the making transmittable of his work in the case of interactive transmission). See Art 23 of the Japanese Copyright Act, 1971, as amended. The English version of the Act is available at the Copyright Research and Information Centre (CRIC) website, at http://www.cric.or.jp/cric_e/clj/clj.html, last viewed on 25th April 2010.

modified to accommodate the advent of digital technology. Under this new Ghanaian Act,[81] the economic rights conferred on copyright owners include the rights of public performance, broadcasting and communication of the work.[82] The right of communication to the public is defined as "the transmission, other than broadcasting, by wire or without wire, of the images or sounds or both of a work, a performance or a sound recording in such a way that the images or sounds can be perceived by persons outside the normal circle of a family and its closest social acquaintants at a place or places so distant from the place where the transmission originates that without the transmission, the images or sounds would not be perceivable irrespective of whether the person can receive images or sounds at the same place and time, or at different places or times individually chosen by them". [83] Unlike the limited scope of the right of communication to the public under Nigerian law, digital online transmissions carried on through the Internet are therefore clearly within the scope of the exclusive rights conferred on copyright owners in Ghana.

Also, the exclusive rights conferred on performers now extend to the right of making available to the public a fixed performance, by wire or wireless means, in a way that members of the public may access it from a place and at a time individually chosen by them.[84] The inclusion of these rights has the advantage of safeguarding copyright works from unauthorised exploitation in the digital environment.

6.2 Anti-Circumvention Measures and Protection of Rights Management Systems

A further issue which needs to be dealt with in the online environment is the taking of reasonable measures to guard against infringement, particularly on a commercial level. In Nigeria, as in many other countries, there is a running battle between copyright owners and the regulatory body on the one hand, and pirates on the other, for the soul of the copyright business.[85] However, the efforts appear to focus more on the physical environment, rather than the online digital environment.

---

[81]   Act No 690 of 2005, hereinafter, "the Ghanaian Act".
[82]   See Section (5) of the Ghanaian Act.
[83]   See Section 76 of the Ghanaian Act.
[84]   See Section 28(1)(f) of the Ghanaian Act. Exceptions to the exclusive rights are dealt with below.
[85]   For information about the Nigerian Copyright Commission's Strategic Action against Piracy (STRAP) initiative, see website of the Commission at http://www.nigcopyright.org/strap.htm.

To correct this imbalance, there is a need to avert to the protection of the legitimate moral and economic rights of copyright owners, to save the copyright sector from the compounding of its woes in the online environment. In this regard, the prohibition of the removal or alteration of rights management information is an important measure, which helps to safeguard the moral rights of paternity and integrity which are accorded to right holders by copyright laws. These provisions are therefore helpful in ensuring that these moral rights are migrated to the digital online environment.

Under the Copyright law of Ghana, there are provisions dealing with the preservation of rights management information and the safeguarding of technological measures to protect online works. With regard to rights management information, the Ghanaian Act prohibits the removal or alteration of any electronic rights management information from a copyright work.[86] It further renders liable anyone who, knowing that electronic rights management information has been removed or altered without authority, distributes, imports for distribution, broadcasts, communicates or makes available to the public, works, performances, copies of fixed performances or sound recordings. [87] Additionally, the manufacture, importation, distribution, exportation, sale, rental, possession for commercial purposes, offering to the public, advertisement, communication or other provision of any device, product or component that is designed or adapted to remove, alter or add electronic rights management information are all prohibited under the law.[88]

Concerning technological protection measures and digital rights management systems, these are technologies for monitoring, identifying, using and enforcing usage terms of intellectual assets in any digital format. [89] Digital rights management systems are therefore the tools that protect intellectual property online, during digital content commerce or other digital activities.[90]

The main reservation against these systems, however, is the threat they pose to the maintenance of the copyright balance as the restriction of access which they afford not only threatens the right to fair dealing,

---

[86] Section 42(1)(e) of the Ghanaian Copyright Act.
[87] Section 42(1)(f).
[88] Section 42(1)(g).
[89] Kristoffer Schollin, (2008), Digital Rights Management: The New Copyright, (Jure Forlag AB) 149. See also, the U.K. Publishers' Association, "Copyright-Digital Rights Management (DRM)", online at http://ec.europa.eu/avpolicy/docs/other_actions/contributions/uk_publishers_annex2_colen_pdf.
[90] Ibid.

but can presumably also be used to unlawfully extend the protection of a copyright work beyond the allotted duration. Thus, while the use of these measures may be justified in certain regards, perhaps more so with regard to entertainment works, their scope, with regard to public interest works, including educational resources needs to be reasonably restricted.

The Ghanaian Act deals with the issue, although with less clarity than would have been desirable. In this regard, the Act provides that it is an offence for anyone to circumvent any technological protection measure applied by a copyright holder to the protected work.[91] Unfortunately, the provision is not very clear about the scope of the prohibited act, and therefore leaves room for speculation. It simply bans the circumvention of technological measures *applied by a copyright holder to the protected work.*[92] Whether such protection is limited to those which guard against infringement of copyright, or extends to those that also prevent access, as obtains under the United States Digital Millenium Copyright Act (DMCA), is not very clear.[93] However, taking into account the need for balance in the digital environment, the former interpretation, i.e., which restricts protection to measures which guard against infringement, appears to be better suited to the realization of the underlying objectives of copyright law. This is because such interpretation ensures that access for permitted purposes, including education and research, is not hindered.

The Ghanaian Act also contains additional provisions which ban devices used for the circumvention of the rights of the copyright owner. To this end, the law renders liable any person who carries out the manufacture, importation, distribution, exportation, sale, rental, possession for commercial purposes, offering to the public, advertisement, communication or otherwise provides without authority, devices, components, services or other means, designed, adapted, or promoted to circumvent such a measure.[94]

Similarly, any person who rents or lends to the public any work where the person performing the act knew or had reasonable grounds to know that the action induces, enables, facilitates or conceals an infringement of any copyright or related right protected under the Act, without the

---

[91] Section 42(1)(h) of the Act

[92] Emphasis laid.

[93] The DMCA prohibits the circumvention of technological measures that effectively control access to copyright works – Section 1201(a)(1)(A) of the Act. Criticisms have trailed the law – see, for example, Pamela Samuelson, (1999), "Intellectual Property And The Digital Economy: Why The Anti-Circumvention Regulations Need To Be Revised", 14 Berkeley Tech. L. J. 519.

[94] Section 42(1)(i) of the Act.

licence or authorisation of the copyright owner or his agent, infringes the protected rights and commits an offence punishable under the Act. [95]

6.3   Limitations and Exceptions to Copyright

To the extent that they provide the necessary window to ensure protection of the interest of the public regarding access to copyright works for education and other related purposes, limitations and exceptions are critical to the balancing of rights and obligations in the digital environment. In fact, to underscore its importance, there have been recommendations for a separate international instrument on limitations and exceptions to copyright,[96] as a means to coordinate, harmonise and balance the new standards of protection of various international intellectual property treaties.[97]

In the meantime, however, developing countries in particular, need to pay attention to the need to amply provide in their national laws for limitations and exceptions to cater for their peculiar needs, notably access to knowledge for information, education and research purposes. In this regard, the Nigerian Copyright Act provides for a wide range of acts which may be carried out without the prior consent or authorisation of the copyright owner. These include use in educational institutions, for educational purposes, and use by or under the direction or control of the government, or by public libraries, non-commercial research or other institutions, where the use is in public interest and no revenue is derived therefrom.[98] These need to be extended to apply to the online environment, as has been done under the Ghanaian law, which provides a broad and quite far-reaching exemption for teaching and research purposes. In this regard, the law exempts from the exclusive rights of copyright owners, use of such works by way of illustration in publications, broadcasts of sound or visual recordings for teaching, as well as the communication of the work for teaching purposes, and its broadcast for use in educational institutions, as well as the utilisation of the work for professional training

---

[95]   Section 43 of the Act stipulates the payment of fines, or terms of imprisonment for offenders.

[96]   See for example, P. Bernt Hugenholtz & Ruth L. Okediji, (2008) "Conceiving an International Instrument on Limitations and Exceptions to Copyright", online at   http://www.ivir.nl/publications/hugenholtz/limitations_exceptions_copyright. pdf, and Gwen Hinze, (2008), "Making Knowledge Accessible Across Borders: the Case for Mandatory Minimum International Copyright Exceptions and Limitations for Education, Capacity Building and Development", Third World Network Briefing Paper No 49, online at www.twnside.org.sg.

[97]   Hugenholtz and Okediji, supra, at p. 11.

[98]   See the 2nd Schedule to the Nigerian Copyright Act.

or public education.[99] However, the source of the work used, as well as the name of the author must be indicated in the relevant publication, broadcast or recording.[100] Also, such use must measure up to the standard of compatibility with fair practice. [101]

On its part, the Ghanaian Act goes further to provide for reproduction, translation and adaptation of works for private and personal use.[102] Also, it specifically and relevantly provides, in the context of the online environment, that the temporary reproduction of a work is not an infringement of copyright if the reproduction is made in order to make a digitally stored work perceptible.[103] Likewise, it is not infringement of copyright where reproduction occurs in the process of a digital transmission by a person or entity that is authorised for that purpose by either the owner of the copyright, or by operation of law; and as an accessory that occurs during the normal operation of the equipment used and which is automatically deleted and is incapable of being retrieved for any other purpose than those referred to in this sub section.[104] Thus, the scope of copyright is limited so as not to interfere with acts which are inevitable in accessing works in the online environment, and to this extent, the provision serves as a good model for developing countries to emulate.

One limitation to the reasonably diverse exemptions provided under the Ghanaian Act, however, is the lack of reference to permitted use of digitised works for libraries and archives. In this regard, although Section 21 of the Act, which deals with library exemptions, refers to reprographic reproductions, there is, however, need to extend the exceptions to cover transmission of works on digital networks. This is because the important role of public libraries and archives to the development of the educational system means such use should not be left to the vagaries of rules of interpretation if the objective of ensuring an appropriate balancing of rights in the digital environment is to remain uncompromised.

7.   EMERGING LEGAL DEVELOPMENTS IN NIGERIA

There are ongoing efforts in Nigeria to respond to some of the issues raised by the online digital environment. The basic policy framework

---

[99] See also Section 19(1)(c) of the Ghanaian Act.
[100] Section 19(4).
[101] Ibid.
[102] Ibid.
[103] Section 19(6) of the Act.
[104] Ibid.

for the response, in one's view, is the National Policy on Information Technology of 2001, which targets the effective utilisation of information technology for the promotion of efficient national development, including in the fields of education and wealth creation.[105] Responsibility for the implementation of the policy lies with the National Information Technology Development Agency (NITDA), whose main mandate is that of addressing the challenges and harnessing the opportunities presented by information and communication technology.[106] It is in furtherance of this mandate that NITDA has partnered with the Nigerian Universities Commission to establish websites for universities in Nigeria, as well as to promote the deployment of IT for promoting access to educational resources through its digitisation projects.

In doing this, there is a need to work closely with the Nigerian Copyright Commission to ensure that copyright laws are upheld, and NITDA is well guided about the possibilities of utilising copyright exceptions and limitations under Nigerian law to public advantage in bridging the digital divide. On its part, the Copyright Commission needs to review the applicable copyright laws and policies, to ensure their balance and conformity with the educational and cultural needs of the country, in the new age of digital technology.

There is also in place a draft Cyber Security and Data Protection Agency Bill, which inter alia, contains provisions criminalising unlawful access to computers, unauthorised disclosure of access information or pass words, and system interference.[107] It further seeks to criminalise the use of computers to violate any intellectual property rights protected under any law or treaty applicable in Nigeria.[108] The Bill is a welcome initiative, which addresses some of the issues relevant to legal protection of intellectual property in the digital age. However, it is clear that it does not address all the issues. Indeed, the Bill only appears to scratch the issues on the surface. This is because the provision simply criminalises the violation of intellectual property rights protected under existing laws and treaties

---

[105]   See Pars 3 & 4 of the Policy. The Policy is available online at http://www. nitda.gov.ng/document/nigeriaitpolicy.pdf
[106]   See the NITDA website at http://nitda.gov.ng/, as well as the National Information Technology Development Agency Act of 2007.
[107]   Titled a 'Bill for an Act to Provide for the Establishment of the Cyber Security and Information Protection Agency Charged with the Responsibility to Secure Computer Systems and Networks and Liason with the Relevant Law Enforcement Agency for the Enforcement of Cyber Crime Laws, and for Related Matters'.
[108]   See Section 21 of the Bill.

applicable in Nigeria. However, to the extent that Nigeria has neither ratified nor domesticated the WIPO Internet treaties, nor otherwise put in place, as yet, provisions to expressly extend protection to the new forms of exploitation online, made possible by advances in digital and communication technology, it can be argued that such online exploitation is not necessarily a violation of intellectual property rights, as presently obtains under Nigerian law.

Beyond these, other related issues which are yet to be clarified and expressly legislated upon include the liability of ISPs for copyright infringement, scope of protection of works, including multimedia works and electronic databases, details regarding the safeguarding of rights management information, as well as legal provisions relating to the circumvention of technological measures.[109]

8.   CONCLUSION

The advent of the digital age presents both opportunities to be harnessed, and challenges to be surmounted. In trying to formulate suitable responses, Nigeria in particular, and the continent of Africa in general, should be guided by the recommendation of the Report of the Commission on Intellectual Property Rights, which advocates that "the crucial issue for developing countries is getting the right balance between protecting copyright and ensuring adequate access to knowledge and knowledge based products . . . to ensure that developing countries have access to knowledge-based products as they seek to bring education to all, facilitate research, improve competitiveness, protect their cultural expressions and reduce poverty".[110] In the same vein, the Report highlights the importance to developing countries of developing mechanisms to protect and benefit from the commercial exploitation of their own past and present creative works.[111]

To achieve these objectives, the rights and freedoms necessary to ensure

---

[109]   Again, in this regard, a new legislation to amend the copyright law to tackle some of these issues is in the pipeline at the National Assembly. One looks forward to its speedy promulgation and effective implementation.

[110]   Commission on Intellectual Property Rights, (2002), "Integrating Intellectual Property Rights and Development Policy", Report of the Commission on Intellectual Property Rights, (2nd Ed), at p. 106. The Report is available online at http://www.iprcommission.org/text/documents/final_report.htmp, last viewed 30th August, 2010.

[111]   Ibid.

socio-economic development in the digital environment need to be put in place. On the one hand, there is a need for the right of copyright owners to extend to the digital environment, to safeguard their works from unauthorised exploitation. On the other hand, and very importantly in the context of the promotion of the education sector, access to the vast resources in the online environment needs to be secured. Measures to achieve the right balance have been identified in this chapter as including the recognition of communication rights in the digital environment, safeguarding of rights management information, limits on technological protection measures, the provision of robust limitations and exceptions for research, educational uses, as well as library and other non-commercial purposes, and exceptions for temporary or incidental copies.

Index